MAGI
The labyrinth of magic

Story & Art by
SHINOBU OHTAKA

A **fantasy adventure** inspired by
One Thousand and One Nights

Deep within the deserts lie the mysterious Dungeons, vast stores of riches there for the taking by anyone lucky enough to find them and brave enough to venture into the depths from where few have ever returned. Plucky young adventurer **Aladdin** means to find the Dungeons and their riches, but Aladdin may be just as mysterious as the treasures he seeks.

S0-AAB-637

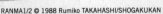

Gosho Aoyama's Mystery Library

66

AKOJURO SENBA

Today I'm introducing you to Agojuro, the famed deduction master of Japan's Edo period! His real name is Akojuro Senba, but his long chin got him the nickname Agojuro, or "Chinjuro." He works at the North Magistrate's Office as the *reikurikata*, an official who researches and records the law, but he usually slacks off. His subordinate Hyoromatsu brings him baffling cases about a chest full of gold coins turning into rusty nails or a person disappearing from a ship without a trace...and that's when he puts his vast knowledge and flexible thinking to use. His rivals at the South Magistrate's Office don't like him. But no matter how you feel about him, don't mention his chin or he'll draw his sword!

The author, Juran Hisao, dictated all his novels. Maybe I should try using dictation too... No, wait! I'm the one who has to draw the artwork! *Heh.*

I recommend *Entobune* (Prison Ship).

Hello, Aoyama here.

Recently I visited an optician in the neighborhood to get a new pair of glasses. I was choosing frames when a sales clerk said, "How about thick frames like Conan wears?" I smiled. "*Ha ha*...I bet he doesn't know I'm the creator of Conan," I thought as I snickered to myself. But then he surprised me by saying, "I was a huge fan of your old series *Yaiba*!" Oh...so he did know. *Heh.*

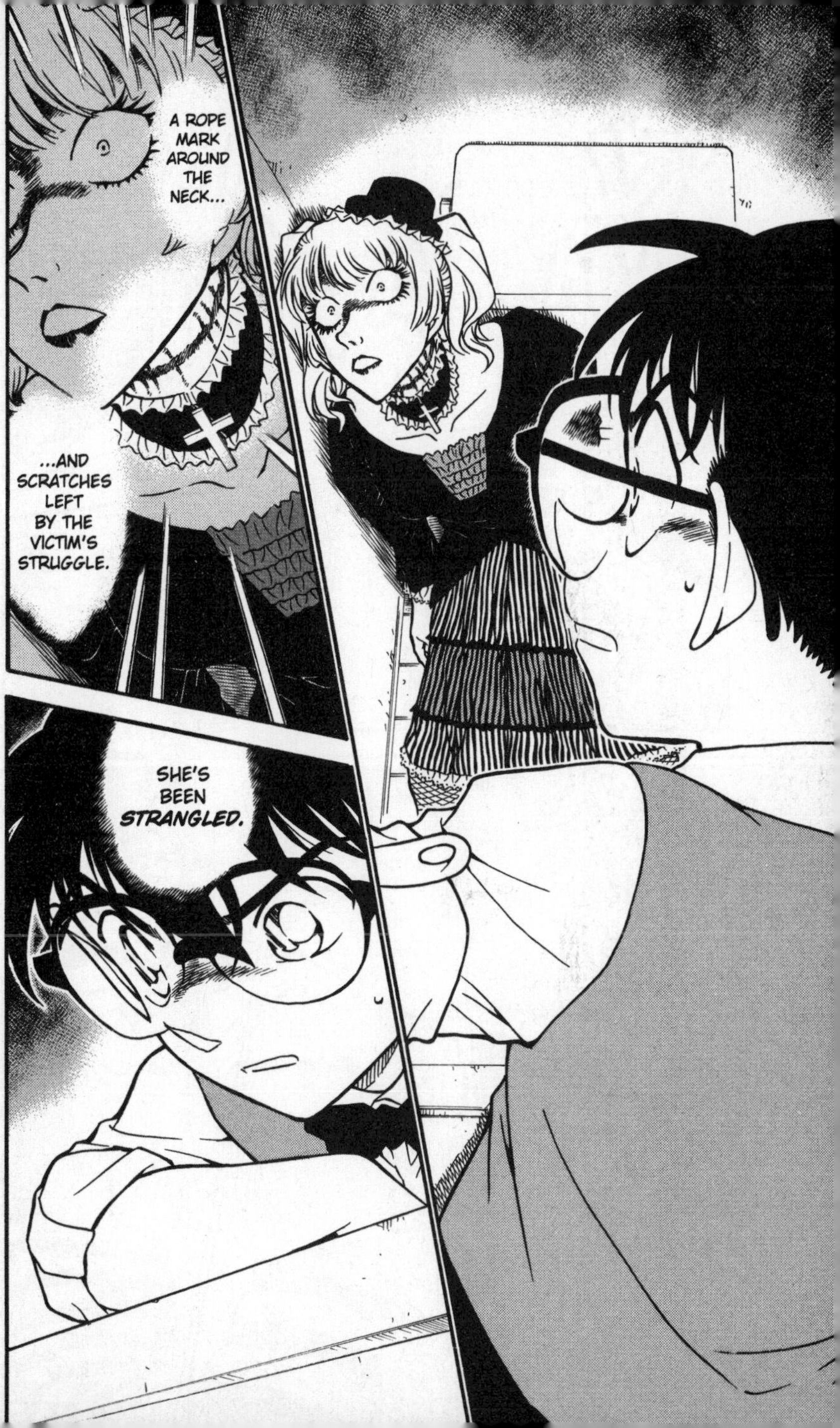
A ROPE MARK AROUND THE NECK...
...AND SCRATCHES LEFT BY THE VICTIM'S STRUGGLE.
SHE'S BEEN STRANGLED.

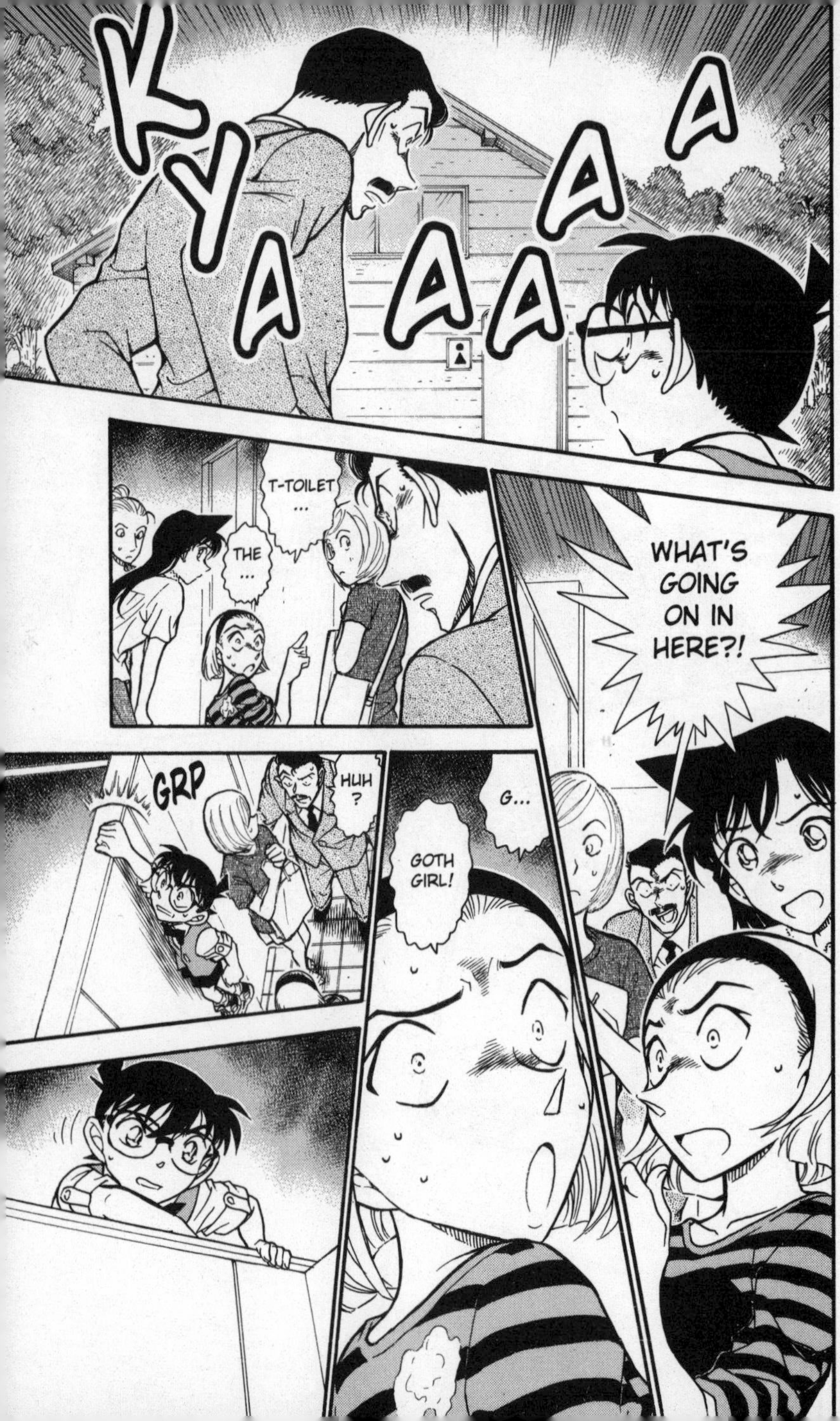
KYAAAAAA
WHAT'S GOING ON IN HERE?!
T-TOILET ...
THE ...
G...
GOTH GIRL!
HUH ?
GRP

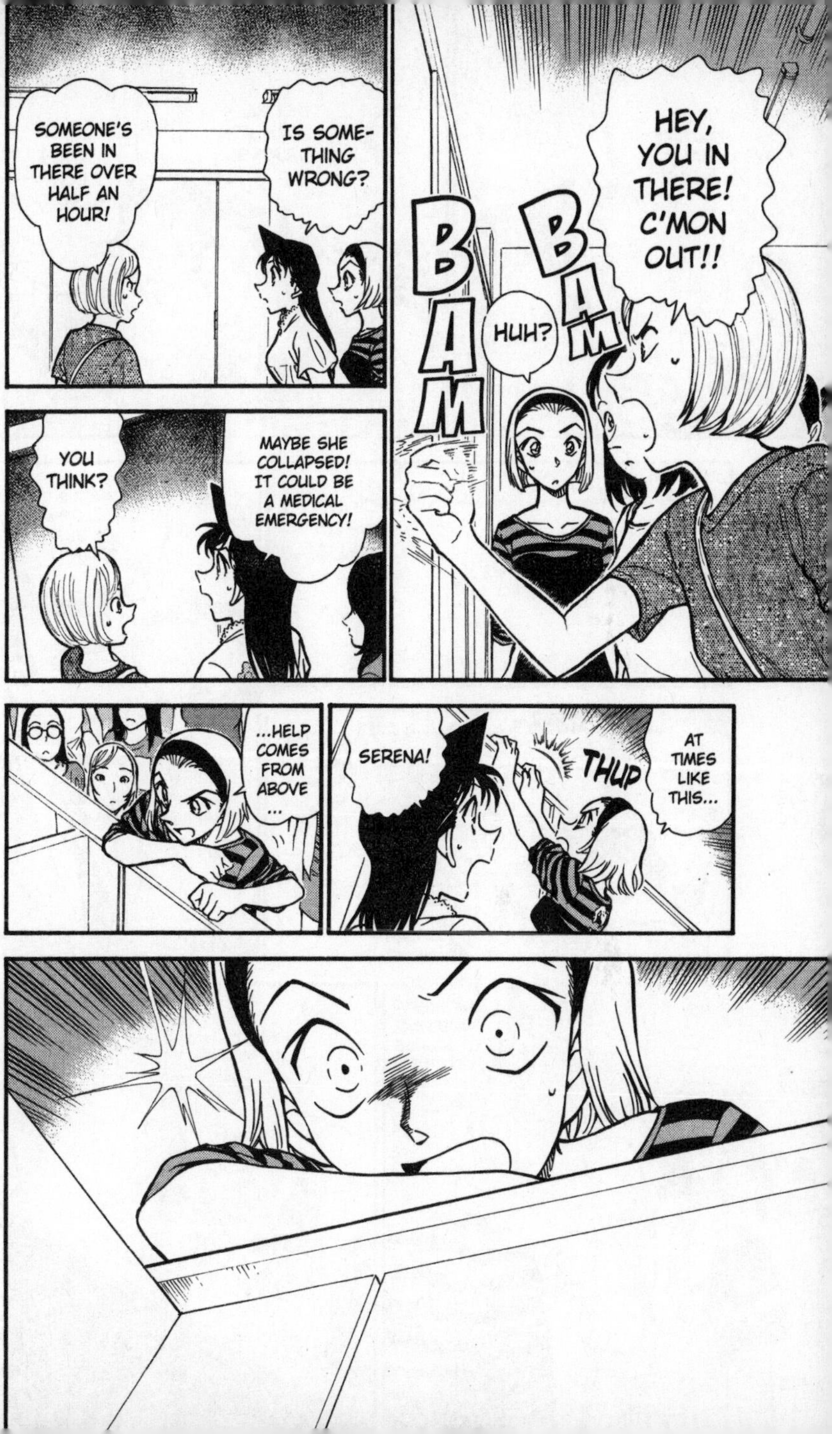
HEY, YOU IN THERE! C'MON OUT!!
BAM
HUH?
BAM
IS SOME-THING WRONG?
SOMEONE'S BEEN IN THERE OVER HALF AN HOUR!
MAYBE SHE COLLAPSED! IT COULD BE A MEDICAL EMERGENCY!
YOU THINK?
AT TIMES LIKE THIS...
THUP
SERENA!
...HELP COMES FROM ABOVE ...

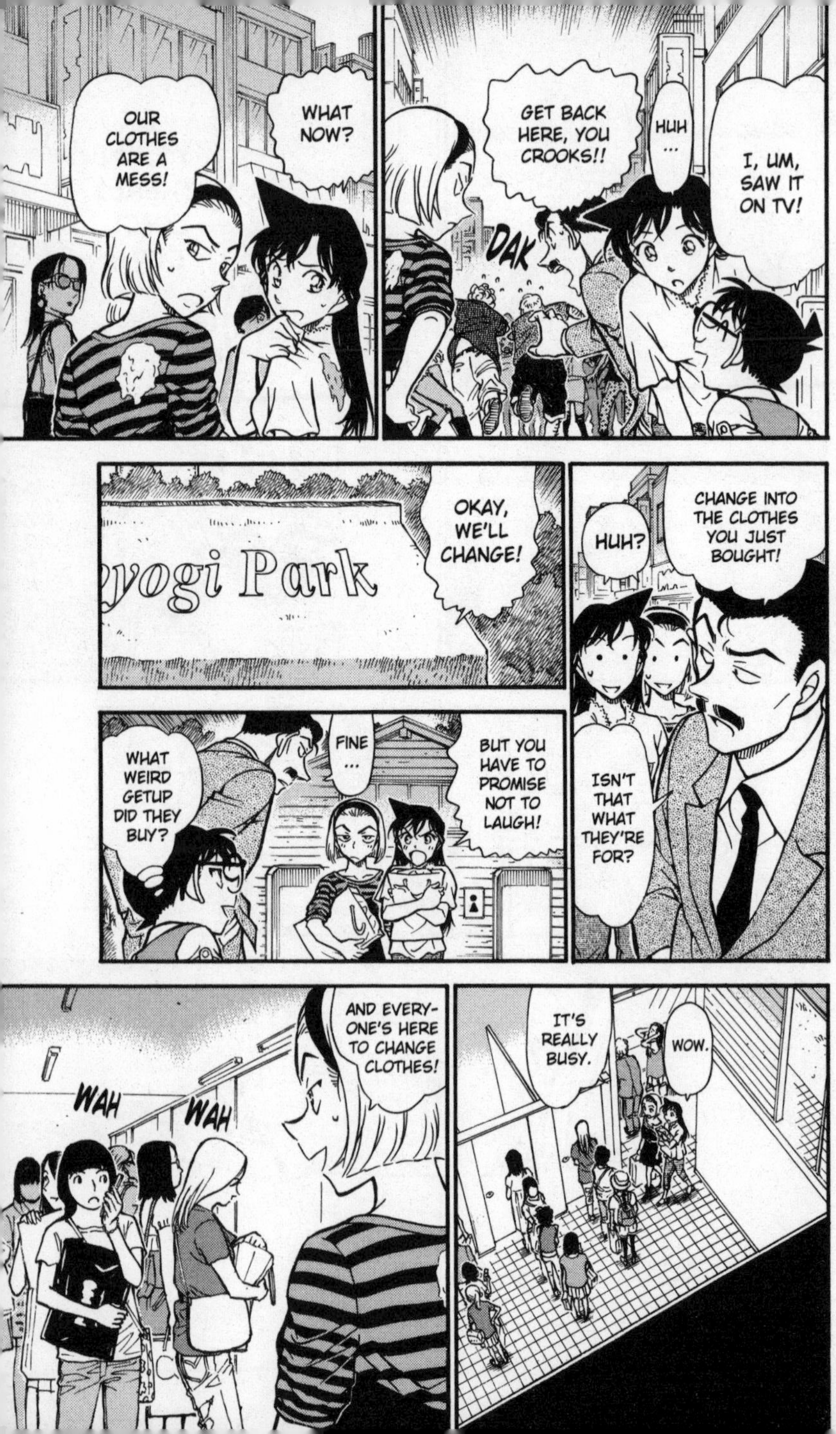
I, UM, SAW IT ON TV!
HUH ...
GET BACK HERE, YOU CROOKS!!
DAK
WHAT NOW?
OUR CLOTHES ARE A MESS!
CHANGE INTO THE CLOTHES YOU JUST BOUGHT!
HUH?
ISN'T THAT WHAT THEY'RE FOR?
OKAY, WE'LL CHANGE!
yogi Park
BUT YOU HAVE TO PROMISE NOT TO LAUGH!
FINE ...
WHAT WEIRD GETUP DID THEY BUY?
WOW.
IT'S REALLY BUSY.
AND EVERYONE'S HERE TO CHANGE CLOTHES!
WAH
WAH

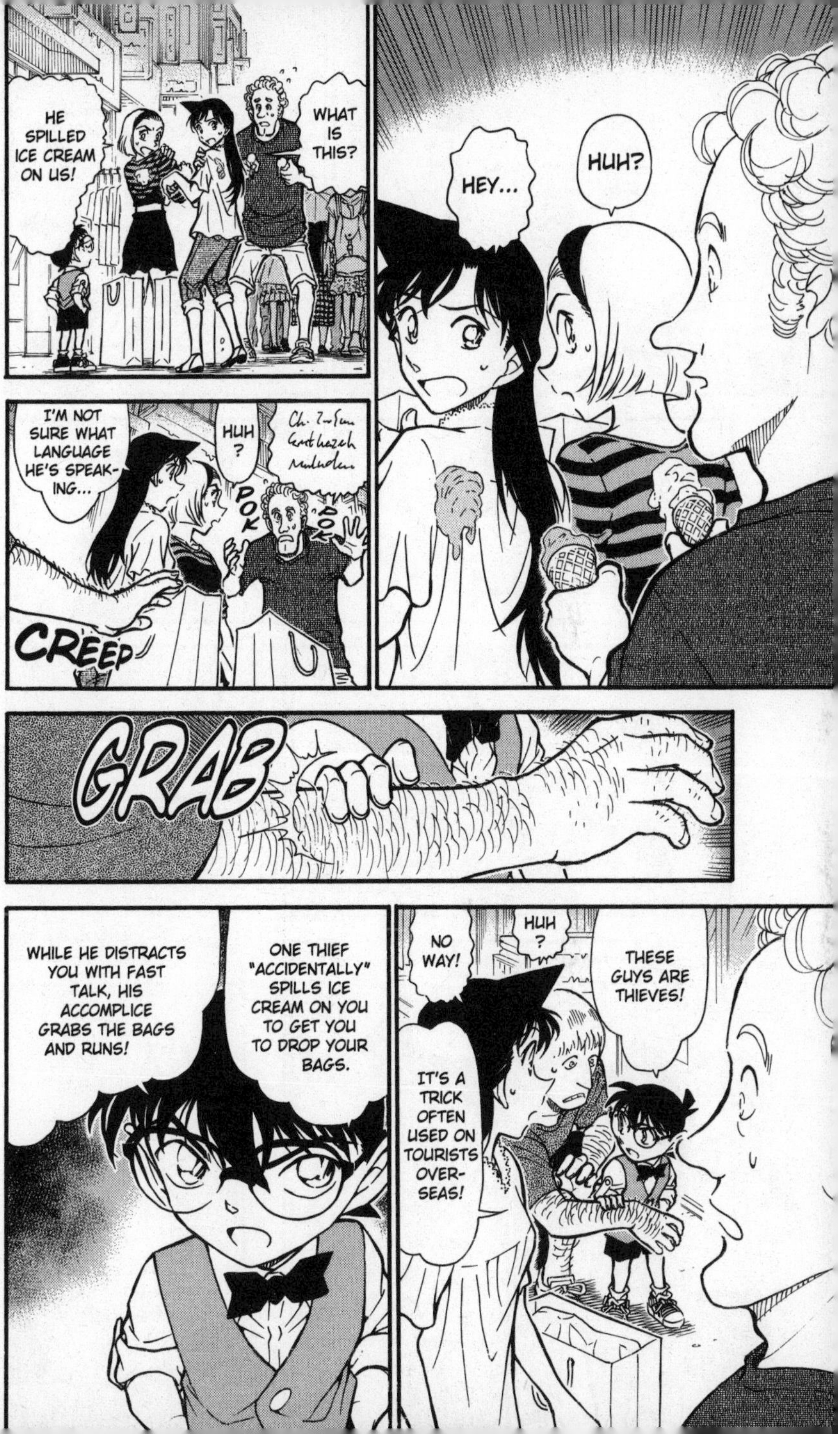
HUH?
HEY...
WHAT IS THIS?
HE SPILLED ICE CREAM ON US!
HUH?
POK
POK
I'M NOT SURE WHAT LANGUAGE HE'S SPEAKING...
CREEP
GRAB
THESE GUYS ARE THIEVES!
HUH?
NO WAY!
IT'S A TRICK OFTEN USED ON TOURISTS OVERSEAS!
ONE THIEF "ACCIDENTALLY" SPILLS ICE CREAM ON YOU TO GET YOU TO DROP YOUR BAGS.
WHILE HE DISTRACTS YOU WITH FAST TALK, HIS ACCOMPLICE GRABS THE BAGS AND RUNS!

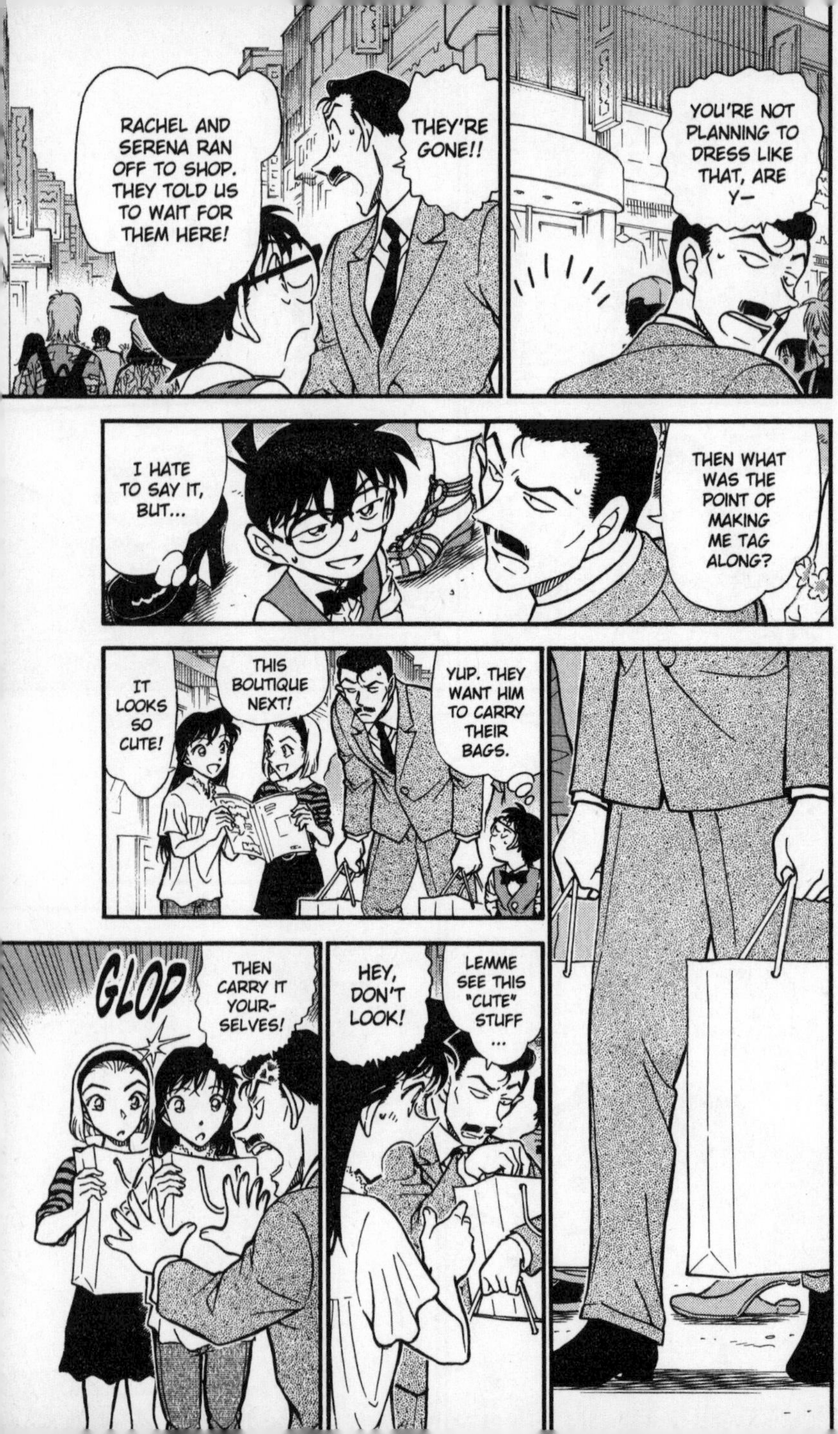
YOU'RE NOT PLANNING TO DRESS LIKE THAT, ARE Y—
THEY'RE GONE!!
RACHEL AND SERENA RAN OFF TO SHOP. THEY TOLD US TO WAIT FOR THEM HERE!
THEN WHAT WAS THE POINT OF MAKING ME TAG ALONG?
I HATE TO SAY IT, BUT...
YUP. THEY WANT HIM TO CARRY THEIR BAGS.
THIS BOUTIQUE NEXT!
IT LOOKS SO CUTE!
LEMME SEE THIS "CUTE" STUFF ...
HEY, DON'T LOOK!
THEN CARRY IT YOURSELVES!
GLOP

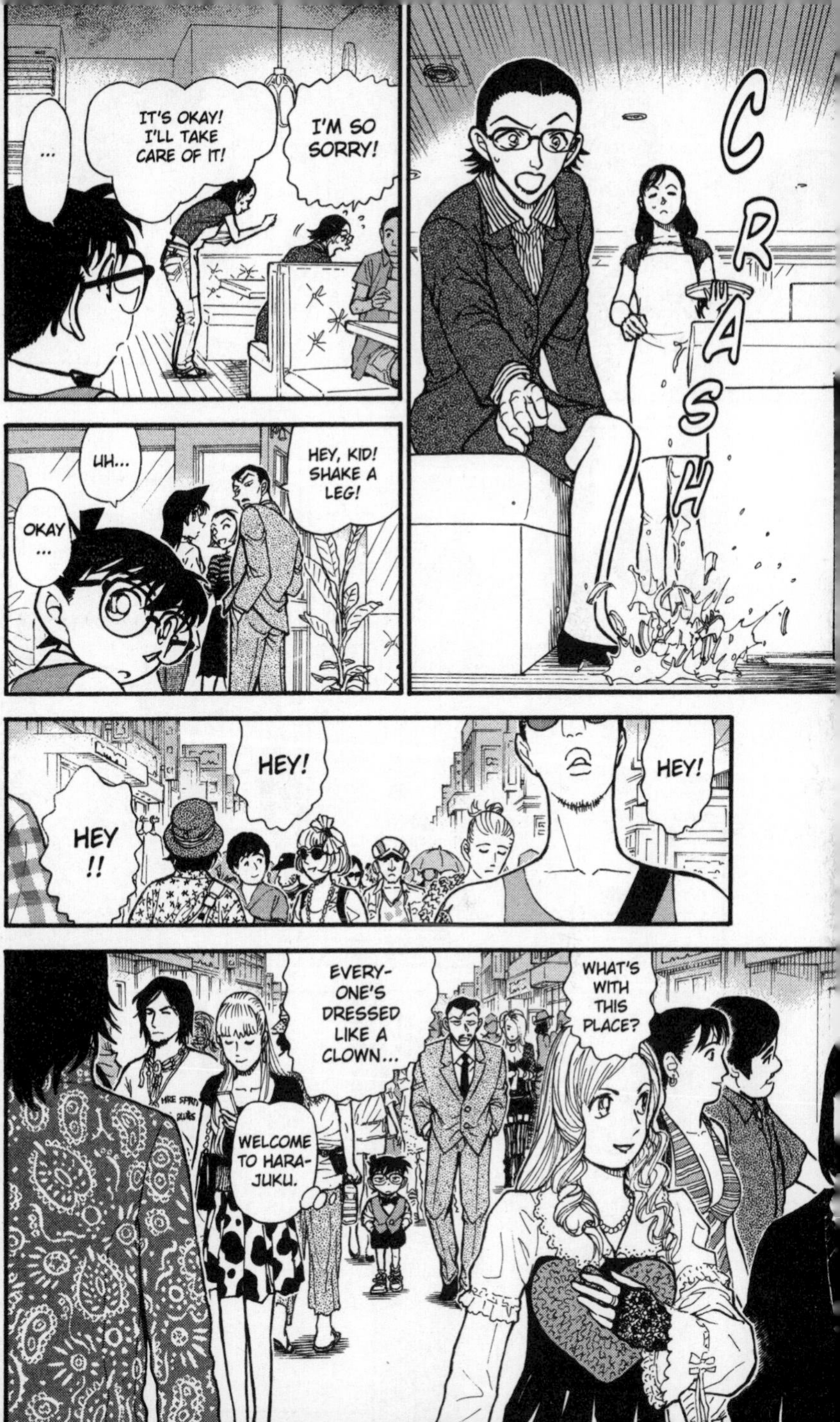
CRASH
I'M SO SORRY!
IT'S OKAY! I'LL TAKE CARE OF IT!
...
HEY, KID! SHAKE A LEG!
UH...
OKAY ...
HEY!
HEY!
HEY !!
WHAT'S WITH THIS PLACE?
EVERY-ONE'S DRESSED LIKE A CLOWN...
WELCOME TO HARA-JUKU.

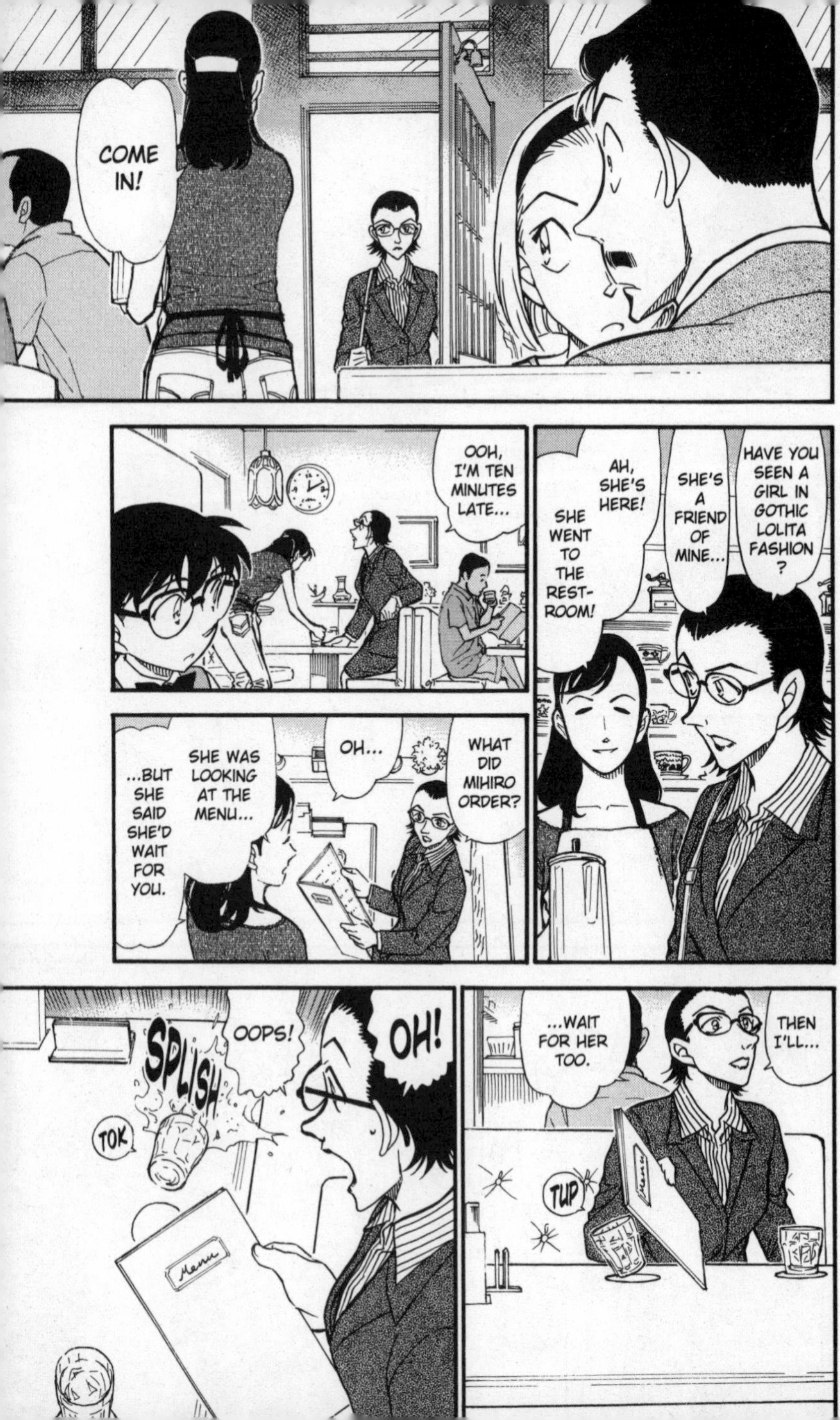
COME IN!
HAVE YOU SEEN A GIRL IN GOTHIC LOLITA FASHION?
SHE'S A FRIEND OF MINE...
AH, SHE'S HERE!
SHE WENT TO THE REST-ROOM!
OOH, I'M TEN MINUTES LATE...
WHAT DID MIHIRO ORDER?
OH...
SHE WAS LOOKING AT THE MENU...
...BUT SHE SAID SHE'D WAIT FOR YOU.
THEN I'LL...
...WAIT FOR HER TOO.
TUP
OH!
OOPS!
SPLISH
TOK

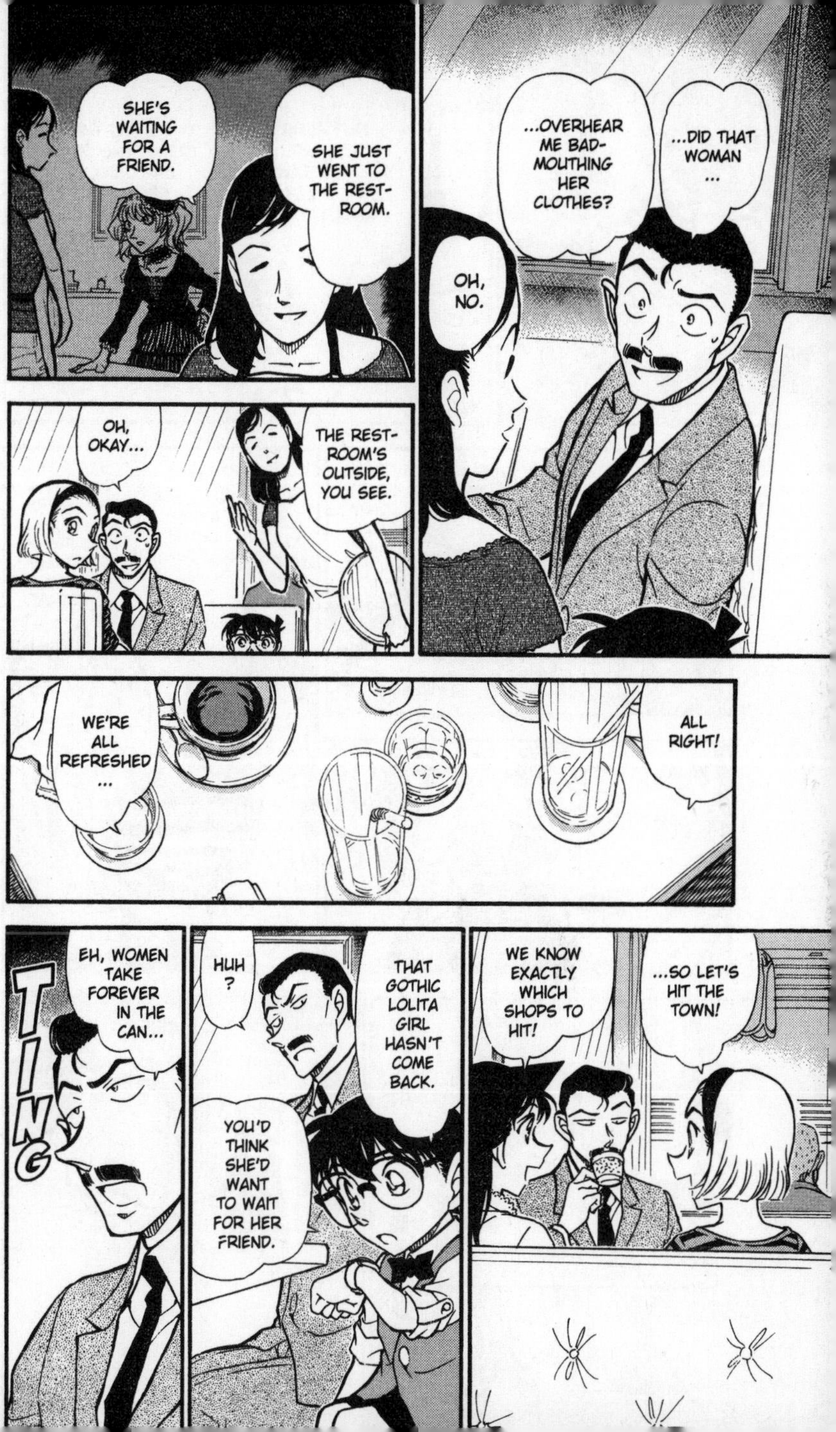
...DID THAT WOMAN ...
...OVERHEAR ME BAD-MOUTHING HER CLOTHES?
OH, NO.
SHE JUST WENT TO THE REST-ROOM.
SHE'S WAITING FOR A FRIEND.
THE REST-ROOM'S OUTSIDE, YOU SEE.
OH, OKAY...
ALL RIGHT!
WE'RE ALL REFRESHED ...
...SO LET'S HIT THE TOWN!
WE KNOW EXACTLY WHICH SHOPS TO HIT!
THAT GOTHIC LOLITA GIRL HASN'T COME BACK.
HUH ?
YOU'D THINK SHE'D WANT TO WAIT FOR HER FRIEND.
EH, WOMEN TAKE FOREVER IN THE CAN...
TING

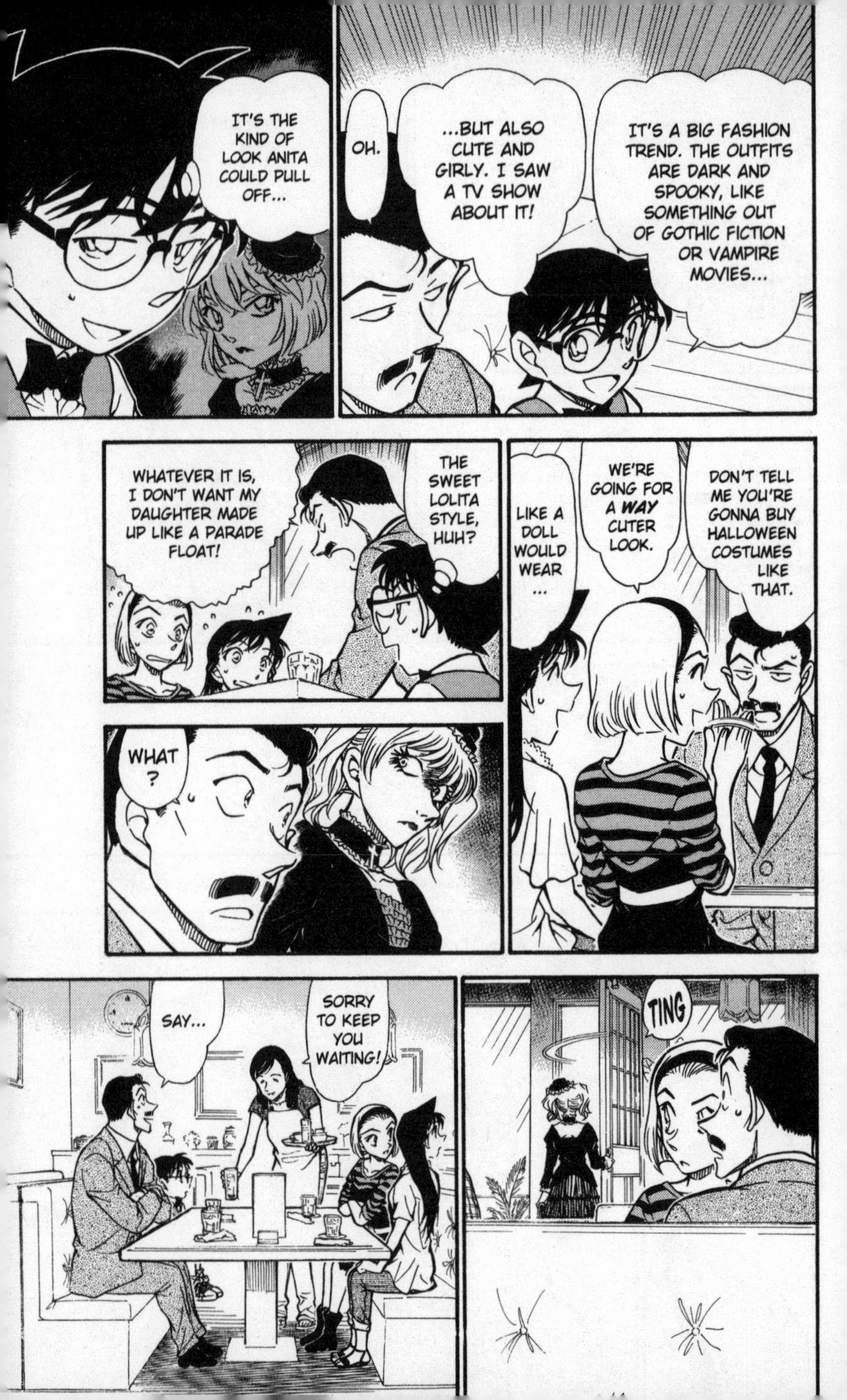
IT'S A BIG FASHION TREND. THE OUTFITS ARE DARK AND SPOOKY, LIKE SOMETHING OUT OF GOTHIC FICTION OR VAMPIRE MOVIES...
...BUT ALSO CUTE AND GIRLY. I SAW A TV SHOW ABOUT IT!
OH.
IT'S THE KIND OF LOOK ANITA COULD PULL OFF...
DON'T TELL ME YOU'RE GONNA BUY HALLOWEEN COSTUMES LIKE THAT.
WE'RE GOING FOR A **WAY** CUTER LOOK.
LIKE A DOLL WOULD WEAR...
THE SWEET LOLITA STYLE, HUH?
WHATEVER IT IS, I DON'T WANT MY DAUGHTER MADE UP LIKE A PARADE FLOAT!
WHAT?
TING
SORRY TO KEEP YOU WAITING!
SAY...

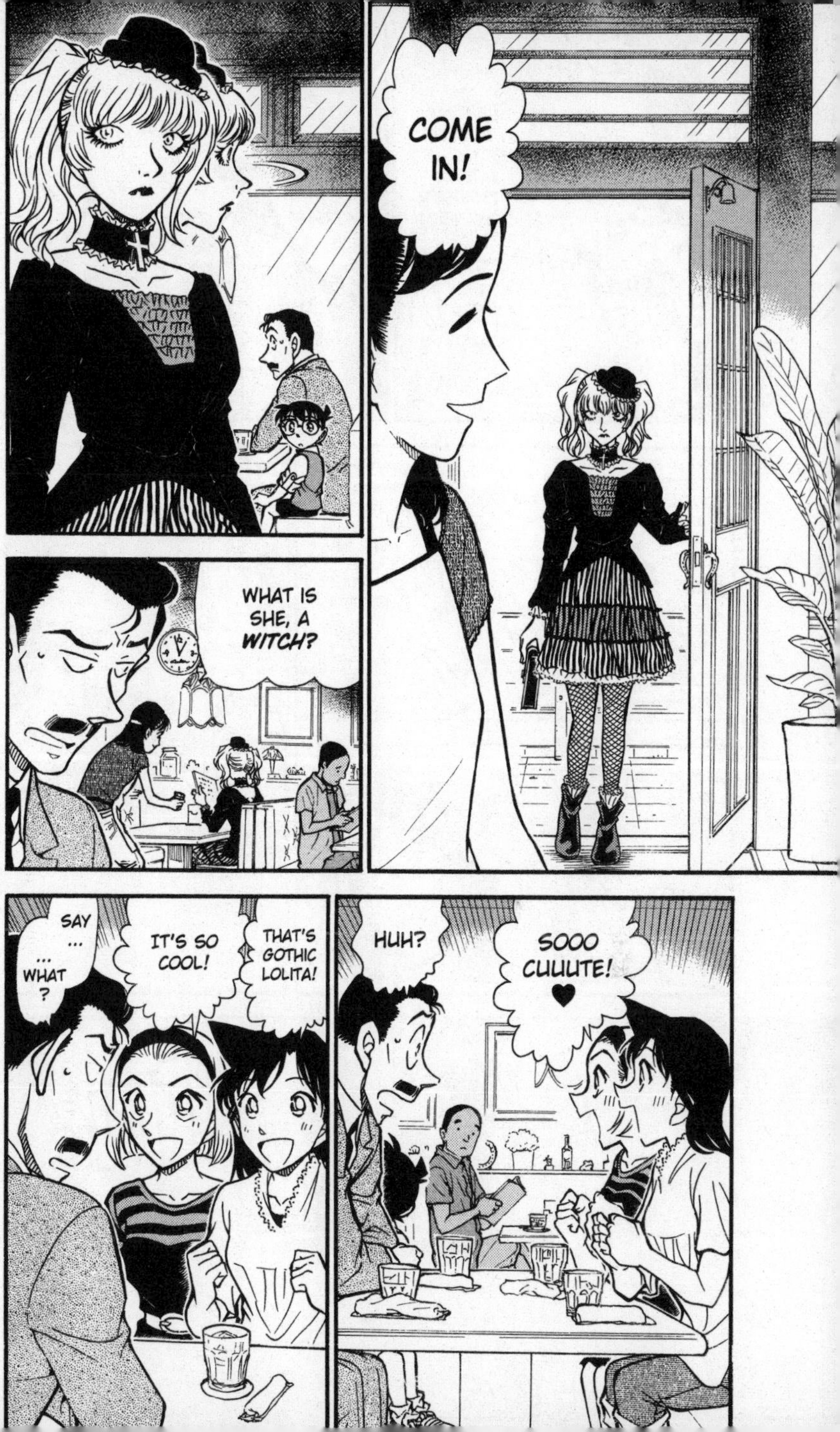

COME IN!
WHAT IS SHE, A WITCH?
SOOO CUUUTE! ♥
HUH?
THAT'S GOTHIC LOLITA!
IT'S SO COOL!
SAY ... ... WHAT ?

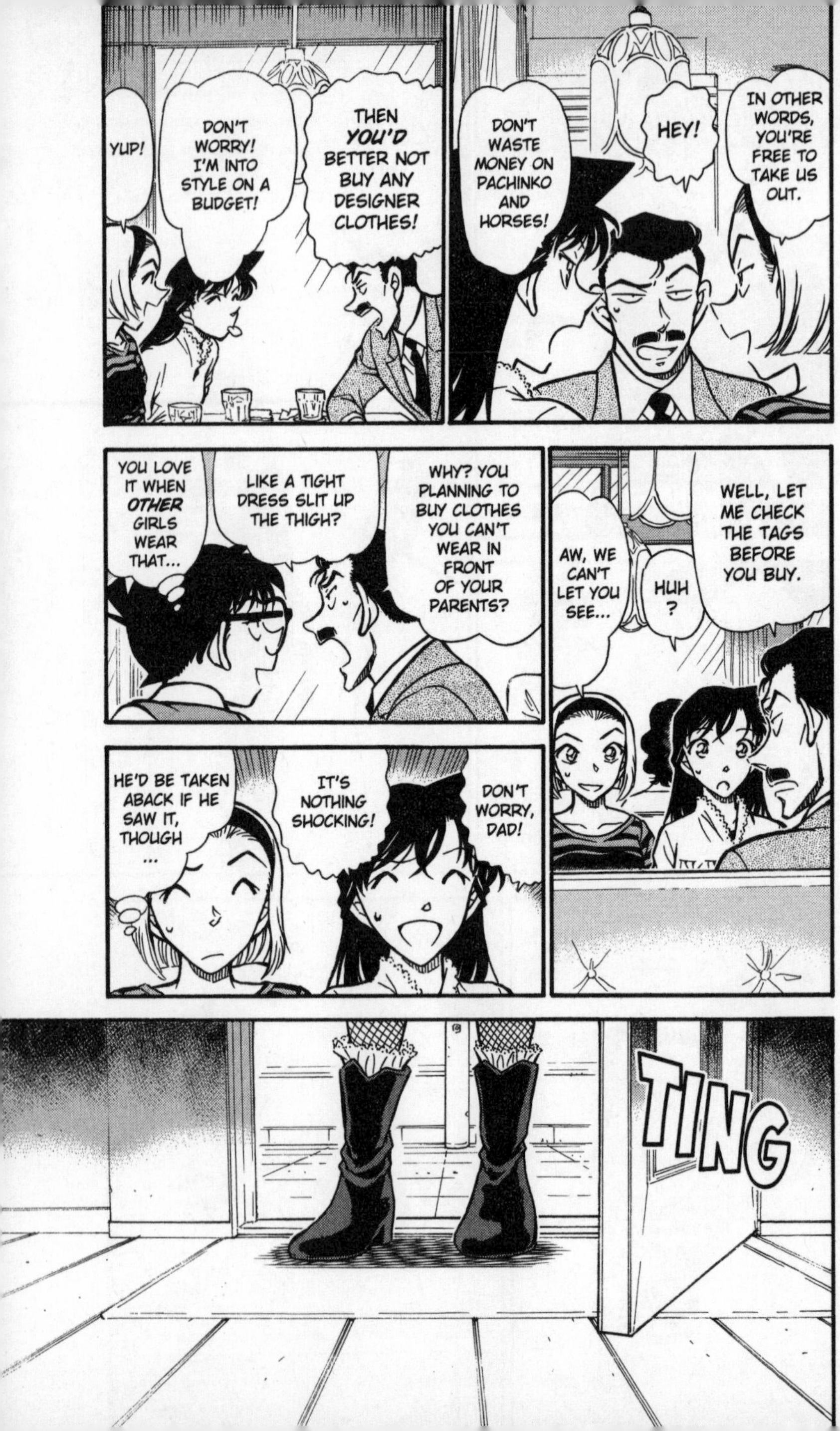
IN OTHER WORDS, YOU'RE FREE TO TAKE US OUT.
HEY!
DON'T WASTE MONEY ON PACHINKO AND HORSES!
THEN *YOU'D* BETTER NOT BUY ANY DESIGNER CLOTHES!
DON'T WORRY! I'M INTO STYLE ON A BUDGET!
YUP!
WELL, LET ME CHECK THE TAGS BEFORE YOU BUY.
HUH?
AW, WE CAN'T LET YOU SEE...
WHY? YOU PLANNING TO BUY CLOTHES YOU CAN'T WEAR IN FRONT OF YOUR PARENTS?
LIKE A TIGHT DRESS SLIT UP THE THIGH?
YOU LOVE IT WHEN *OTHER* GIRLS WEAR THAT...
DON'T WORRY, DAD!
IT'S NOTHING SHOCKING!
HE'D BE TAKEN ABACK IF HE SAW IT, THOUGH ...
TING

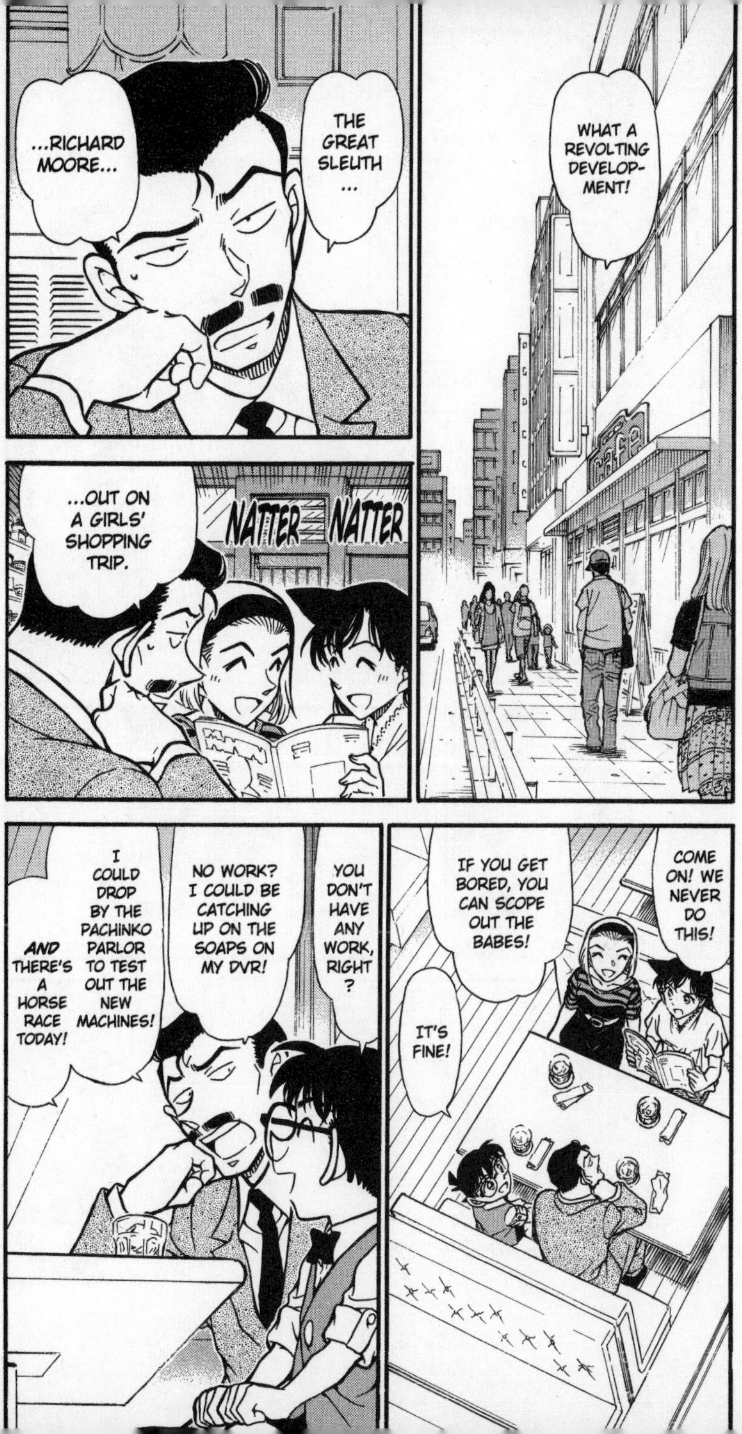
WHAT A REVOLTING DEVELOPMENT!
THE GREAT SLEUTH ...
...RICHARD MOORE...
...OUT ON A GIRLS' SHOPPING TRIP.
NATTER NATTER
COME ON! WE NEVER DO THIS!
IF YOU GET BORED, YOU CAN SCOPE OUT THE BABES!
IT'S FINE!
YOU DON'T HAVE ANY WORK, RIGHT?
NO WORK? I COULD BE CATCHING UP ON THE SOAPS ON MY DVR!
I COULD DROP BY THE PACHINKO PARLOR TO TEST OUT THE NEW MACHINES!
AND THERE'S A HORSE RACE TODAY!

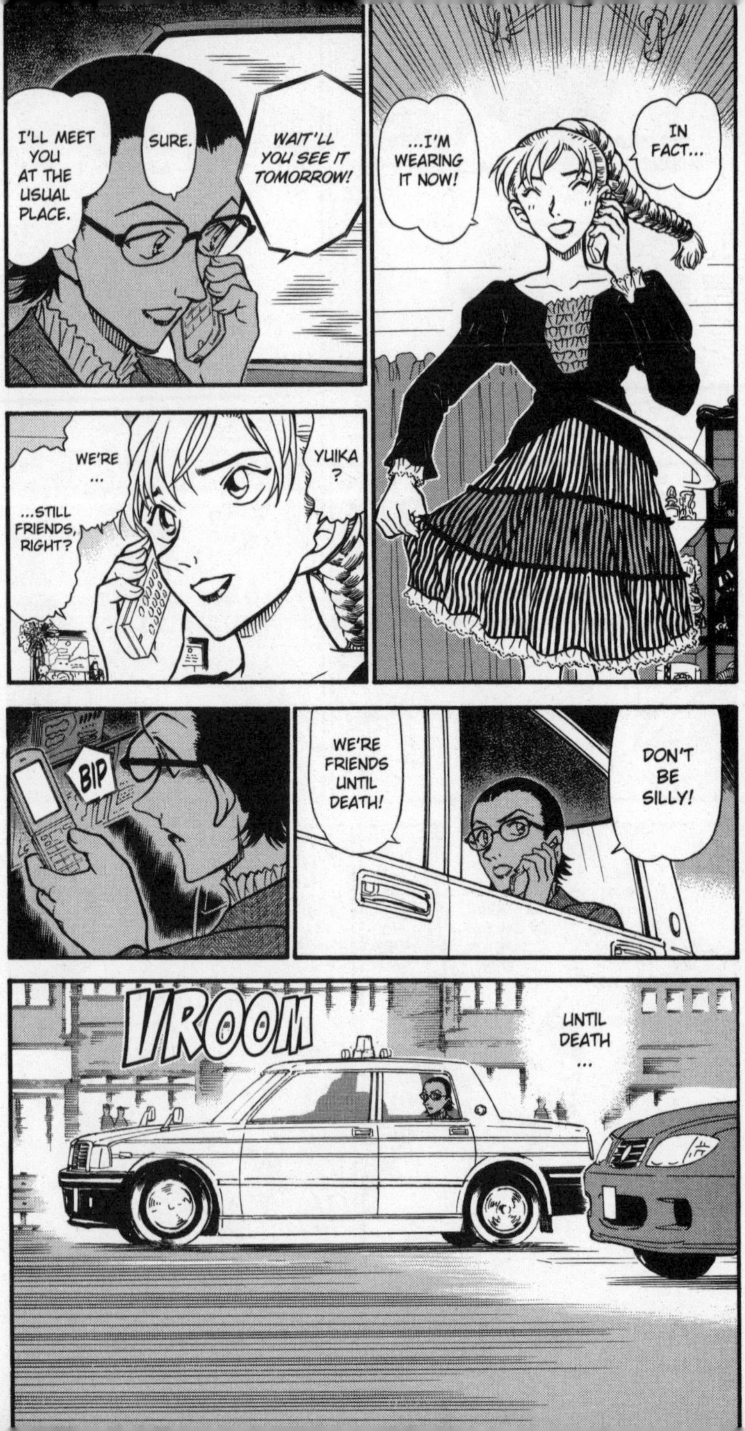
IN FACT...
...I'M WEARING IT NOW!
WAIT'LL YOU SEE IT TOMORROW!
SURE.
I'LL MEET YOU AT THE USUAL PLACE.
YUIKA?
WE'RE...
...STILL FRIENDS, RIGHT?
DON'T BE SILLY!
WE'RE FRIENDS UNTIL DEATH!
BIP
UNTIL DEATH...
VROOM

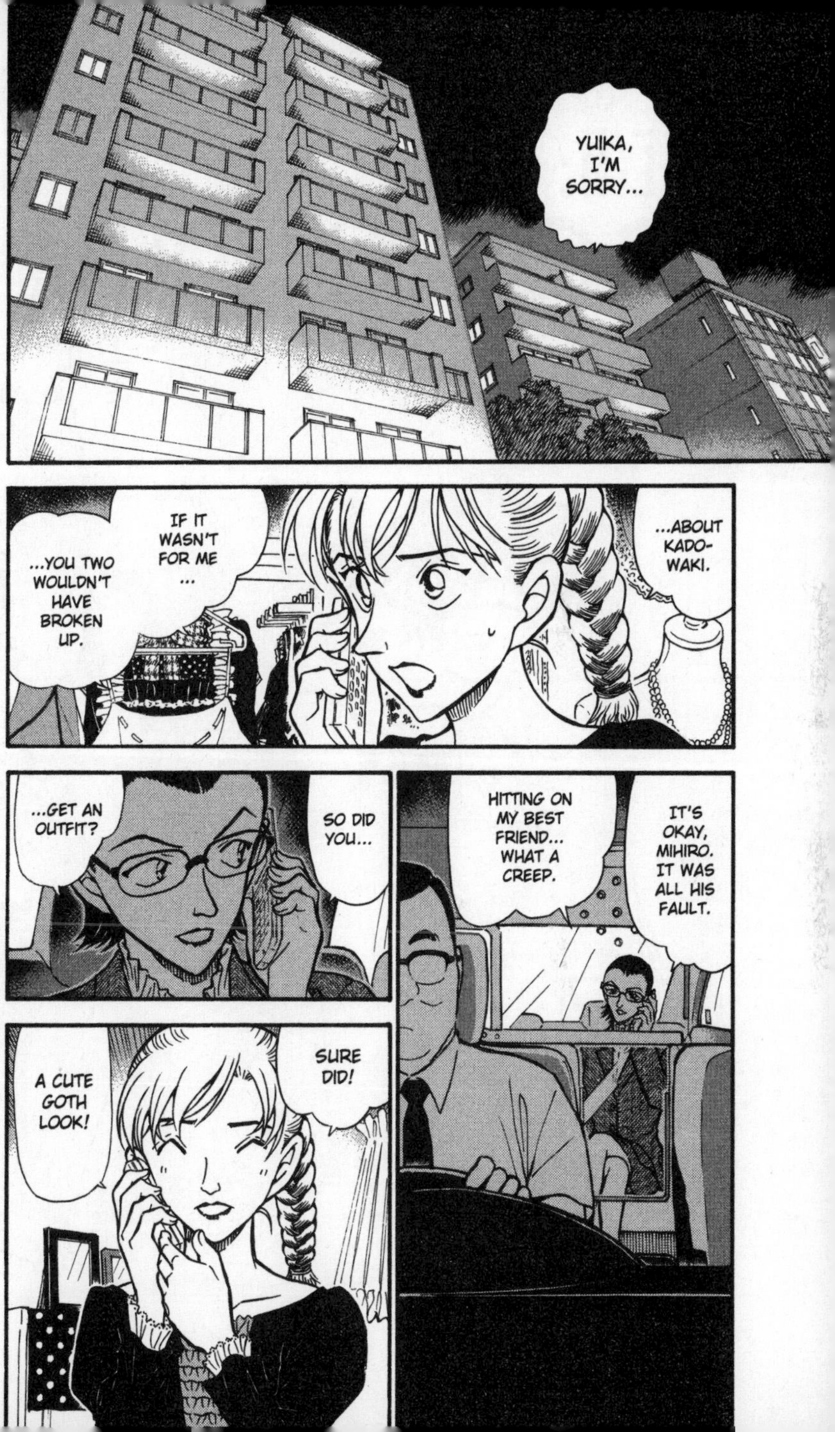
YUIKA, I'M SORRY...
...ABOUT KADO-WAKI.
IF IT WASN'T FOR ME ...
...YOU TWO WOULDN'T HAVE BROKEN UP.
IT'S OKAY, MIHIRO. IT WAS ALL HIS FAULT.
HITTING ON MY BEST FRIEND... WHAT A CREEP.
SO DID YOU...
...GET AN OUTFIT?
SURE DID!
A CUTE GOTH LOOK!

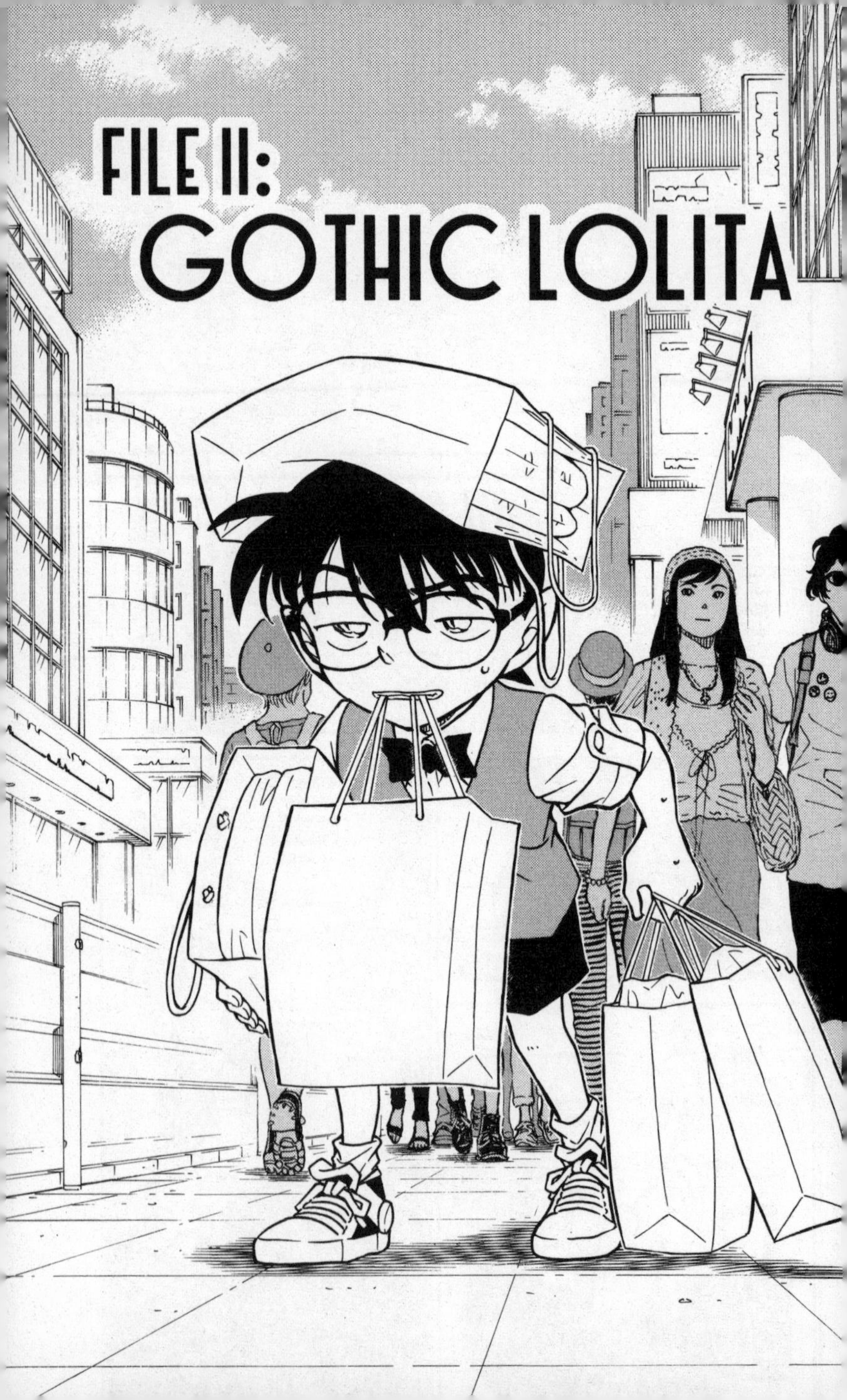
FILE 11:
GOTHIC LOLITA

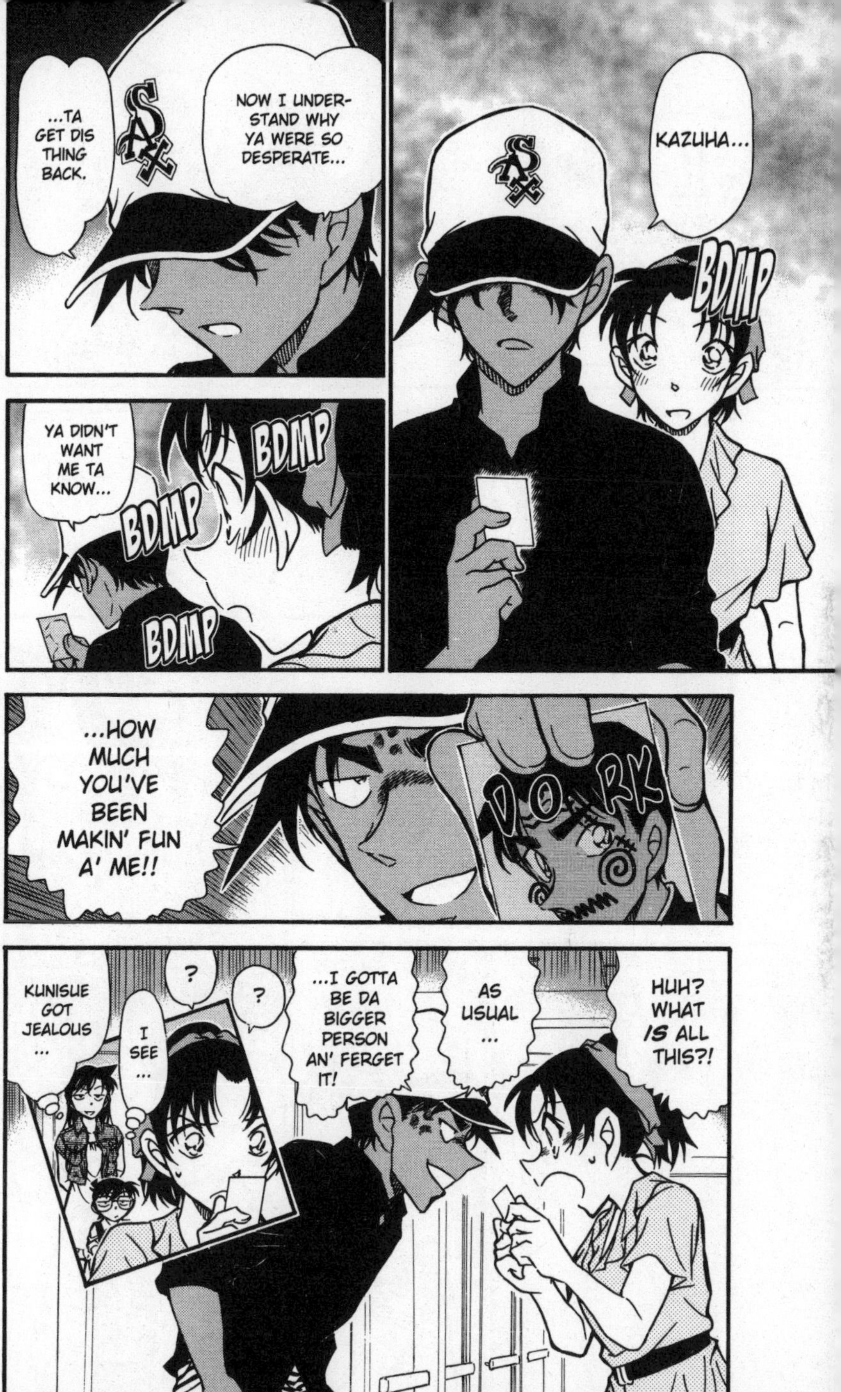
KAZUHA...
BDMP
NOW I UNDER-STAND WHY YA WERE SO DESPERATE...
...TA GET DIS THING BACK.
BDMP
YA DIDN'T WANT ME TA KNOW...
BDMP
BDMP
...HOW MUCH YOU'VE BEEN MAKIN' FUN A' ME!!
DORK
HUH? WHAT IS ALL THIS?!
AS USUAL...
...I GOTTA BE DA BIGGER PERSON AN' FERGET IT!
?
?
I SEE...
KUNISUE GOT JEALOUS...

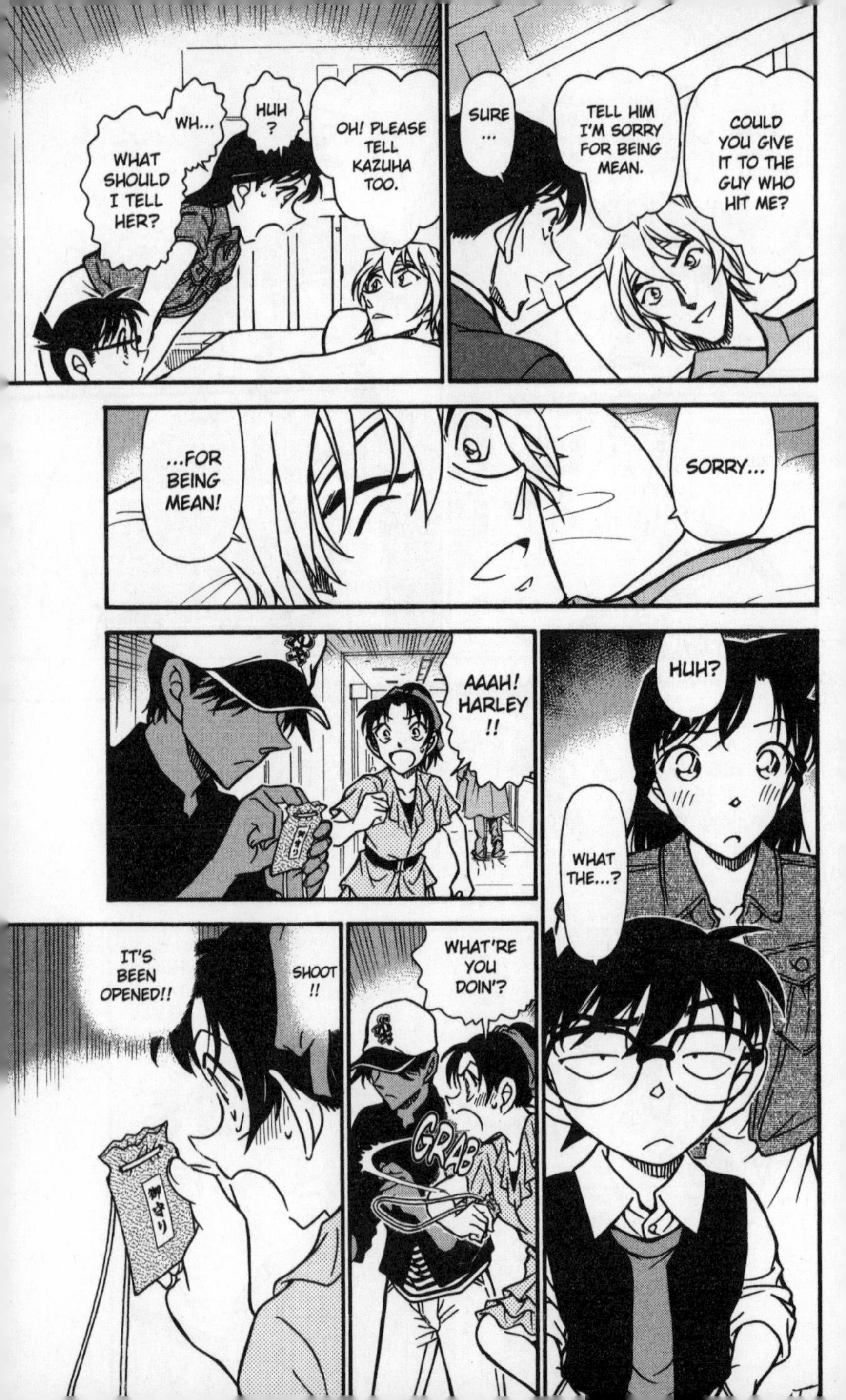
COULD YOU GIVE IT TO THE GUY WHO HIT ME?
TELL HIM I'M SORRY FOR BEING MEAN.
SURE...
OH! PLEASE TELL KAZUHA TOO.
HUH?
WH...
WHAT SHOULD I TELL HER?
SORRY...
...FOR BEING MEAN!
HUH?
WHAT THE...?
AAAH! HARLEY !!
WHAT'RE YOU DOIN'?
GRAB
SHOOT !!
IT'S BEEN OPENED!!
御守り

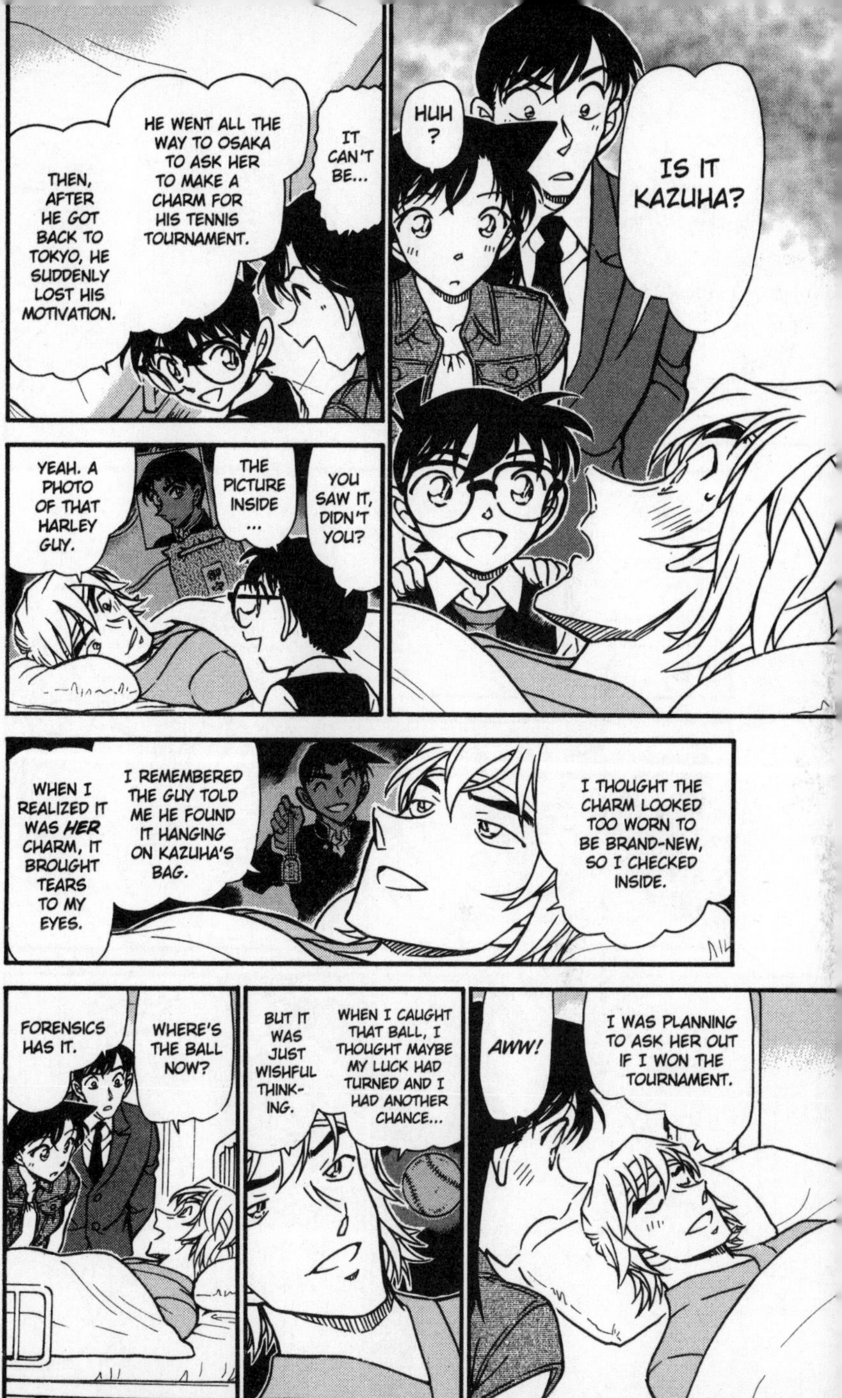
IS IT KAZUHA?
HUH?
IT CAN'T BE...
HE WENT ALL THE WAY TO OSAKA TO ASK HER TO MAKE A CHARM FOR HIS TENNIS TOURNAMENT.
THEN, AFTER HE GOT BACK TO TOKYO, HE SUDDENLY LOST HIS MOTIVATION.
YOU SAW IT, DIDN'T YOU?
THE PICTURE INSIDE ...
YEAH. A PHOTO OF THAT HARLEY GUY.
I THOUGHT THE CHARM LOOKED TOO WORN TO BE BRAND-NEW, SO I CHECKED INSIDE.
I REMEMBERED THE GUY TOLD ME HE FOUND IT HANGING ON KAZUHA'S BAG.
WHEN I REALIZED IT WAS *HER* CHARM, IT BROUGHT TEARS TO MY EYES.
I WAS PLANNING TO ASK HER OUT IF I WON THE TOURNAMENT.
AWW!
WHEN I CAUGHT THAT BALL, I THOUGHT MAYBE MY LUCK HAD TURNED AND I HAD ANOTHER CHANCE...
BUT IT WAS JUST WISHFUL THINK-ING.
WHERE'S THE BALL NOW?
FORENSICS HAS IT.

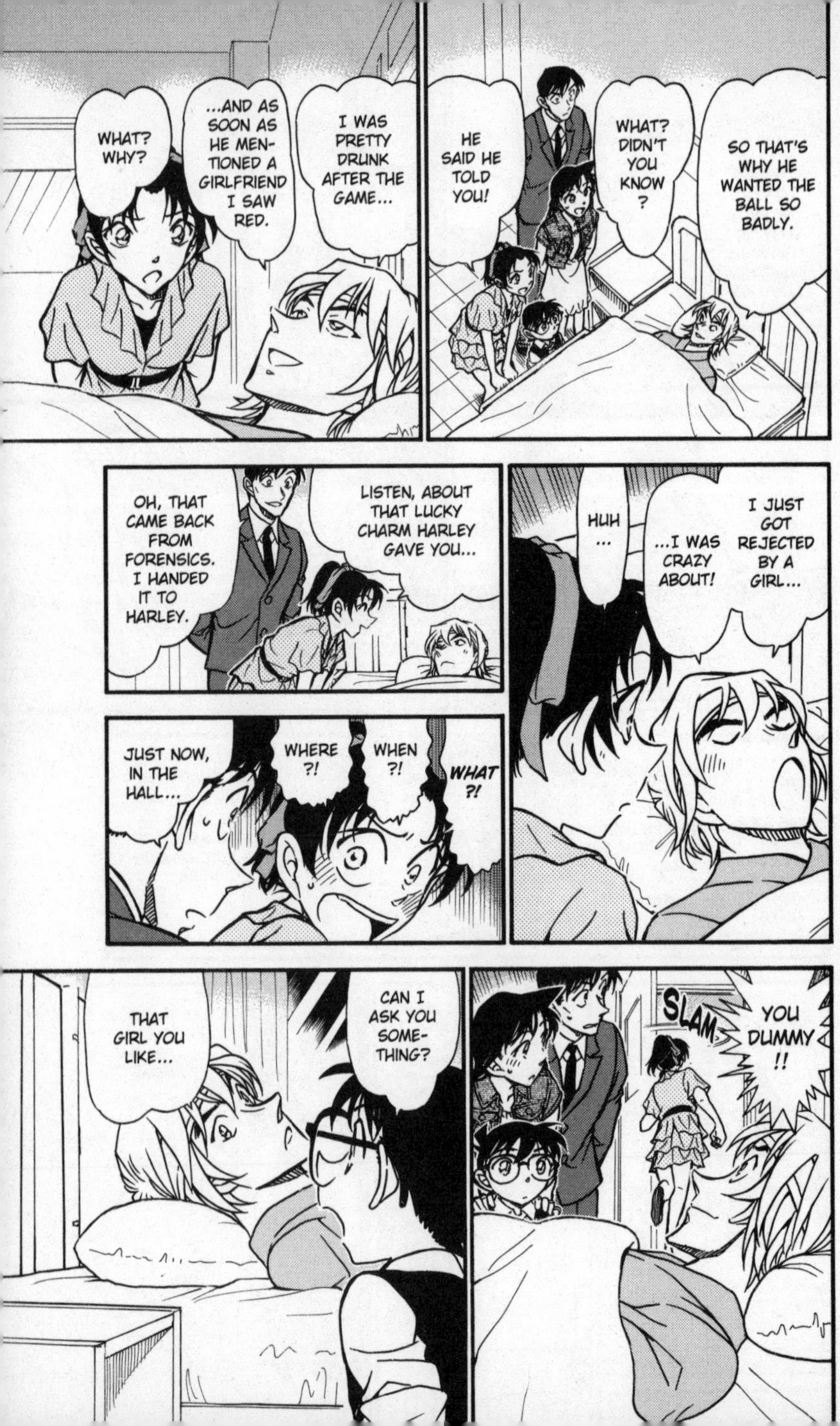
SO THAT'S WHY HE WANTED THE BALL SO BADLY.
WHAT? DIDN'T YOU KNOW ?
HE SAID HE TOLD YOU!
I WAS PRETTY DRUNK AFTER THE GAME...
...AND AS SOON AS HE MEN-TIONED A GIRLFRIEND I SAW RED.
WHAT? WHY?
I JUST GOT REJECTED BY A GIRL...
...I WAS CRAZY ABOUT!
HUH ...
LISTEN, ABOUT THAT LUCKY CHARM HARLEY GAVE YOU...
OH, THAT CAME BACK FROM FORENSICS. I HANDED IT TO HARLEY.
WHAT ?!
WHEN ?!
WHERE ?!
JUST NOW, IN THE HALL...
SLAM
YOU DUMMY !!
CAN I ASK YOU SOME-THING?
THAT GIRL YOU LIKE...

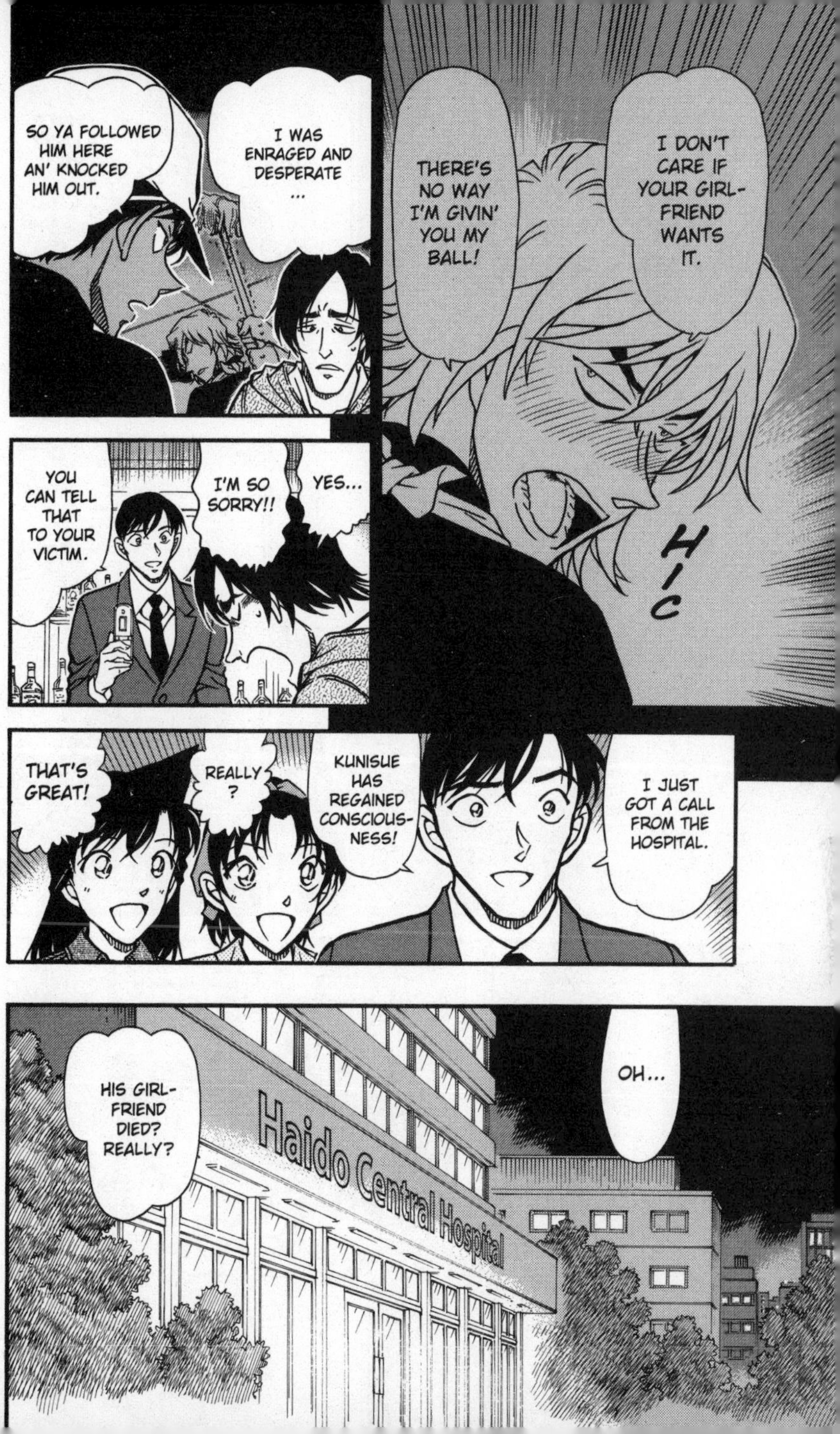
I DON'T CARE IF YOUR GIRL-FRIEND WANTS IT.
THERE'S NO WAY I'M GIVIN' YOU MY BALL!
HIC
I WAS ENRAGED AND DESPERATE ...
SO YA FOLLOWED HIM HERE AN' KNOCKED HIM OUT.
YES...
I'M SO SORRY!!
YOU CAN TELL THAT TO YOUR VICTIM.
I JUST GOT A CALL FROM THE HOSPITAL.
KUNISUE HAS REGAINED CONSCIOUS-NESS!
REALLY?
THAT'S GREAT!
OH...
Haido Central Hospital
HIS GIRL-FRIEND DIED? REALLY?

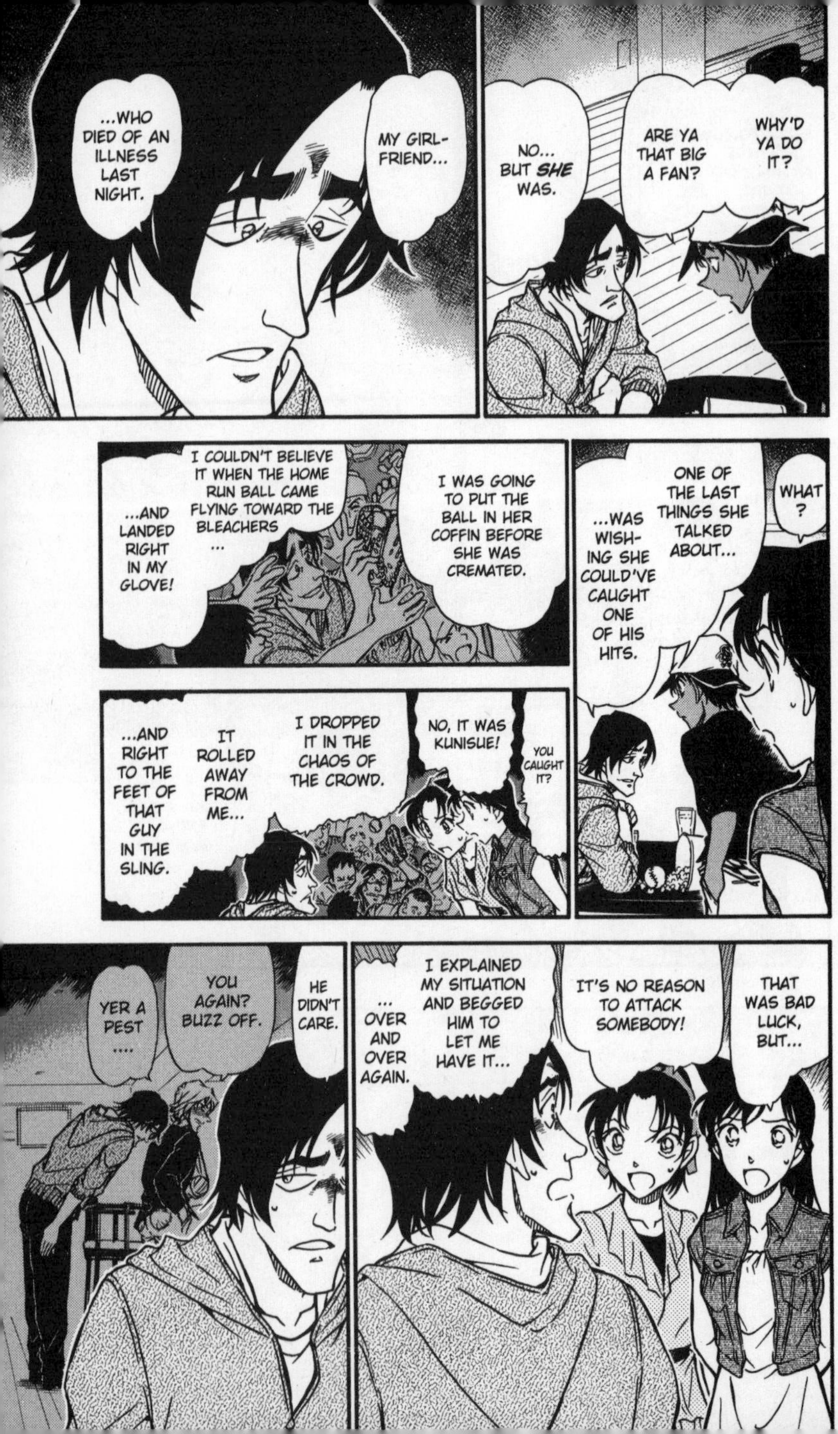
WHY'D YA DO IT?
ARE YA THAT BIG A FAN?
NO... BUT *SHE* WAS.
MY GIRL-FRIEND...
...WHO DIED OF AN ILLNESS LAST NIGHT.
WHAT?
ONE OF THE LAST THINGS SHE TALKED ABOUT...
...WAS WISHING SHE COULD'VE CAUGHT ONE OF HIS HITS.
I WAS GOING TO PUT THE BALL IN HER COFFIN BEFORE SHE WAS CREMATED.
I COULDN'T BELIEVE IT WHEN THE HOME RUN BALL CAME FLYING TOWARD THE BLEACHERS...
...AND LANDED RIGHT IN MY GLOVE!
YOU CAUGHT IT?
NO, IT WAS KUNISUE!
I DROPPED IT IN THE CHAOS OF THE CROWD.
IT ROLLED AWAY FROM ME...
...AND RIGHT TO THE FEET OF THAT GUY IN THE SLING.
THAT WAS BAD LUCK, BUT...
IT'S NO REASON TO ATTACK SOMEBODY!
I EXPLAINED MY SITUATION AND BEGGED HIM TO LET ME HAVE IT...
...OVER AND OVER AGAIN.
HE DIDN'T CARE.
YOU AGAIN? BUZZ OFF.
YER A PEST....

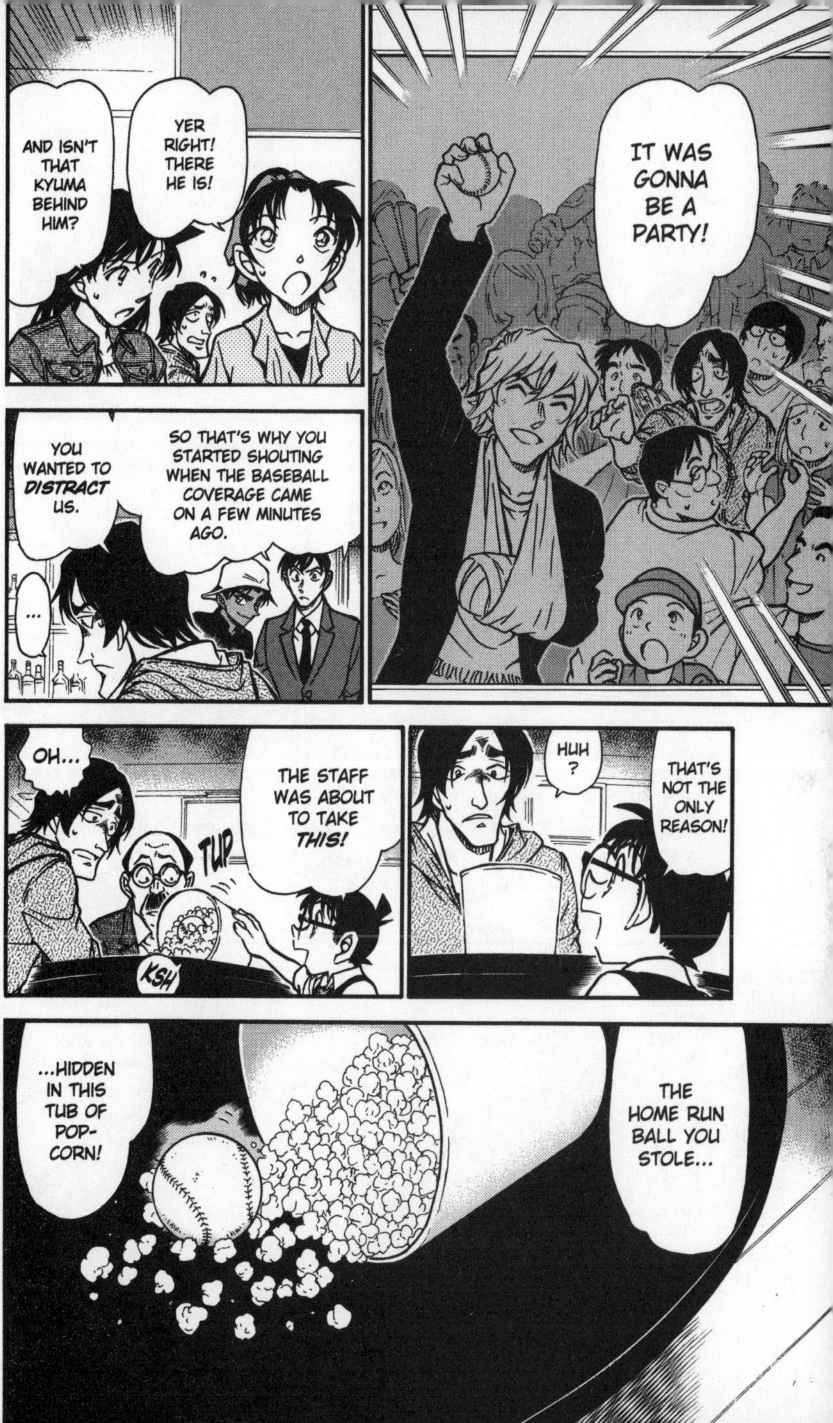
IT WAS GONNA BE A PARTY!
YER RIGHT! THERE HE IS!
AND ISN'T THAT KYUMA BEHIND HIM?
SO THAT'S WHY YOU STARTED SHOUTING WHEN THE BASEBALL COVERAGE CAME ON A FEW MINUTES AGO.
YOU WANTED TO *DISTRACT* US.
...
THAT'S NOT THE ONLY REASON!
HUH?
THE STAFF WAS ABOUT TO TAKE *THIS!*
TUP
OH...
KSH
THE HOME RUN BALL YOU STOLE...
...HIDDEN IN THIS TUB OF POP-CORN!

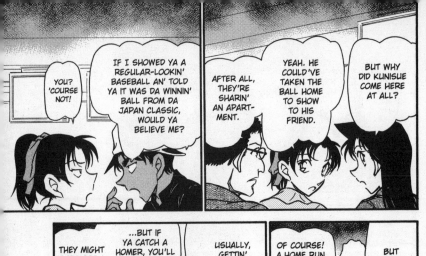

BUT WHY DID KUNISUE COME HERE AT ALL?
YEAH. HE COULD'VE TAKEN THE BALL HOME TO SHOW TO HIS FRIEND.
AFTER ALL, THEY'RE SHARIN' AN APART-MENT.
IF I SHOWED YA A REGULAR-LOOKIN' BASEBALL AN' TOLD YA IT WAS DA WINNIN' BALL FROM DA JAPAN CLASSIC, WOULD YA BELIEVE ME?
YOU? 'COURSE NOT!
BUT WHAT IF I HAD VIDEO PROOF?
PROOF?
OF COURSE! A HOME RUN WOULD GET REPLAYED ON THE SPORTS CHANNELS!
USUALLY, GETTIN' CAUGHT ON TV AT A GAME IS PURE LUCK...
...BUT IF YA CATCH A HOMER, YOU'LL DEFINITELY BE ON CAMERA!
THEY MIGHT EVEN GET A CLOSE-UP OF A GUY CHEERIN' WITH HIS ARM IN A SLING!
DAT'S WHY KUNISUE WANTED TA HIT A SPORTS BAR.
TIME FOR TODAY'S HOME RUN HIGH-LIGHT! ♪
WAK
HE WAS GONNA SHOW HIS FRIEND AN' DA WHOLE BAR...
...DA HOME RUN BALL HE CAUGHT ...
...ALONG WITH DA FOOTAGE ON TV.
WAAAA

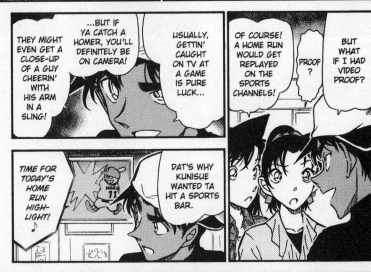

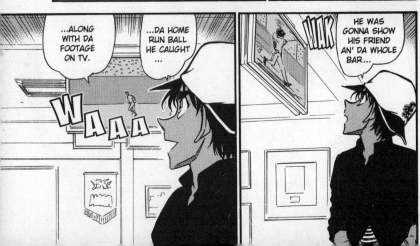

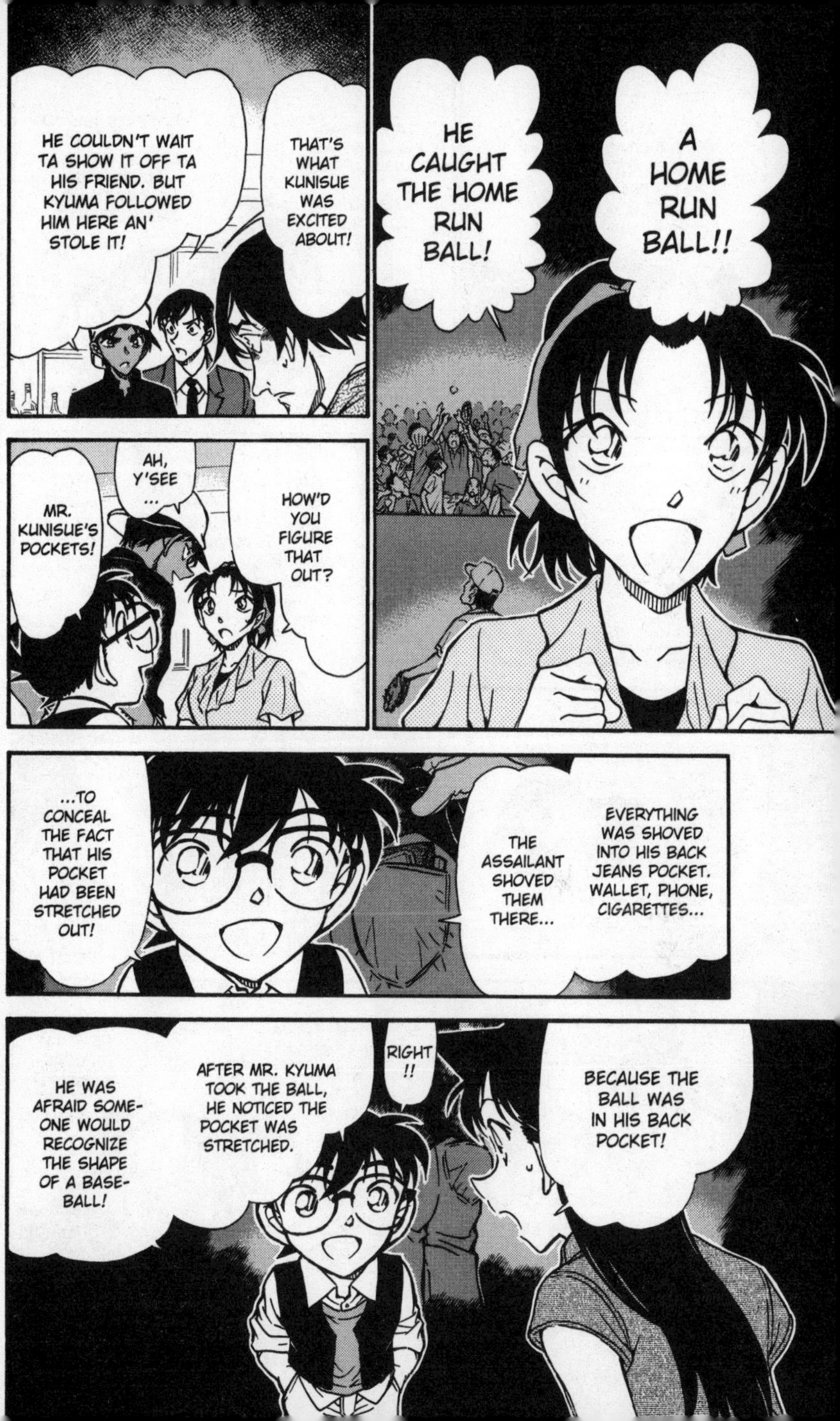
A HOME RUN BALL!!
HE CAUGHT THE HOME RUN BALL!
THAT'S WHAT KUNISUE WAS EXCITED ABOUT!
HE COULDN'T WAIT TA SHOW IT OFF TA HIS FRIEND. BUT KYUMA FOLLOWED HIM HERE AN' STOLE IT!
HOW'D YOU FIGURE THAT OUT?
AH, Y'SEE ...
MR. KUNISUE'S POCKETS!
EVERYTHING WAS SHOVED INTO HIS BACK JEANS POCKET. WALLET, PHONE, CIGARETTES...
THE ASSAILANT SHOVED THEM THERE...
...TO CONCEAL THE FACT THAT HIS POCKET HAD BEEN STRETCHED OUT!
BECAUSE THE BALL WAS IN HIS BACK POCKET!
RIGHT !!
AFTER MR. KYUMA TOOK THE BALL, HE NOTICED THE POCKET WAS STRETCHED.
HE WAS AFRAID SOME-ONE WOULD RECOGNIZE THE SHAPE OF A BASE-BALL!

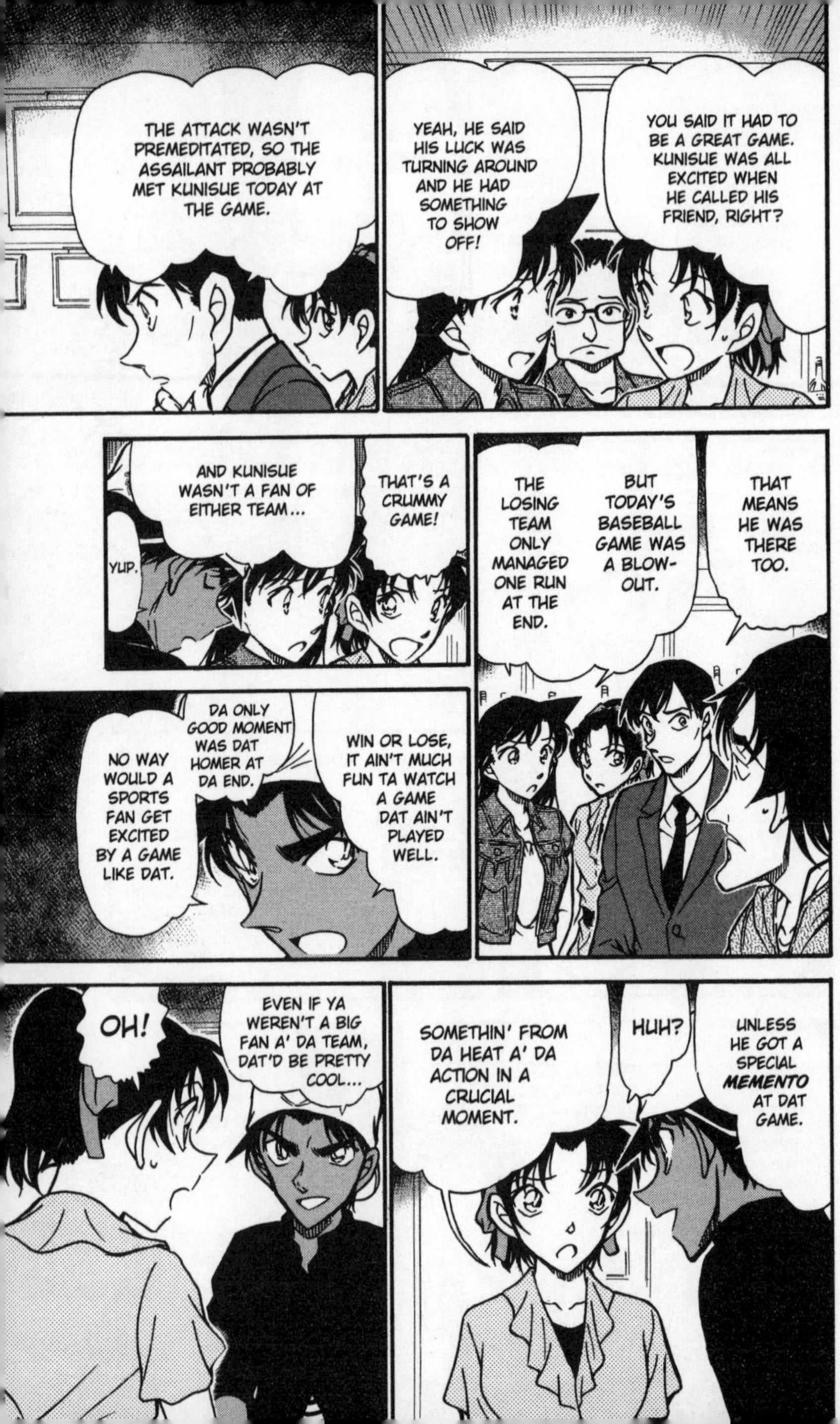
YOU SAID IT HAD TO BE A GREAT GAME. KUNISUE WAS ALL EXCITED WHEN HE CALLED HIS FRIEND, RIGHT?
YEAH, HE SAID HIS LUCK WAS TURNING AROUND AND HE HAD SOMETHING TO SHOW OFF!
THE ATTACK WASN'T PREMEDITATED, SO THE ASSAILANT PROBABLY MET KUNISUE TODAY AT THE GAME.
THAT MEANS HE WAS THERE TOO.
BUT TODAY'S BASEBALL GAME WAS A BLOW-OUT.
THE LOSING TEAM ONLY MANAGED ONE RUN AT THE END.
THAT'S A CRUMMY GAME!
AND KUNISUE WASN'T A FAN OF EITHER TEAM...
YUP.
WIN OR LOSE, IT AIN'T MUCH FUN TA WATCH A GAME DAT AIN'T PLAYED WELL.
DA ONLY GOOD MOMENT WAS DAT HOMER AT DA END.
NO WAY WOULD A SPORTS FAN GET EXCITED BY A GAME LIKE DAT.
UNLESS HE GOT A SPECIAL *MEMENTO* AT DAT GAME.
HUH?
SOMETHIN' FROM DA HEAT A' DA ACTION IN A CRUCIAL MOMENT.
EVEN IF YA WEREN'T A BIG FAN A' DA TEAM, DAT'D BE PRETTY COOL...
OH!

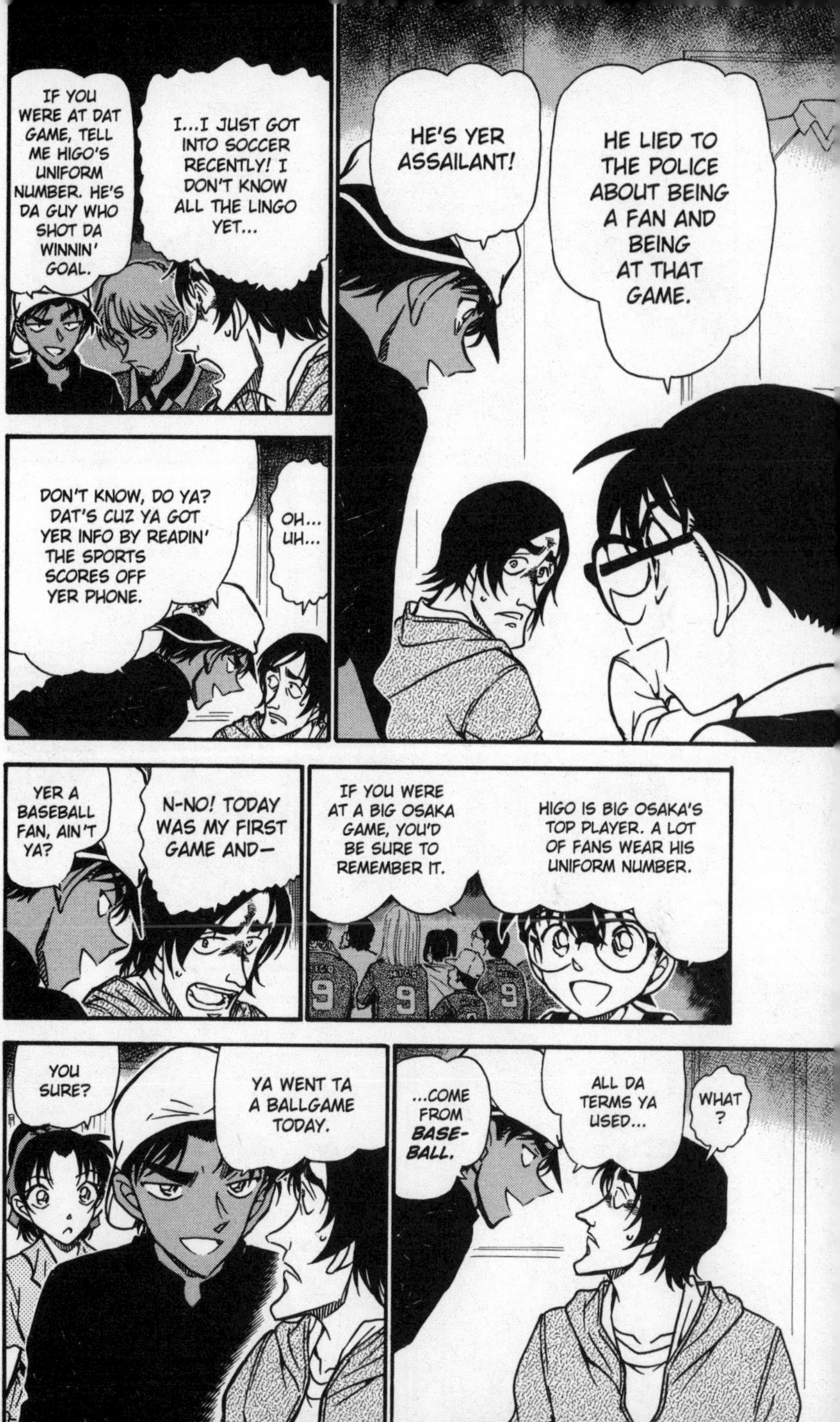
HE LIED TO THE POLICE ABOUT BEING A FAN AND BEING AT THAT GAME.
HE'S YER ASSAILANT!
IF YOU WERE AT DAT GAME, TELL ME HIGO'S UNIFORM NUMBER. HE'S DA GUY WHO SHOT DA WINNIN' GOAL.
I...I JUST GOT INTO SOCCER RECENTLY! I DON'T KNOW ALL THE LINGO YET...
DON'T KNOW, DO YA? DAT'S CUZ YA GOT YER INFO BY READIN' THE SPORTS SCORES OFF YER PHONE.
OH... UH...
HIGO IS BIG OSAKA'S TOP PLAYER. A LOT OF FANS WEAR HIS UNIFORM NUMBER.
IF YOU WERE AT A BIG OSAKA GAME, YOU'D BE SURE TO REMEMBER IT.
YER A BASEBALL FAN, AIN'T YA?
N-NO! TODAY WAS MY FIRST GAME AND—
WHAT?
ALL DA TERMS YA USED...
...COME FROM BASEBALL.
YA WENT TA A BALLGAME TODAY.
YOU SURE?

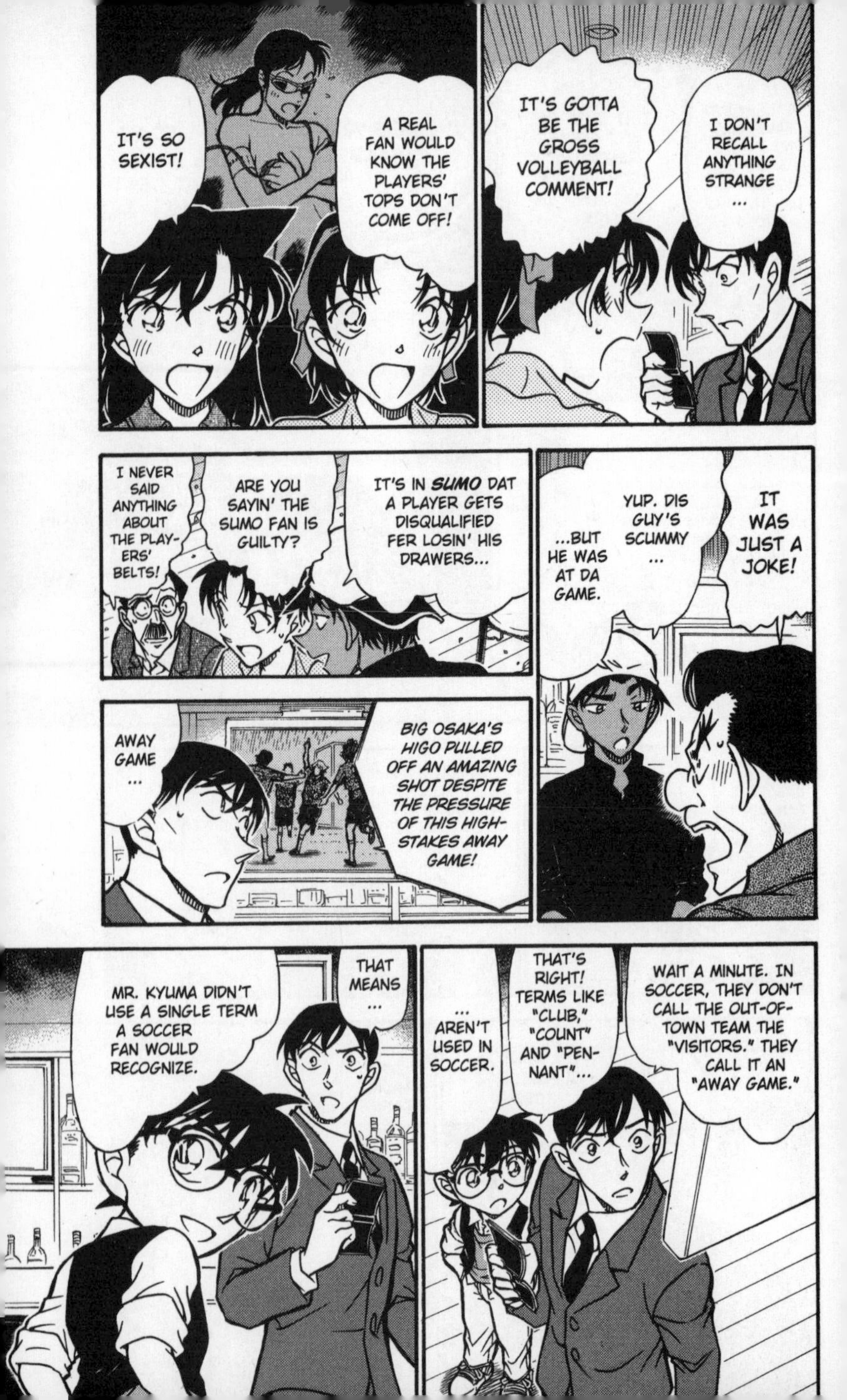
I DON'T RECALL ANYTHING STRANGE ...
IT'S GOTTA BE THE GROSS VOLLEYBALL COMMENT!
A REAL FAN WOULD KNOW THE PLAYERS' TOPS DON'T COME OFF!
IT'S SO SEXIST!
IT WAS JUST A JOKE!
YUP. DIS GUY'S SCUMMY ...
...BUT HE WAS AT DA GAME.
IT'S IN **SUMO** DAT A PLAYER GETS DISQUALIFIED FER LOSIN' HIS DRAWERS...
ARE YOU SAYIN' THE SUMO FAN IS GUILTY?
I NEVER SAID ANYTHING ABOUT THE PLAY-ERS' BELTS!
BIG OSAKA'S HIGO PULLED OFF AN AMAZING SHOT DESPITE THE PRESSURE OF THIS HIGH-STAKES AWAY GAME!
AWAY GAME ...
WAIT A MINUTE. IN SOCCER, THEY DON'T CALL THE OUT-OF-TOWN TEAM THE "VISITORS." THEY CALL IT AN "AWAY GAME."
THAT'S RIGHT! TERMS LIKE "CLUB," "COUNT" AND "PEN-NANT"...
... AREN'T USED IN SOCCER.
THAT MEANS ...
MR. KYUMA DIDN'T USE A SINGLE TERM A SOCCER FAN WOULD RECOGNIZE.

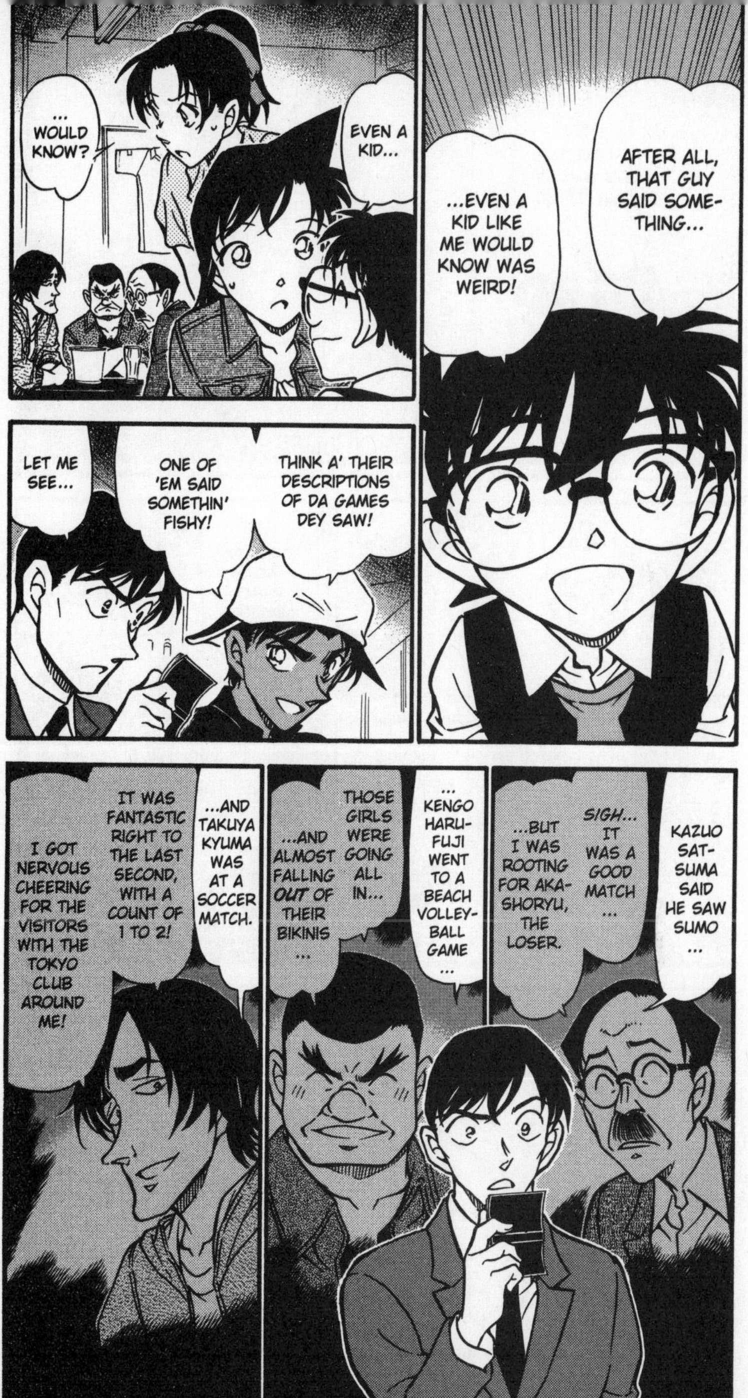
AFTER ALL, THAT GUY SAID SOMETHING...
...EVEN A KID LIKE ME WOULD KNOW WAS WEIRD!
EVEN A KID...
... WOULD KNOW?
THINK A' THEIR DESCRIPTIONS OF DA GAMES DEY SAW!
ONE OF 'EM SAID SOMETHIN' FISHY!
LET ME SEE...
KAZUO SATSUMA SAID HE SAW SUMO ...
SIGH... IT WAS A GOOD MATCH ...
...BUT I WAS ROOTING FOR AKASHORYU, THE LOSER.
... KENGO HARUFUJI WENT TO A BEACH VOLLEYBALL GAME ...
THOSE GIRLS WERE GOING ALL IN...
...AND ALMOST FALLING *OUT* OF THEIR BIKINIS ...
...AND TAKUYA KYUMA WAS AT A SOCCER MATCH.
IT WAS FANTASTIC RIGHT TO THE LAST SECOND, WITH A COUNT OF 1 TO 2!
I GOT NERVOUS CHEERING FOR THE VISITORS WITH THE TOKYO CLUB AROUND ME!

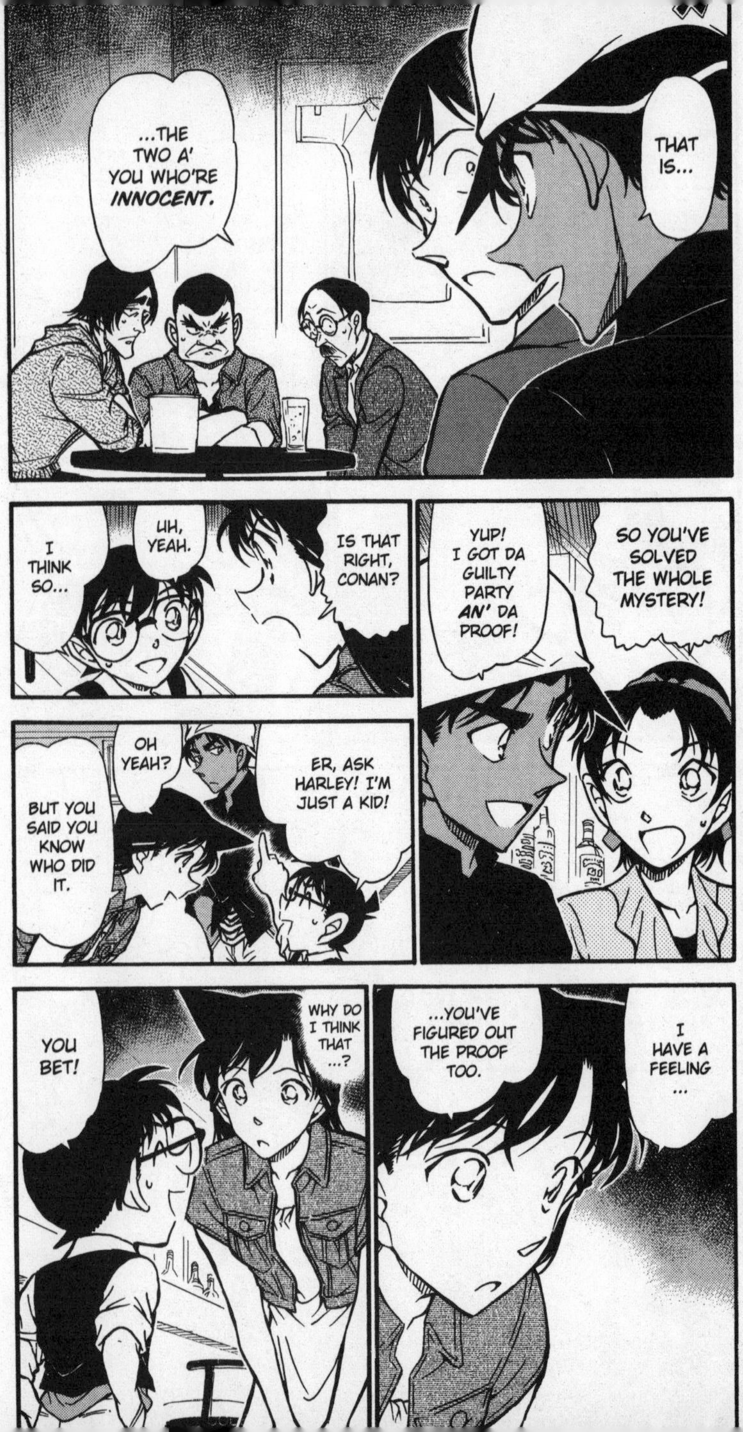
THAT IS...
...THE TWO A' YOU WHO'RE *INNOCENT.*
SO YOU'VE SOLVED THE WHOLE MYSTERY!
YUP! I GOT DA GUILTY PARTY *AN'* DA PROOF!
IS THAT RIGHT, CONAN?
UH, YEAH.
I THINK SO...
ER, ASK HARLEY! I'M JUST A KID!
OH YEAH?
BUT YOU SAID YOU KNOW WHO DID IT.
I HAVE A FEELING...
...YOU'VE FIGURED OUT THE PROOF TOO.
WHY DO I THINK THAT...?
YOU BET!

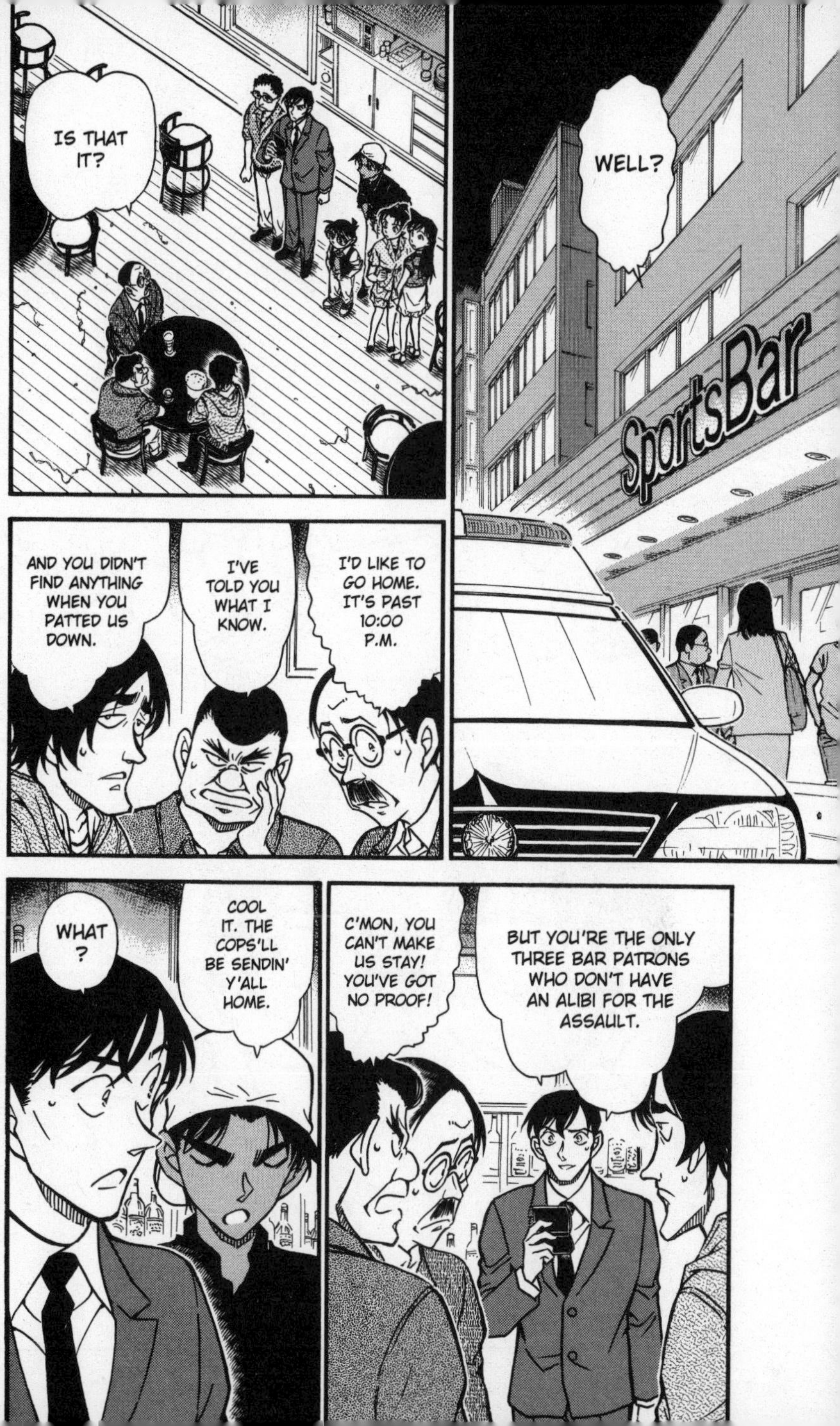
WELL?
IS THAT IT?
I'D LIKE TO GO HOME. IT'S PAST 10:00 P.M.
I'VE TOLD YOU WHAT I KNOW.
AND YOU DIDN'T FIND ANYTHING WHEN YOU PATTED US DOWN.
BUT YOU'RE THE ONLY THREE BAR PATRONS WHO DON'T HAVE AN ALIBI FOR THE ASSAULT.
C'MON, YOU CAN'T MAKE US STAY! YOU'VE GOT NO PROOF!
COOL IT. THE COPS'LL BE SENDIN' Y'ALL HOME.
WHAT?

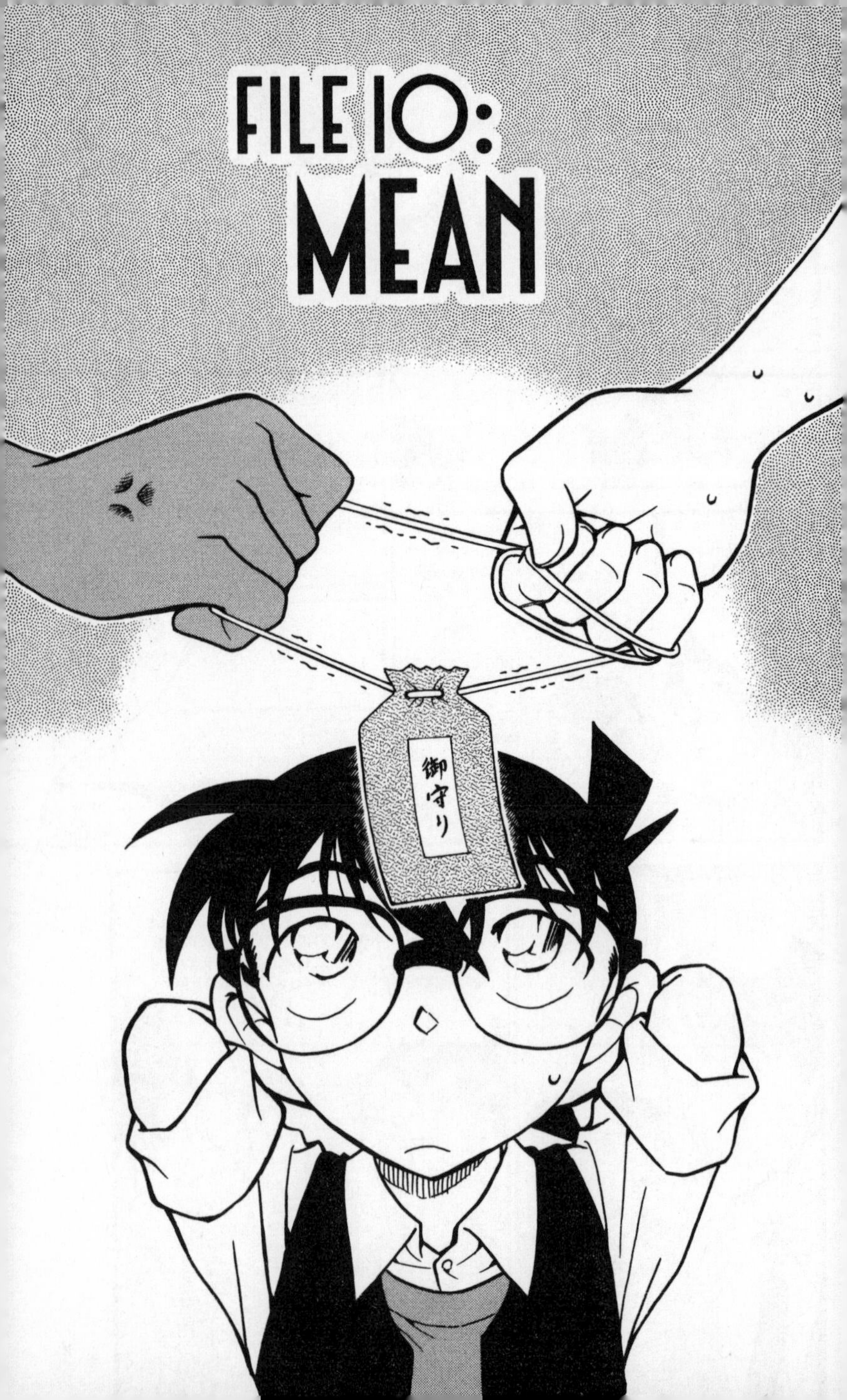
FILE 10:
MEAN
御守り

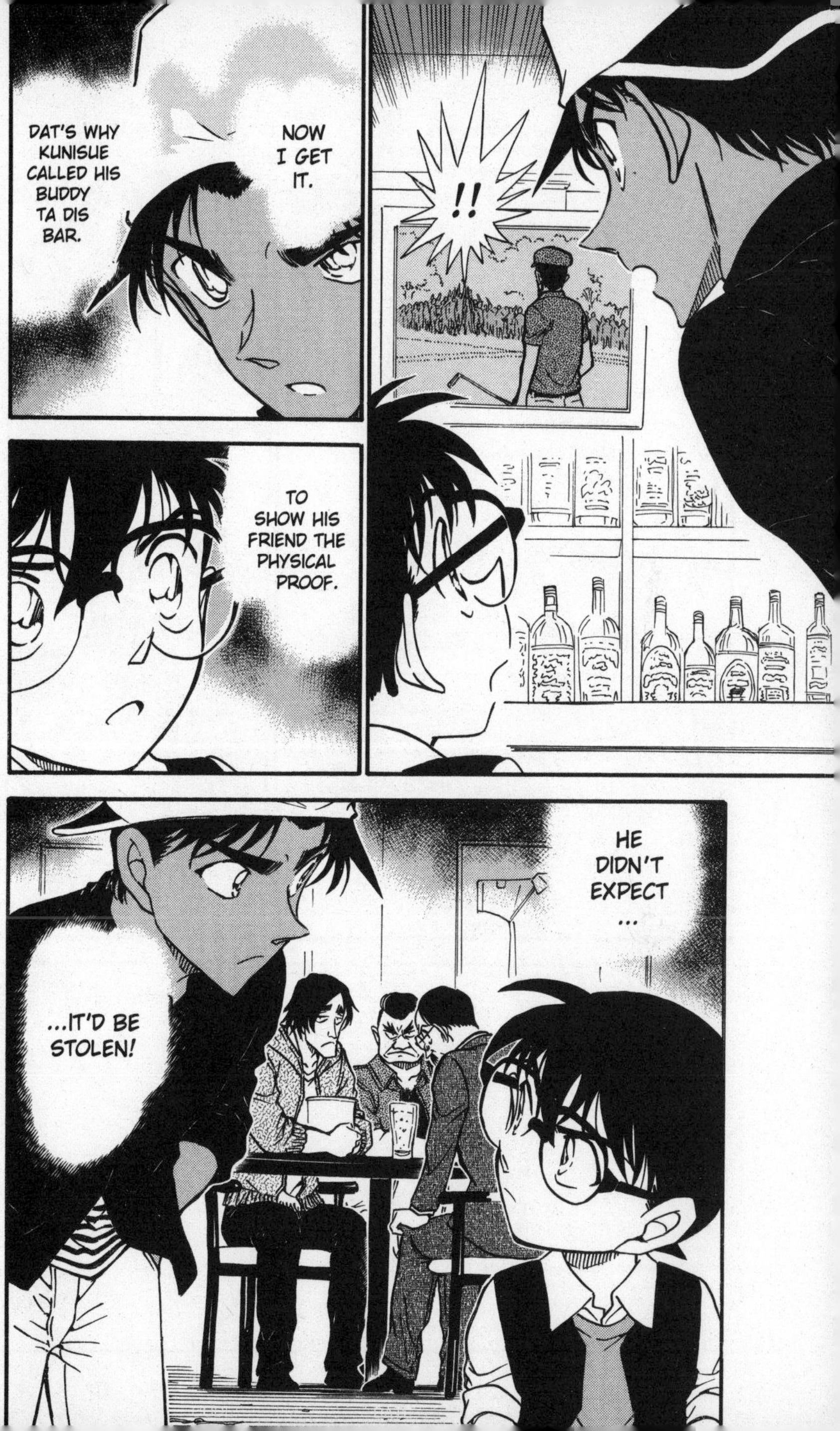
!!
NOW I GET IT.
DAT'S WHY KUNISUE CALLED HIS BUDDY TA DIS BAR.
TO SHOW HIS FRIEND THE PHYSICAL PROOF.
HE DIDN'T EXPECT ...
...IT'D BE STOLEN!

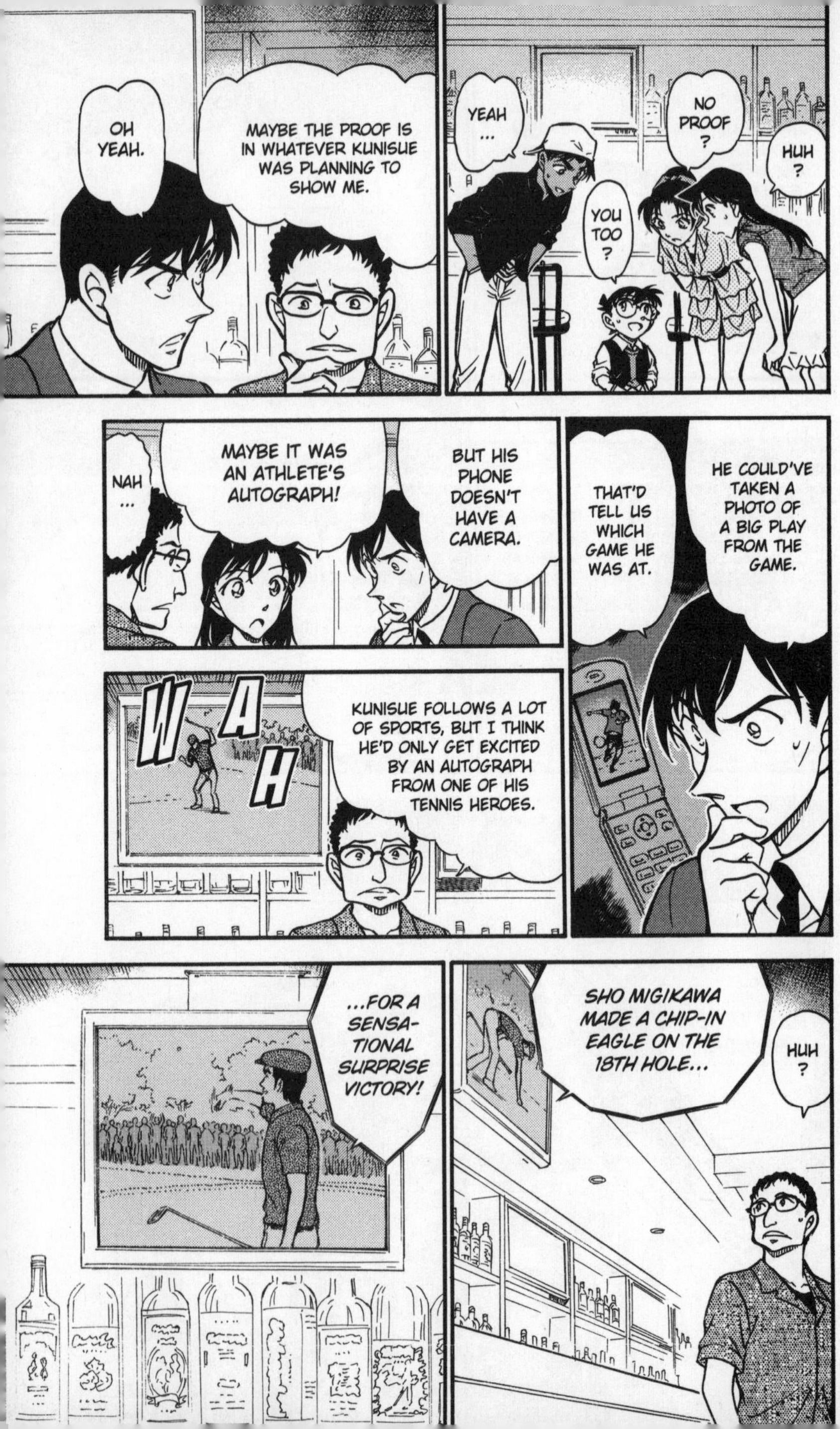
HUH ?
NO PROOF ?
YEAH ...
YOU TOO ?
MAYBE THE PROOF IS IN WHATEVER KUNISUE WAS PLANNING TO SHOW ME.
OH YEAH.
HE COULD'VE TAKEN A PHOTO OF A BIG PLAY FROM THE GAME.
THAT'D TELL US WHICH GAME HE WAS AT.
BUT HIS PHONE DOESN'T HAVE A CAMERA.
MAYBE IT WAS AN ATHLETE'S AUTOGRAPH!
NAH ...
KUNISUE FOLLOWS A LOT OF SPORTS, BUT I THINK HE'D ONLY GET EXCITED BY AN AUTOGRAPH FROM ONE OF HIS TENNIS HEROES.
WAH
HUH ?
SHO MIGIKAWA MADE A CHIP-IN EAGLE ON THE 18TH HOLE...
...FOR A SENSA-TIONAL SURPRISE VICTORY!

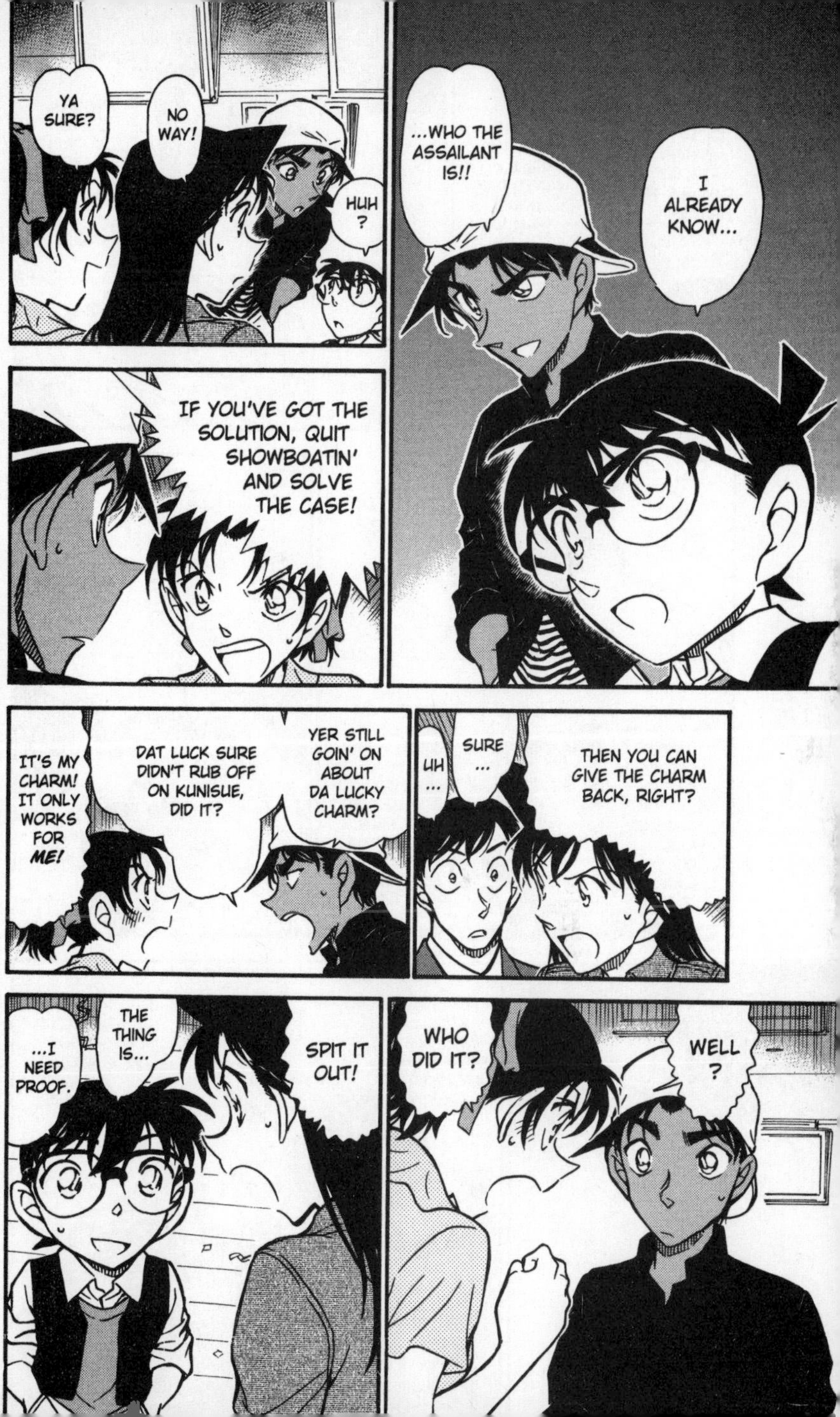
I ALREADY KNOW...
...WHO THE ASSAILANT IS!!
HUH ?
NO WAY!
YA SURE?
IF YOU'VE GOT THE SOLUTION, QUIT SHOWBOATIN' AND SOLVE THE CASE!
THEN YOU CAN GIVE THE CHARM BACK, RIGHT?
SURE ...
UH ...
YER STILL GOIN' ON ABOUT DA LUCKY CHARM?
DAT LUCK SURE DIDN'T RUB OFF ON KUNISUE, DID IT?
IT'S MY CHARM! IT ONLY WORKS FOR *ME!*
WELL ?
WHO DID IT?
SPIT IT OUT!
THE THING IS...
...I NEED PROOF.

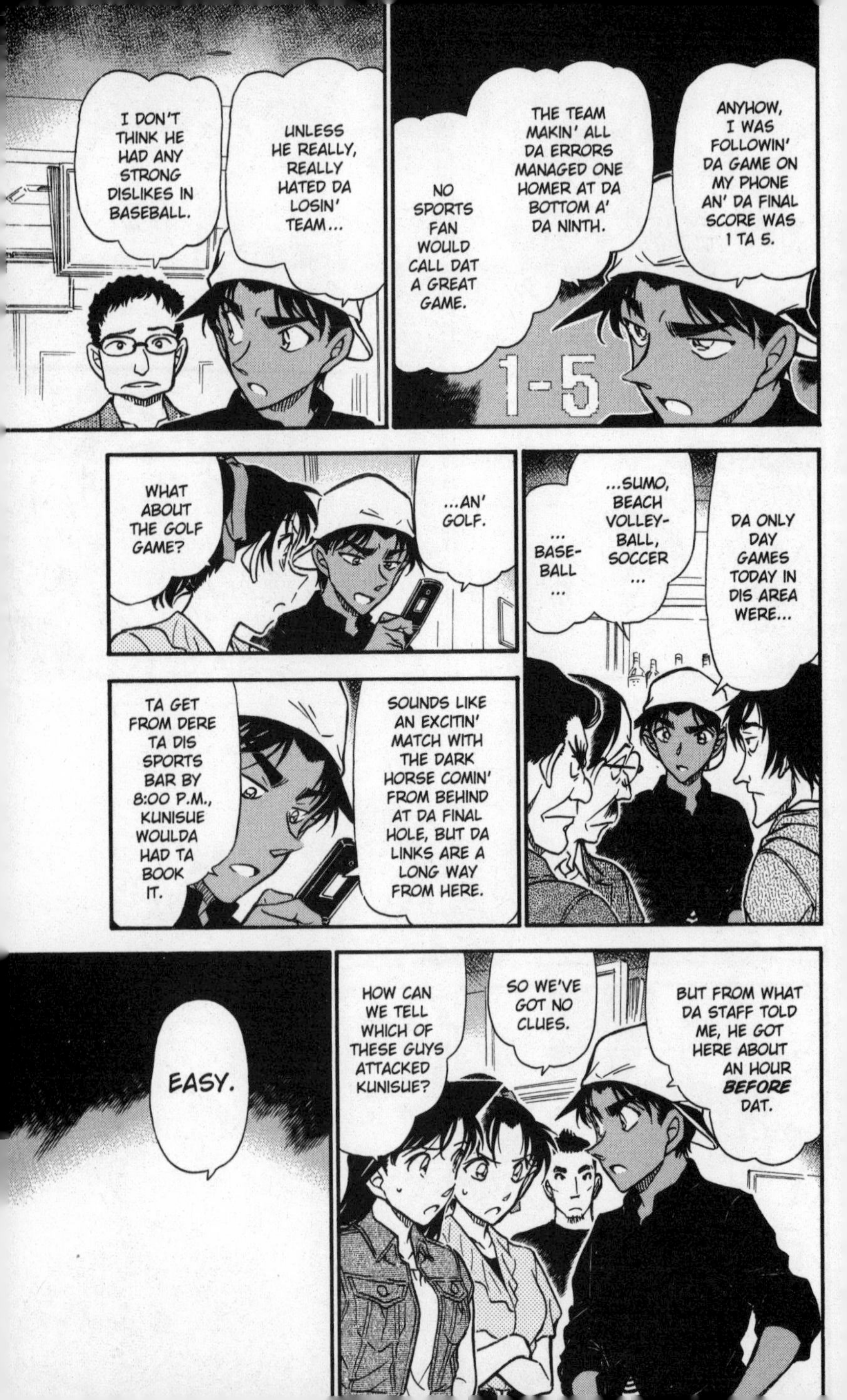
ANYHOW, I WAS FOLLOWIN' DA GAME ON MY PHONE AN' DA FINAL SCORE WAS 1 TA 5.
THE TEAM MAKIN' ALL DA ERRORS MANAGED ONE HOMER AT DA BOTTOM A' DA NINTH.
NO SPORTS FAN WOULD CALL DAT A GREAT GAME.
1-5
UNLESS HE REALLY, REALLY HATED DA LOSIN' TEAM...
I DON'T THINK HE HAD ANY STRONG DISLIKES IN BASEBALL.
DA ONLY DAY GAMES TODAY IN DIS AREA WERE...
...SUMO, BEACH VOLLEY-BALL, SOCCER...
...BASE-BALL...
...AN' GOLF.
WHAT ABOUT THE GOLF GAME?
SOUNDS LIKE AN EXCITIN' MATCH WITH THE DARK HORSE COMIN' FROM BEHIND AT DA FINAL HOLE, BUT DA LINKS ARE A LONG WAY FROM HERE.
TA GET FROM DERE TA DIS SPORTS BAR BY 8:00 P.M., KUNISUE WOULDA HAD TA BOOK IT.
BUT FROM WHAT DA STAFF TOLD ME, HE GOT HERE ABOUT AN HOUR *BEFORE* DAT.
SO WE'VE GOT NO CLUES.
HOW CAN WE TELL WHICH OF THESE GUYS ATTACKED KUNISUE?
EASY.

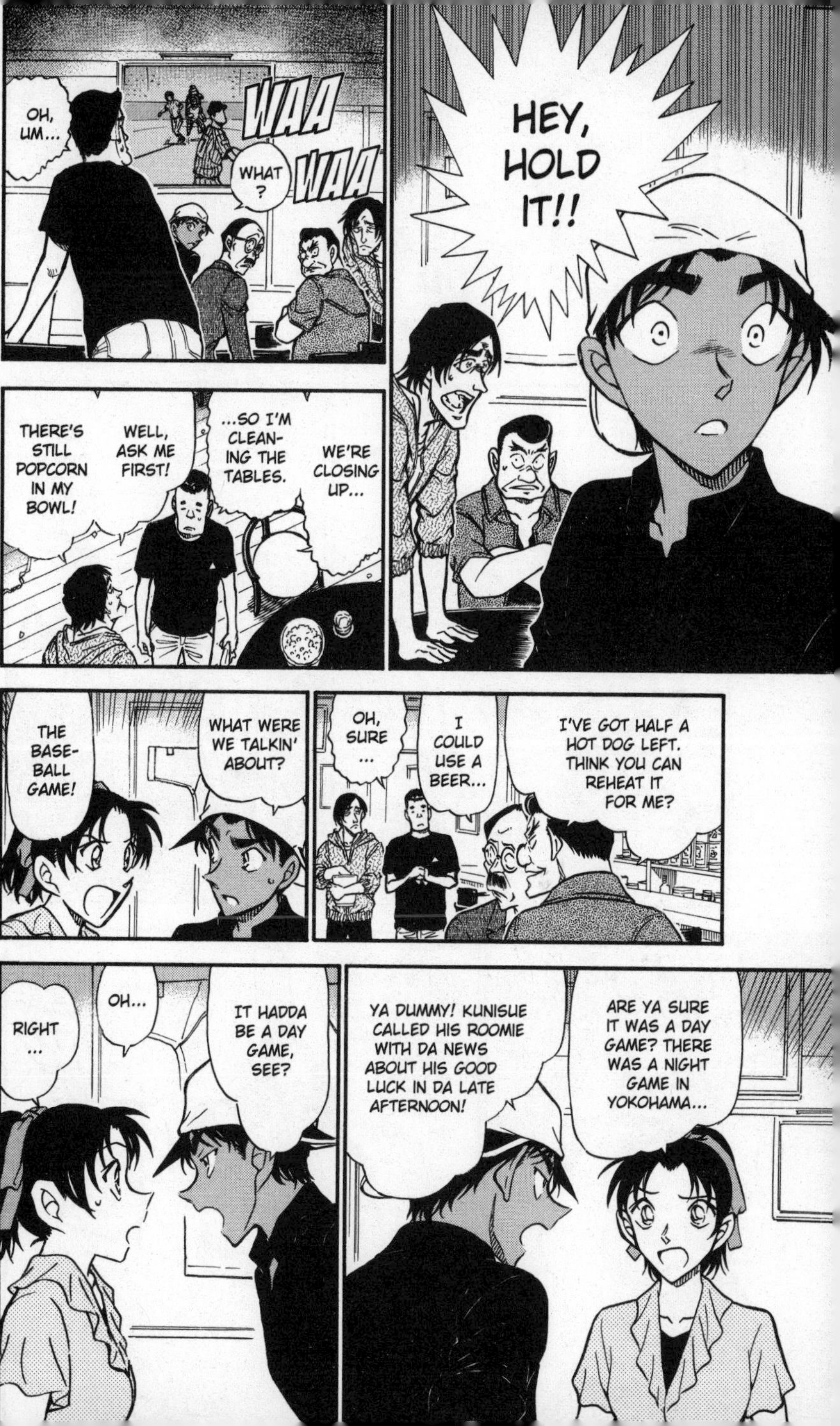
HEY, HOLD IT!!
WAA WAA
WHAT?
OH, UM...
WE'RE CLOSING UP...
...SO I'M CLEANING THE TABLES.
WELL, ASK ME FIRST!
THERE'S STILL POPCORN IN MY BOWL!
I'VE GOT HALF A HOT DOG LEFT. THINK YOU CAN REHEAT IT FOR ME?
I COULD USE A BEER...
OH, SURE...
WHAT WERE WE TALKIN' ABOUT?
THE BASEBALL GAME!
ARE YA SURE IT WAS A DAY GAME? THERE WAS A NIGHT GAME IN YOKOHAMA...
YA DUMMY! KUNISUE CALLED HIS ROOMIE WITH DA NEWS ABOUT HIS GOOD LUCK IN DA LATE AFTERNOON!
IT HADDA BE A DAY GAME, SEE?
OH...
RIGHT...

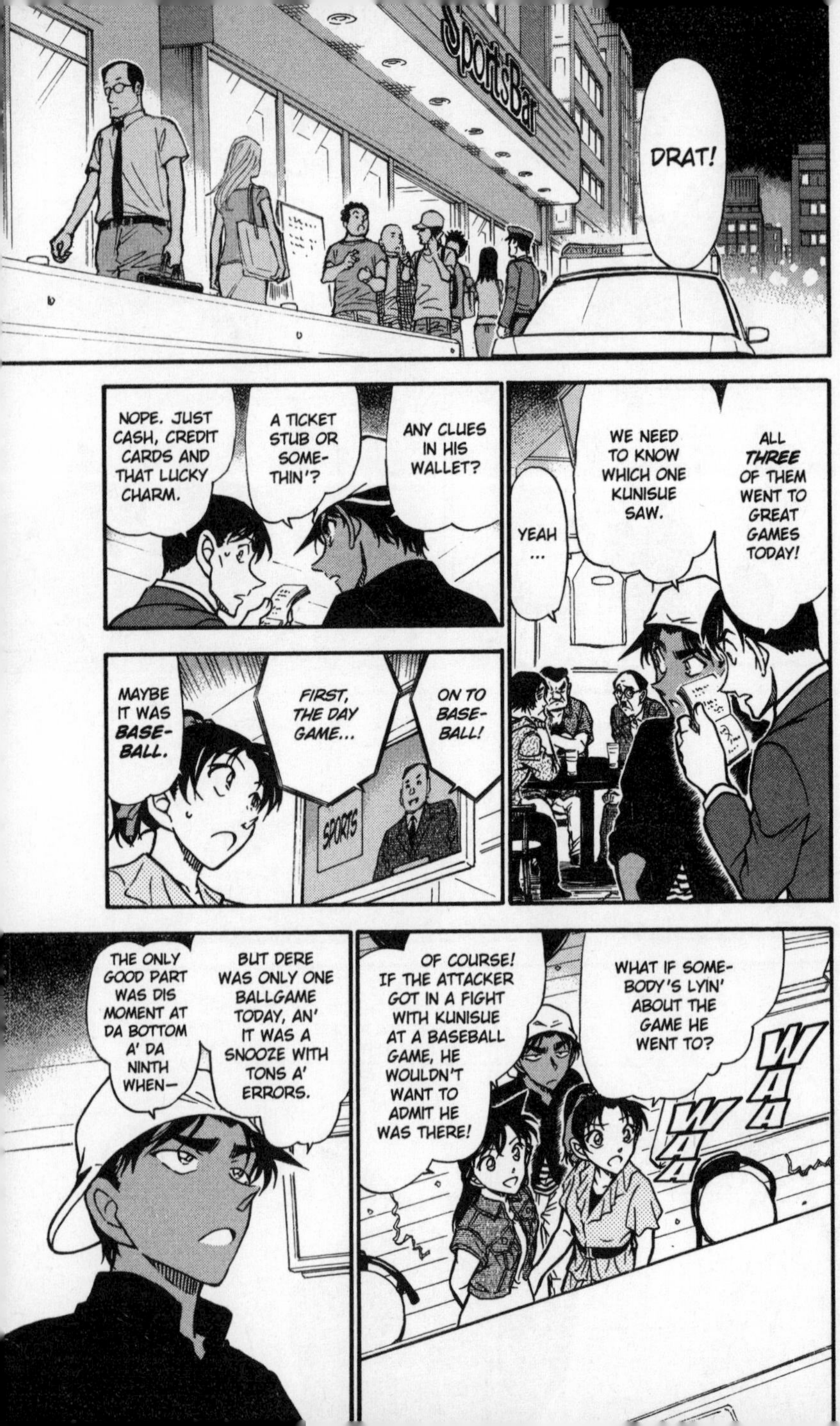
SportsBar
DRAT!
ALL THREE OF THEM WENT TO GREAT GAMES TODAY!
WE NEED TO KNOW WHICH ONE KUNISUE SAW.
YEAH ...
ANY CLUES IN HIS WALLET?
A TICKET STUB OR SOME-THIN'?
NOPE. JUST CASH, CREDIT CARDS AND THAT LUCKY CHARM.
ON TO BASE-BALL!
FIRST, THE DAY GAME...
SPORTS
MAYBE IT WAS BASE-BALL.
WHAT IF SOME-BODY'S LYIN' ABOUT THE GAME HE WENT TO?
WAA
WAA
OF COURSE! IF THE ATTACKER GOT IN A FIGHT WITH KUNISUE AT A BASEBALL GAME, HE WOULDN'T WANT TO ADMIT HE WAS THERE!
BUT DERE WAS ONLY ONE BALLGAME TODAY, AN' IT WAS A SNOOZE WITH TONS A' ERRORS.
THE ONLY GOOD PART WAS DIS MOMENT AT DA BOTTOM A' DA NINTH WHEN—

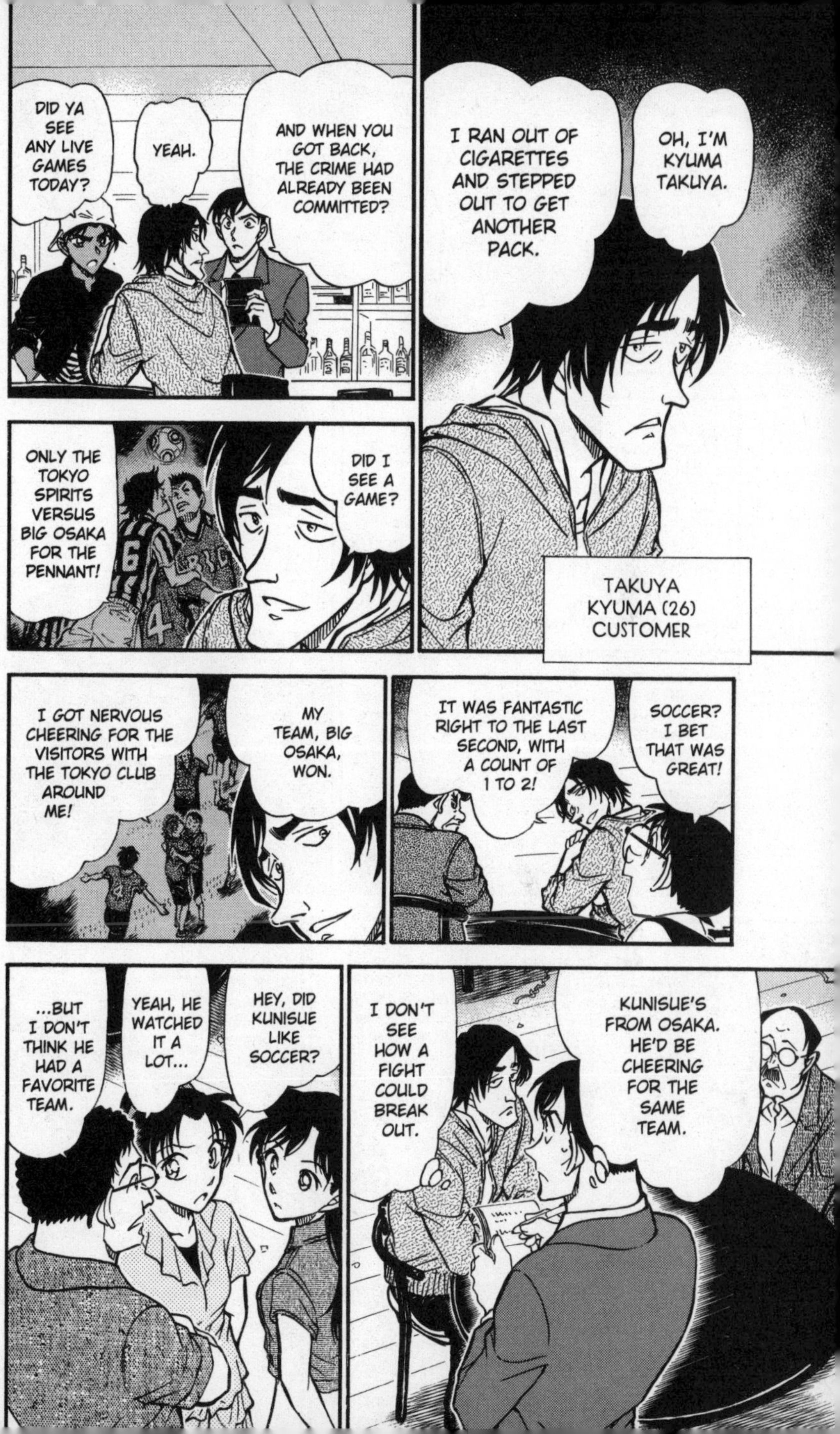
OH, I'M KYUMA TAKUYA.
I RAN OUT OF CIGARETTES AND STEPPED OUT TO GET ANOTHER PACK.
TAKUYA KYUMA (26) CUSTOMER
AND WHEN YOU GOT BACK, THE CRIME HAD ALREADY BEEN COMMITTED?
YEAH.
DID YA SEE ANY LIVE GAMES TODAY?
DID I SEE A GAME?
ONLY THE TOKYO SPIRITS VERSUS BIG OSAKA FOR THE PENNANT!
SOCCER? I BET THAT WAS GREAT!
IT WAS FANTASTIC RIGHT TO THE LAST SECOND, WITH A COUNT OF 1 TO 2!
MY TEAM, BIG OSAKA, WON.
I GOT NERVOUS CHEERING FOR THE VISITORS WITH THE TOKYO CLUB AROUND ME!
KUNISUE'S FROM OSAKA. HE'D BE CHEERING FOR THE SAME TEAM.
I DON'T SEE HOW A FIGHT COULD BREAK OUT.
HEY, DID KUNISUE LIKE SOCCER?
YEAH, HE WATCHED IT A LOT...
...BUT I DON'T THINK HE HAD A FAVORITE TEAM.

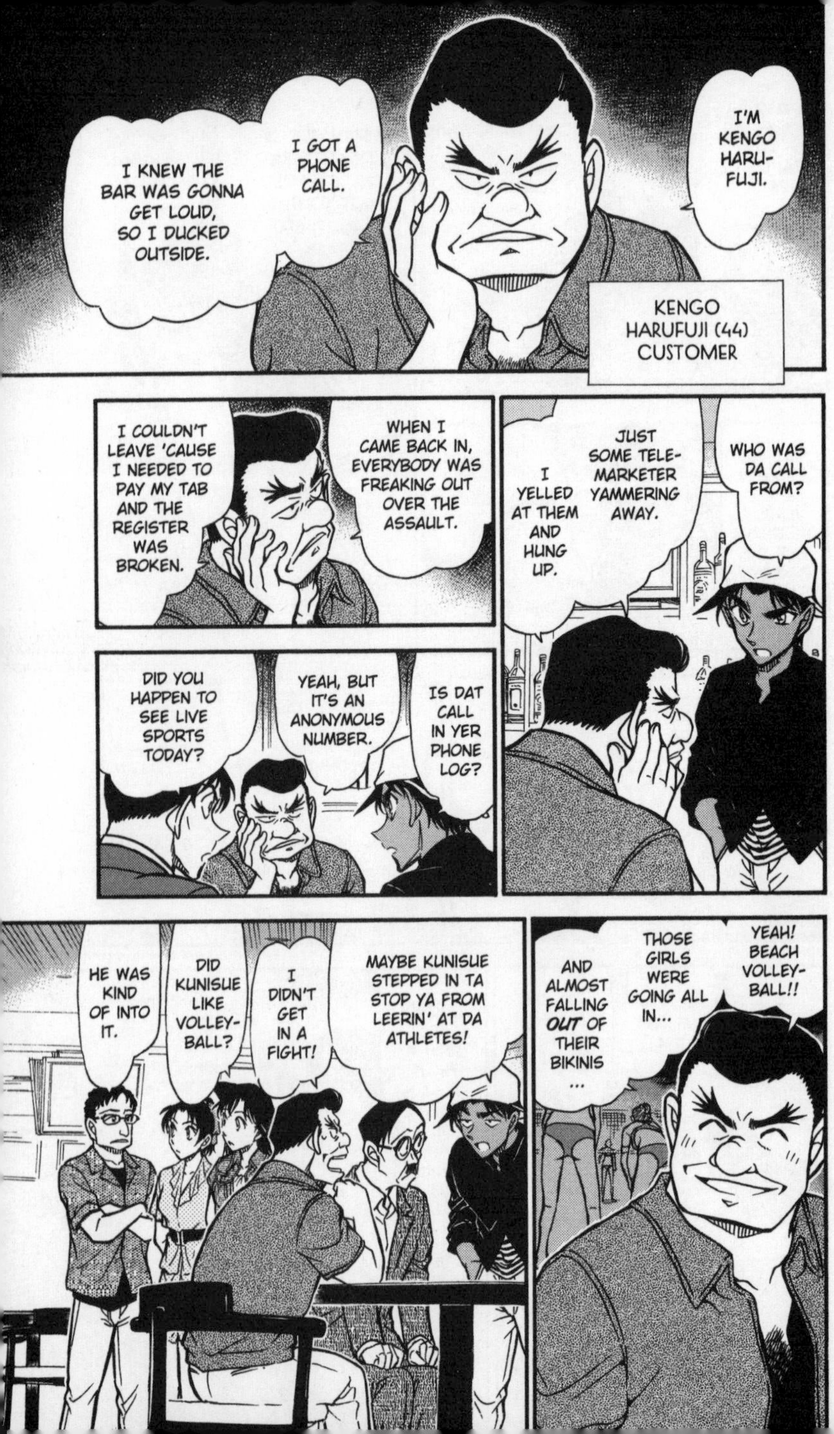
I'M KENGO HARUFUJI.
KENGO HARUFUJI (44) CUSTOMER
I GOT A PHONE CALL.
I KNEW THE BAR WAS GONNA GET LOUD, SO I DUCKED OUTSIDE.
WHO WAS DA CALL FROM?
JUST SOME TELEMARKETER YAMMERING AWAY.
I YELLED AT THEM AND HUNG UP.
WHEN I CAME BACK IN, EVERYBODY WAS FREAKING OUT OVER THE ASSAULT.
I COULDN'T LEAVE 'CAUSE I NEEDED TO PAY MY TAB AND THE REGISTER WAS BROKEN.
IS DAT CALL IN YER PHONE LOG?
YEAH, BUT IT'S AN ANONYMOUS NUMBER.
DID YOU HAPPEN TO SEE LIVE SPORTS TODAY?
YEAH! BEACH VOLLEYBALL!!
THOSE GIRLS WERE GOING ALL IN...
AND ALMOST FALLING *OUT* OF THEIR BIKINIS ...
MAYBE KUNISUE STEPPED IN TA STOP YA FROM LEERIN' AT DA ATHLETES!
I DIDN'T GET IN A FIGHT!
DID KUNISUE LIKE VOLLEYBALL?
HE WAS KIND OF INTO IT.

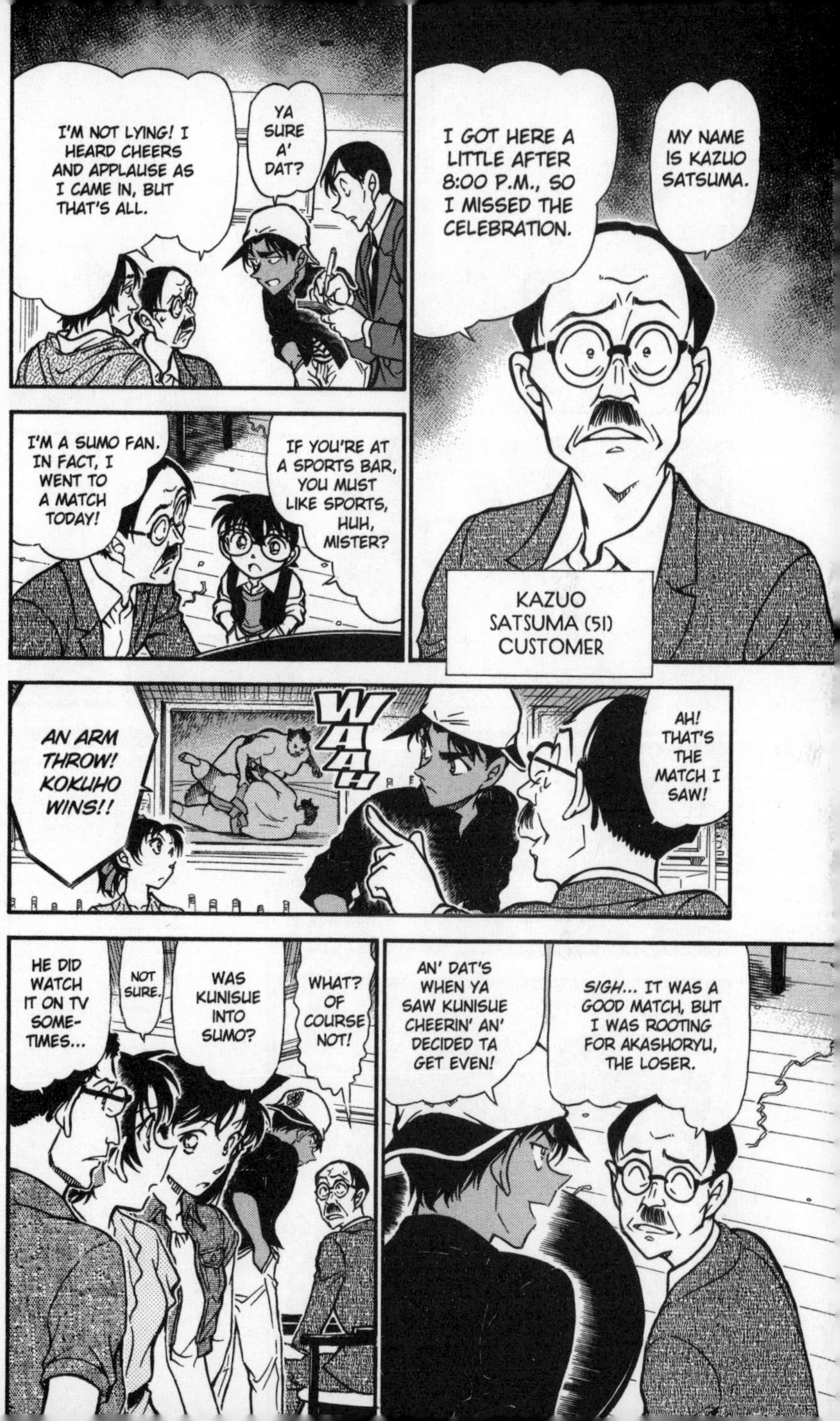
MY NAME IS KAZUO SATSUMA.
I GOT HERE A LITTLE AFTER 8:00 P.M., SO I MISSED THE CELEBRATION.
KAZUO SATSUMA (51) CUSTOMER
YA SURE A' DAT?
I'M NOT LYING! I HEARD CHEERS AND APPLAUSE AS I CAME IN, BUT THAT'S ALL.
IF YOU'RE AT A SPORTS BAR, YOU MUST LIKE SPORTS, HUH, MISTER?
I'M A SUMO FAN. IN FACT, I WENT TO A MATCH TODAY!
AH! THAT'S THE MATCH I SAW!
WAAH
AN ARM THROW! KOKUHO WINS!!
SIGH... IT WAS A GOOD MATCH, BUT I WAS ROOTING FOR AKASHORYU, THE LOSER.
AN' DAT'S WHEN YA SAW KUNISUE CHEERIN' AN' DECIDED TA GET EVEN!
WHAT? OF COURSE NOT!
WAS KUNISUE INTO SUMO?
NOT SURE.
HE DID WATCH IT ON TV SOME-TIMES...

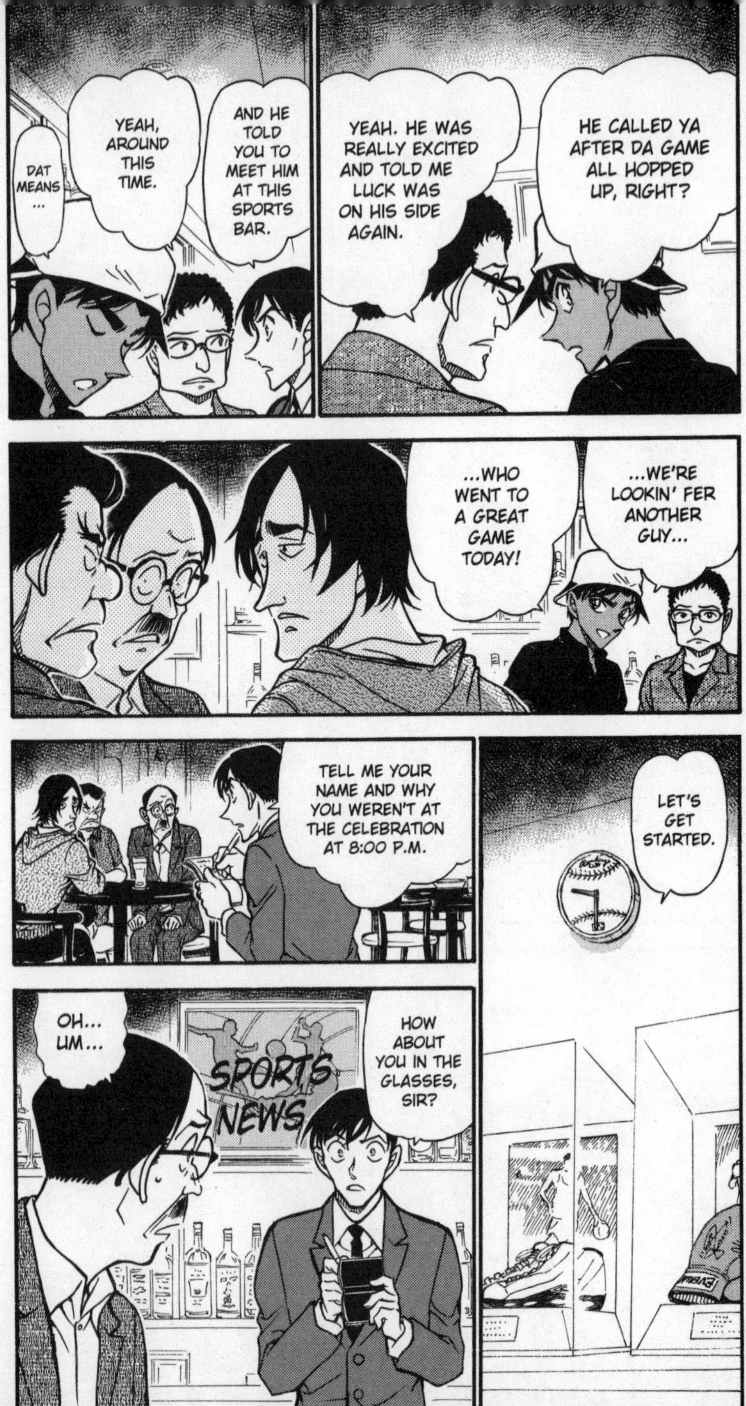
HE CALLED YA AFTER DA GAME ALL HOPPED UP, RIGHT?
YEAH. HE WAS REALLY EXCITED AND TOLD ME LUCK WAS ON HIS SIDE AGAIN.
AND HE TOLD YOU TO MEET HIM AT THIS SPORTS BAR.
YEAH, AROUND THIS TIME.
DAT MEANS ...
...WE'RE LOOKIN' FER ANOTHER GUY...
...WHO WENT TO A GREAT GAME TODAY!
LET'S GET STARTED.
TELL ME YOUR NAME AND WHY YOU WEREN'T AT THE CELEBRATION AT 8:00 P.M.
HOW ABOUT YOU IN THE GLASSES, SIR?
SPORTS NEWS
OH... UM...

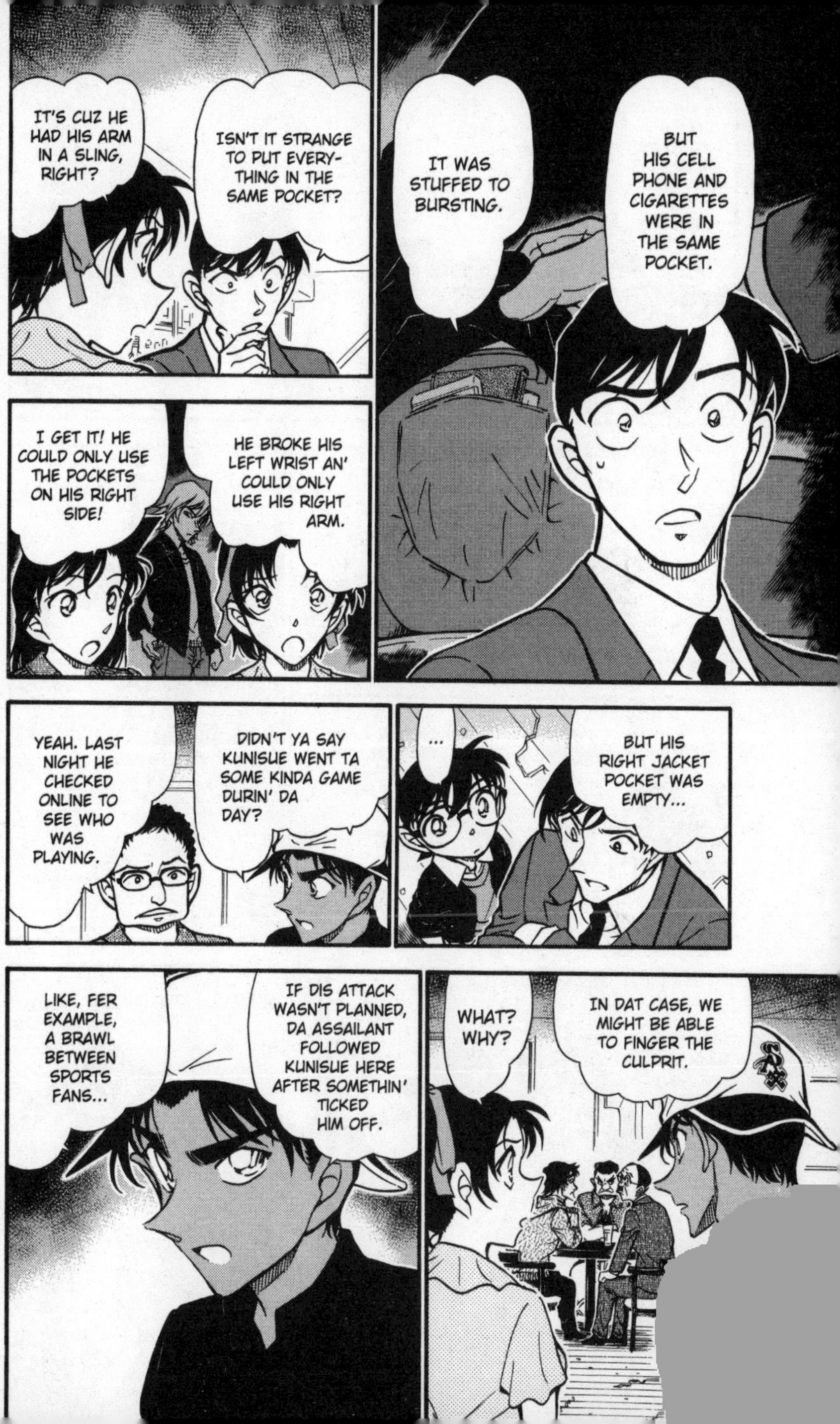
BUT HIS CELL PHONE AND CIGARETTES WERE IN THE SAME POCKET.
IT WAS STUFFED TO BURSTING.
ISN'T IT STRANGE TO PUT EVERY-THING IN THE SAME POCKET?
IT'S CUZ HE HAD HIS ARM IN A SLING, RIGHT?
HE BROKE HIS LEFT WRIST AN' COULD ONLY USE HIS RIGHT ARM.
I GET IT! HE COULD ONLY USE THE POCKETS ON HIS RIGHT SIDE!
BUT HIS RIGHT JACKET POCKET WAS EMPTY...
...
DIDN'T YA SAY KUNISUE WENT TA SOME KINDA GAME DURIN' DA DAY?
YEAH. LAST NIGHT HE CHECKED ONLINE TO SEE WHO WAS PLAYING.
IN DAT CASE, WE MIGHT BE ABLE TO FINGER THE CULPRIT.
WHAT? WHY?
IF DIS ATTACK WASN'T PLANNED, DA ASSAILANT FOLLOWED KUNISUE HERE AFTER SOMETHIN' TICKED HIM OFF.
LIKE, FER EXAMPLE, A BRAWL BETWEEN SPORTS FANS...

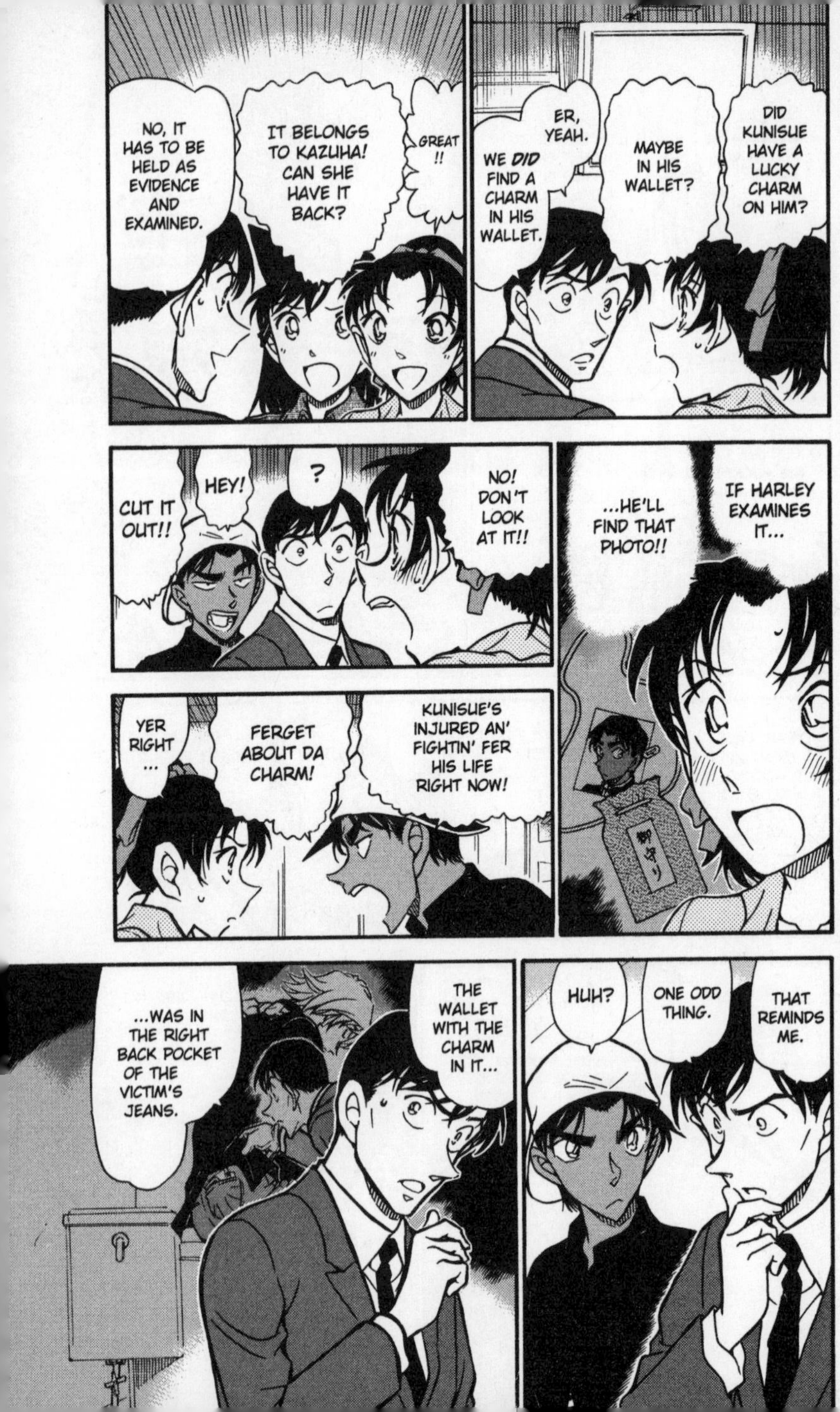
DID KUNISUE HAVE A LUCKY CHARM ON HIM?
MAYBE IN HIS WALLET?
ER, YEAH.
WE *DID* FIND A CHARM IN HIS WALLET.
GREAT!!
IT BELONGS TO KAZUHA! CAN SHE HAVE IT BACK?
NO, IT HAS TO BE HELD AS EVIDENCE AND EXAMINED.
IF HARLEY EXAMINES IT...
...HE'LL FIND THAT PHOTO!!
御守り
NO! DON'T LOOK AT IT!!
?
HEY!
CUT IT OUT!!
KUNISUE'S INJURED AN' FIGHTIN' FER HIS LIFE RIGHT NOW!
FERGET ABOUT DA CHARM!
YER RIGHT ...
THAT REMINDS ME.
ONE ODD THING.
HUH?
THE WALLET WITH THE CHARM IN IT...
...WAS IN THE RIGHT BACK POCKET OF THE VICTIM'S JEANS.

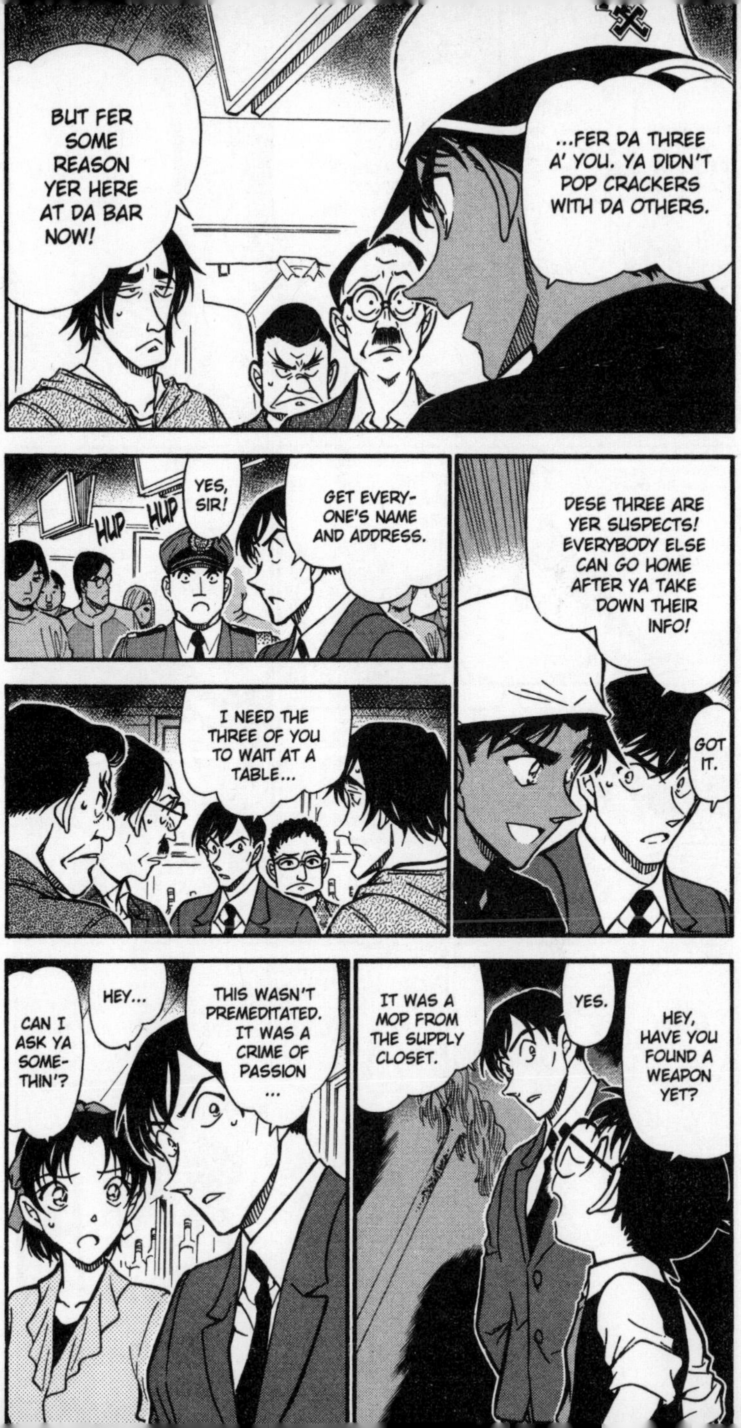
...FER DA THREE A' YOU. YA DIDN'T POP CRACKERS WITH DA OTHERS.
BUT FER SOME REASON YER HERE AT DA BAR NOW!
DESE THREE ARE YER SUSPECTS! EVERYBODY ELSE CAN GO HOME AFTER YA TAKE DOWN THEIR INFO!
GOT IT.
GET EVERY-ONE'S NAME AND ADDRESS.
YES, SIR!
HUP
HUP
I NEED THE THREE OF YOU TO WAIT AT A TABLE...
HEY, HAVE YOU FOUND A WEAPON YET?
YES.
IT WAS A MOP FROM THE SUPPLY CLOSET.
THIS WASN'T PREMEDITATED. IT WAS A CRIME OF PASSION ...
HEY...
CAN I ASK YA SOME-THIN'?

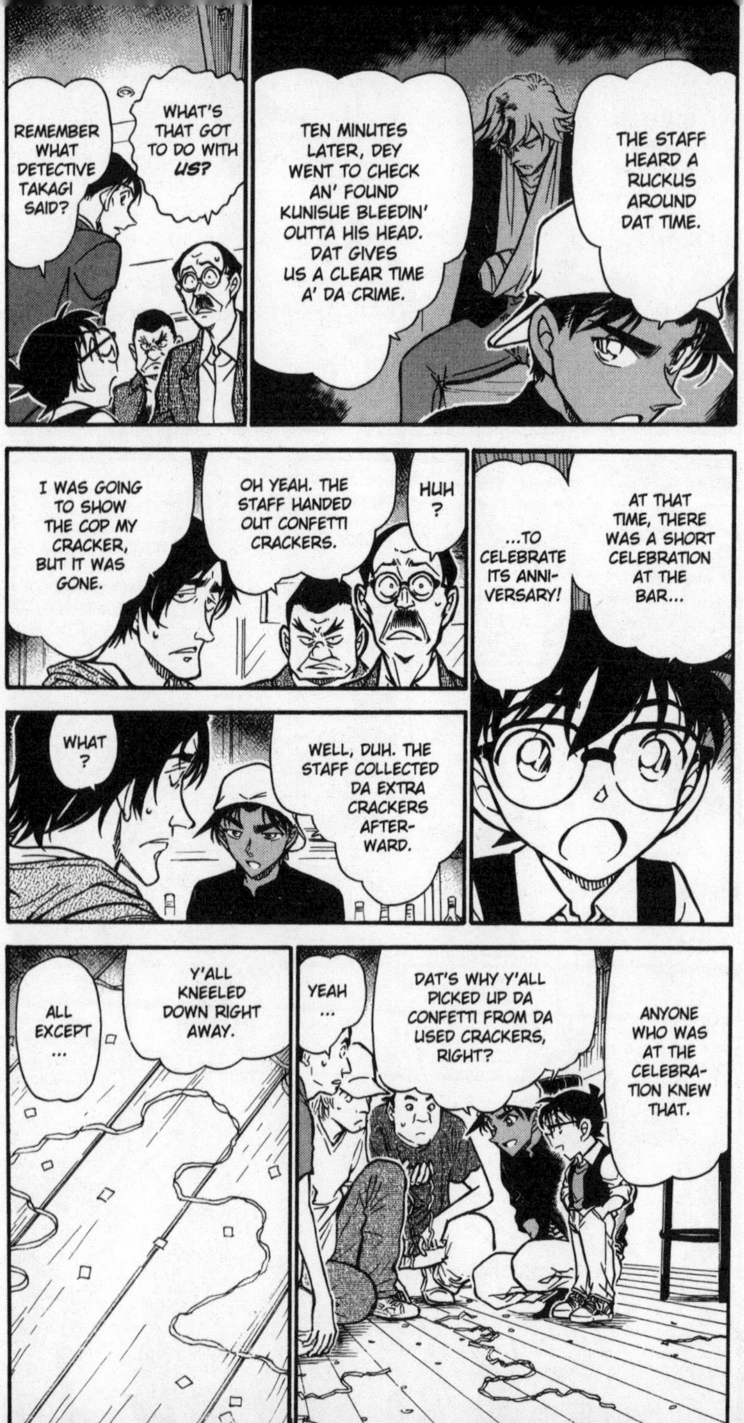
THE STAFF HEARD A RUCKUS AROUND DAT TIME.
TEN MINUTES LATER, DEY WENT TO CHECK AN' FOUND KUNISUE BLEEDIN' OUTTA HIS HEAD. DAT GIVES US A CLEAR TIME A' DA CRIME.
WHAT'S THAT GOT TO DO WITH *US?*
REMEMBER WHAT DETECTIVE TAKAGI SAID?
AT THAT TIME, THERE WAS A SHORT CELEBRATION AT THE BAR...
...TO CELEBRATE ITS ANNIVERSARY!
HUH?
OH YEAH. THE STAFF HANDED OUT CONFETTI CRACKERS.
I WAS GOING TO SHOW THE COP MY CRACKER, BUT IT WAS GONE.
WELL, DUH. THE STAFF COLLECTED DA EXTRA CRACKERS AFTERWARD.
WHAT?
ANYONE WHO WAS AT THE CELEBRATION KNEW THAT.
DAT'S WHY Y'ALL PICKED UP DA CONFETTI FROM DA USED CRACKERS, RIGHT?
YEAH...
Y'ALL KNEELED DOWN RIGHT AWAY.
ALL EXCEPT...

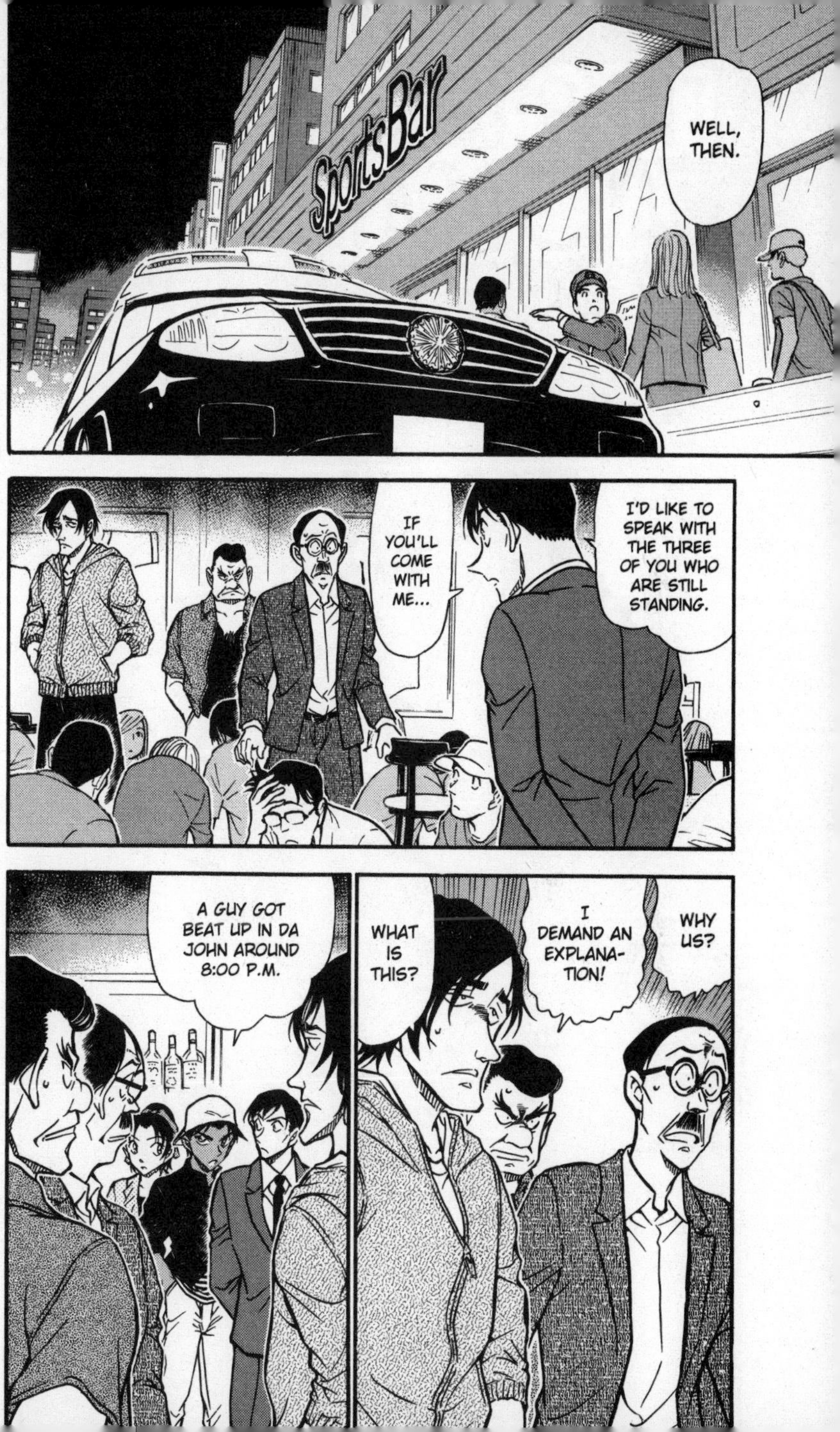
SportsBar
WELL, THEN.
I'D LIKE TO SPEAK WITH THE THREE OF YOU WHO ARE STILL STANDING.
IF YOU'LL COME WITH ME...
WHY US?
I DEMAND AN EXPLANATION!
WHAT IS THIS?
A GUY GOT BEAT UP IN DA JOHN AROUND 8:00 P.M.

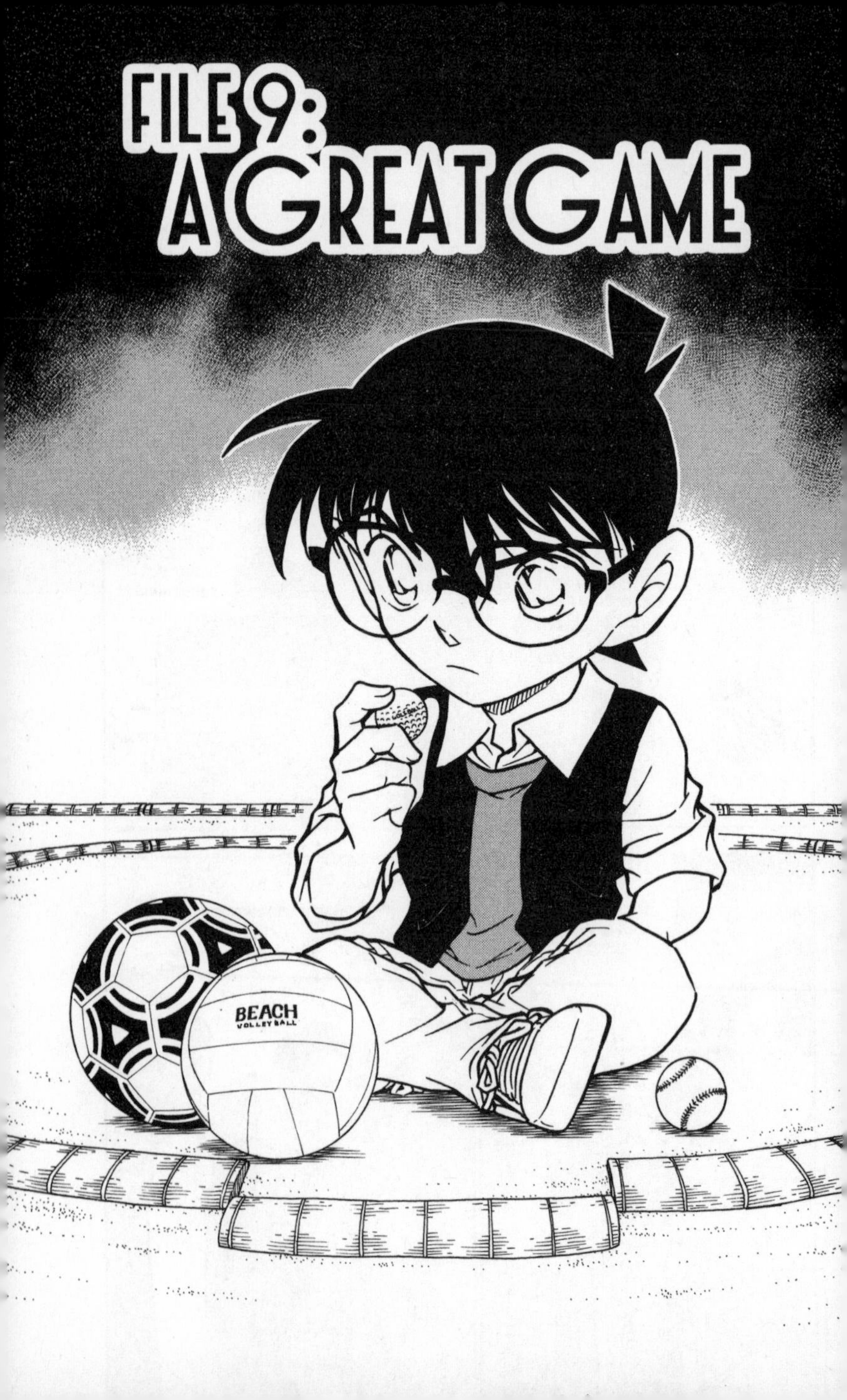
FILE 9:
A GREAT GAME
BEACH
VOLLEYBALL

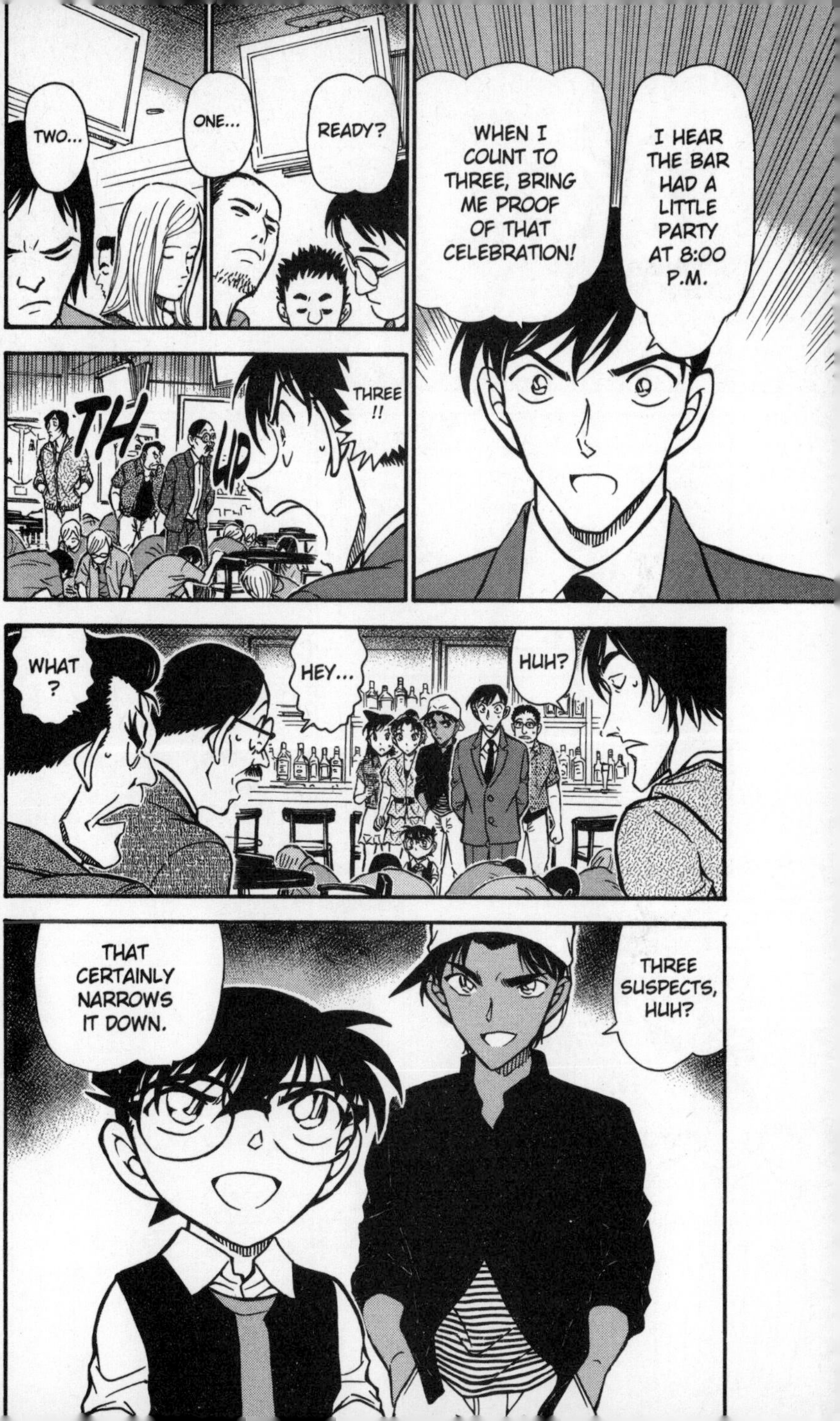
I HEAR THE BAR HAD A LITTLE PARTY AT 8:00 P.M.
WHEN I COUNT TO THREE, BRING ME PROOF OF THAT CELEBRATION!
READY?
ONE...
TWO...
THREE !!
THUP
HUH?
HEY...
WHAT ?
THREE SUSPECTS, HUH?
THAT CERTAINLY NARROWS IT DOWN.

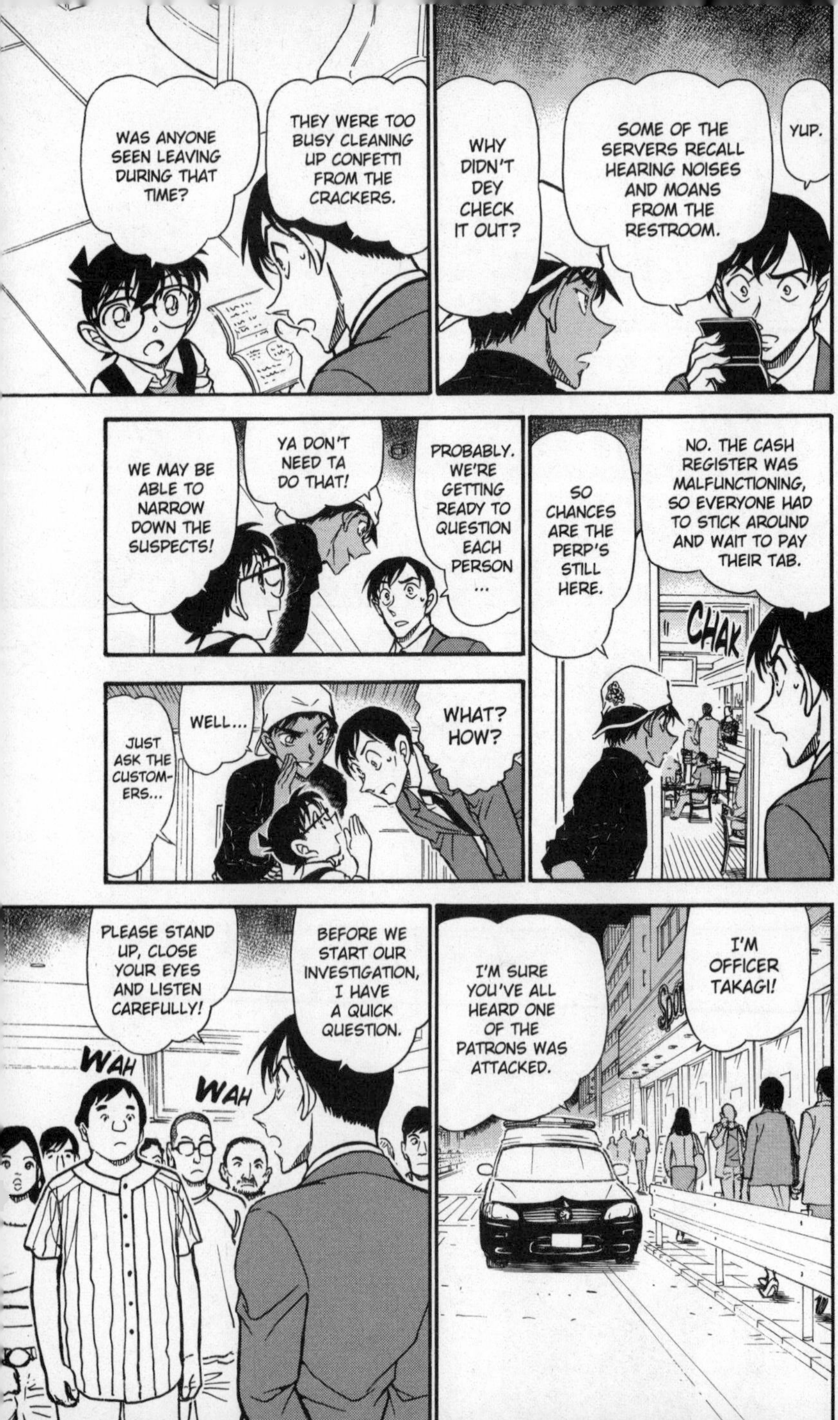
YUP.
SOME OF THE SERVERS RECALL HEARING NOISES AND MOANS FROM THE RESTROOM.
WHY DIDN'T DEY CHECK IT OUT?
THEY WERE TOO BUSY CLEANING UP CONFETTI FROM THE CRACKERS.
WAS ANYONE SEEN LEAVING DURING THAT TIME?
NO. THE CASH REGISTER WAS MALFUNCTIONING, SO EVERYONE HAD TO STICK AROUND AND WAIT TO PAY THEIR TAB.
SO CHANCES ARE THE PERP'S STILL HERE.
CHAK
PROBABLY. WE'RE GETTING READY TO QUESTION EACH PERSON ...
YA DON'T NEED TA DO THAT!
WE MAY BE ABLE TO NARROW DOWN THE SUSPECTS!
WHAT? HOW?
WELL...
JUST ASK THE CUSTOM-ERS...
I'M OFFICER TAKAGI!
I'M SURE YOU'VE ALL HEARD ONE OF THE PATRONS WAS ATTACKED.
BEFORE WE START OUR INVESTIGATION, I HAVE A QUICK QUESTION.
PLEASE STAND UP, CLOSE YOUR EYES AND LISTEN CAREFULLY!
WAH
WAH

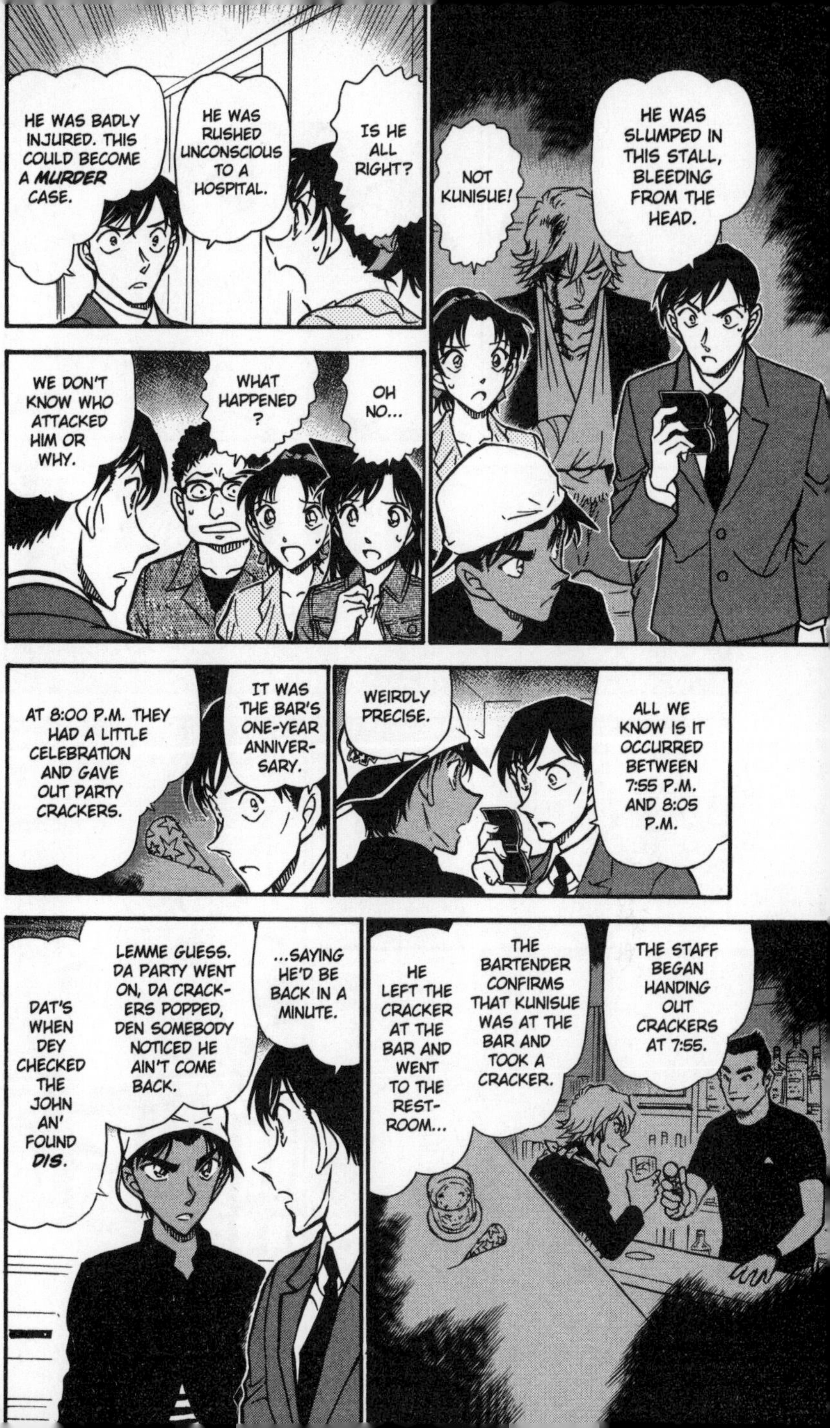
HE WAS SLUMPED IN THIS STALL, BLEEDING FROM THE HEAD.
NOT KUNISUE!
IS HE ALL RIGHT?
HE WAS RUSHED UNCONSCIOUS TO A HOSPITAL.
HE WAS BADLY INJURED. THIS COULD BECOME A ***MURDER*** CASE.
OH NO...
WHAT HAPPENED?
WE DON'T KNOW WHO ATTACKED HIM OR WHY.
ALL WE KNOW IS IT OCCURRED BETWEEN 7:55 P.M. AND 8:05 P.M.
WEIRDLY PRECISE.
IT WAS THE BAR'S ONE-YEAR ANNIVERSARY.
AT 8:00 P.M. THEY HAD A LITTLE CELEBRATION AND GAVE OUT PARTY CRACKERS.
THE STAFF BEGAN HANDING OUT CRACKERS AT 7:55.
THE BARTENDER CONFIRMS THAT KUNISUE WAS AT THE BAR AND TOOK A CRACKER.
HE LEFT THE CRACKER AT THE BAR AND WENT TO THE REST-ROOM...
...SAYING HE'D BE BACK IN A MINUTE.
LEMME GUESS. DA PARTY WENT ON, DA CRACK-ERS POPPED, DEN SOMEBODY NOTICED HE AIN'T COME BACK.
DAT'S WHEN DEY CHECKED THE JOHN AN' FOUND ***DIS***.

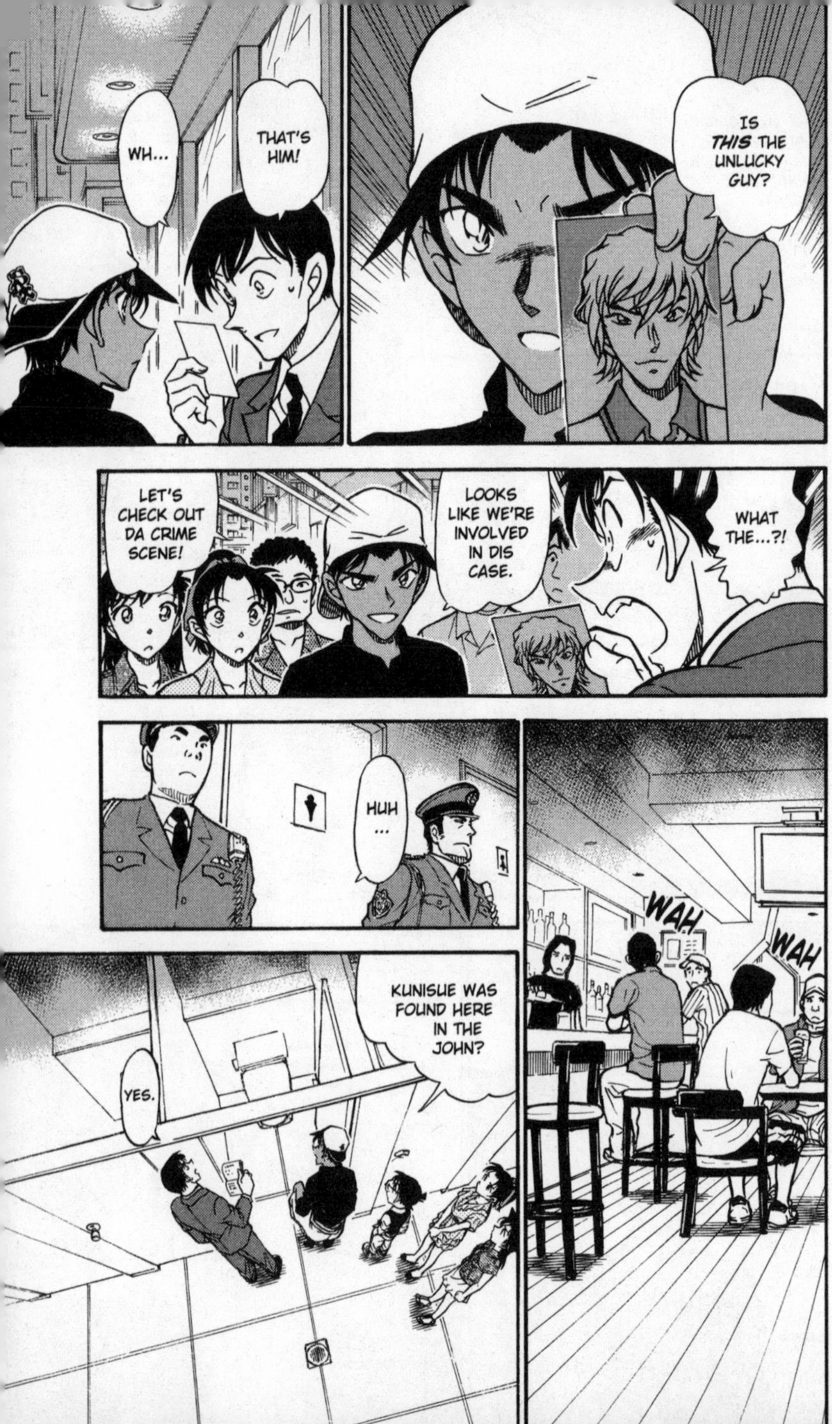
IS *THIS* THE UNLUCKY GUY?
THAT'S HIM!
WH...
WHAT THE...?!
LOOKS LIKE WE'RE INVOLVED IN DIS CASE.
LET'S CHECK OUT DA CRIME SCENE!
WAH
WAH
HUH...
KUNISUE WAS FOUND HERE IN THE JOHN?
YES.

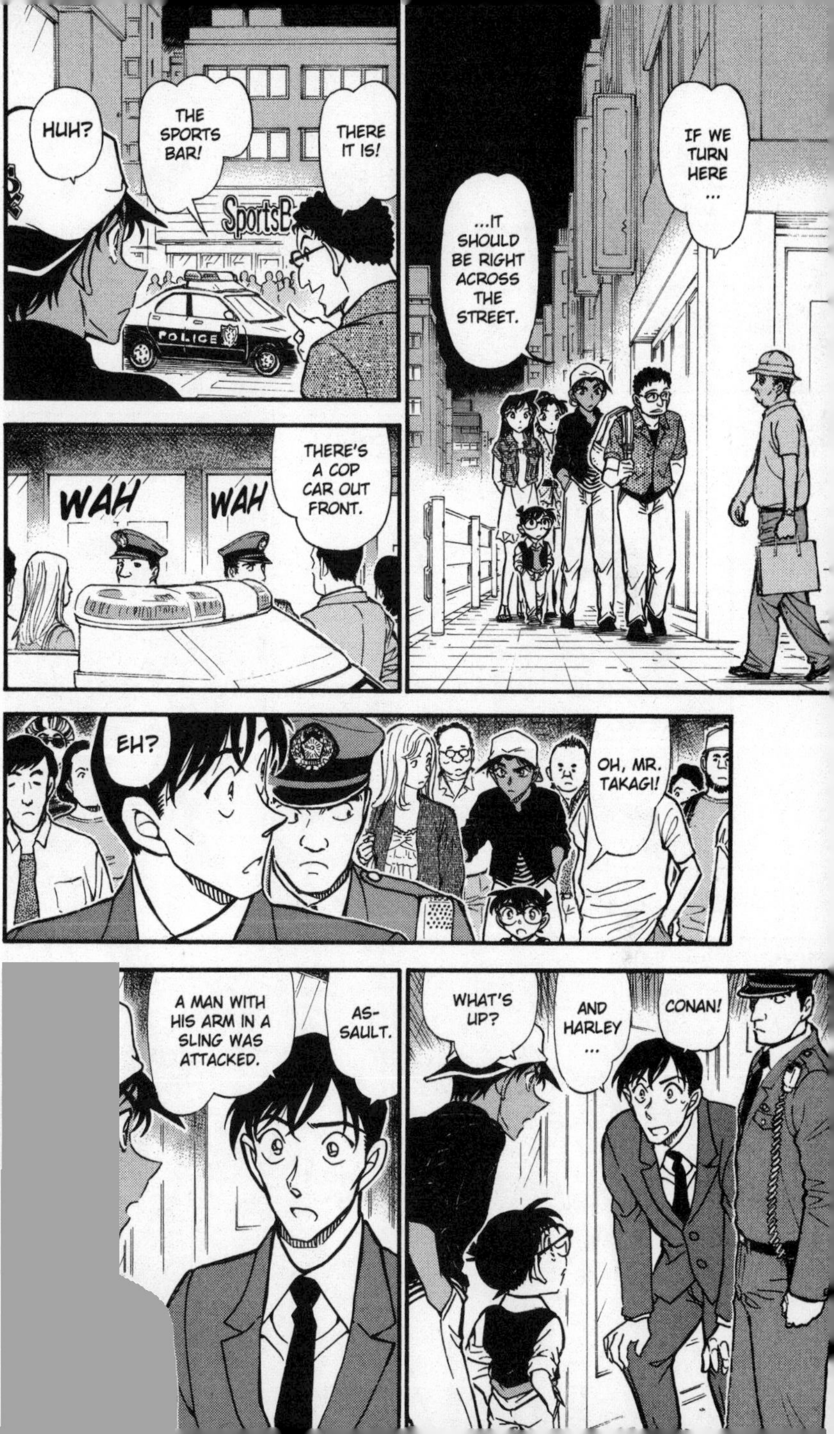
IF WE TURN HERE ...
...IT SHOULD BE RIGHT ACROSS THE STREET.
THERE IT IS!
THE SPORTS BAR!
HUH?
SportsB
POLICE
THERE'S A COP CAR OUT FRONT.
WAH
WAH
OH, MR. TAKAGI!
EH?
CONAN!
AND HARLEY ...
WHAT'S UP?
AS-SAULT.
A MAN WITH HIS ARM IN A SLING WAS ATTACKED.

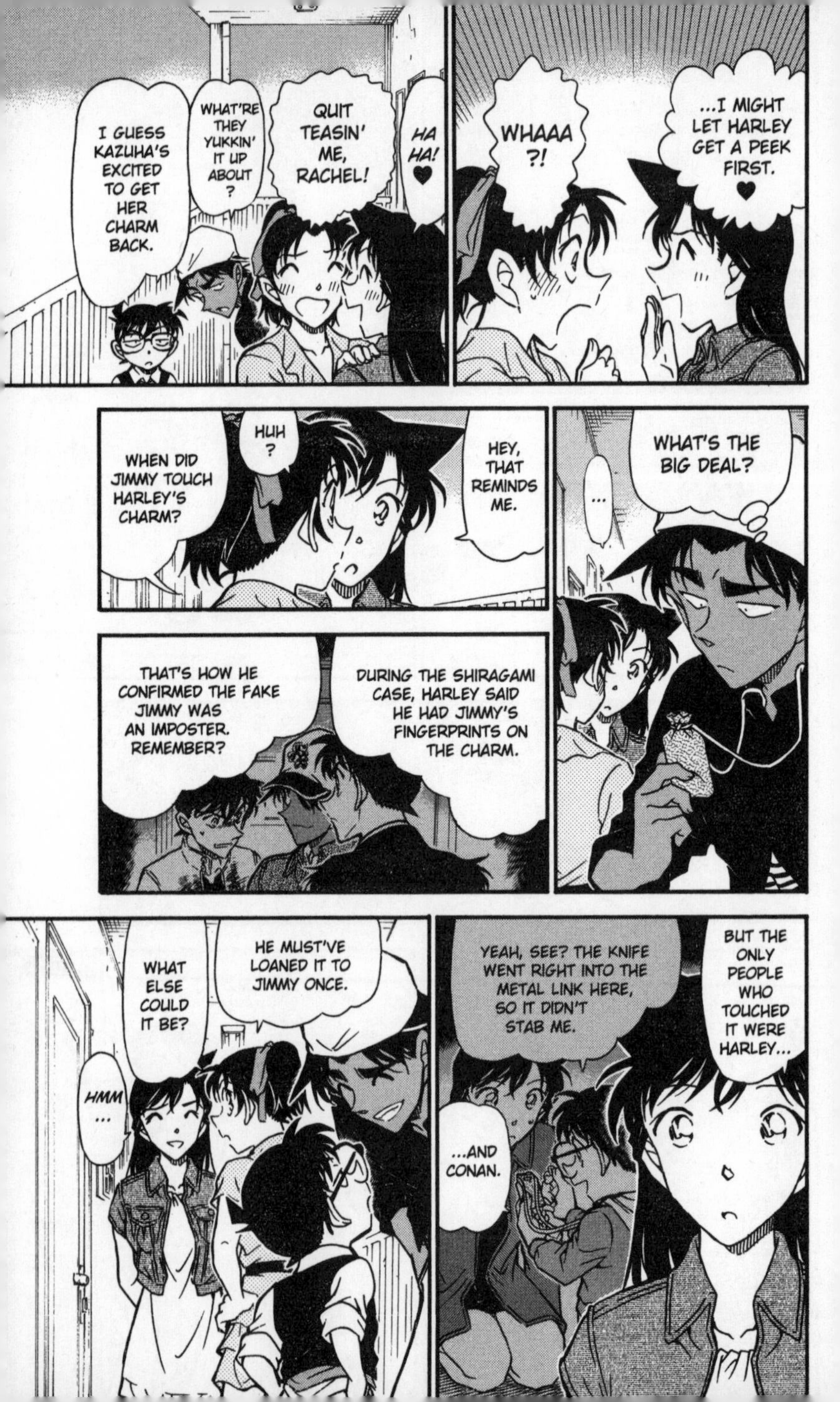
...I MIGHT LET HARLEY GET A PEEK FIRST. ♥
WHAAA ?!
HA HA! ♥
QUIT TEASIN' ME, RACHEL!
WHAT'RE THEY YUKKIN' IT UP ABOUT?
I GUESS KAZUHA'S EXCITED TO GET HER CHARM BACK.
WHAT'S THE BIG DEAL?
...
HEY, THAT REMINDS ME.
HUH?
WHEN DID JIMMY TOUCH HARLEY'S CHARM?
DURING THE SHIRAGAMI CASE, HARLEY SAID HE HAD JIMMY'S FINGERPRINTS ON THE CHARM.
THAT'S HOW HE CONFIRMED THE FAKE JIMMY WAS AN IMPOSTER. REMEMBER?
BUT THE ONLY PEOPLE WHO TOUCHED IT WERE HARLEY...
YEAH, SEE? THE KNIFE WENT RIGHT INTO THE METAL LINK HERE, SO IT DIDN'T STAB ME.
...AND CONAN.
HE MUST'VE LOANED IT TO JIMMY ONCE.
WHAT ELSE COULD IT BE?
HMM...

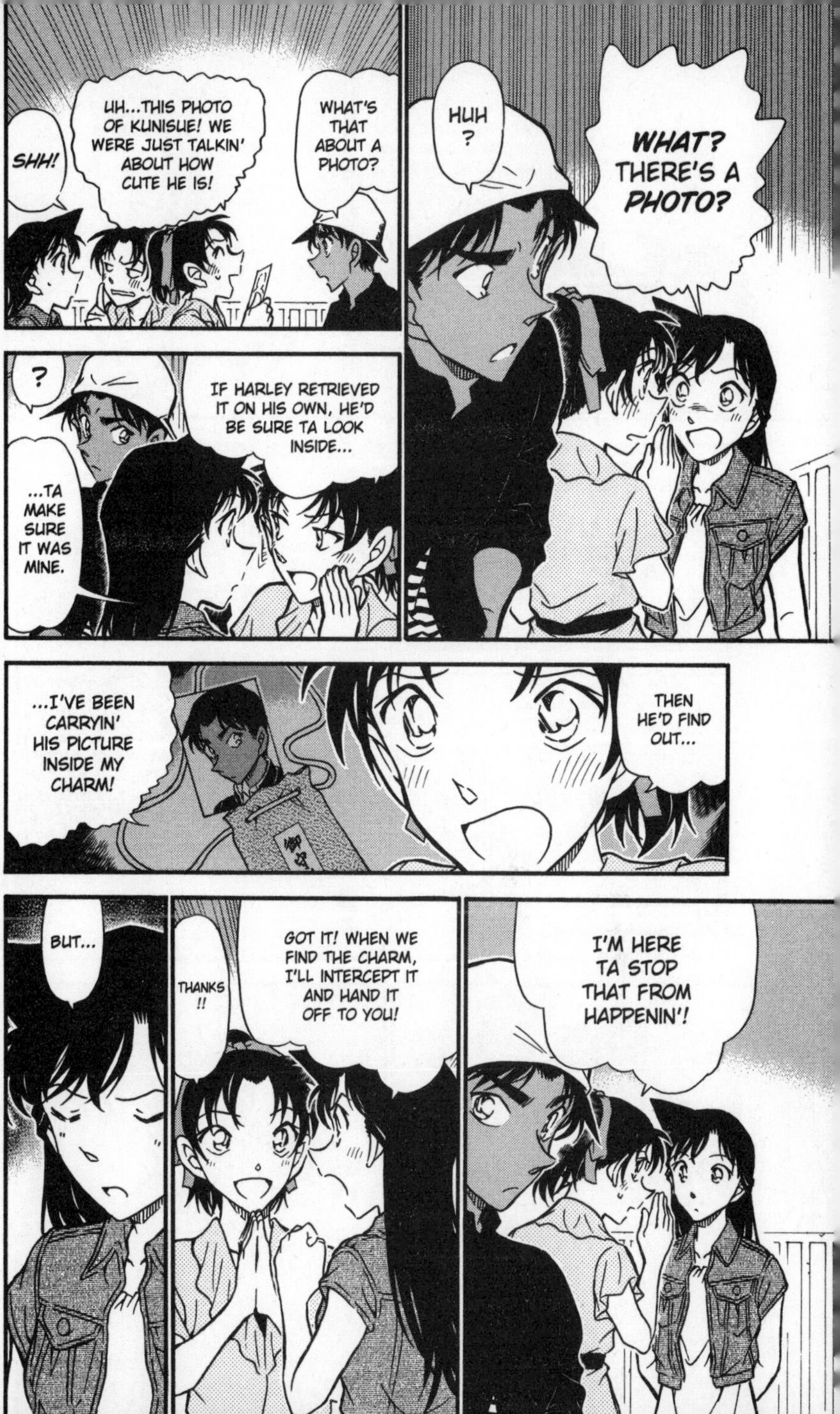
WHAT? THERE'S A PHOTO?
HUH?
WHAT'S THAT ABOUT A PHOTO?
UH...THIS PHOTO OF KUNISUE! WE WERE JUST TALKIN' ABOUT HOW CUTE HE IS!
SHH!
IF HARLEY RETRIEVED IT ON HIS OWN, HE'D BE SURE TA LOOK INSIDE...
?
...TA MAKE SURE IT WAS MINE.
THEN HE'D FIND OUT...
...I'VE BEEN CARRYIN' HIS PICTURE INSIDE MY CHARM!
I'M HERE TA STOP THAT FROM HAPPENIN'!
GOT IT! WHEN WE FIND THE CHARM, I'LL INTERCEPT IT AND HAND IT OFF TO YOU!
THANKS!!
BUT...

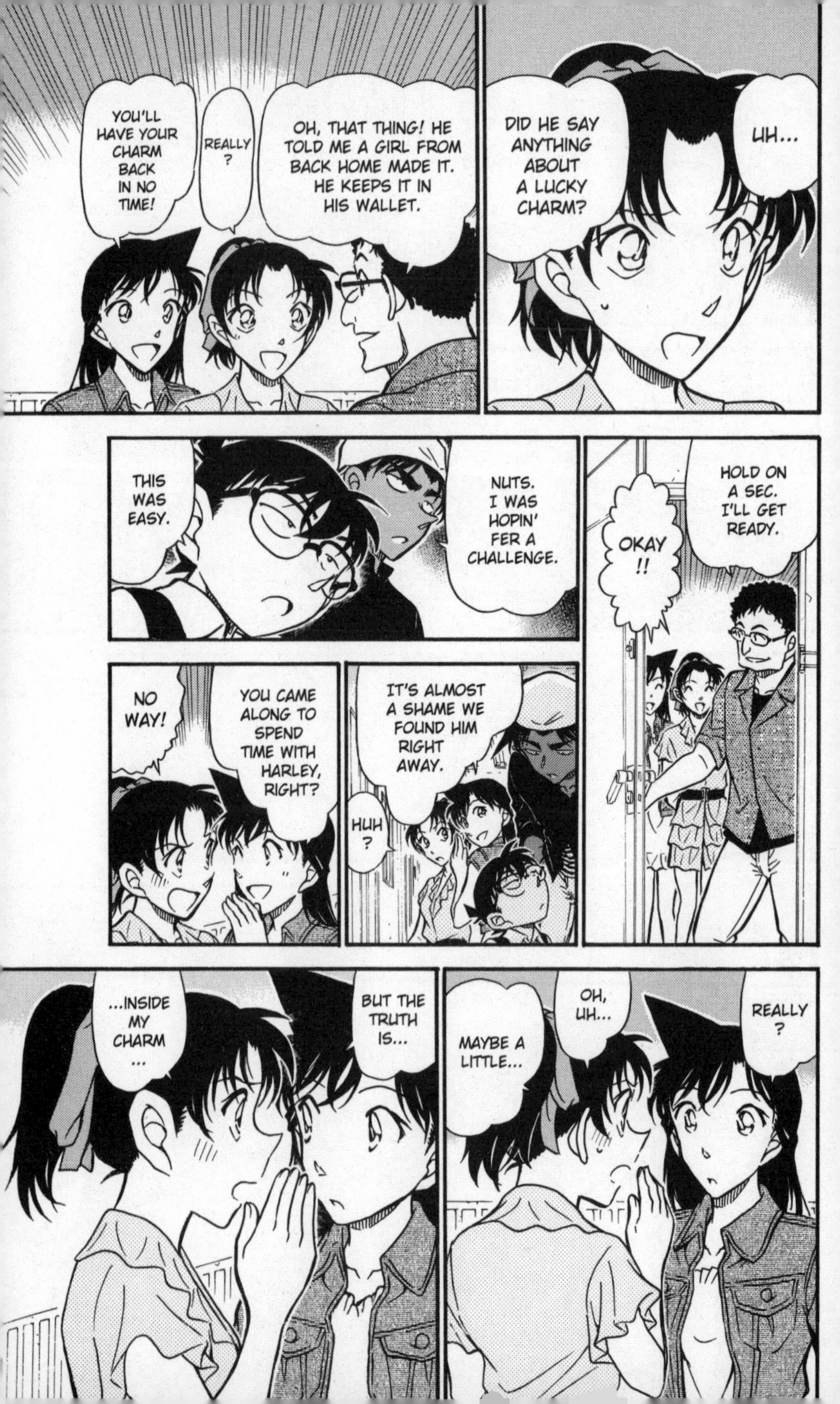
UH...
DID HE SAY ANYTHING ABOUT A LUCKY CHARM?
OH, THAT THING! HE TOLD ME A GIRL FROM BACK HOME MADE IT. HE KEEPS IT IN HIS WALLET.
REALLY?
YOU'LL HAVE YOUR CHARM BACK IN NO TIME!
HOLD ON A SEC. I'LL GET READY.
OKAY!!
NUTS. I WAS HOPIN' FER A CHALLENGE.
THIS WAS EASY.
IT'S ALMOST A SHAME WE FOUND HIM RIGHT AWAY.
HUH?
YOU CAME ALONG TO SPEND TIME WITH HARLEY, RIGHT?
NO WAY!
REALLY?
OH, UH...
MAYBE A LITTLE...
BUT THE TRUTH IS...
...INSIDE MY CHARM...

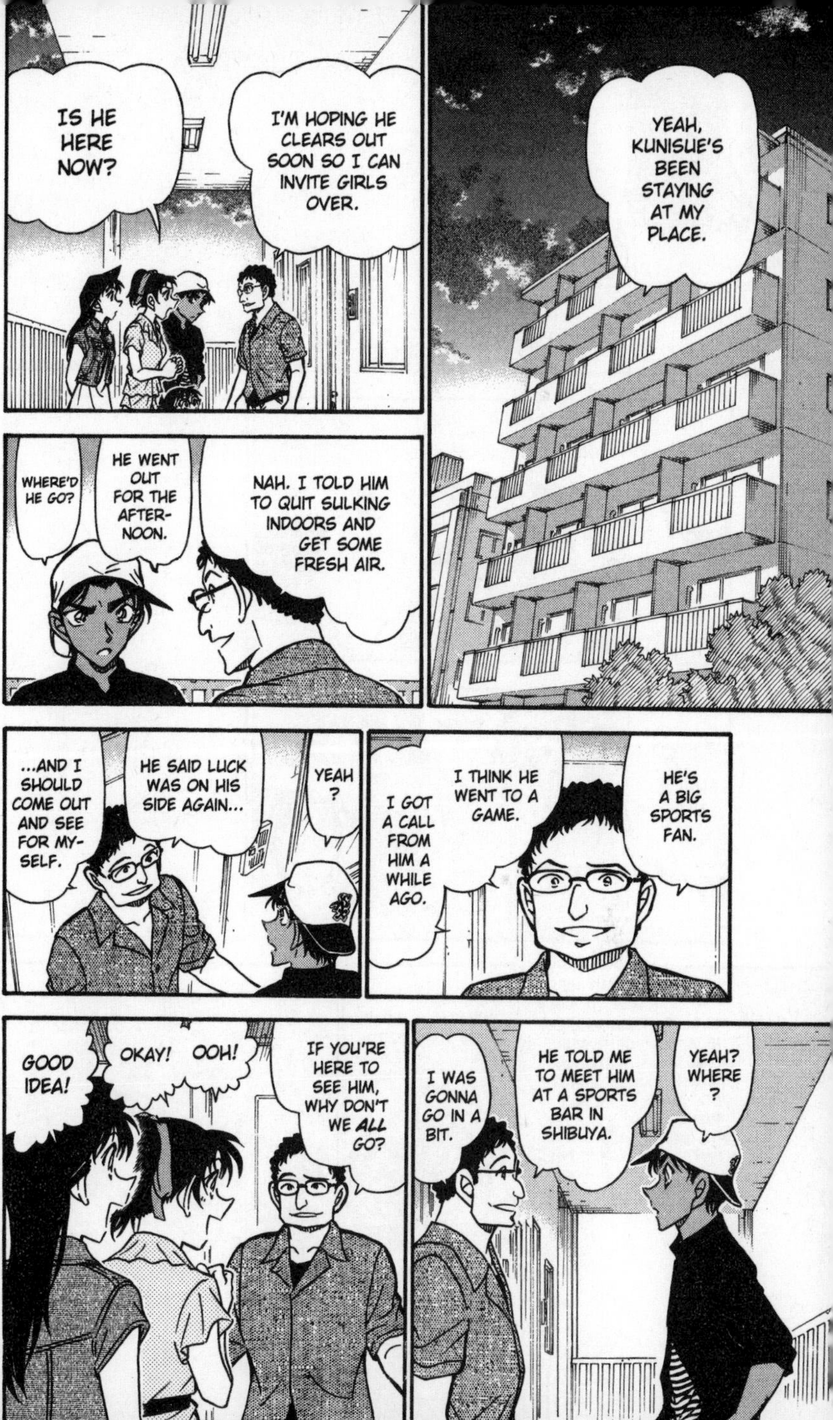
YEAH, KUNISUE'S BEEN STAYING AT MY PLACE.
I'M HOPING HE CLEARS OUT SOON SO I CAN INVITE GIRLS OVER.
IS HE HERE NOW?
NAH. I TOLD HIM TO QUIT SULKING INDOORS AND GET SOME FRESH AIR.
HE WENT OUT FOR THE AFTER-NOON.
WHERE'D HE GO?
HE'S A BIG SPORTS FAN.
I THINK HE WENT TO A GAME.
I GOT A CALL FROM HIM A WHILE AGO.
YEAH?
HE SAID LUCK WAS ON HIS SIDE AGAIN...
...AND I SHOULD COME OUT AND SEE FOR MY-SELF.
YEAH? WHERE?
HE TOLD ME TO MEET HIM AT A SPORTS BAR IN SHIBUYA.
I WAS GONNA GO IN A BIT.
IF YOU'RE HERE TO SEE HIM, WHY DON'T WE *ALL* GO?
OOH!
OKAY!
GOOD IDEA!

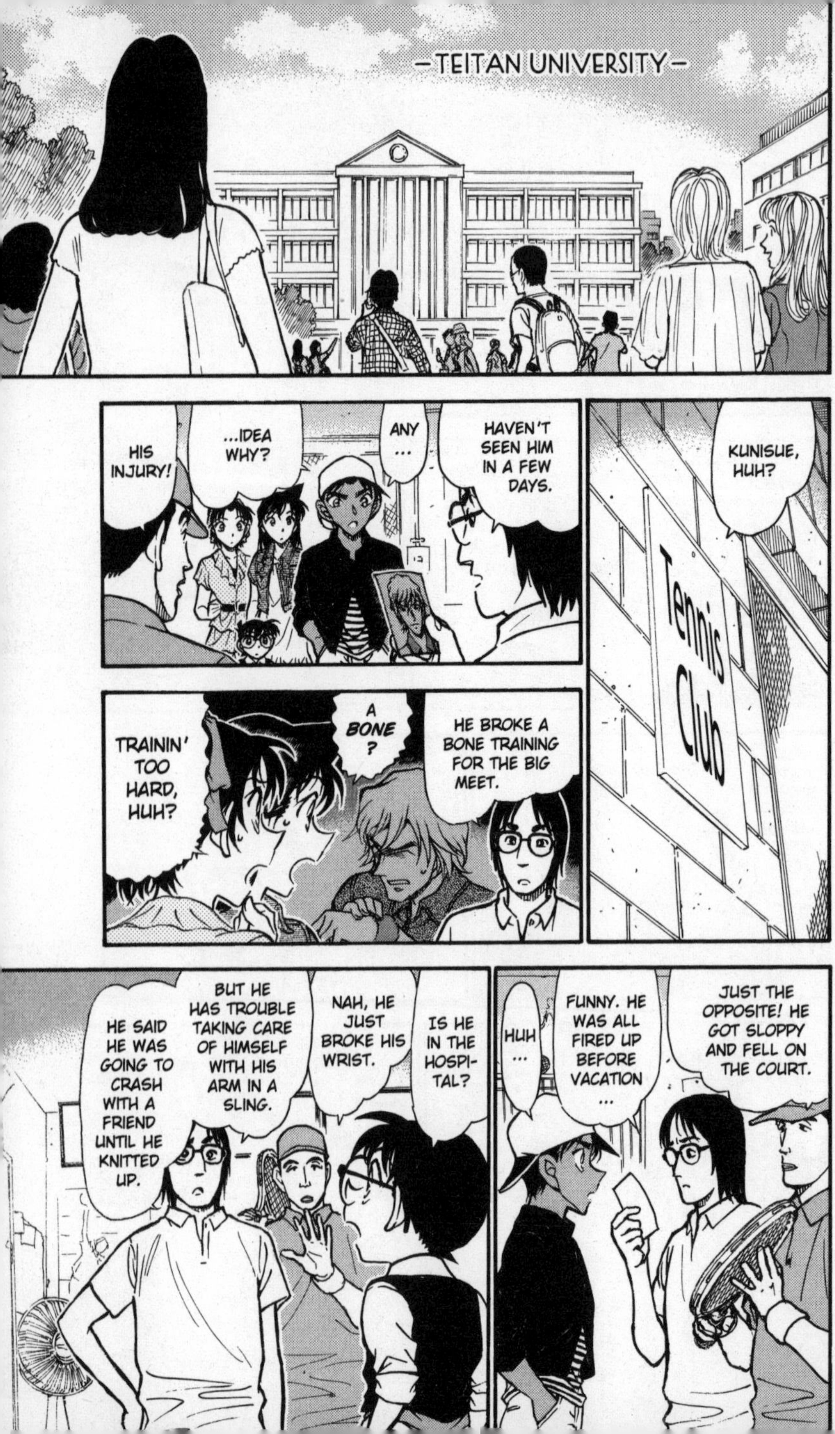
-TEITAN UNIVERSITY-
Tennis Club
KUNISUE, HUH?
HAVEN'T SEEN HIM IN A FEW DAYS.
ANY...
...IDEA WHY?
HIS INJURY!
HE BROKE A BONE TRAINING FOR THE BIG MEET.
A *BONE*?
TRAININ' TOO HARD, HUH?
JUST THE OPPOSITE! HE GOT SLOPPY AND FELL ON THE COURT.
FUNNY. HE WAS ALL FIRED UP BEFORE VACATION...
HUH...
IS HE IN THE HOSPI-TAL?
NAH, HE JUST BROKE HIS WRIST.
BUT HE HAS TROUBLE TAKING CARE OF HIMSELF WITH HIS ARM IN A SLING.
HE SAID HE WAS GOING TO CRASH WITH A FRIEND UNTIL HE KNITTED UP.

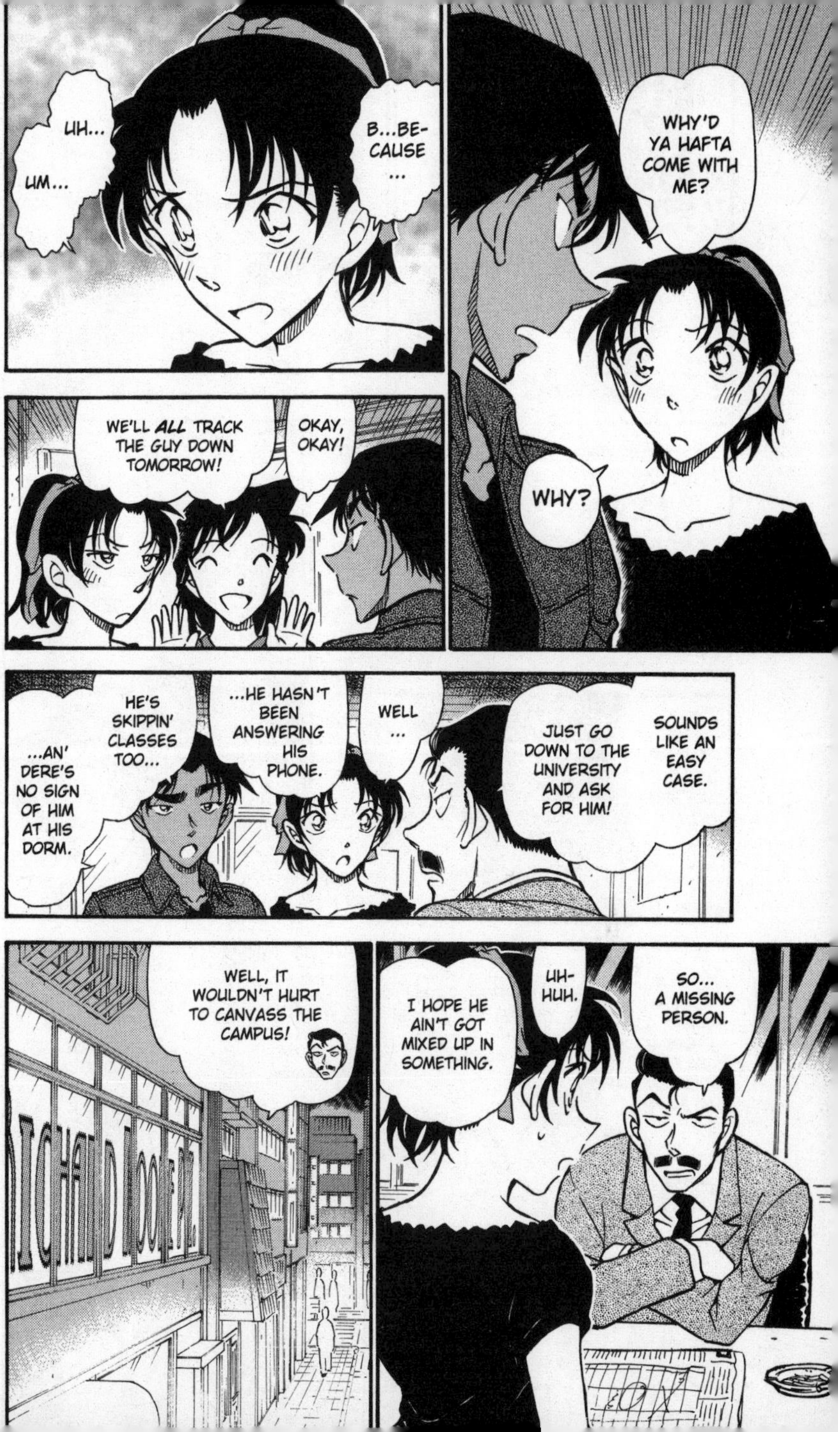
WHY'D YA HAFTA COME WITH ME?
WHY?
B...BE-CAUSE ...
UH...
UM...
OKAY, OKAY!
WE'LL ALL TRACK THE GUY DOWN TOMORROW!
SOUNDS LIKE AN EASY CASE.
JUST GO DOWN TO THE UNIVERSITY AND ASK FOR HIM!
WELL ...
...HE HASN'T BEEN ANSWERING HIS PHONE.
HE'S SKIPPIN' CLASSES TOO...
...AN' DERE'S NO SIGN OF HIM AT HIS DORM.
SO... A MISSING PERSON.
UH-HUH.
I HOPE HE AIN'T GOT MIXED UP IN SOMETHING.
WELL, IT WOULDN'T HURT TO CANVASS THE CAMPUS!

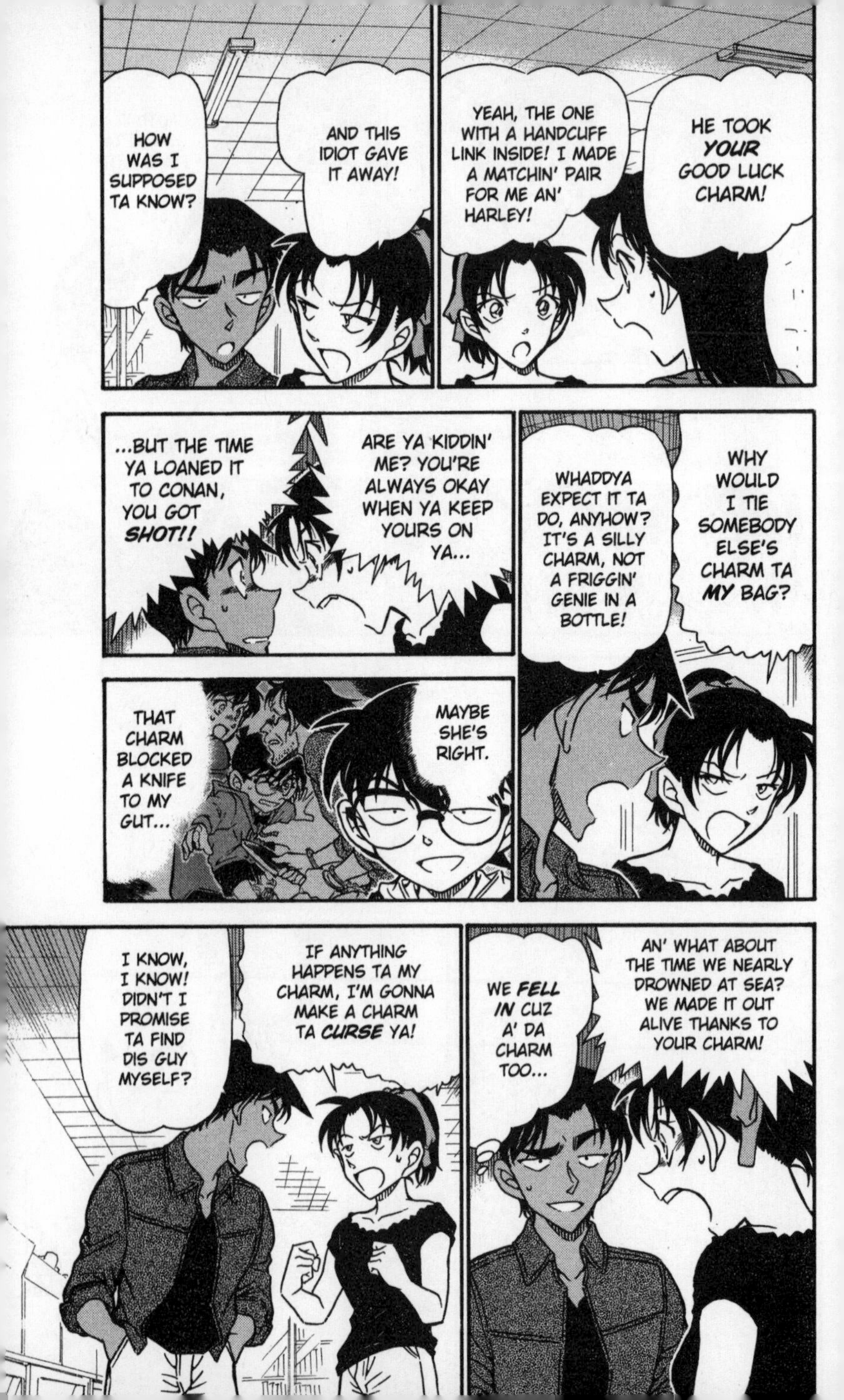
HE TOOK YOUR GOOD LUCK CHARM!
YEAH, THE ONE WITH A HANDCUFF LINK INSIDE! I MADE A MATCHIN' PAIR FOR ME AN' HARLEY!
AND THIS IDIOT GAVE IT AWAY!
HOW WAS I SUPPOSED TA KNOW?
WHY WOULD I TIE SOMEBODY ELSE'S CHARM TA MY BAG?
WHADDYA EXPECT IT TA DO, ANYHOW? IT'S A SILLY CHARM, NOT A FRIGGIN' GENIE IN A BOTTLE!
ARE YA KIDDIN' ME? YOU'RE ALWAYS OKAY WHEN YA KEEP YOURS ON YA...
...BUT THE TIME YA LOANED IT TO CONAN, YOU GOT SHOT!!
MAYBE SHE'S RIGHT.
THAT CHARM BLOCKED A KNIFE TO MY GUT...
AN' WHAT ABOUT THE TIME WE NEARLY DROWNED AT SEA? WE MADE IT OUT ALIVE THANKS TO YOUR CHARM!
WE FELL IN CUZ A' DA CHARM TOO...
IF ANYTHING HAPPENS TA MY CHARM, I'M GONNA MAKE A CHARM TA CURSE YA!
I KNOW, I KNOW! DIDN'T I PROMISE TA FIND DIS GUY MYSELF?

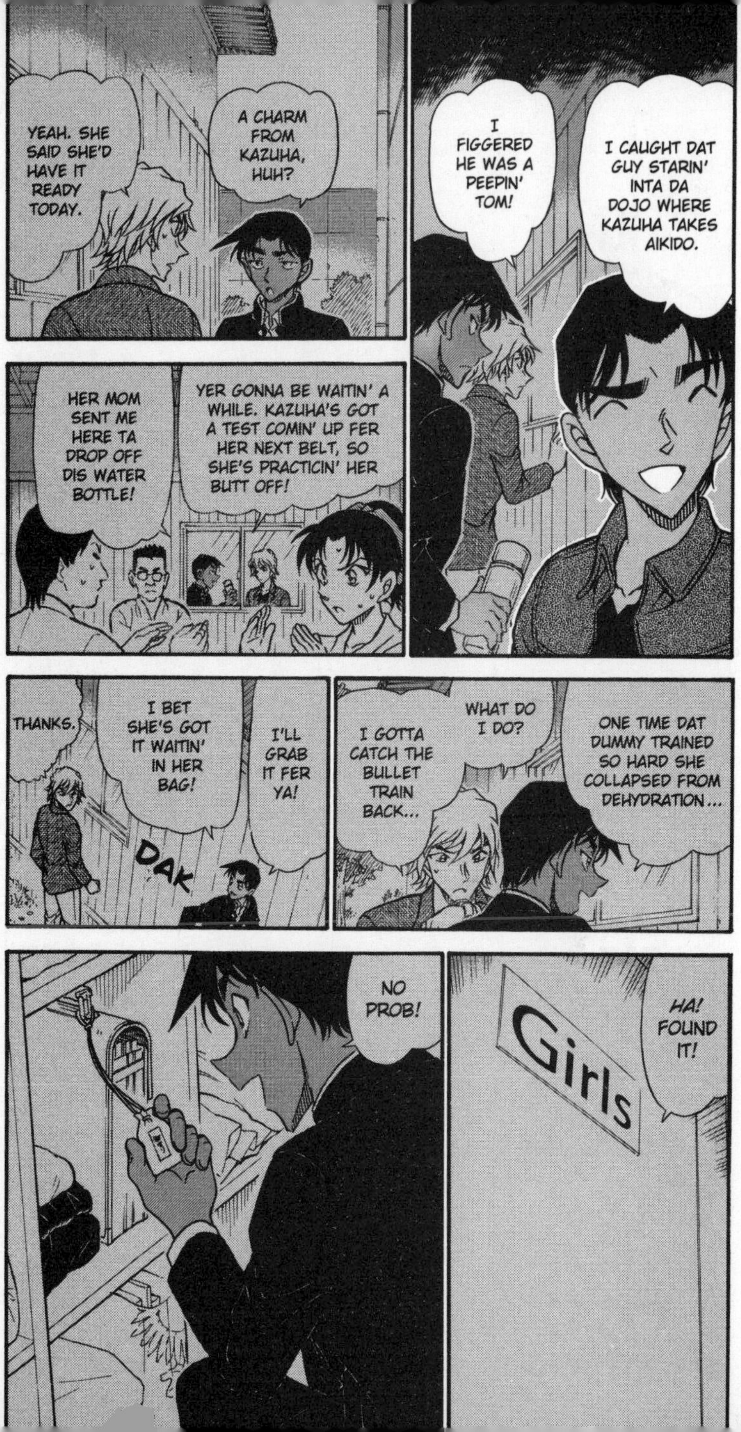

I CAUGHT DAT GUY STARIN' INTA DA DOJO WHERE KAZUHA TAKES AIKIDO.
I FIGGERED HE WAS A PEEPIN' TOM!
A CHARM FROM KAZUHA, HUH?
YEAH. SHE SAID SHE'D HAVE IT READY TODAY.
YER GONNA BE WAITIN' A WHILE. KAZUHA'S GOT A TEST COMIN' UP FER HER NEXT BELT, SO SHE'S PRACTICIN' HER BUTT OFF!
HER MOM SENT ME HERE TA DROP OFF DIS WATER BOTTLE!
ONE TIME DAT DUMMY TRAINED SO HARD SHE COLLAPSED FROM DEHYDRATION...
WHAT DO I DO?
I GOTTA CATCH THE BULLET TRAIN BACK...
I BET SHE'S GOT IT WAITIN' IN HER BAG!
I'LL GRAB IT FER YA!
THANKS.
DAK
Girls
HA! FOUND IT!
NO PROB!

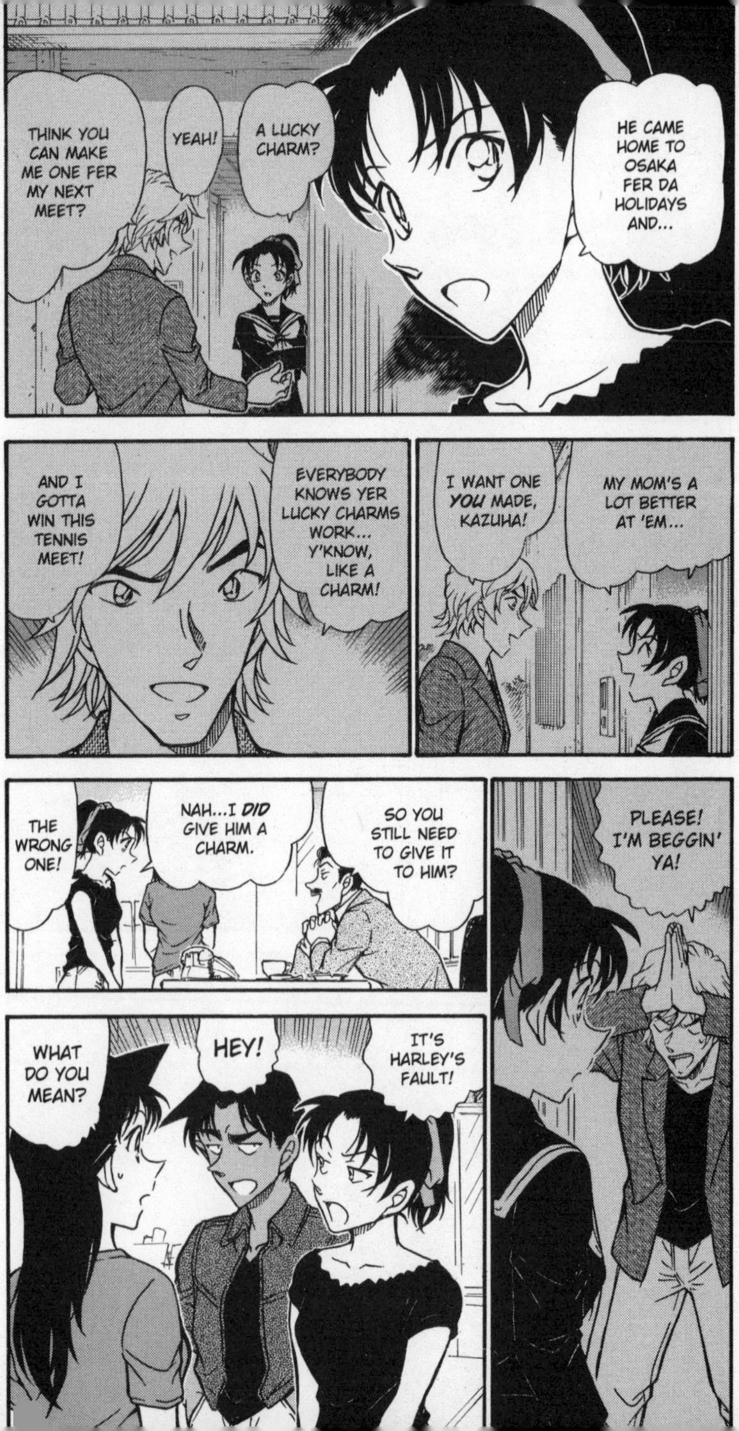

HE CAME HOME TO OSAKA FER DA HOLIDAYS AND...
A LUCKY CHARM?
YEAH!
THINK YOU CAN MAKE ME ONE FER MY NEXT MEET?
MY MOM'S A LOT BETTER AT 'EM...
I WANT ONE *YOU* MADE, KAZUHA!
EVERYBODY KNOWS YER LUCKY CHARMS WORK... Y'KNOW, LIKE A CHARM!
AND I GOTTA WIN THIS TENNIS MEET!
PLEASE! I'M BEGGIN' YA!
SO YOU STILL NEED TO GIVE IT TO HIM?
NAH...I *DID* GIVE HIM A CHARM.
THE WRONG ONE!
IT'S HARLEY'S FAULT!
HEY!
WHAT DO YOU MEAN?

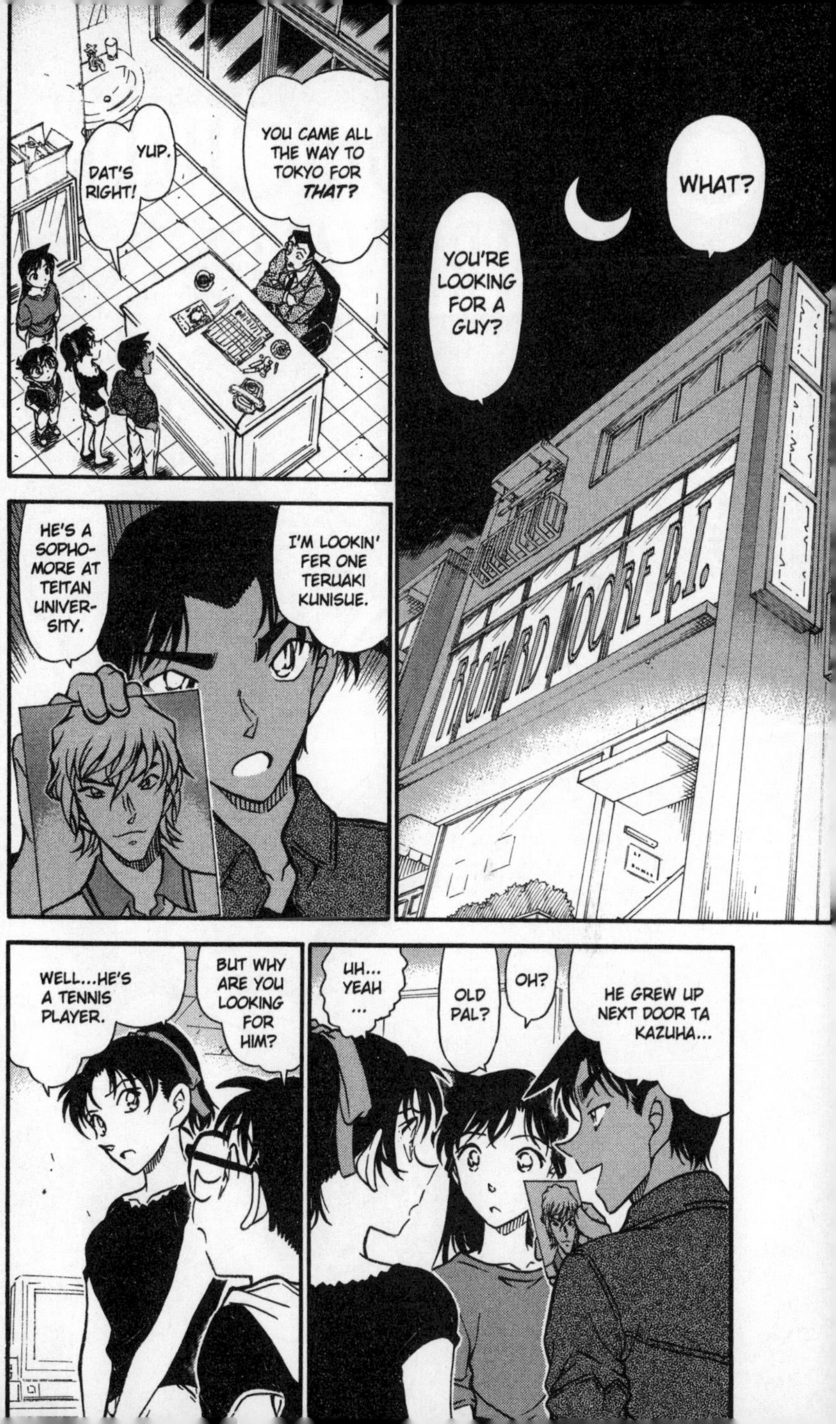
WHAT?
YOU'RE LOOKING FOR A GUY?
RICHARD MOORE P.I.
YOU CAME ALL THE WAY TO TOKYO FOR *THAT?*
YUP. DAT'S RIGHT!
I'M LOOKIN' FER ONE TERUAKI KUNISUE.
HE'S A SOPHOMORE AT TEITAN UNIVERSITY.
HE GREW UP NEXT DOOR TA KAZUHA...
OH?
OLD PAL?
UH... YEAH ...
BUT WHY ARE YOU LOOKING FOR HIM?
WELL...HE'S A TENNIS PLAYER.

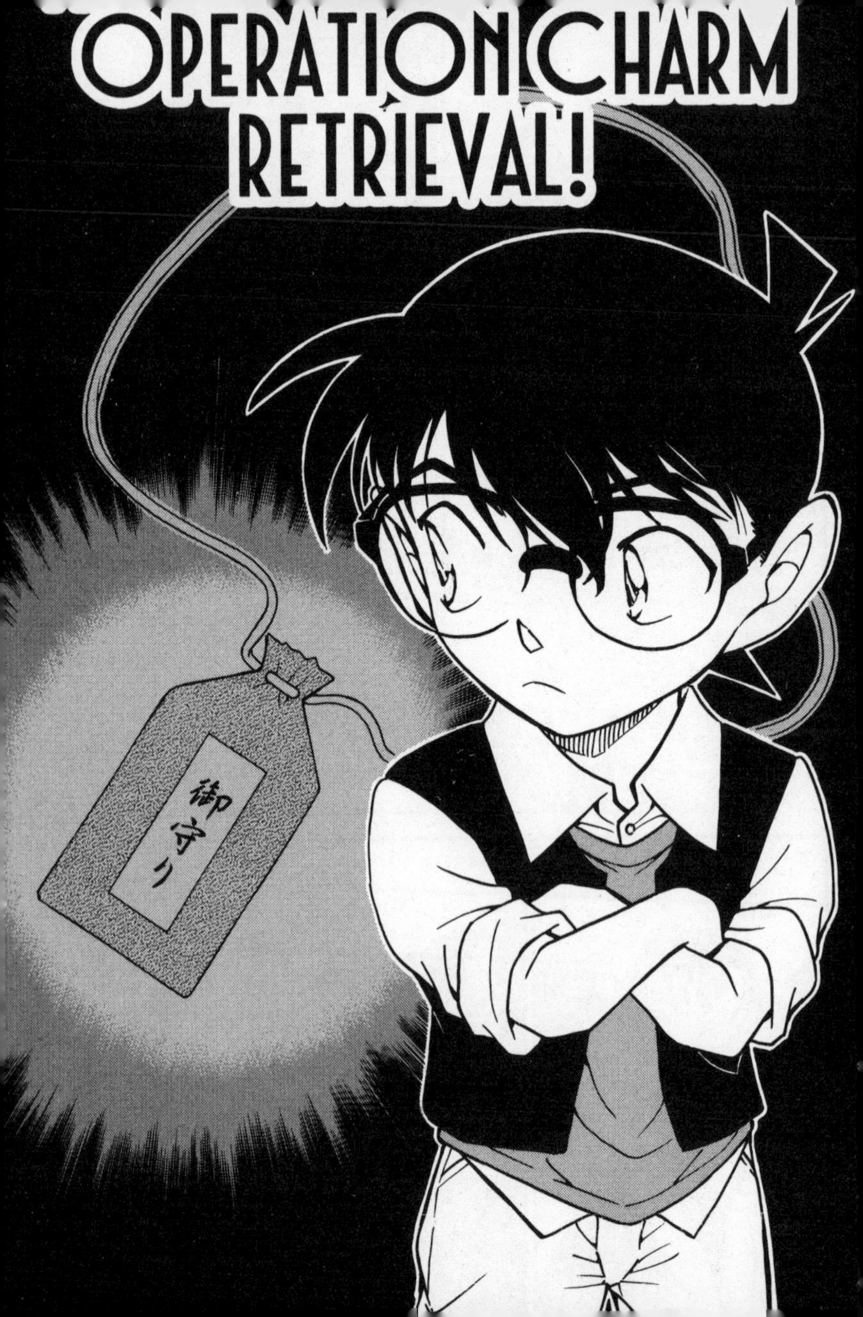
OPERATION CHARM RETRIEVAL!
御守り

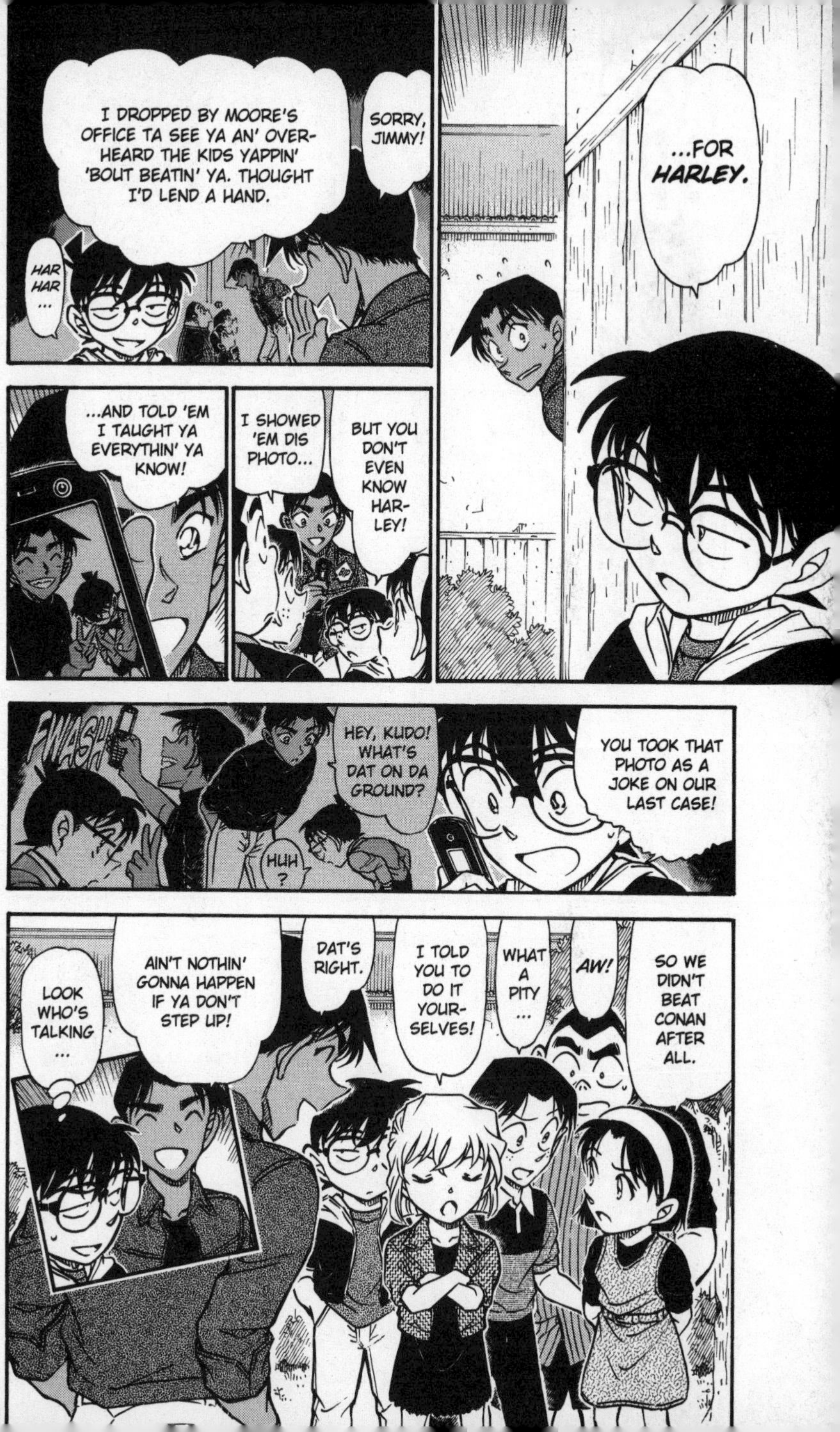
...FOR HARLEY.
SORRY, JIMMY!
I DROPPED BY MOORE'S OFFICE TA SEE YA AN' OVER-HEARD THE KIDS YAPPIN' 'BOUT BEATIN' YA. THOUGHT I'D LEND A HAND.
HAR HAR ...
BUT YOU DON'T EVEN KNOW HARLEY!
I SHOWED 'EM DIS PHOTO...
...AND TOLD 'EM I TAUGHT YA EVERYTHIN' YA KNOW!
YOU TOOK THAT PHOTO AS A JOKE ON OUR LAST CASE!
HEY, KUDO! WHAT'S DAT ON DA GROUND?
HUH ?
FWASH
SO WE DIDN'T BEAT CONAN AFTER ALL.
AW!
WHAT A PITY ...
I TOLD YOU TO DO IT YOUR-SELVES!
DAT'S RIGHT.
AIN'T NOTHIN' GONNA HAPPEN IF YA DON'T STEP UP!
LOOK WHO'S TALKING ...

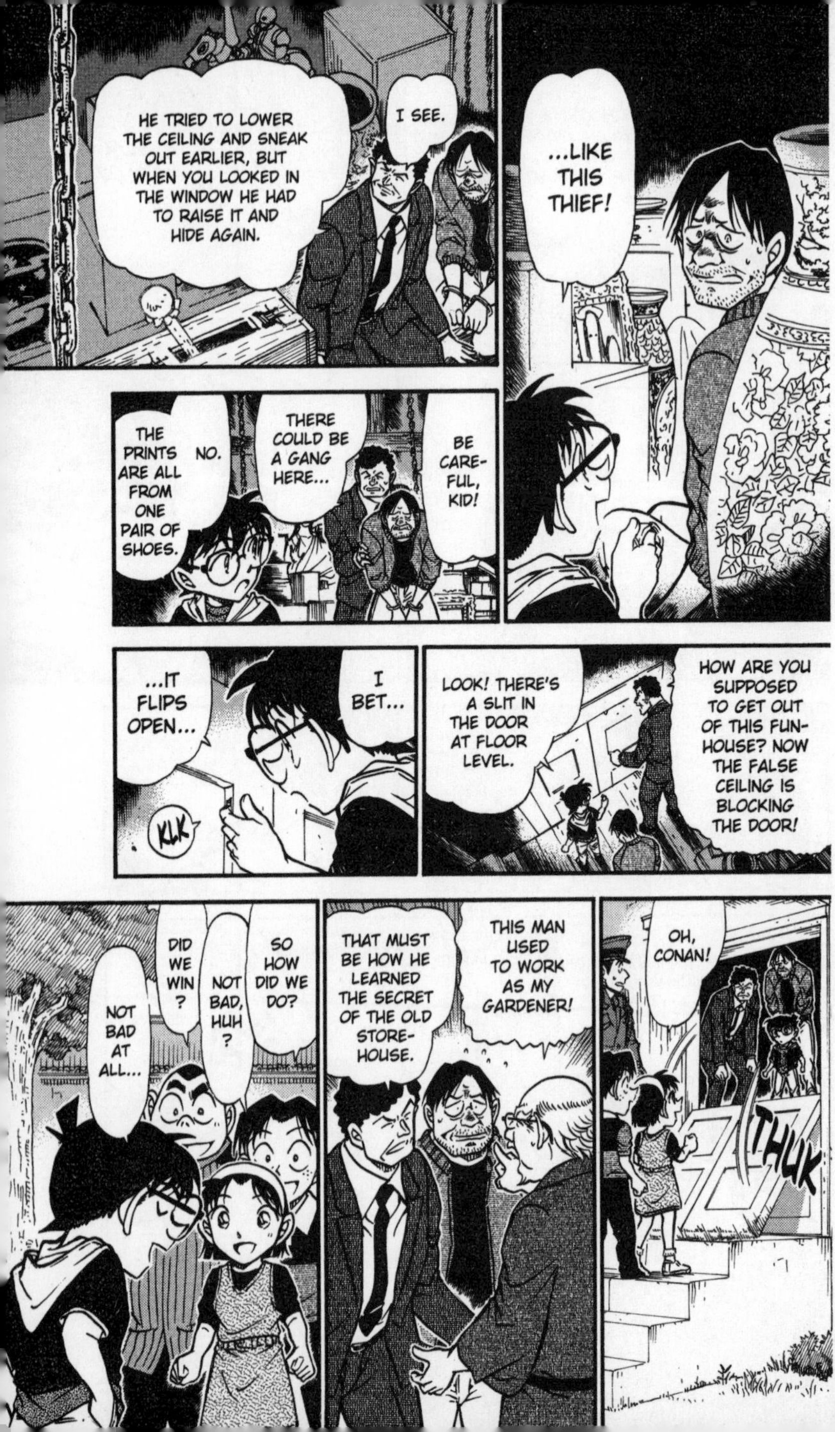
...LIKE THIS THIEF!
I SEE.
HE TRIED TO LOWER THE CEILING AND SNEAK OUT EARLIER, BUT WHEN YOU LOOKED IN THE WINDOW HE HAD TO RAISE IT AND HIDE AGAIN.
BE CARE-FUL, KID!
THERE COULD BE A GANG HERE...
NO.
THE PRINTS ARE ALL FROM ONE PAIR OF SHOES.
HOW ARE YOU SUPPOSED TO GET OUT OF THIS FUN-HOUSE? NOW THE FALSE CEILING IS BLOCKING THE DOOR!
LOOK! THERE'S A SLIT IN THE DOOR AT FLOOR LEVEL.
I BET...
...IT FLIPS OPEN...
KLK
OH, CONAN!
THUK
THIS MAN USED TO WORK AS MY GARDENER!
THAT MUST BE HOW HE LEARNED THE SECRET OF THE OLD STORE-HOUSE.
SO HOW DID WE DO?
DID WE WIN?
NOT BAD, HUH?
NOT BAD AT ALL...

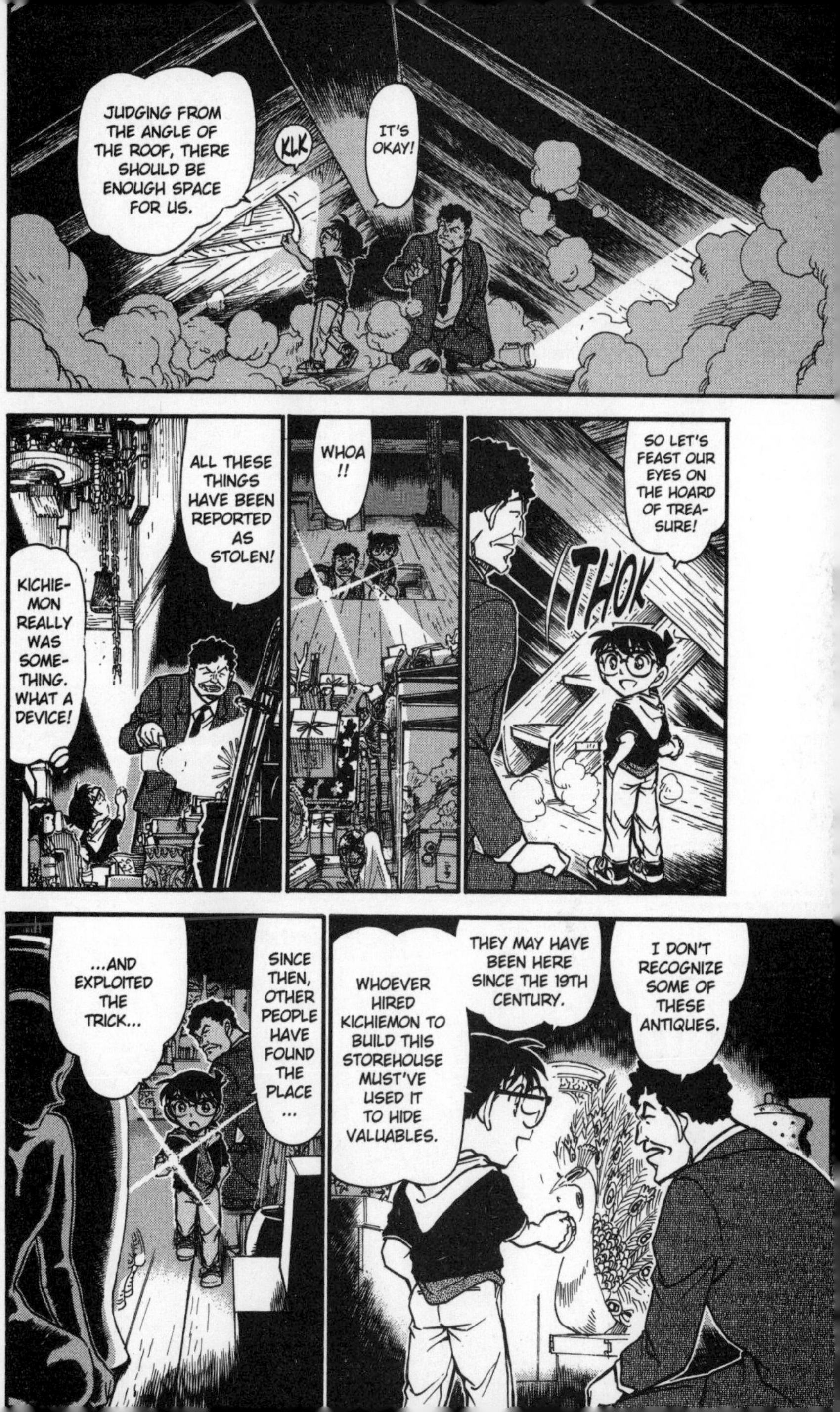
IT'S OKAY!
KLK
JUDGING FROM THE ANGLE OF THE ROOF, THERE SHOULD BE ENOUGH SPACE FOR US.
SO LET'S FEAST OUR EYES ON THE HOARD OF TREA-SURE!
THOK
WHOA !!
ALL THESE THINGS HAVE BEEN REPORTED AS STOLEN!
KICHIE-MON REALLY WAS SOME-THING. WHAT A DEVICE!
I DON'T RECOGNIZE SOME OF THESE ANTIQUES.
THEY MAY HAVE BEEN HERE SINCE THE 19TH CENTURY.
WHOEVER HIRED KICHIEMON TO BUILD THIS STOREHOUSE MUST'VE USED IT TO HIDE VALUABLES.
SINCE THEN, OTHER PEOPLE HAVE FOUND THE PLACE ...
...AND EXPLOITED THE TRICK...

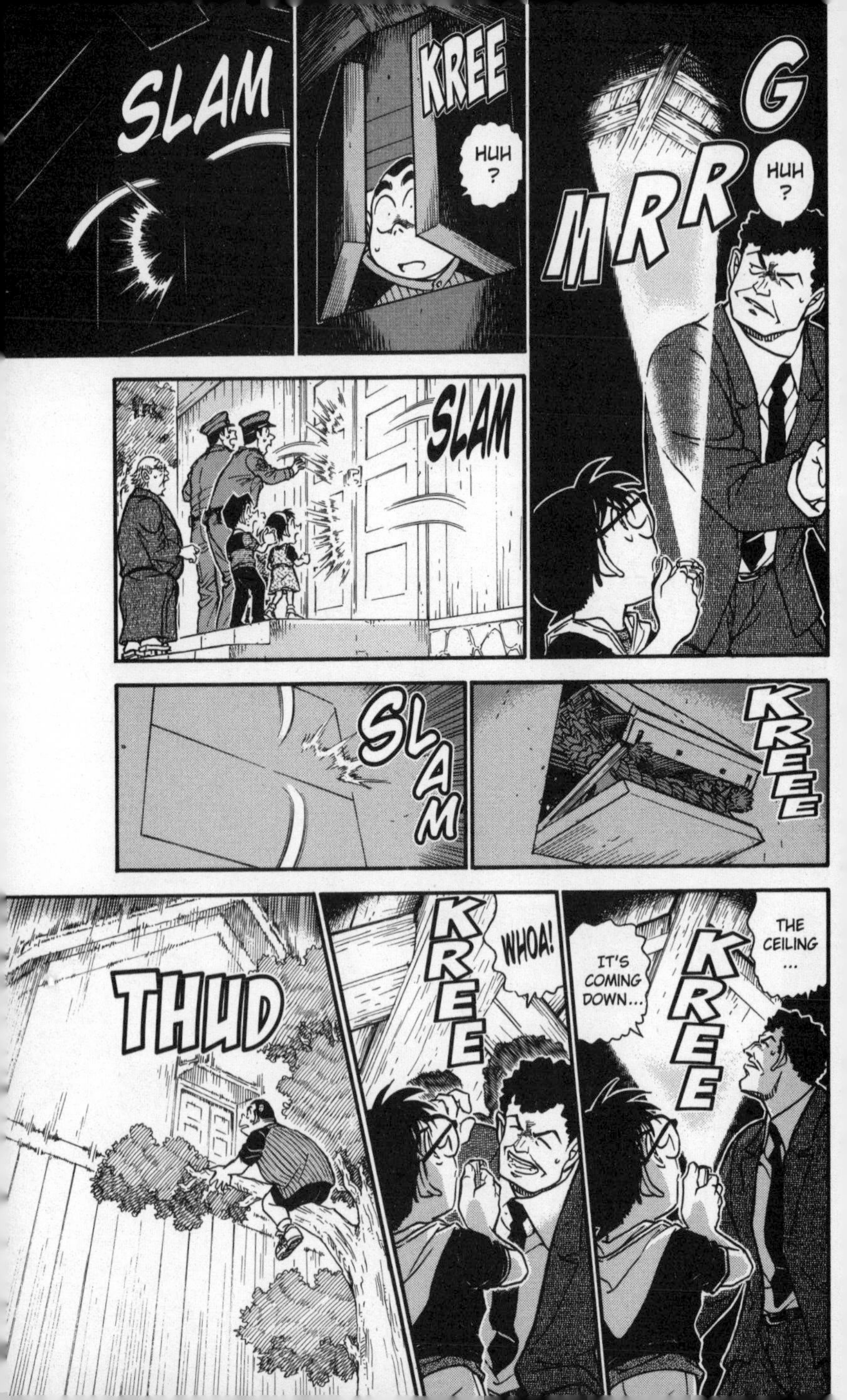
MRRRG
HUH?
KREE
HUH?
SLAM
SLAM
KREEE
SLAM
THE CEILING...
KREE
IT'S COMING DOWN...
WHOA!
KREE
THUD

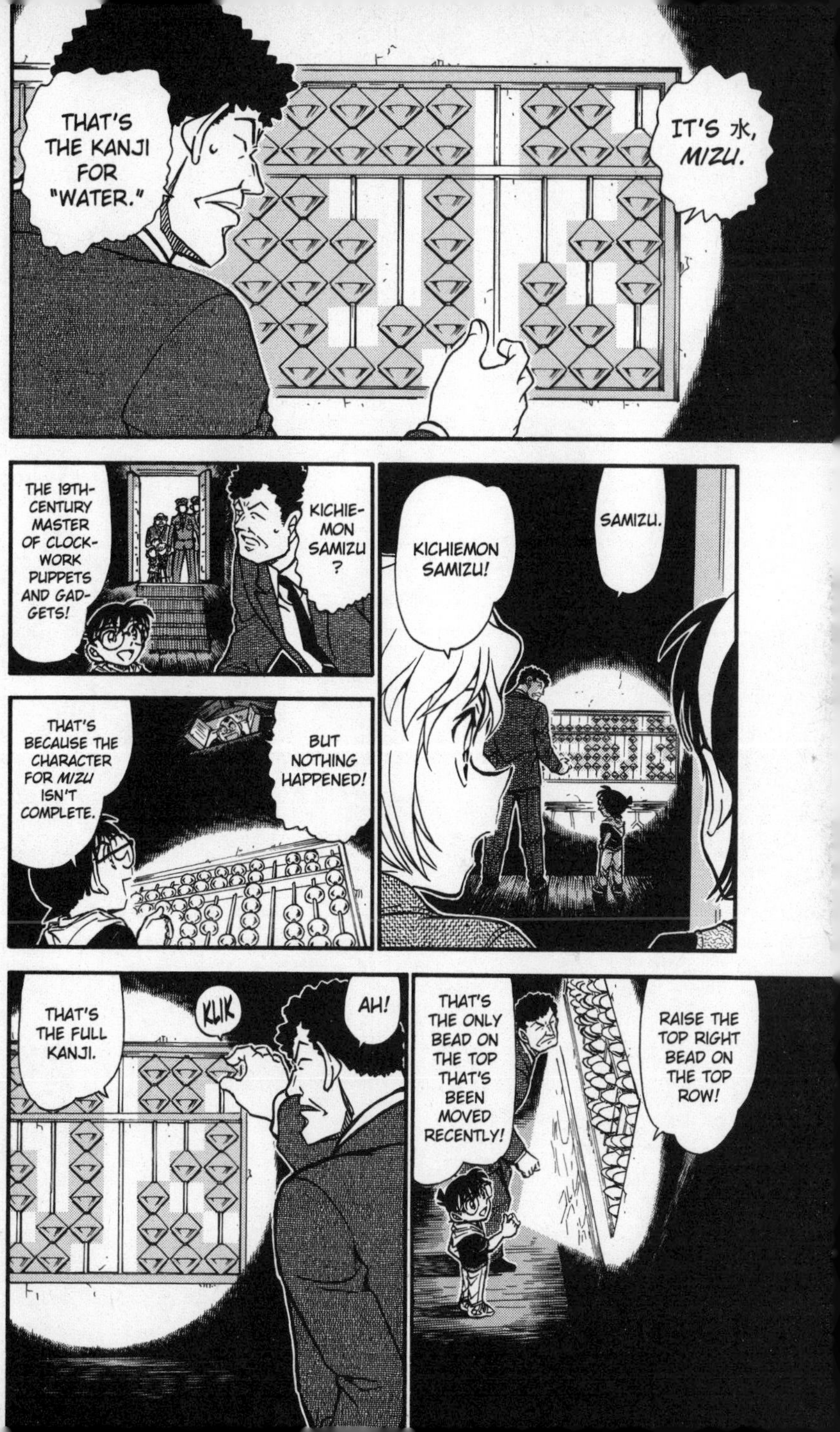

IT'S 水, *MIZU*.
THAT'S THE KANJI FOR "WATER."
SAMIZU.
KICHIEMON SAMIZU!
KICHIEMON SAMIZU?
THE 19TH-CENTURY MASTER OF CLOCKWORK PUPPETS AND GADGETS!
BUT NOTHING HAPPENED!
THAT'S BECAUSE THE CHARACTER FOR *MIZU* ISN'T COMPLETE.
RAISE THE TOP RIGHT BEAD ON THE TOP ROW!
THAT'S THE ONLY BEAD ON THE TOP THAT'S BEEN MOVED RECENTLY!
AH!
KLIK
THAT'S THE FULL KANJI.

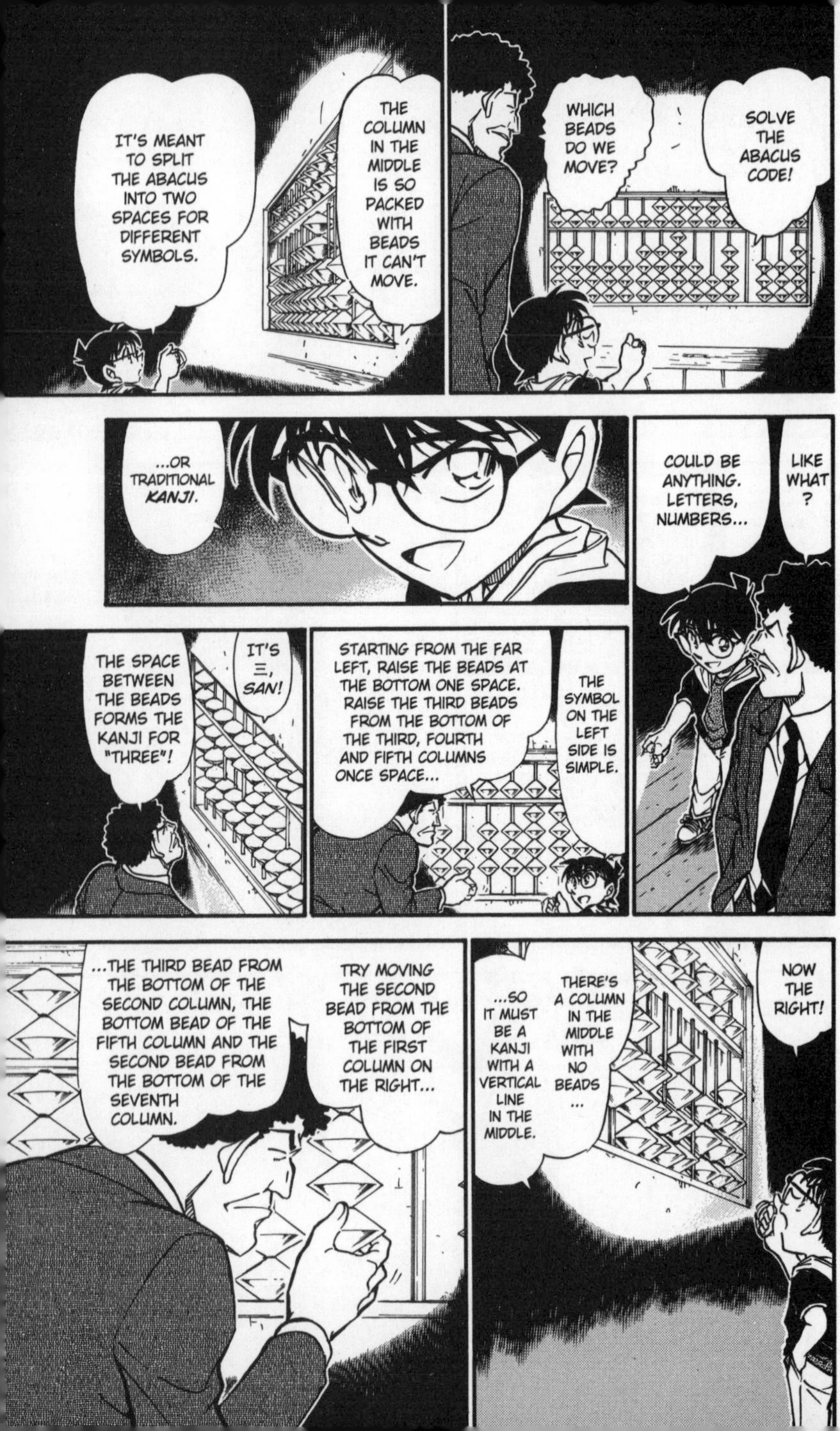
SOLVE THE ABACUS CODE!
WHICH BEADS DO WE MOVE?
THE COLUMN IN THE MIDDLE IS SO PACKED WITH BEADS IT CAN'T MOVE.
IT'S MEANT TO SPLIT THE ABACUS INTO TWO SPACES FOR DIFFERENT SYMBOLS.
LIKE WHAT?
COULD BE ANYTHING. LETTERS, NUMBERS...
...OR TRADITIONAL *KANJI*.
THE SYMBOL ON THE LEFT SIDE IS SIMPLE.
STARTING FROM THE FAR LEFT, RAISE THE BEADS AT THE BOTTOM ONE SPACE. RAISE THE THIRD BEADS FROM THE BOTTOM OF THE THIRD, FOURTH AND FIFTH COLUMNS ONCE SPACE...
IT'S 三, *SAN*!
THE SPACE BETWEEN THE BEADS FORMS THE KANJI FOR "THREE"!
NOW THE RIGHT!
THERE'S A COLUMN IN THE MIDDLE WITH NO BEADS...
...SO IT MUST BE A KANJI WITH A VERTICAL LINE IN THE MIDDLE.
TRY MOVING THE SECOND BEAD FROM THE BOTTOM OF THE FIRST COLUMN ON THE RIGHT...
...THE THIRD BEAD FROM THE BOTTOM OF THE SECOND COLUMN, THE BOTTOM BEAD OF THE FIFTH COLUMN AND THE SECOND BEAD FROM THE BOTTOM OF THE SEVENTH COLUMN.

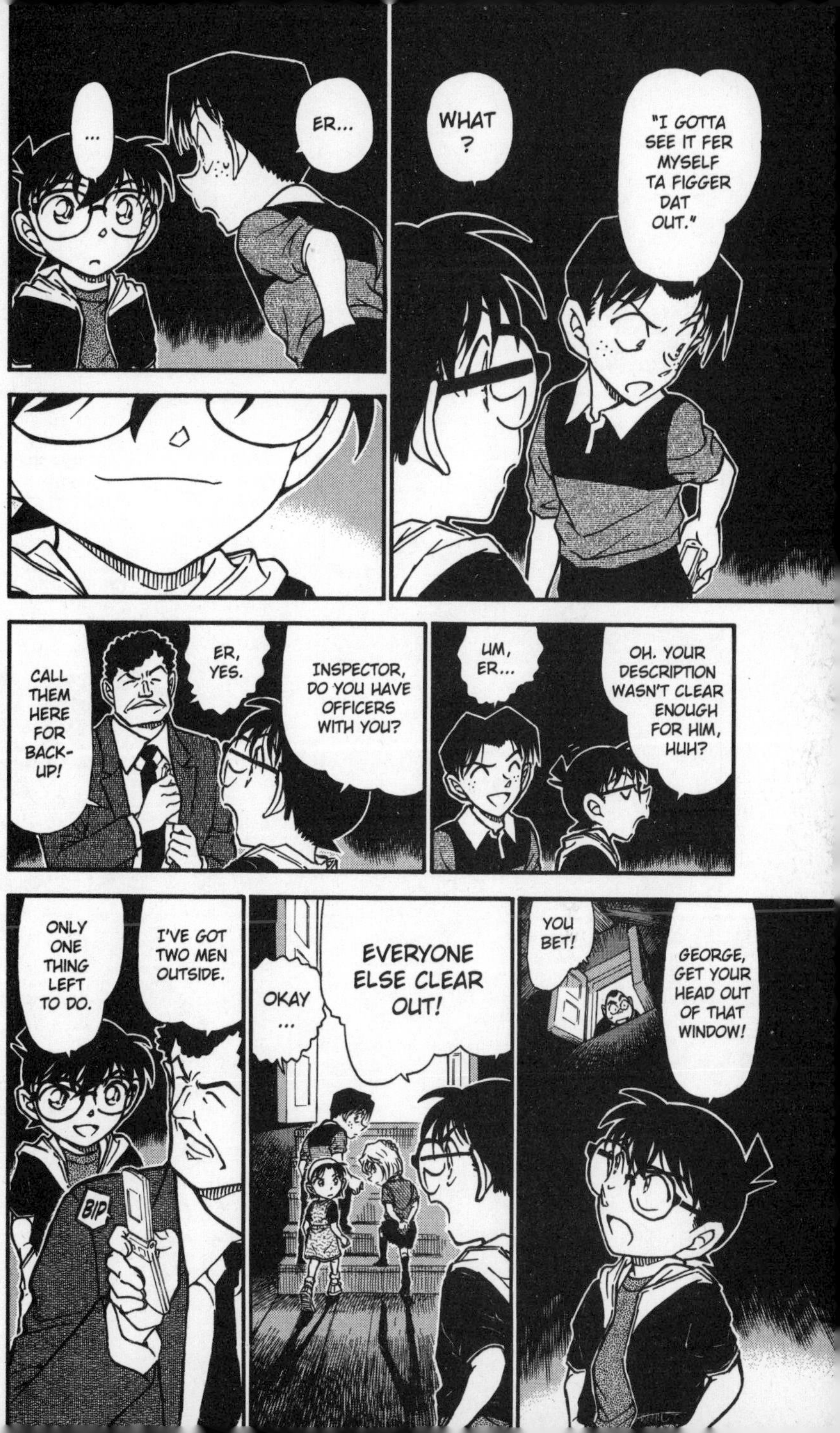
"I GOTTA SEE IT FER MYSELF TA FIGGER DAT OUT."
WHAT ?
ER...
...
OH. YOUR DESCRIPTION WASN'T CLEAR ENOUGH FOR HIM, HUH?
UM, ER...
INSPECTOR, DO YOU HAVE OFFICERS WITH YOU?
ER, YES.
CALL THEM HERE FOR BACK-UP!
GEORGE, GET YOUR HEAD OUT OF THAT WINDOW!
YOU BET!
EVERYONE ELSE CLEAR OUT!
OKAY ...
I'VE GOT TWO MEN OUTSIDE.
ONLY ONE THING LEFT TO DO.
BIP

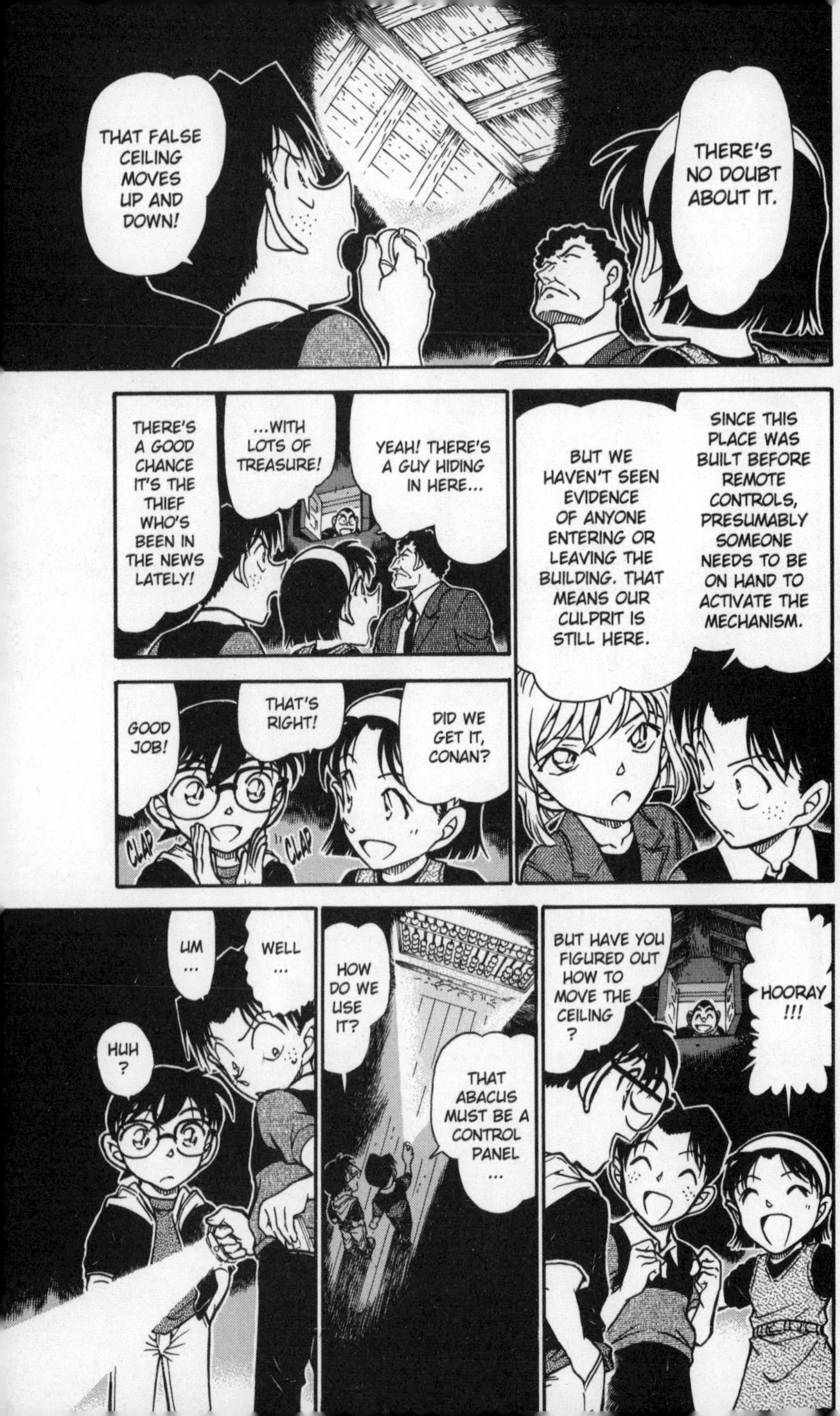
THERE'S NO DOUBT ABOUT IT.
THAT FALSE CEILING MOVES UP AND DOWN!
SINCE THIS PLACE WAS BUILT BEFORE REMOTE CONTROLS, PRESUMABLY SOMEONE NEEDS TO BE ON HAND TO ACTIVATE THE MECHANISM.
BUT WE HAVEN'T SEEN EVIDENCE OF ANYONE ENTERING OR LEAVING THE BUILDING. THAT MEANS OUR CULPRIT IS STILL HERE.
YEAH! THERE'S A GUY HIDING IN HERE...
...WITH LOTS OF TREASURE!
THERE'S A GOOD CHANCE IT'S THE THIEF WHO'S BEEN IN THE NEWS LATELY!
DID WE GET IT, CONAN?
THAT'S RIGHT!
GOOD JOB!
CLAP
CLAP
HOORAY!!!
BUT HAVE YOU FIGURED OUT HOW TO MOVE THE CEILING?
HOW DO WE USE IT?
THAT ABACUS MUST BE A CONTROL PANEL...
WELL...
UM...
HUH?

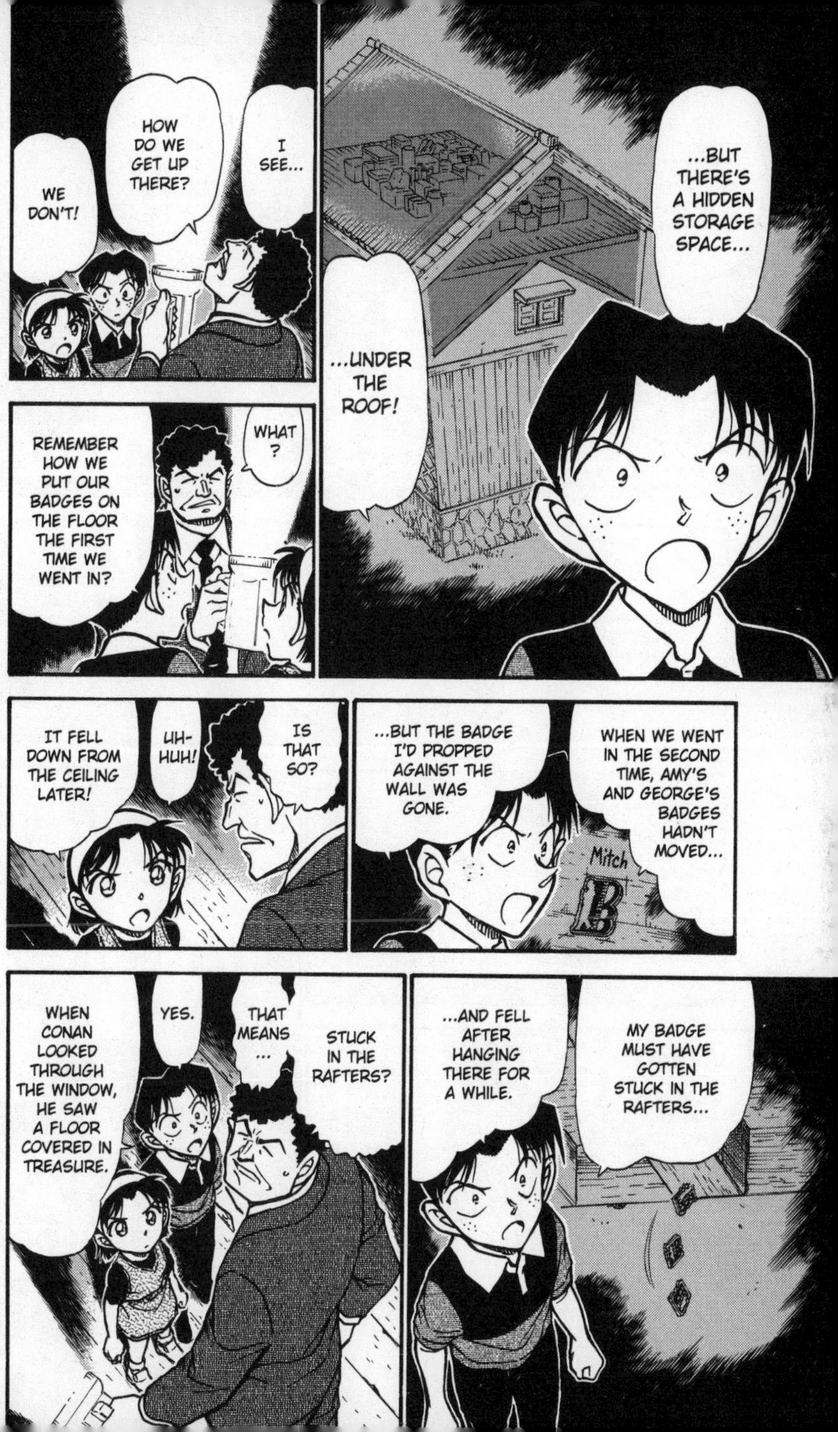
...BUT THERE'S A HIDDEN STORAGE SPACE...
...UNDER THE ROOF!
I SEE...
HOW DO WE GET UP THERE?
WE DON'T!
WHAT?
REMEMBER HOW WE PUT OUR BADGES ON THE FLOOR THE FIRST TIME WE WENT IN?
WHEN WE WENT IN THE SECOND TIME, AMY'S AND GEORGE'S BADGES HADN'T MOVED...
...BUT THE BADGE I'D PROPPED AGAINST THE WALL WAS GONE.
Mitch
IS THAT SO?
UH-HUH!
IT FELL DOWN FROM THE CEILING LATER!
MY BADGE MUST HAVE GOTTEN STUCK IN THE RAFTERS...
...AND FELL AFTER HANGING THERE FOR A WHILE.
STUCK IN THE RAFTERS?
THAT MEANS...
YES.
WHEN CONAN LOOKED THROUGH THE WINDOW, HE SAW A FLOOR COVERED IN TREASURE.

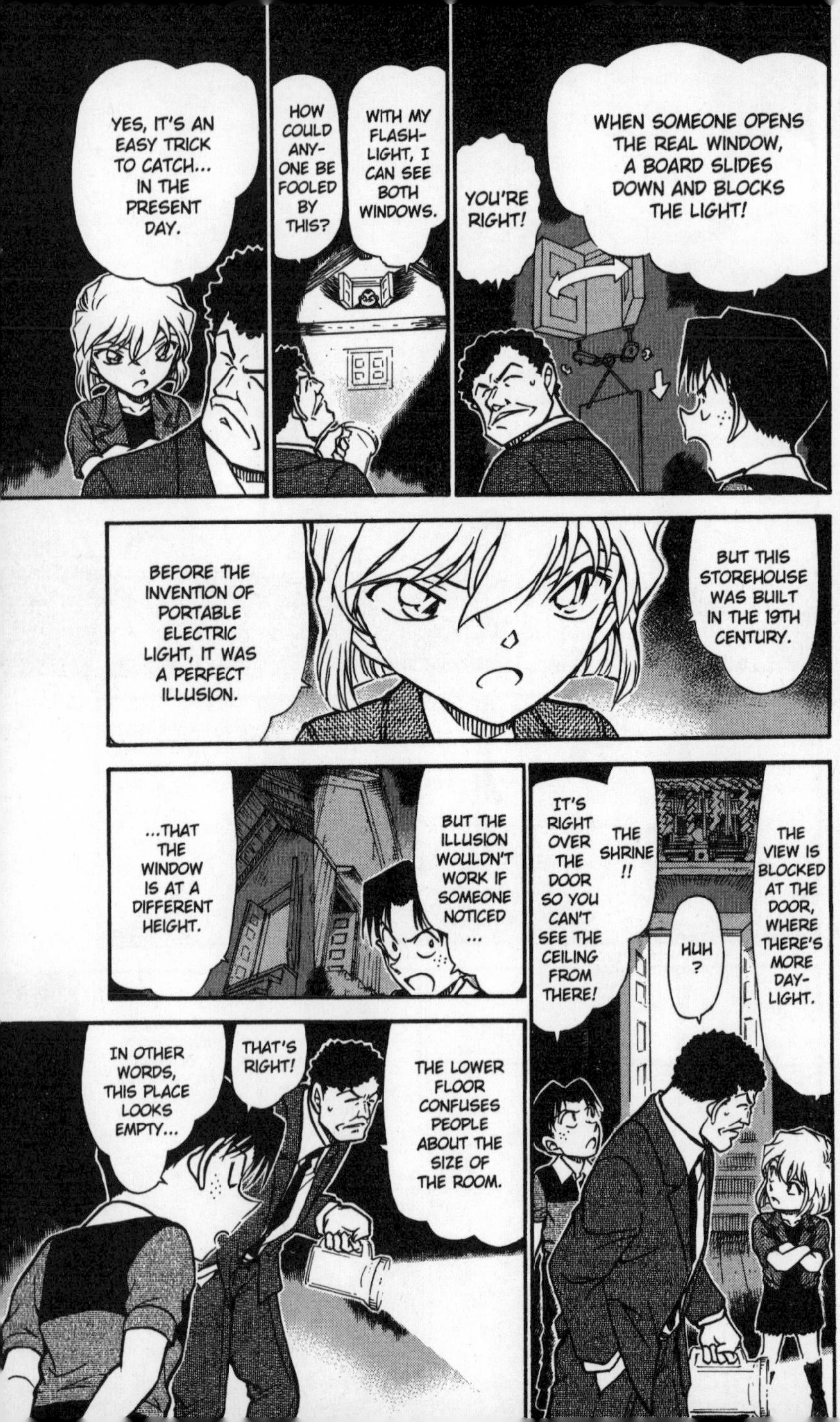
WHEN SOMEONE OPENS THE REAL WINDOW, A BOARD SLIDES DOWN AND BLOCKS THE LIGHT!
YOU'RE RIGHT!
WITH MY FLASHLIGHT, I CAN SEE BOTH WINDOWS.
HOW COULD ANYONE BE FOOLED BY THIS?
YES, IT'S AN EASY TRICK TO CATCH... IN THE PRESENT DAY.
BUT THIS STOREHOUSE WAS BUILT IN THE 19TH CENTURY.
BEFORE THE INVENTION OF PORTABLE ELECTRIC LIGHT, IT WAS A PERFECT ILLUSION.
THE VIEW IS BLOCKED AT THE DOOR, WHERE THERE'S MORE DAYLIGHT.
HUH?
THE SHRINE!!
IT'S RIGHT OVER THE DOOR SO YOU CAN'T SEE THE CEILING FROM THERE!
BUT THE ILLUSION WOULDN'T WORK IF SOMEONE NOTICED...
...THAT THE WINDOW IS AT A DIFFERENT HEIGHT.
THE LOWER FLOOR CONFUSES PEOPLE ABOUT THE SIZE OF THE ROOM.
THAT'S RIGHT!
IN OTHER WORDS, THIS PLACE LOOKS EMPTY...

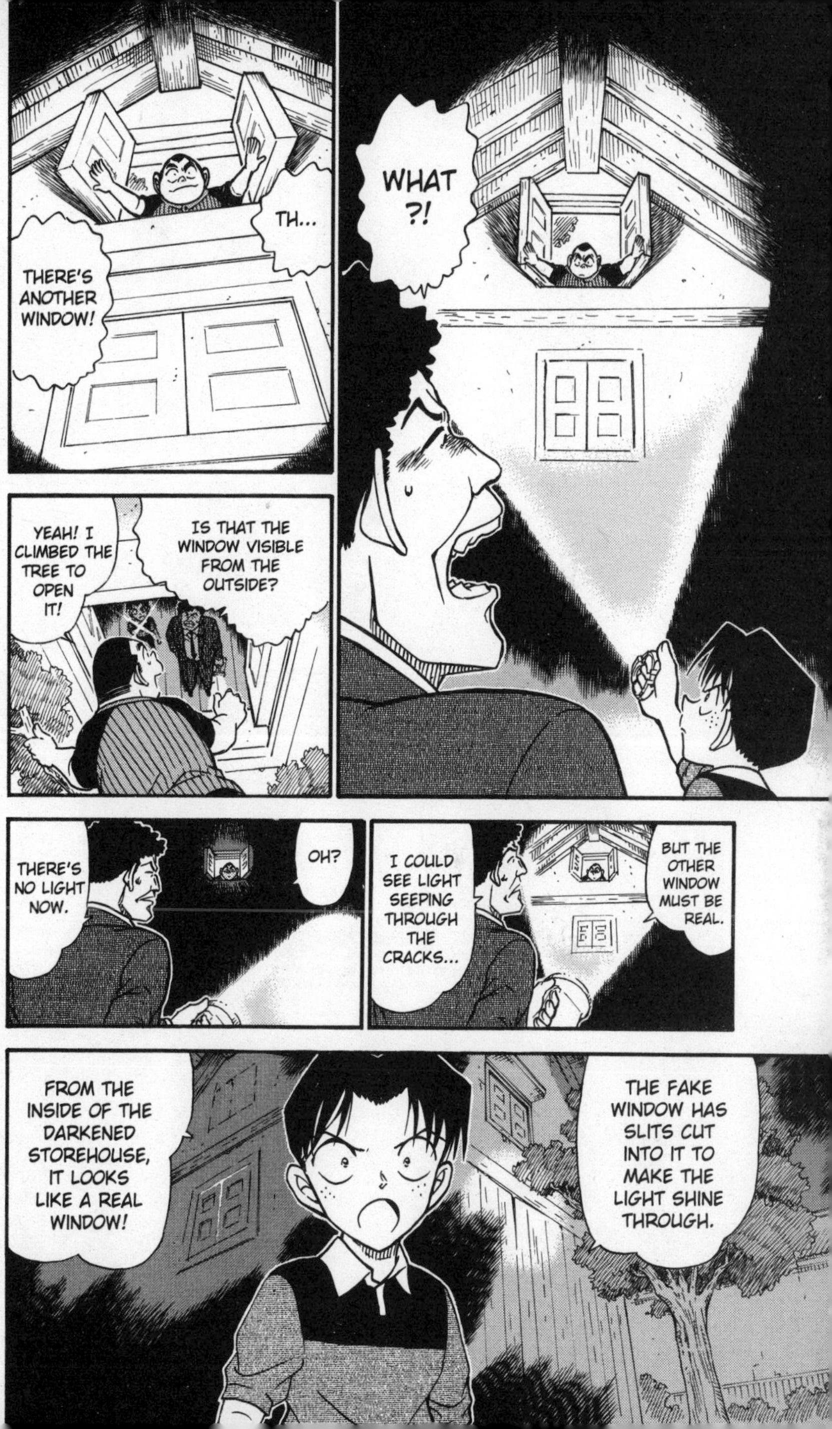
WHAT?!
TH...
THERE'S ANOTHER WINDOW!
IS THAT THE WINDOW VISIBLE FROM THE OUTSIDE?
YEAH! I CLIMBED THE TREE TO OPEN IT!
BUT THE OTHER WINDOW MUST BE REAL.
I COULD SEE LIGHT SEEPING THROUGH THE CRACKS...
OH?
THERE'S NO LIGHT NOW.
THE FAKE WINDOW HAS SLITS CUT INTO IT TO MAKE THE LIGHT SHINE THROUGH.
FROM THE INSIDE OF THE DARKENED STOREHOUSE, IT LOOKS LIKE A REAL WINDOW!

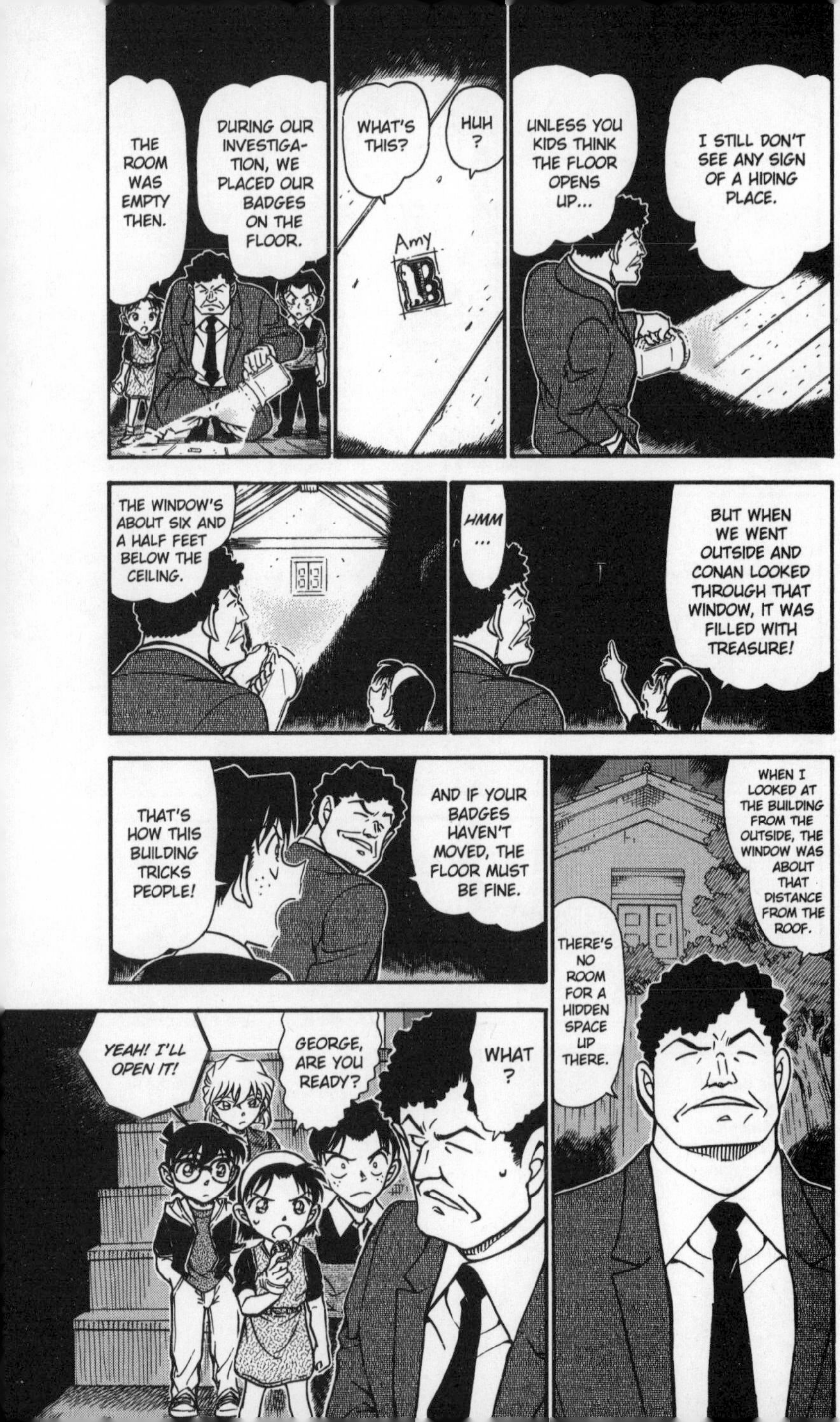
I STILL DON'T SEE ANY SIGN OF A HIDING PLACE.
UNLESS YOU KIDS THINK THE FLOOR OPENS UP...
HUH?
WHAT'S THIS?
Amy
DURING OUR INVESTIGATION, WE PLACED OUR BADGES ON THE FLOOR.
THE ROOM WAS EMPTY THEN.
BUT WHEN WE WENT OUTSIDE AND CONAN LOOKED THROUGH THAT WINDOW, IT WAS FILLED WITH TREASURE!
HMM...
THE WINDOW'S ABOUT SIX AND A HALF FEET BELOW THE CEILING.
WHEN I LOOKED AT THE BUILDING FROM THE OUTSIDE, THE WINDOW WAS ABOUT THAT DISTANCE FROM THE ROOF.
THERE'S NO ROOM FOR A HIDDEN SPACE UP THERE.
AND IF YOUR BADGES HAVEN'T MOVED, THE FLOOR MUST BE FINE.
THAT'S HOW THIS BUILDING TRICKS PEOPLE!
WHAT?
GEORGE, ARE YOU READY?
YEAH! I'LL OPEN IT!

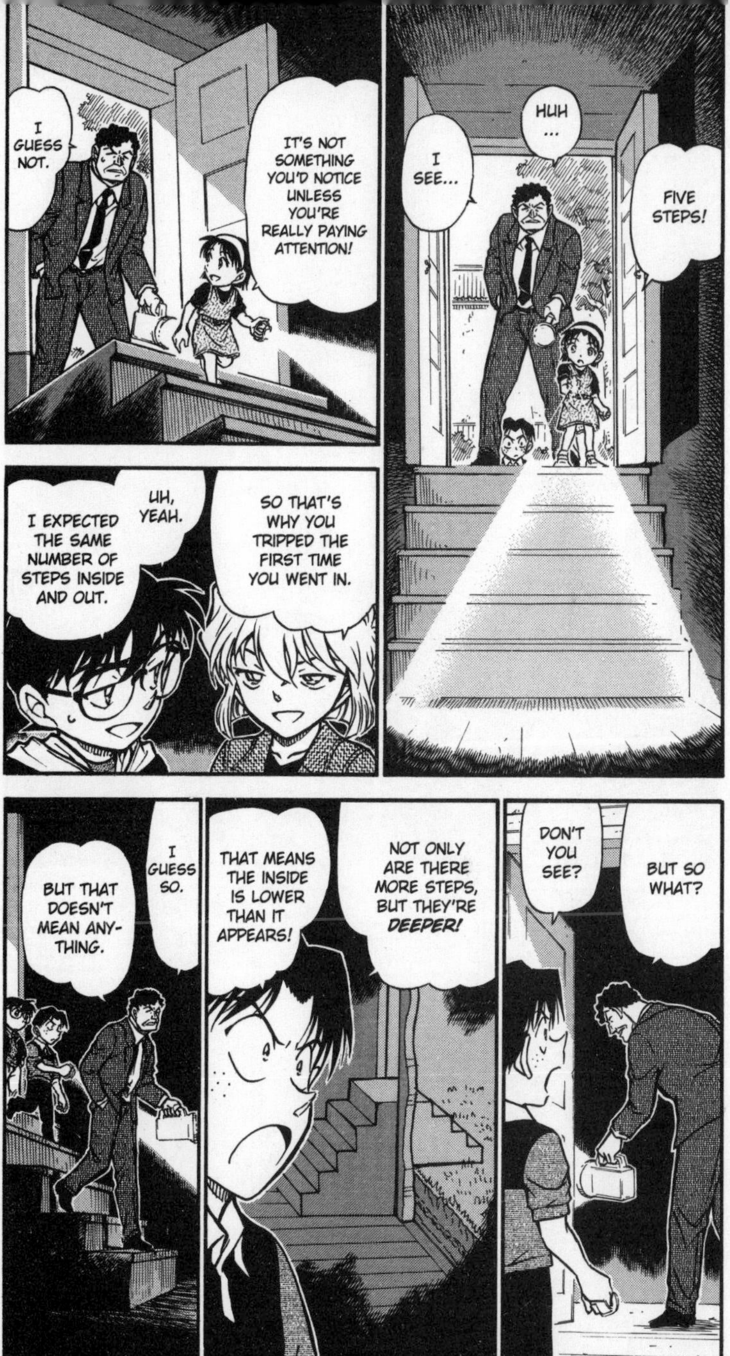
FIVE STEPS!
HUH ...
I SEE...
IT'S NOT SOMETHING YOU'D NOTICE UNLESS YOU'RE REALLY PAYING ATTENTION!
I GUESS NOT.
SO THAT'S WHY YOU TRIPPED THE FIRST TIME YOU WENT IN.
UH, YEAH.
I EXPECTED THE SAME NUMBER OF STEPS INSIDE AND OUT.
BUT SO WHAT?
DON'T YOU SEE?
NOT ONLY ARE THERE MORE STEPS, BUT THEY'RE *DEEPER!*
THAT MEANS THE INSIDE IS LOWER THAN IT APPEARS!
I GUESS SO.
BUT THAT DOESN'T MEAN ANY-THING.

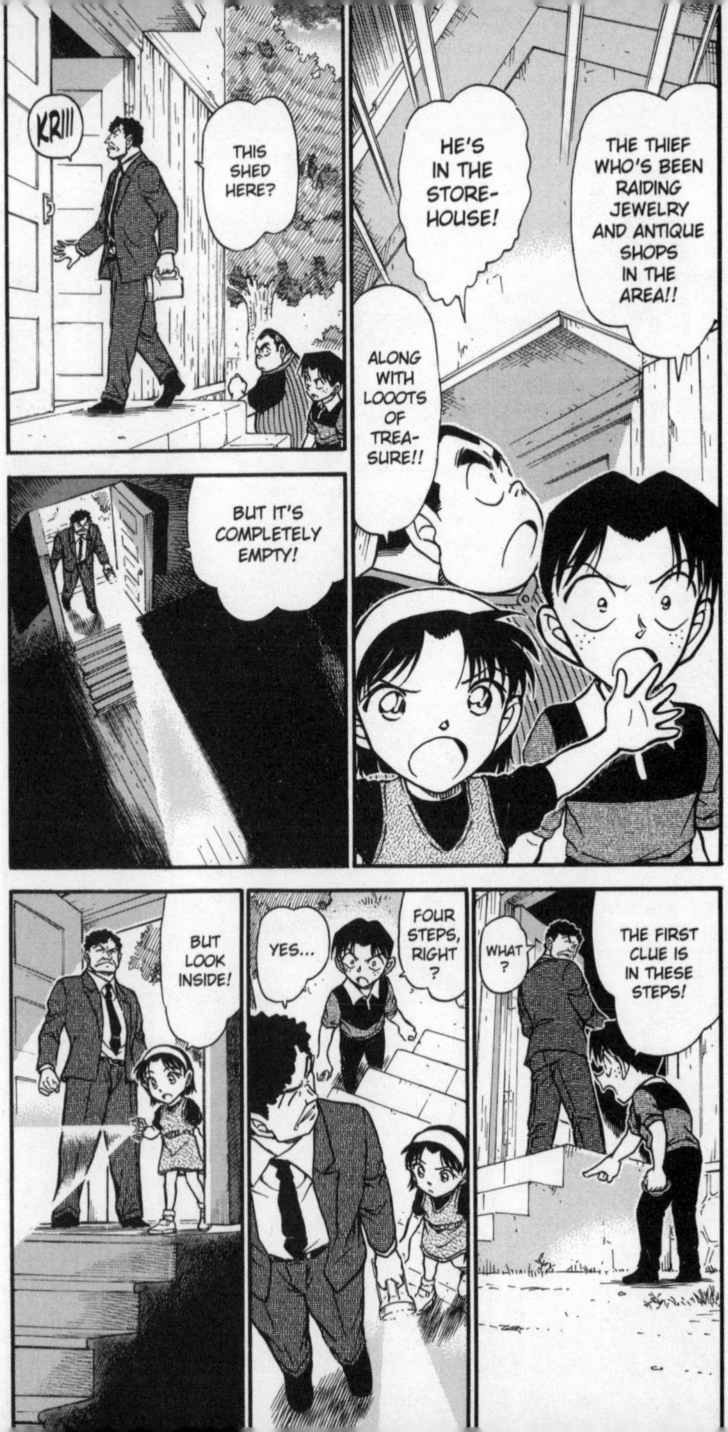
THE THIEF WHO'S BEEN RAIDING JEWELRY AND ANTIQUE SHOPS IN THE AREA!!
HE'S IN THE STORE-HOUSE!
ALONG WITH LOOOTS OF TREA-SURE!!
KRIII
THIS SHED HERE?
BUT IT'S COMPLETELY EMPTY!
THE FIRST CLUE IS IN THESE STEPS!
WHAT?
FOUR STEPS, RIGHT?
YES...
BUT LOOK INSIDE!

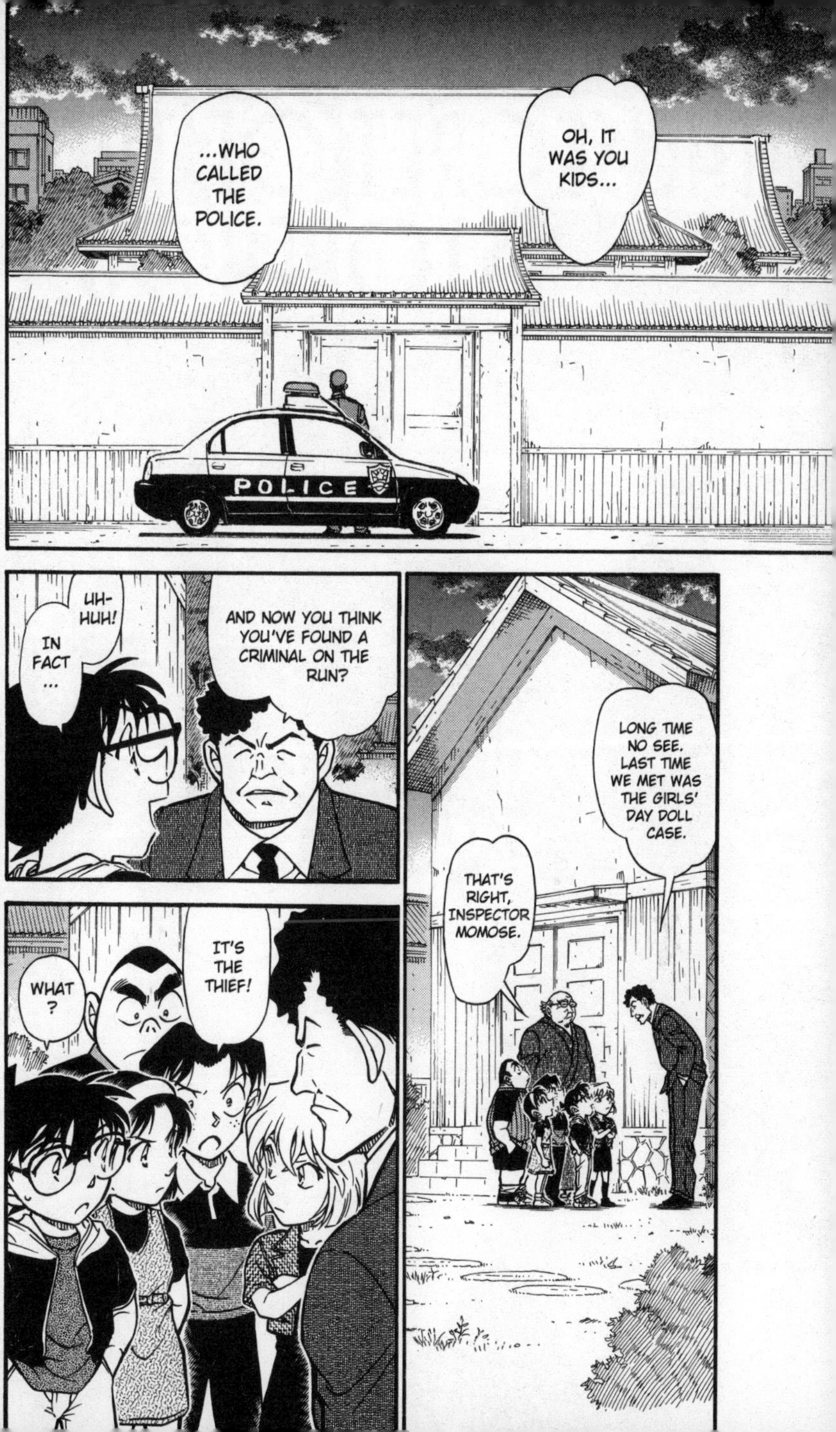
OH, IT WAS YOU KIDS...
...WHO CALLED THE POLICE.
POLICE
LONG TIME NO SEE. LAST TIME WE MET WAS THE GIRLS' DAY DOLL CASE.
THAT'S RIGHT, INSPECTOR MOMOSE.
AND NOW YOU THINK YOU'VE FOUND A CRIMINAL ON THE RUN?
UH-HUH!
IN FACT ...
IT'S THE THIEF!
WHAT?

FILE 7: THE SECRET OF THE STOREHOUSE

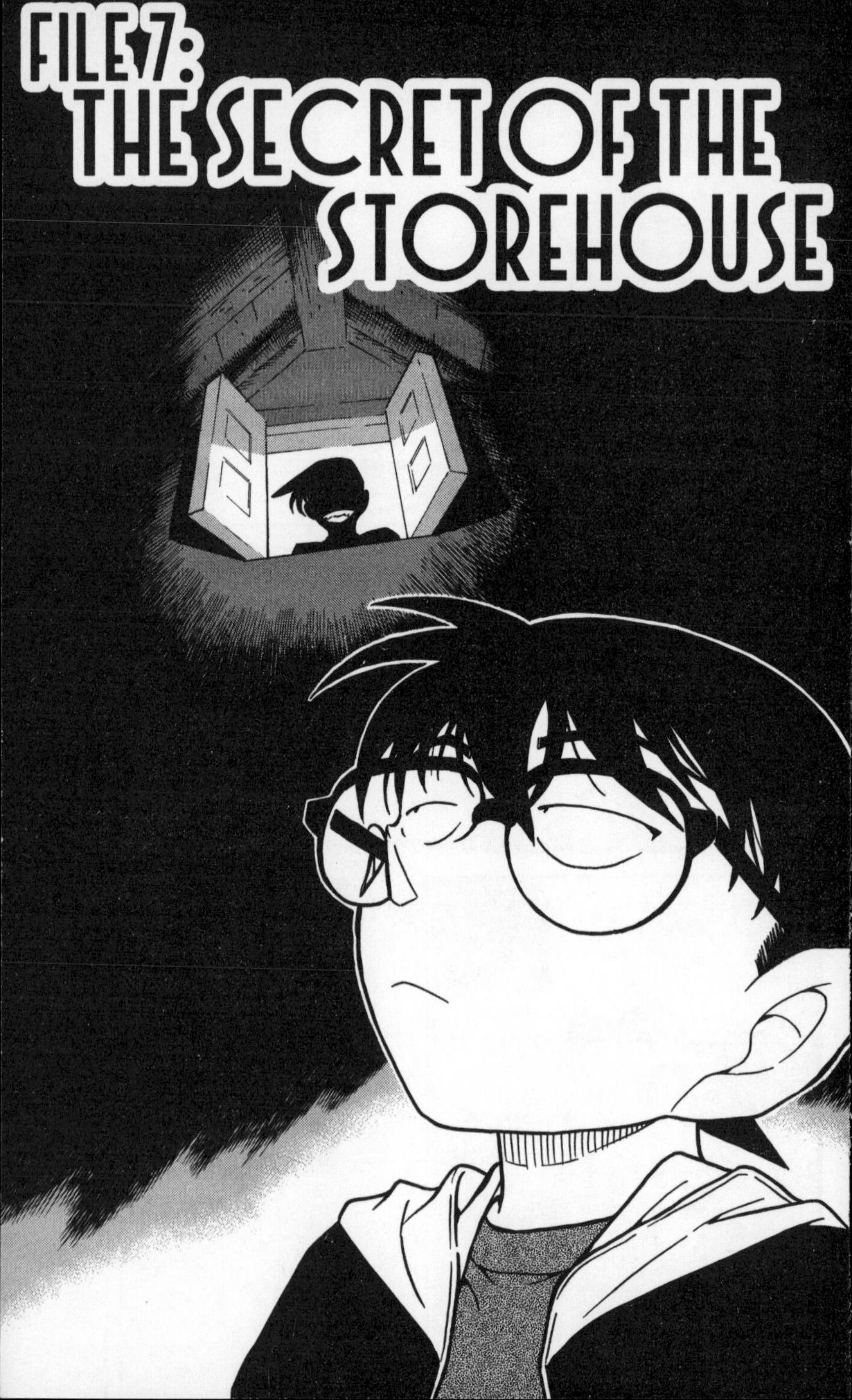

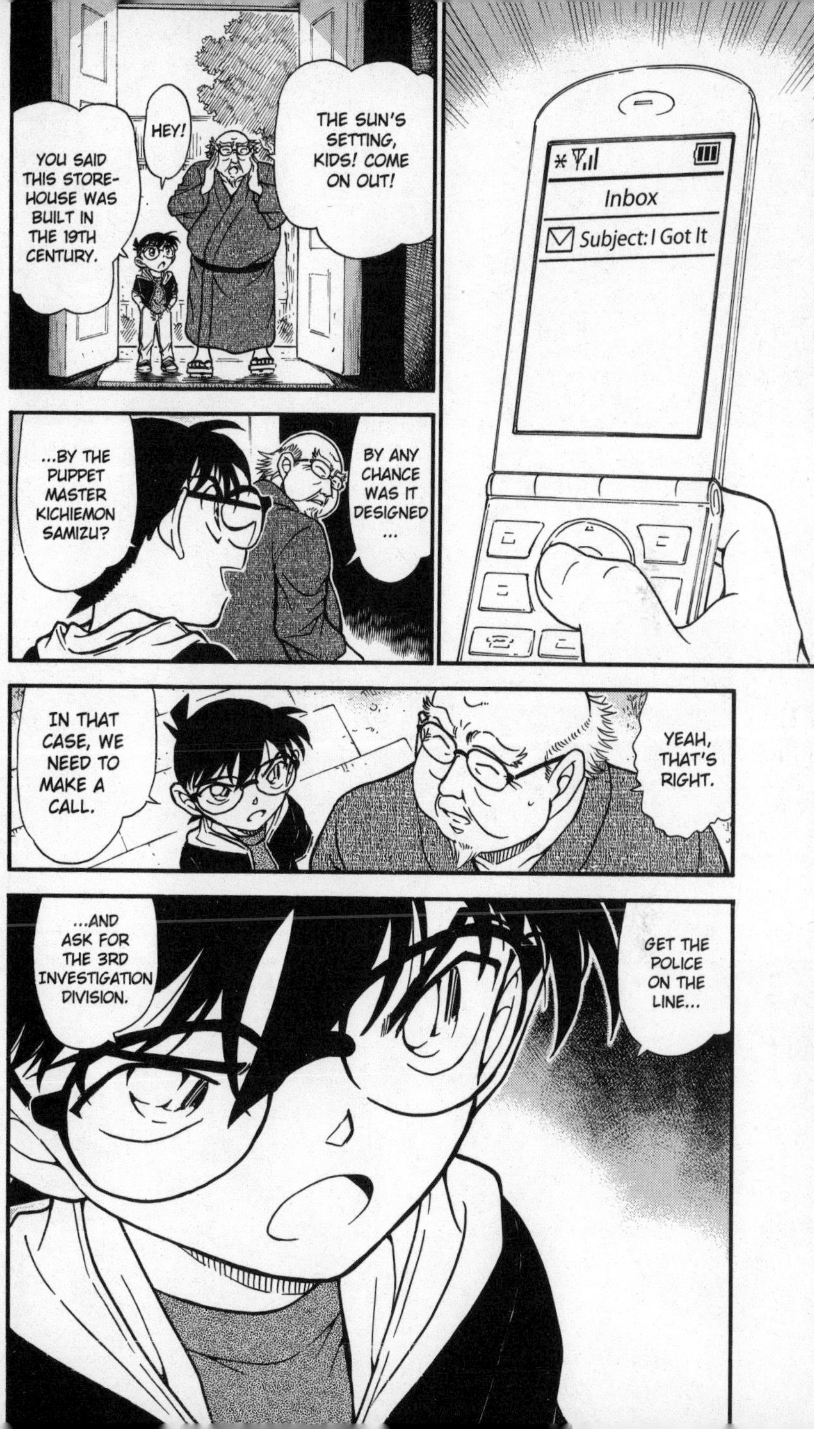
Inbox
Subject: I Got It
THE SUN'S SETTING, KIDS! COME ON OUT!
HEY!
YOU SAID THIS STORE-HOUSE WAS BUILT IN THE 19TH CENTURY.
BY ANY CHANCE WAS IT DESIGNED ...
...BY THE PUPPET MASTER KICHIEMON SAMIZU?
YEAH, THAT'S RIGHT.
IN THAT CASE, WE NEED TO MAKE A CALL.
GET THE POLICE ON THE LINE...
...AND ASK FOR THE 3RD INVESTIGATION DIVISION.

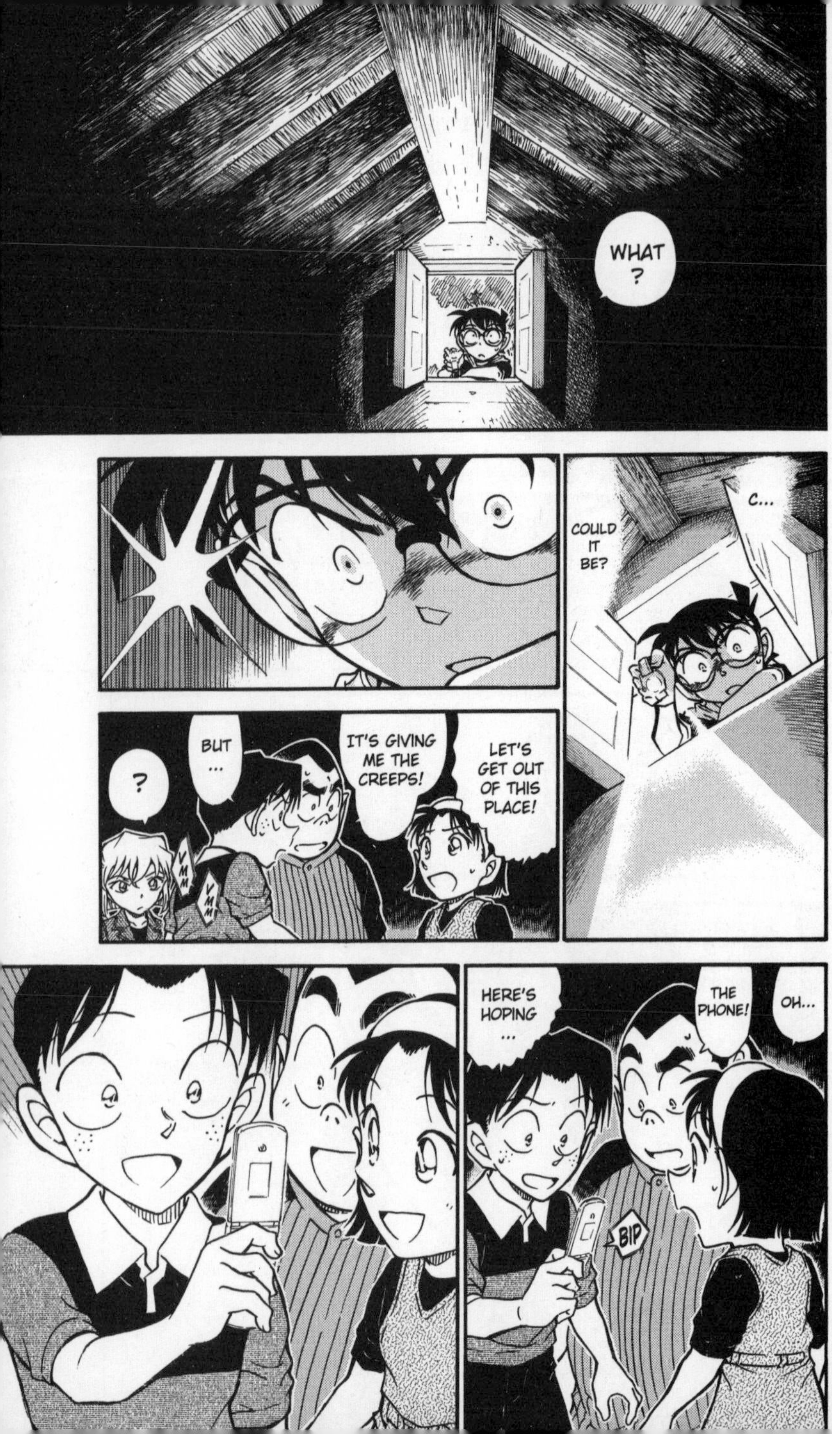
WHAT ?
C...
COULD IT BE?
LET'S GET OUT OF THIS PLACE!
IT'S GIVING ME THE CREEPS!
BUT ...
?
VMM
VMM
OH...
THE PHONE!
HERE'S HOPING ...
BIP

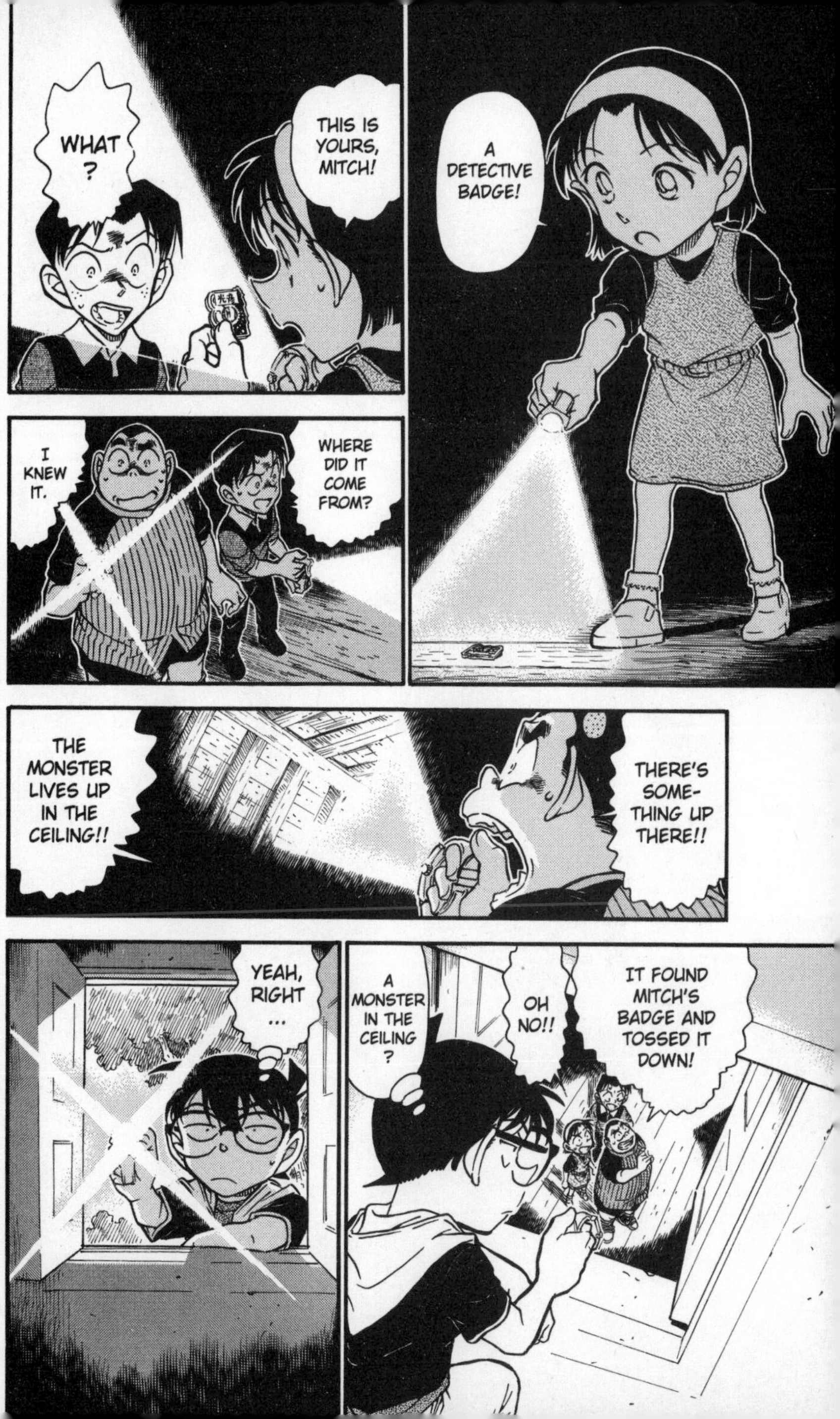
A DETECTIVE BADGE!
THIS IS YOURS, MITCH!
WHAT?
WHERE DID IT COME FROM?
I KNEW IT.
THERE'S SOMETHING UP THERE!!
THE MONSTER LIVES UP IN THE CEILING!!
IT FOUND MITCH'S BADGE AND TOSSED IT DOWN!
OH NO!!
A MONSTER IN THE CEILING?
YEAH, RIGHT...

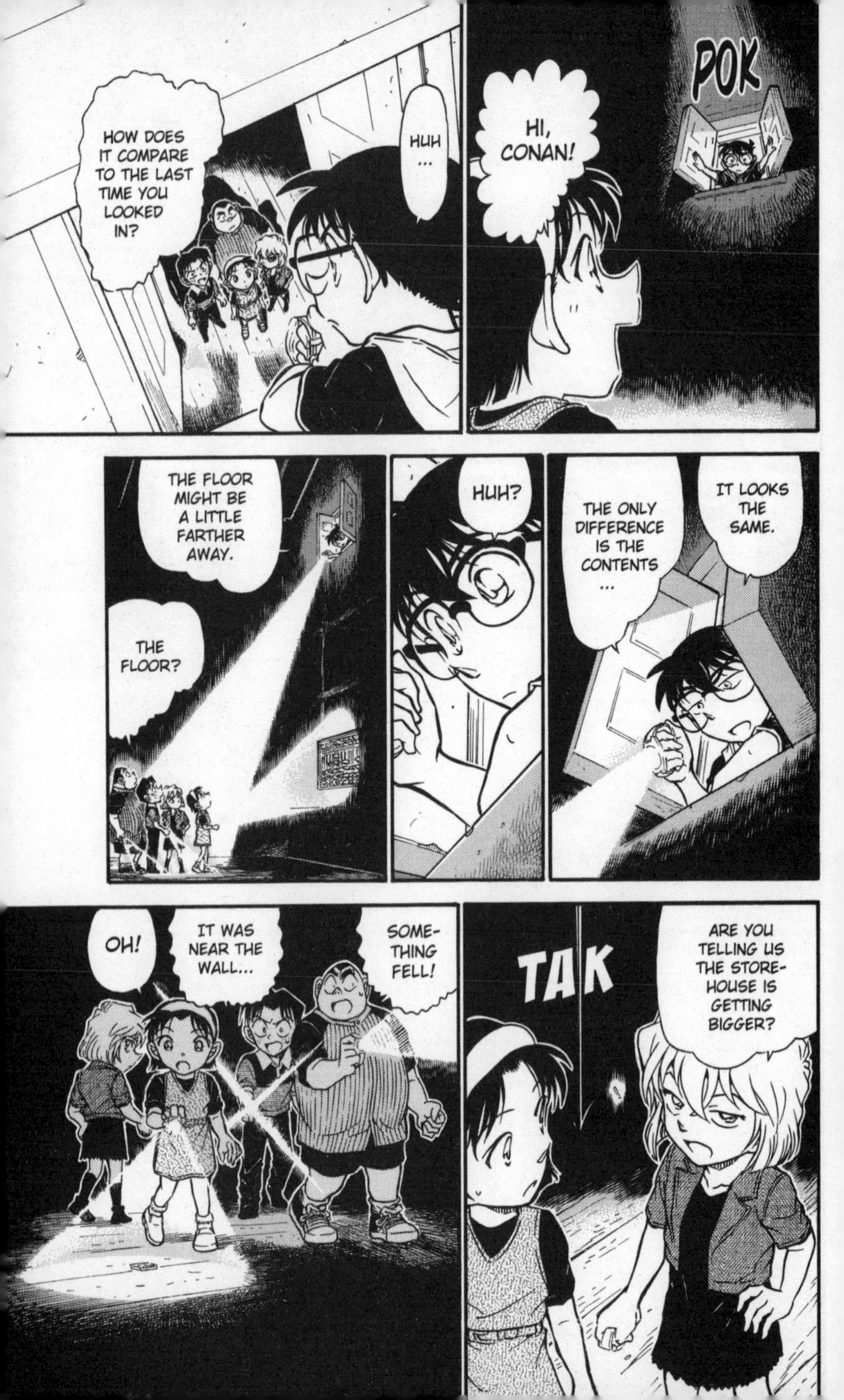
POK
HI, CONAN!
HUH ...
HOW DOES IT COMPARE TO THE LAST TIME YOU LOOKED IN?
IT LOOKS THE SAME.
THE ONLY DIFFERENCE IS THE CONTENTS ...
HUH?
THE FLOOR MIGHT BE A LITTLE FARTHER AWAY.
THE FLOOR?
ARE YOU TELLING US THE STORE-HOUSE IS GETTING BIGGER?
TAK
SOME-THING FELL!
IT WAS NEAR THE WALL...
OH!

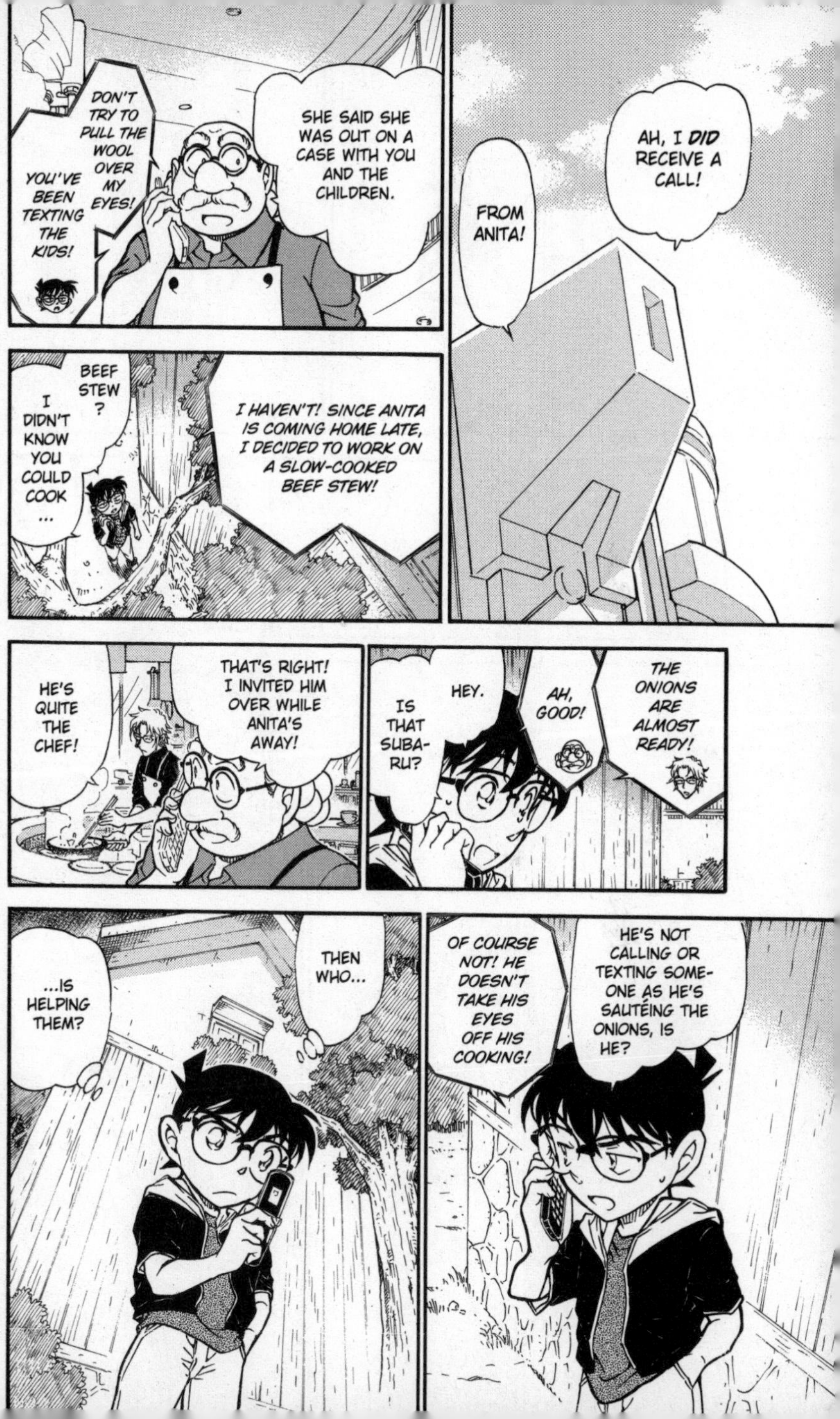
AH, I *DID* RECEIVE A CALL!
FROM ANITA!
SHE SAID SHE WAS OUT ON A CASE WITH YOU AND THE CHILDREN.
DON'T TRY TO PULL THE WOOL OVER MY EYES!
YOU'VE BEEN TEXTING THE KIDS!
I HAVEN'T! SINCE ANITA IS COMING HOME LATE, I DECIDED TO WORK ON A SLOW-COOKED BEEF STEW!
BEEF STEW?
I DIDN'T KNOW YOU COULD COOK...
THE ONIONS ARE ALMOST READY!
AH, GOOD!
HEY.
IS THAT SUBA-RU?
THAT'S RIGHT! I INVITED HIM OVER WHILE ANITA'S AWAY!
HE'S QUITE THE CHEF!
HE'S NOT CALLING OR TEXTING SOME-ONE AS HE'S SAUTÉING THE ONIONS, IS HE?
OF COURSE NOT! HE DOESN'T TAKE HIS EYES OFF HIS COOKING!
THEN WHO...
...IS HELPING THEM?

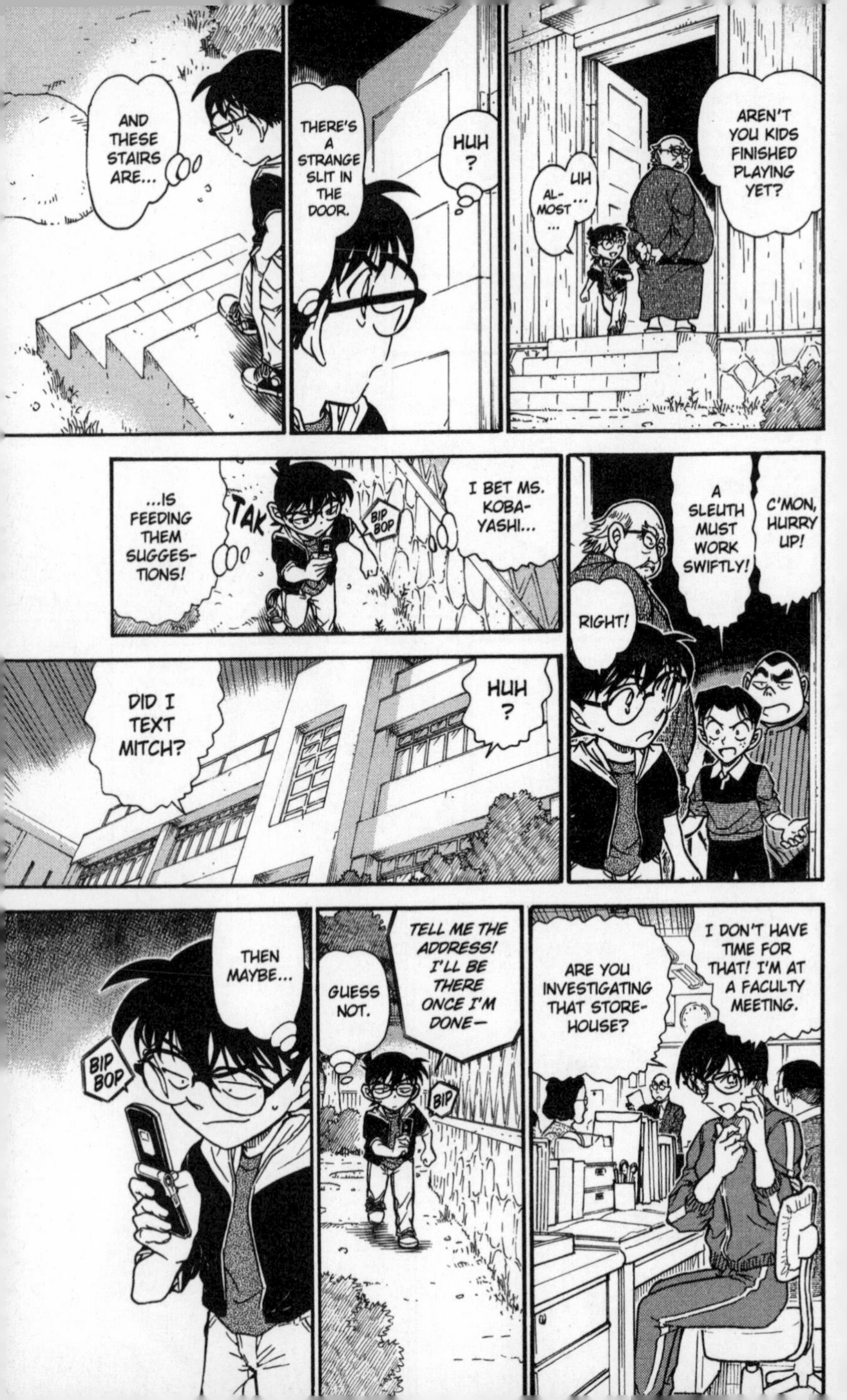
AREN'T YOU KIDS FINISHED PLAYING YET?
UH... AL-MOST...
HUH?
THERE'S A STRANGE SLIT IN THE DOOR.
AND THESE STAIRS ARE...
C'MON, HURRY UP!
A SLEUTH MUST WORK SWIFTLY!
RIGHT!
I BET MS. KOBA-YASHI...
BIP BOP
TAK
...IS FEEDING THEM SUGGES-TIONS!
HUH?
DID I TEXT MITCH?
I DON'T HAVE TIME FOR THAT! I'M AT A FACULTY MEETING.
ARE YOU INVESTIGATING THAT STORE-HOUSE?
TELL ME THE ADDRESS! I'LL BE THERE ONCE I'M DONE—
GUESS NOT.
BIP
THEN MAYBE...
BIP BOP

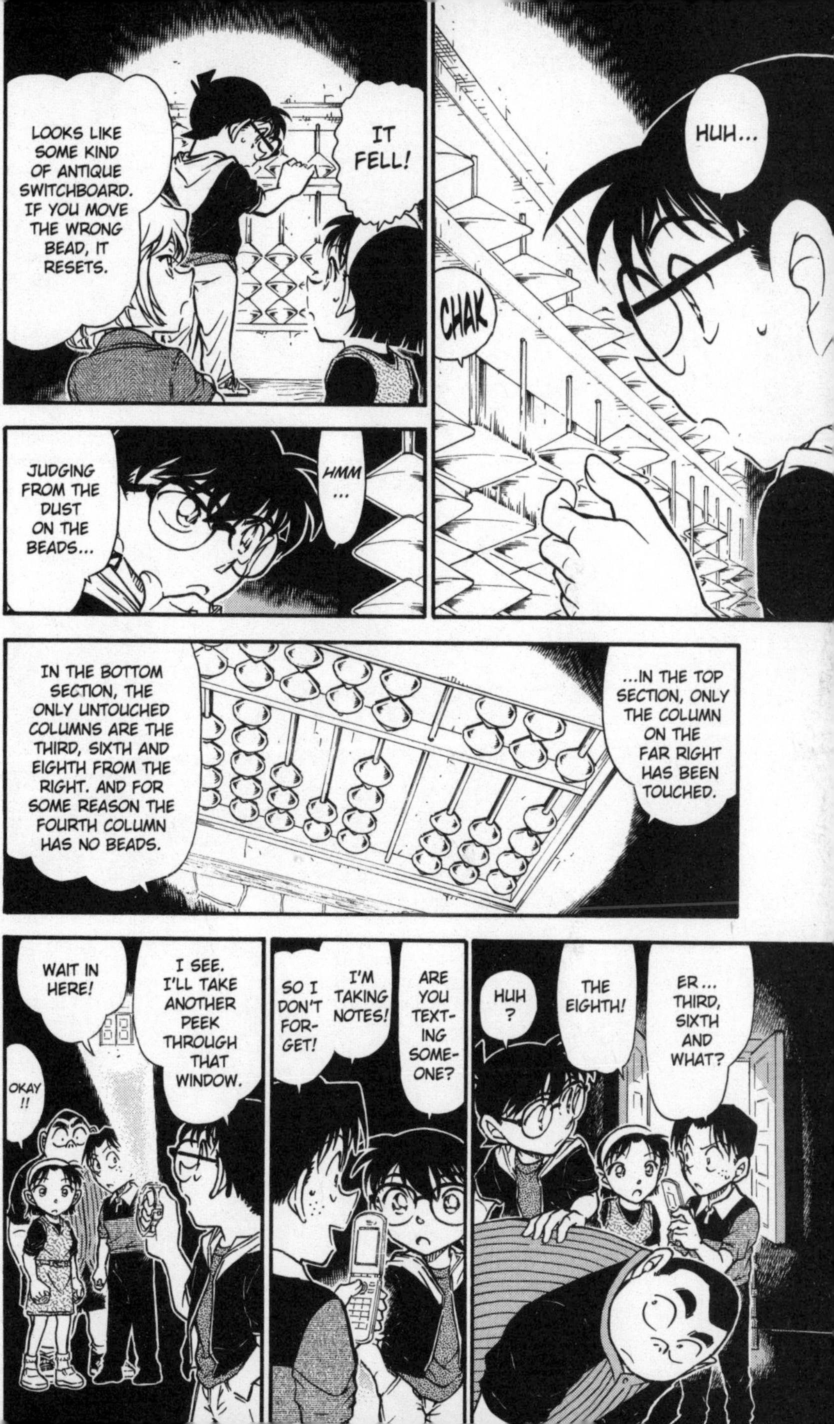
HUH...
CHAK
IT FELL!
LOOKS LIKE SOME KIND OF ANTIQUE SWITCHBOARD. IF YOU MOVE THE WRONG BEAD, IT RESETS.
HMM ...
JUDGING FROM THE DUST ON THE BEADS...
...IN THE TOP SECTION, ONLY THE COLUMN ON THE FAR RIGHT HAS BEEN TOUCHED.
IN THE BOTTOM SECTION, THE ONLY UNTOUCHED COLUMNS ARE THE THIRD, SIXTH AND EIGHTH FROM THE RIGHT. AND FOR SOME REASON THE FOURTH COLUMN HAS NO BEADS.
ER... THIRD, SIXTH AND WHAT?
THE EIGHTH!
HUH ?
ARE YOU TEXT-ING SOME-ONE?
I'M TAKING NOTES!
SO I DON'T FOR-GET!
I SEE. I'LL TAKE ANOTHER PEEK THROUGH THAT WINDOW.
WAIT IN HERE!
OKAY !!

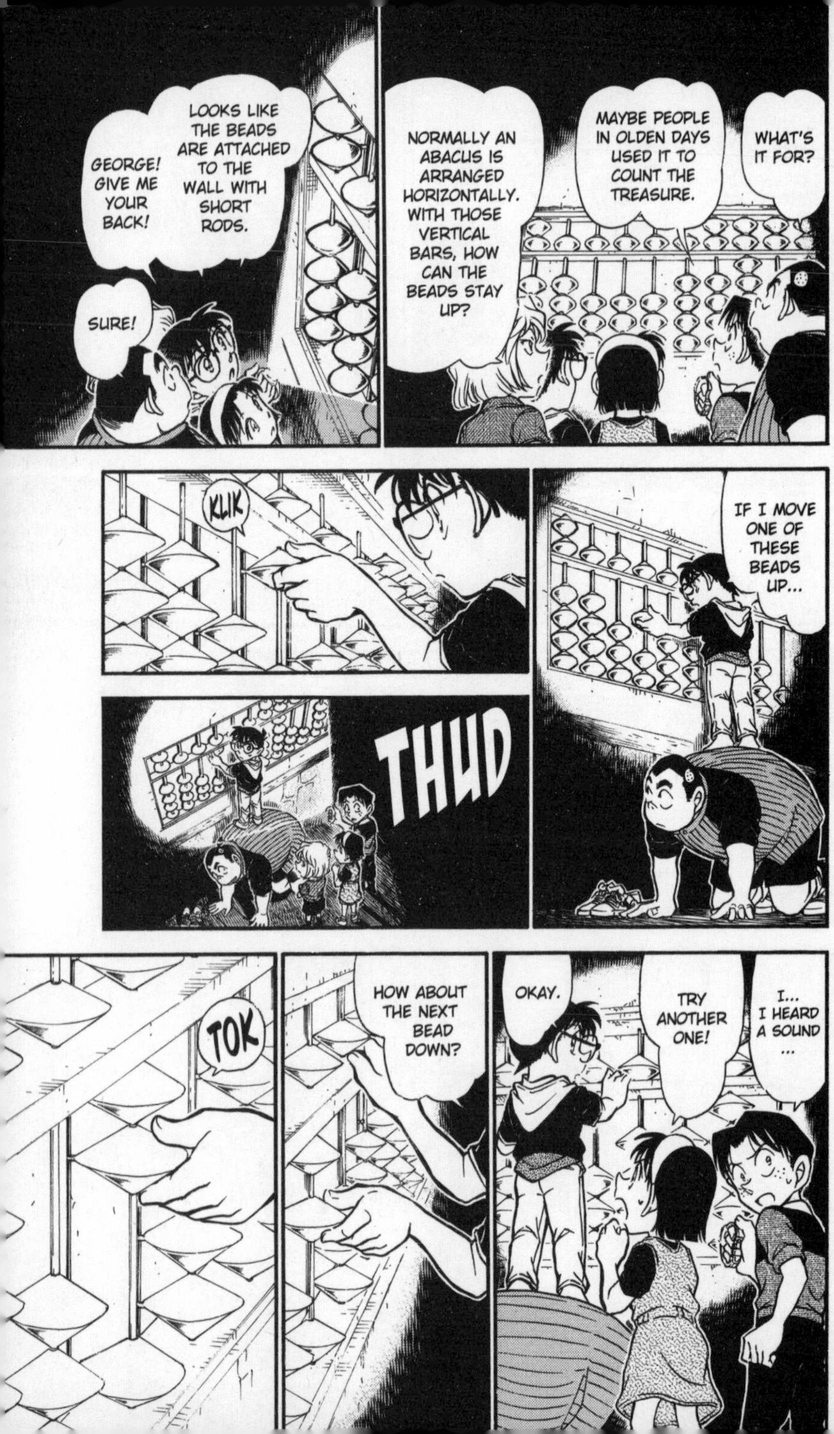
WHAT'S IT FOR?
MAYBE PEOPLE IN OLDEN DAYS USED IT TO COUNT THE TREASURE.
NORMALLY AN ABACUS IS ARRANGED HORIZONTALLY. WITH THOSE VERTICAL BARS, HOW CAN THE BEADS STAY UP?
LOOKS LIKE THE BEADS ARE ATTACHED TO THE WALL WITH SHORT RODS.
GEORGE! GIVE ME YOUR BACK!
SURE!
IF I MOVE ONE OF THESE BEADS UP...
KLIK
THUD
I... I HEARD A SOUND ...
TRY ANOTHER ONE!
OKAY.
HOW ABOUT THE NEXT BEAD DOWN?
TOK

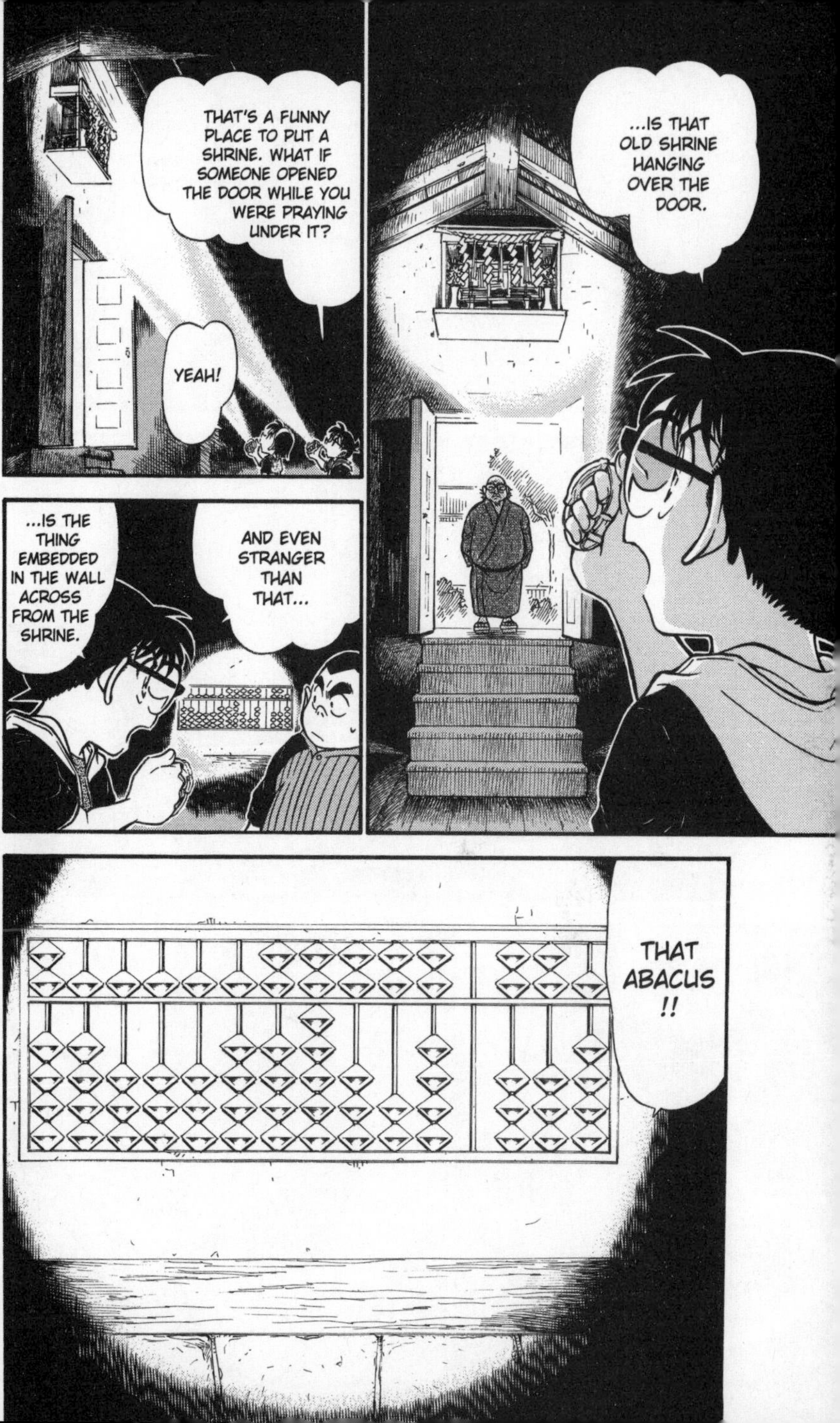
...IS THAT OLD SHRINE HANGING OVER THE DOOR.
THAT'S A FUNNY PLACE TO PUT A SHRINE. WHAT IF SOMEONE OPENED THE DOOR WHILE YOU WERE PRAYING UNDER IT?
YEAH!
AND EVEN STRANGER THAN THAT...
...IS THE THING EMBEDDED IN THE WALL ACROSS FROM THE SHRINE.
THAT ABACUS !!

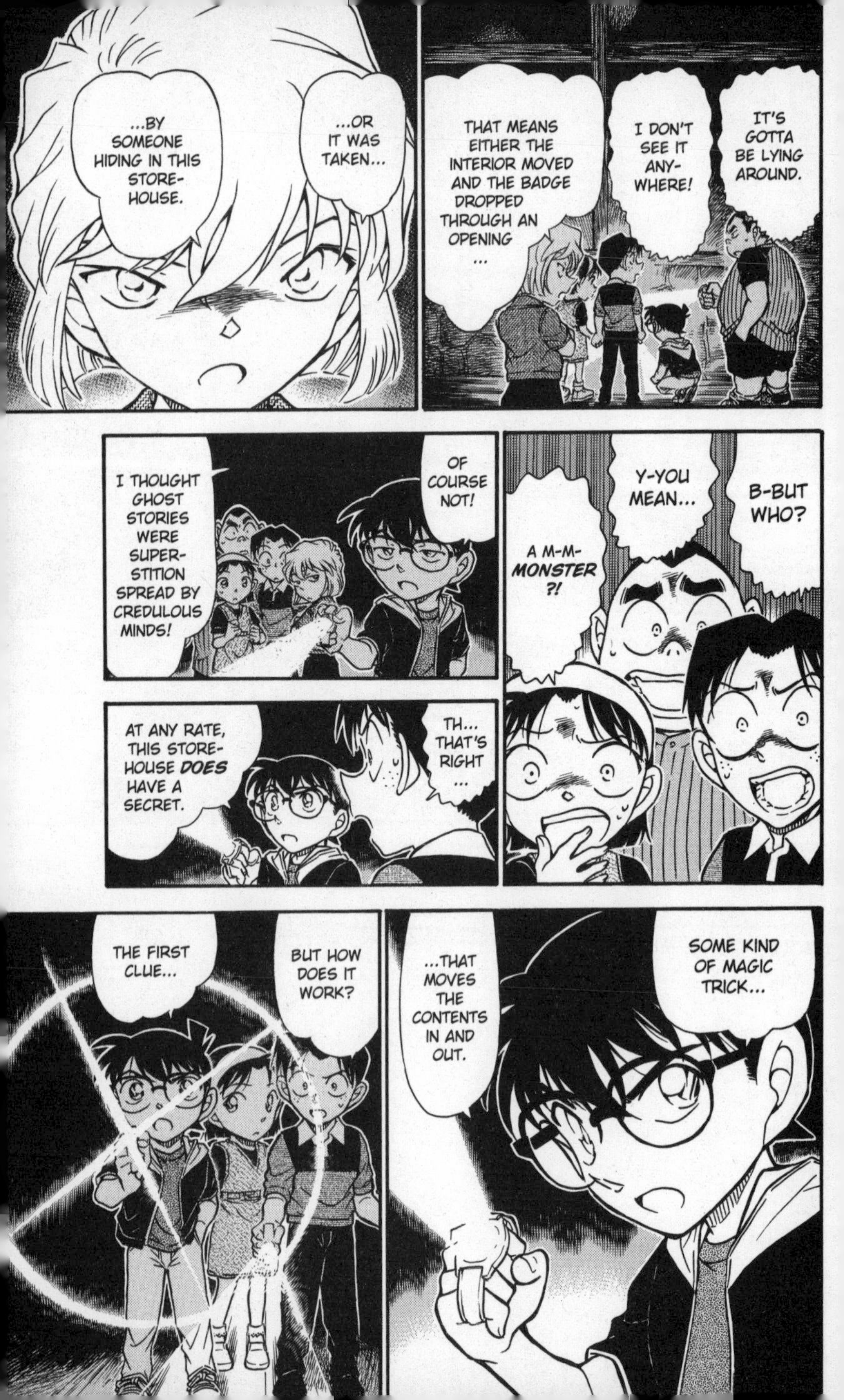
IT'S GOTTA BE LYING AROUND.
I DON'T SEE IT ANYWHERE!
THAT MEANS EITHER THE INTERIOR MOVED AND THE BADGE DROPPED THROUGH AN OPENING ...
...OR IT WAS TAKEN...
...BY SOMEONE HIDING IN THIS STOREHOUSE.
B-BUT WHO?
Y-YOU MEAN...
A M-M-*MONSTER*?!
OF COURSE NOT!
I THOUGHT GHOST STORIES WERE SUPERSTITION SPREAD BY CREDULOUS MINDS!
TH... THAT'S RIGHT ...
AT ANY RATE, THIS STOREHOUSE *DOES* HAVE A SECRET.
SOME KIND OF MAGIC TRICK...
...THAT MOVES THE CONTENTS IN AND OUT.
BUT HOW DOES IT WORK?
THE FIRST CLUE...

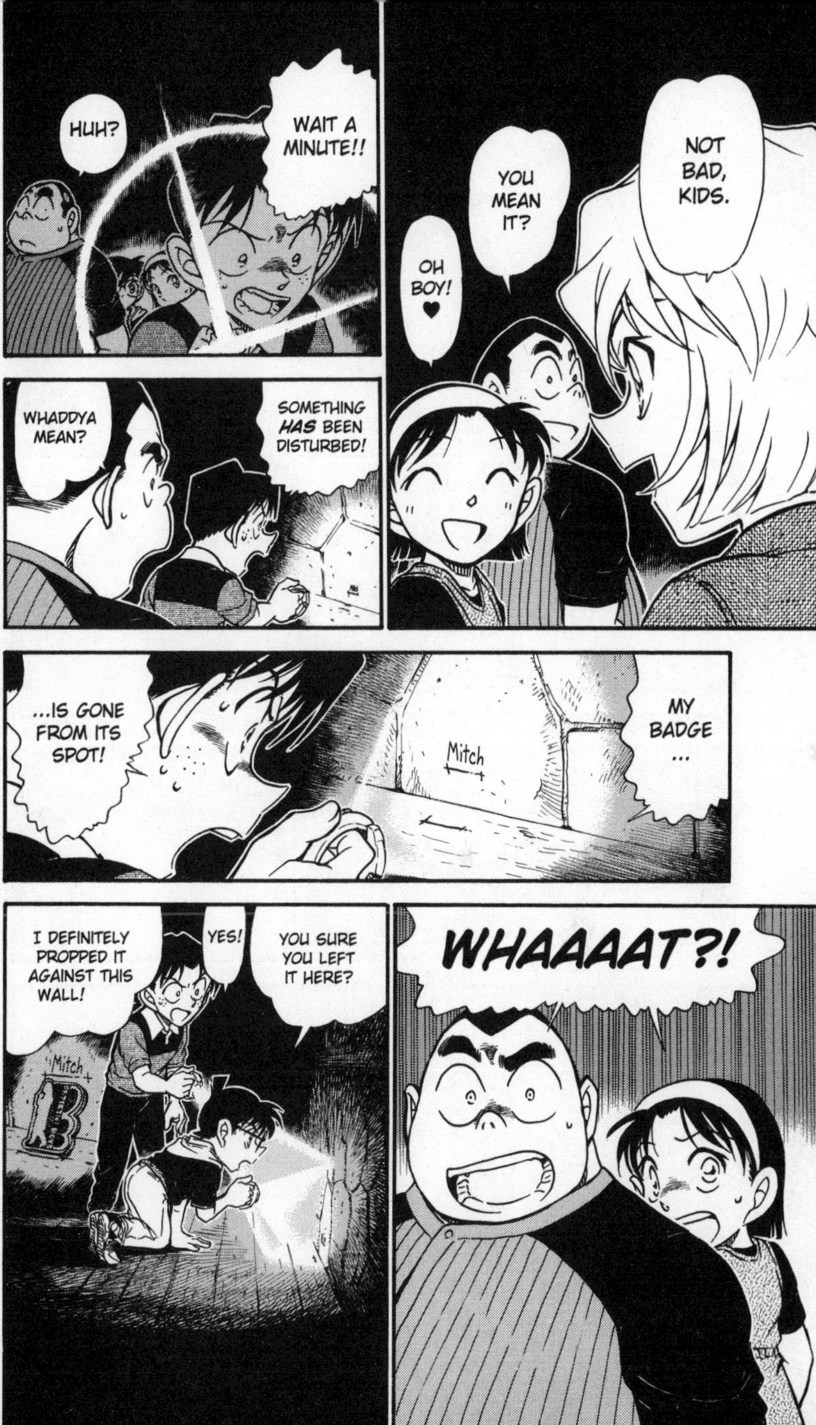
NOT BAD, KIDS.
YOU MEAN IT?
OH BOY! ♥
WAIT A MINUTE!!
HUH?
SOMETHING *HAS* BEEN DISTURBED!
WHADDYA MEAN?
MY BADGE ...
Mitch
...IS GONE FROM ITS SPOT!
WHAAAAT?!
YOU SURE YOU LEFT IT HERE?
YES!
I DEFINITELY PROPPED IT AGAINST THIS WALL!
Mitch

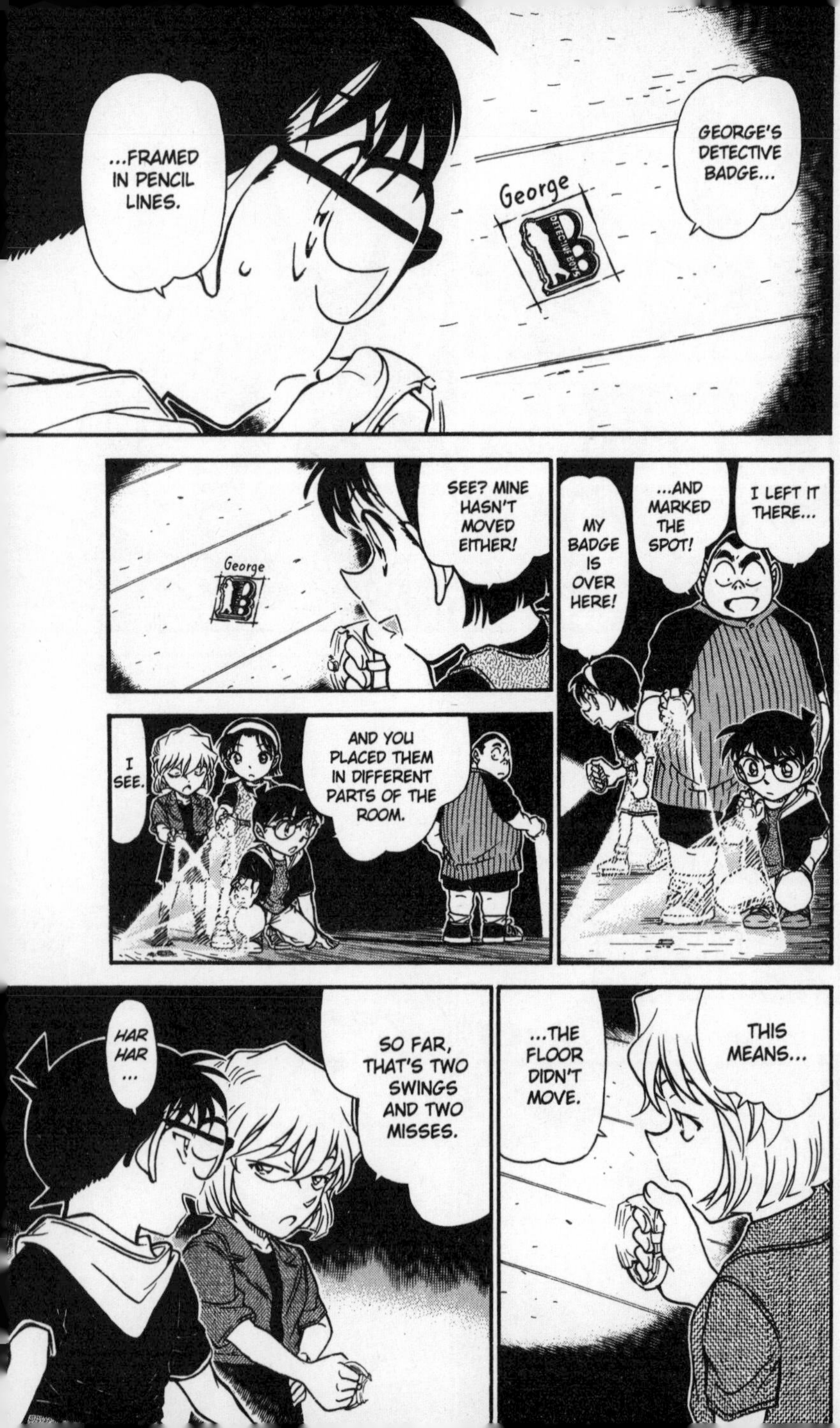
GEORGE'S DETECTIVE BADGE...
George
...FRAMED IN PENCIL LINES.
I LEFT IT THERE...
...AND MARKED THE SPOT!
MY BADGE IS OVER HERE!
SEE? MINE HASN'T MOVED EITHER!
George
AND YOU PLACED THEM IN DIFFERENT PARTS OF THE ROOM.
I SEE.
THIS MEANS...
...THE FLOOR DIDN'T MOVE.
SO FAR, THAT'S TWO SWINGS AND TWO MISSES.
HAR HAR ...

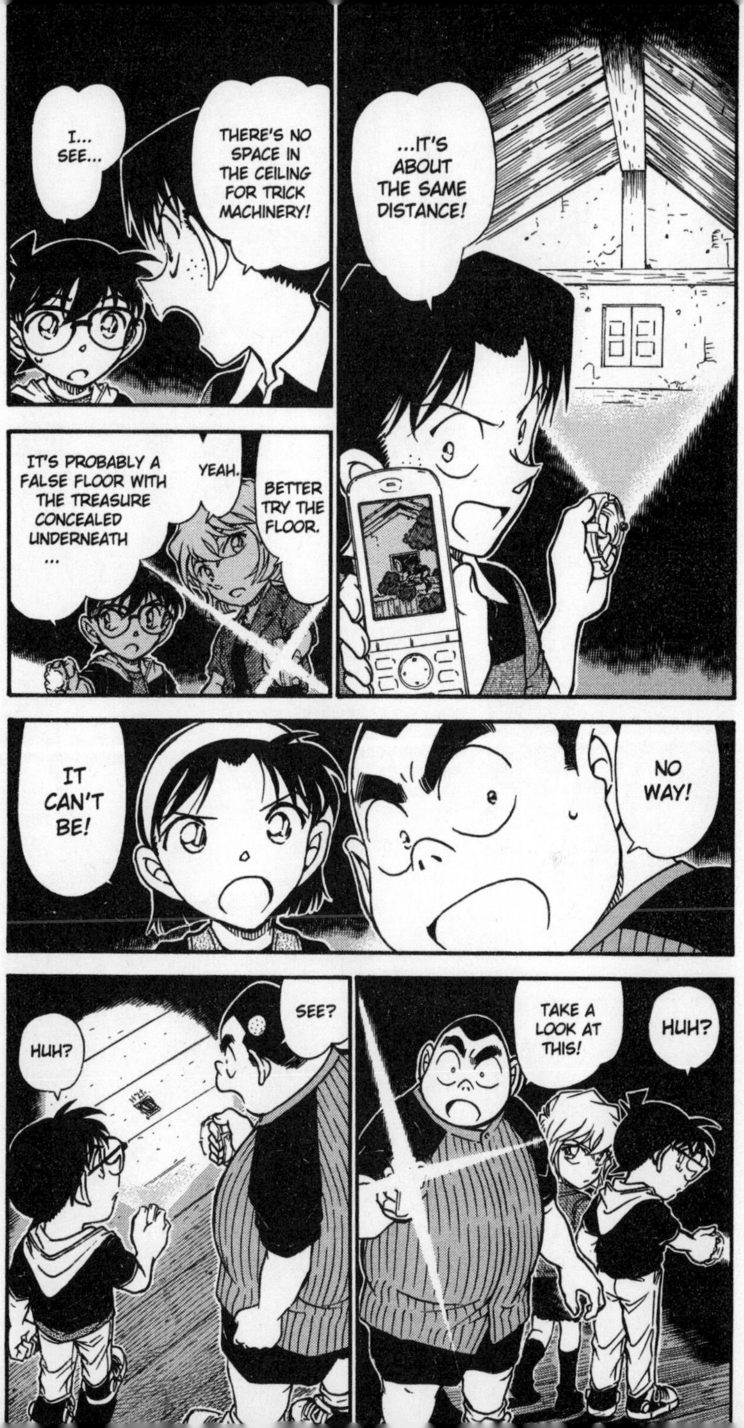
...IT'S ABOUT THE SAME DISTANCE!
THERE'S NO SPACE IN THE CEILING FOR TRICK MACHINERY!
I... SEE...
BETTER TRY THE FLOOR.
YEAH.
IT'S PROBABLY A FALSE FLOOR WITH THE TREASURE CONCEALED UNDERNEATH ...
NO WAY!
IT CAN'T BE!
HUH?
TAKE A LOOK AT THIS!
SEE?
HUH?

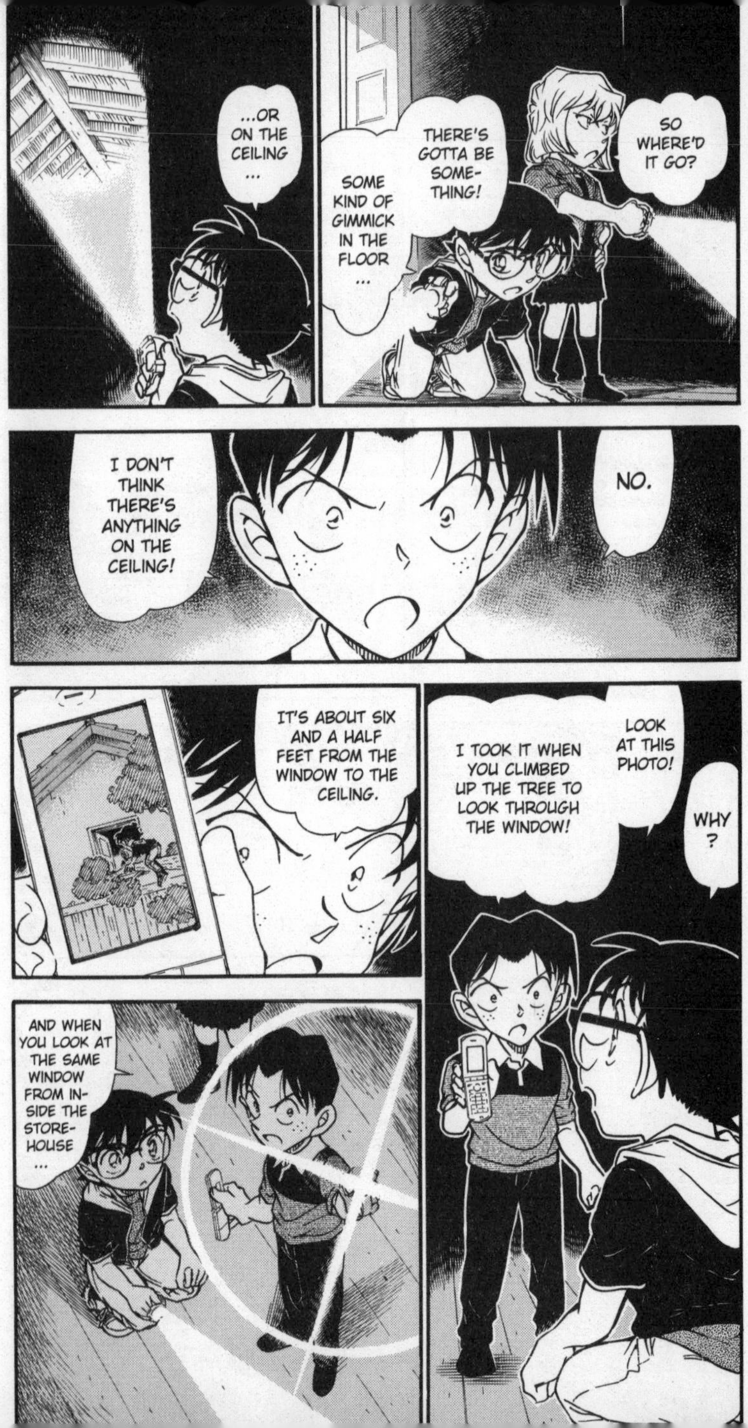
SO WHERE'D IT GO?
THERE'S GOTTA BE SOME-THING!
SOME KIND OF GIMMICK IN THE FLOOR ...
...OR ON THE CEILING ...
NO.
I DON'T THINK THERE'S ANYTHING ON THE CEILING!
WHY ?
LOOK AT THIS PHOTO!
I TOOK IT WHEN YOU CLIMBED UP THE TREE TO LOOK THROUGH THE WINDOW!
IT'S ABOUT SIX AND A HALF FEET FROM THE WINDOW TO THE CEILING.
AND WHEN YOU LOOK AT THE SAME WINDOW FROM IN-SIDE THE STORE-HOUSE ...

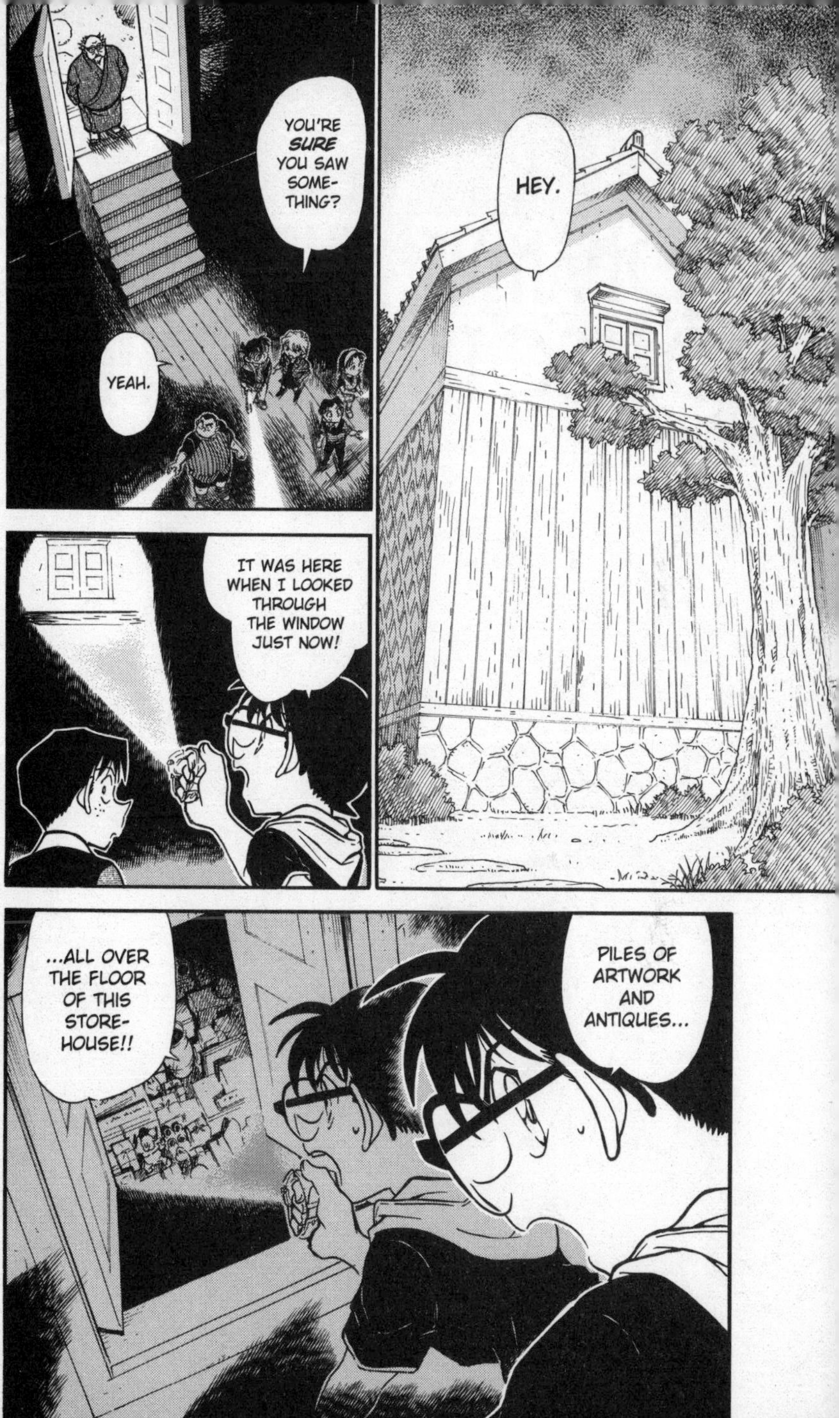
HEY.
YOU'RE SURE YOU SAW SOME-THING?
YEAH.
IT WAS HERE WHEN I LOOKED THROUGH THE WINDOW JUST NOW!
PILES OF ARTWORK AND ANTIQUES...
...ALL OVER THE FLOOR OF THIS STORE-HOUSE!!

CONAN VS. THE JUNIOR DETECTIVE LEAGUE

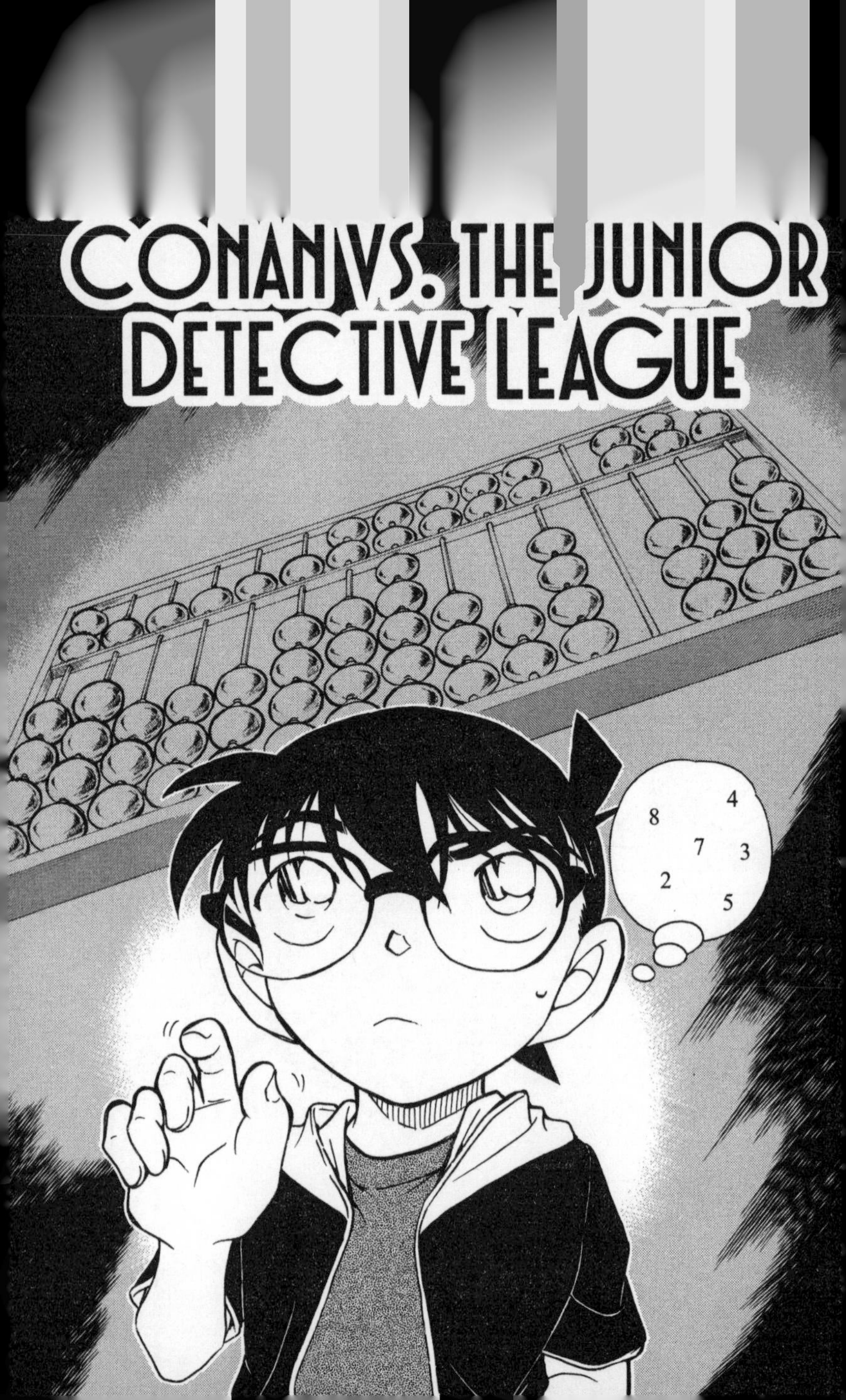
8 4 7 3 2 5

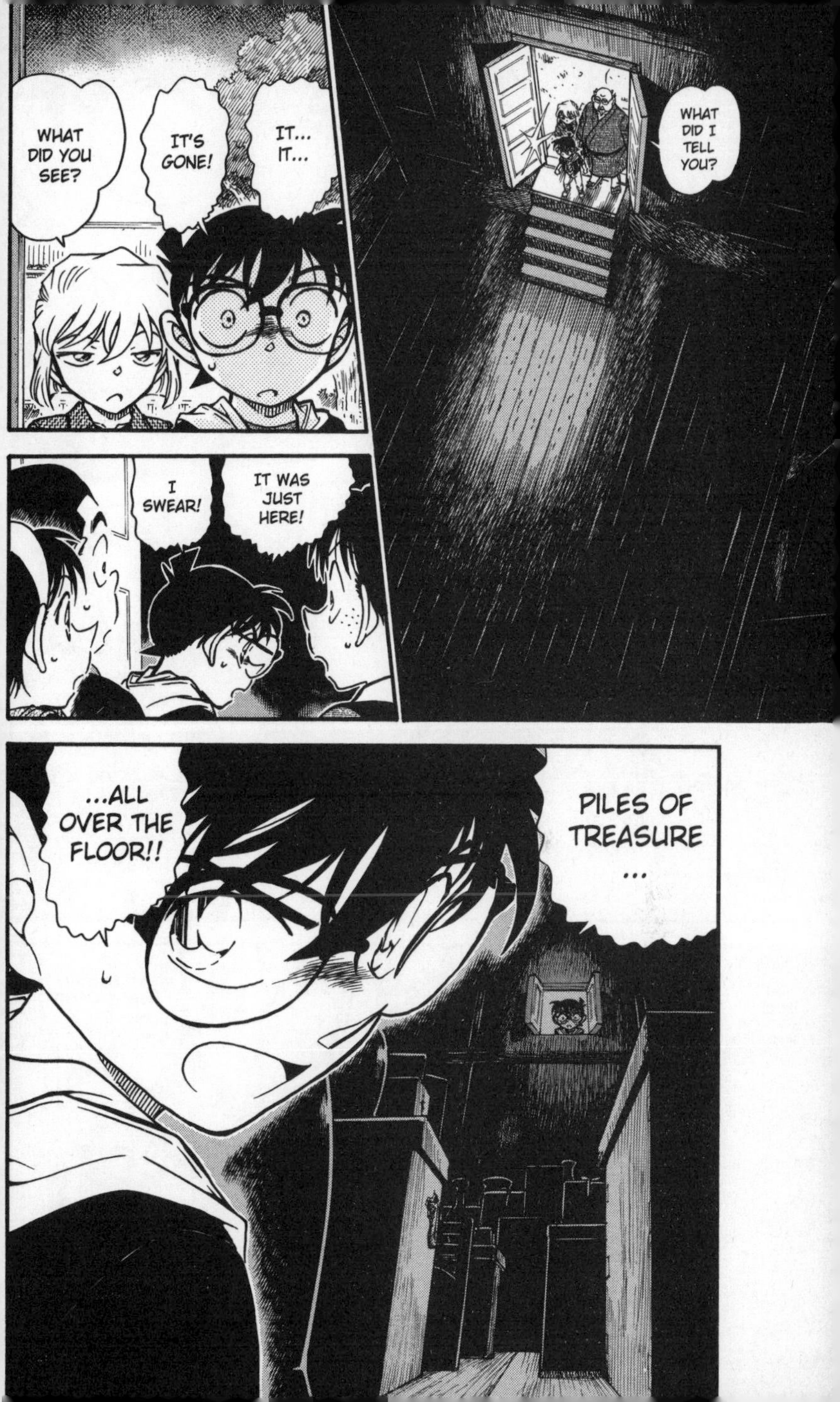
WHAT DID I TELL YOU?
IT... IT...
IT'S GONE!
WHAT DID YOU SEE?
IT WAS JUST HERE!
I SWEAR!
PILES OF TREASURE ...
...ALL OVER THE FLOOR!!

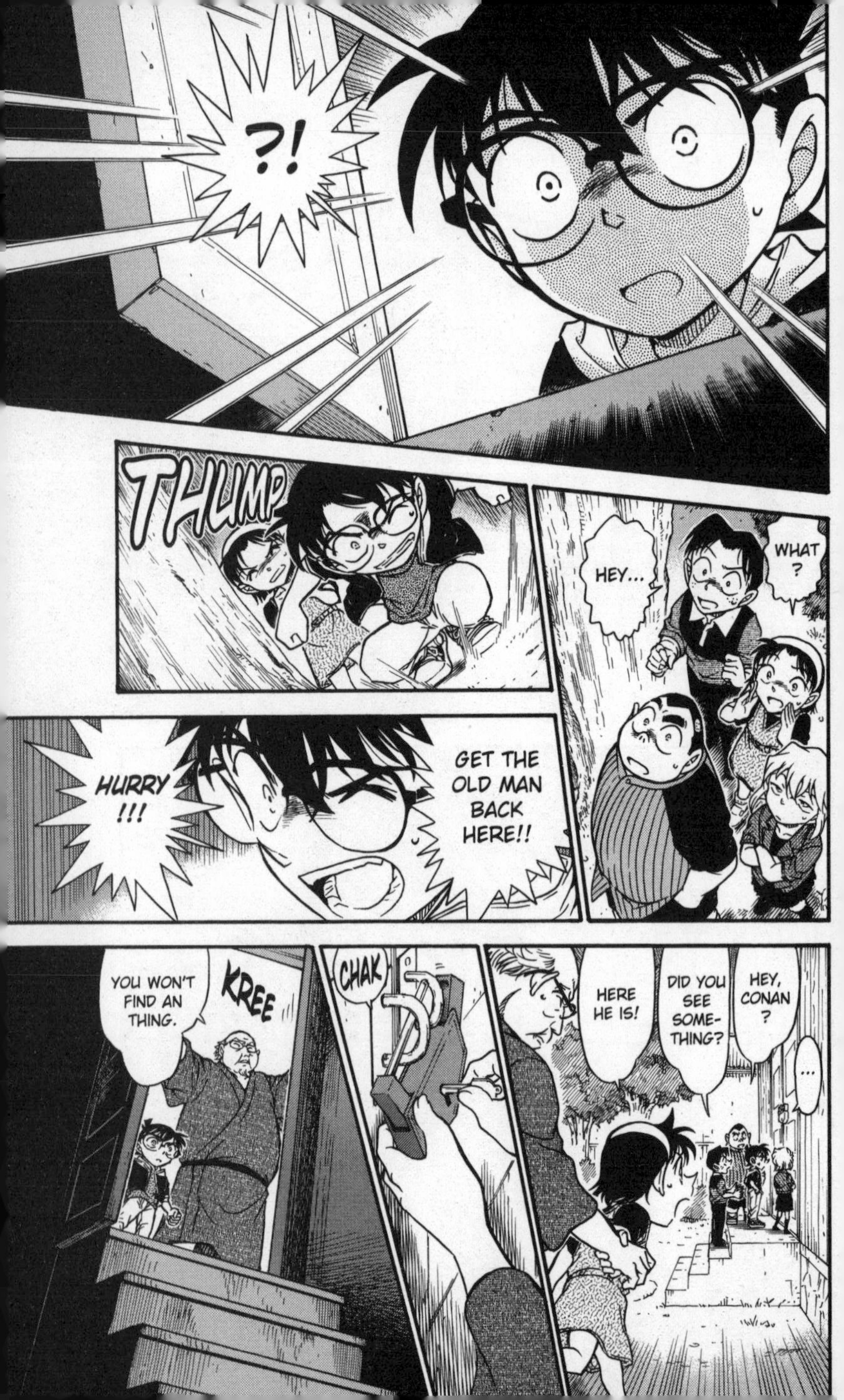
?!
WHAT ?
HEY...
THUMP
GET THE OLD MAN BACK HERE!!
HURRY !!!
HEY, CONAN ?
DID YOU SEE SOME-THING?
HERE HE IS!
...
CHAK
KREE
YOU WON'T FIND AN THING.

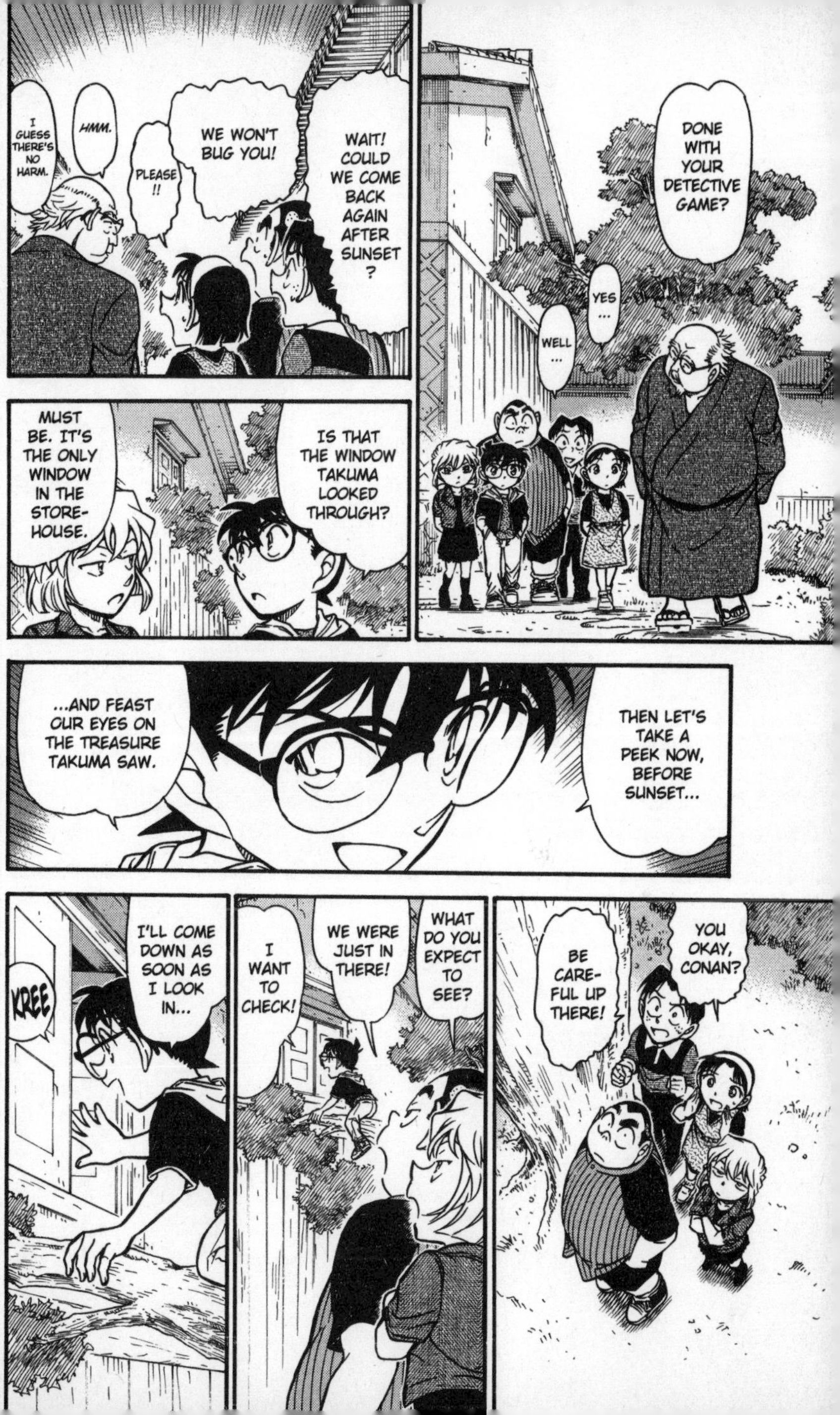
DONE WITH YOUR DETECTIVE GAME?
YES...
WELL...
WAIT! COULD WE COME BACK AGAIN AFTER SUNSET?
WE WON'T BUG YOU!
PLEASE!!
HMM.
I GUESS THERE'S NO HARM.
IS THAT THE WINDOW TAKUMA LOOKED THROUGH?
MUST BE. IT'S THE ONLY WINDOW IN THE STOREHOUSE.
THEN LET'S TAKE A PEEK NOW, BEFORE SUNSET...
...AND FEAST OUR EYES ON THE TREASURE TAKUMA SAW.
YOU OKAY, CONAN?
BE CAREFUL UP THERE!
WHAT DO YOU EXPECT TO SEE?
WE WERE JUST IN THERE!
I WANT TO CHECK!
I'LL COME DOWN AS SOON AS I LOOK IN...
KREE

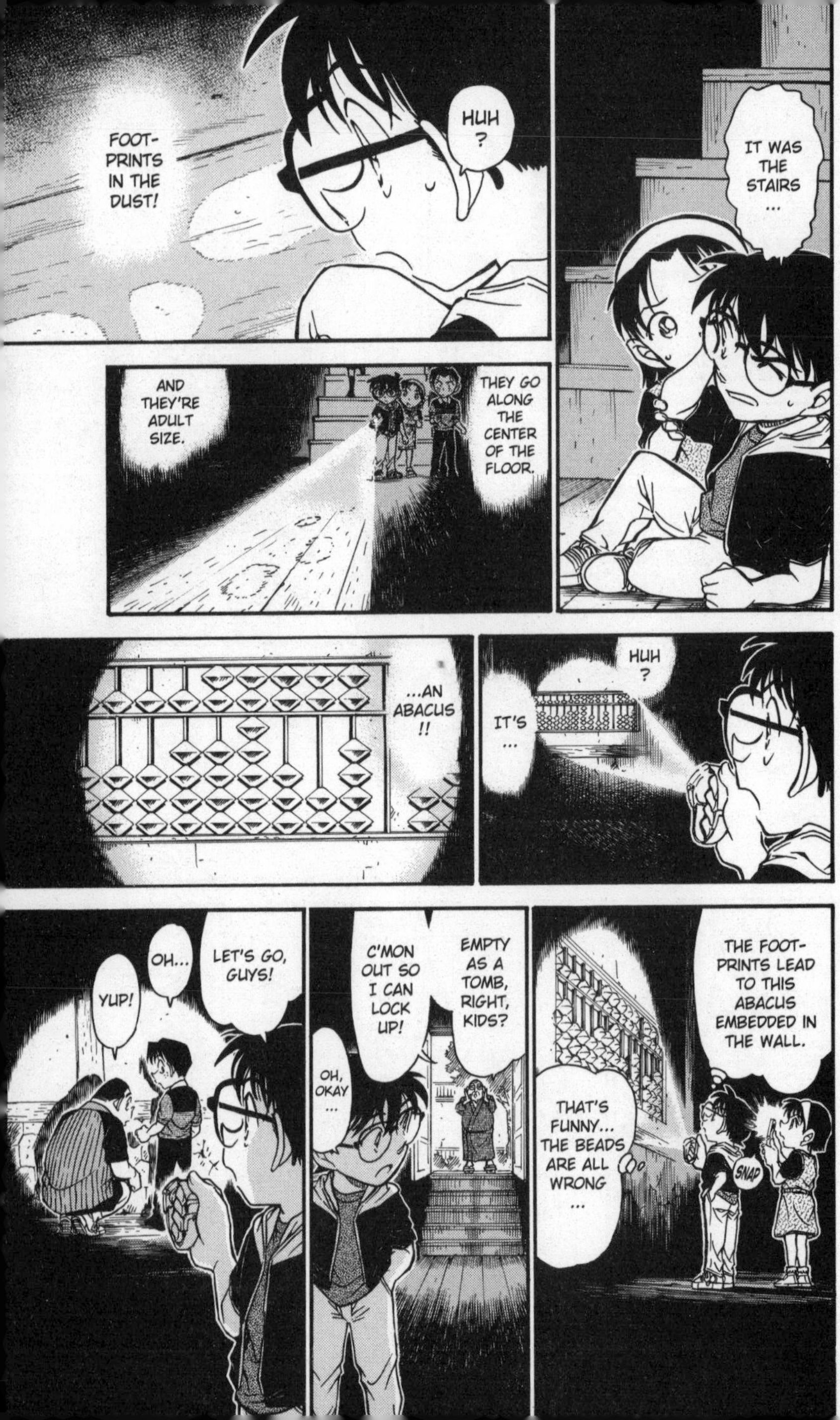

IT WAS THE STAIRS ...
HUH ?
FOOT-PRINTS IN THE DUST!
THEY GO ALONG THE CENTER OF THE FLOOR.
AND THEY'RE ADULT SIZE.
HUH ?
IT'S ...
...AN ABACUS !!
THE FOOT-PRINTS LEAD TO THIS ABACUS EMBEDDED IN THE WALL.
THAT'S FUNNY... THE BEADS ARE ALL WRONG ...
SNAP
EMPTY AS A TOMB, RIGHT, KIDS?
C'MON OUT SO I CAN LOCK UP!
OH, OKAY ...
LET'S GO, GUYS!
OH...
YUP!

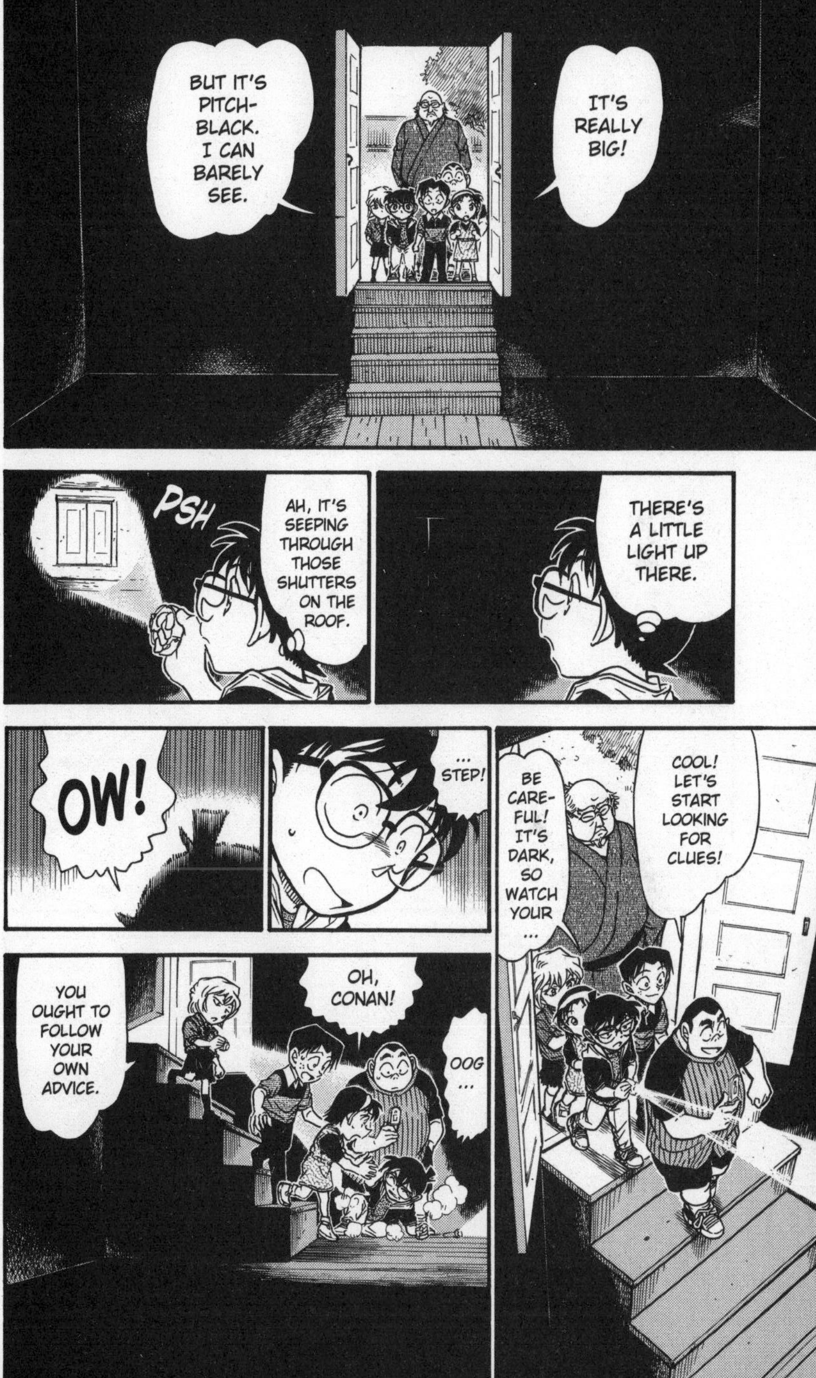
IT'S REALLY BIG!
BUT IT'S PITCH-BLACK. I CAN BARELY SEE.
THERE'S A LITTLE LIGHT UP THERE.
PSH
AH, IT'S SEEPING THROUGH THOSE SHUTTERS ON THE ROOF.
COOL! LET'S START LOOKING FOR CLUES!
BE CARE-FUL! IT'S DARK, SO WATCH YOUR ...
... STEP!
OW!
OH, CONAN!
OOG ...
YOU OUGHT TO FOLLOW YOUR OWN ADVICE.

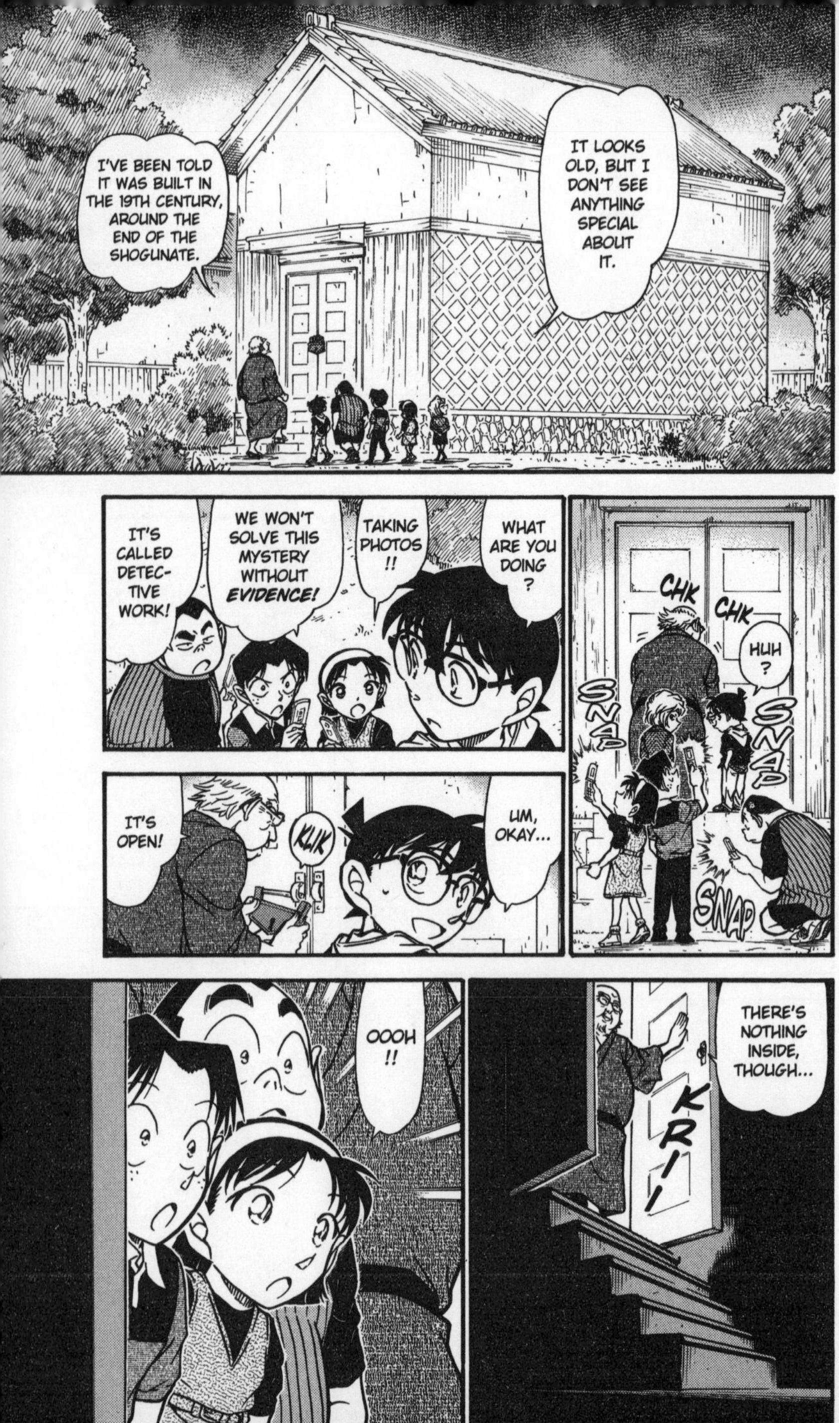
IT LOOKS OLD, BUT I DON'T SEE ANYTHING SPECIAL ABOUT IT.
I'VE BEEN TOLD IT WAS BUILT IN THE 19TH CENTURY, AROUND THE END OF THE SHOGUNATE.
CHK
CHK
HUH?
SNAP
SNAP
SNAP
WHAT ARE YOU DOING?
TAKING PHOTOS!!
WE WON'T SOLVE THIS MYSTERY WITHOUT EVIDENCE!
IT'S CALLED DETECTIVE WORK!
UM, OKAY...
KLIK
IT'S OPEN!
THERE'S NOTHING INSIDE, THOUGH...
KRI!
OOOH!!

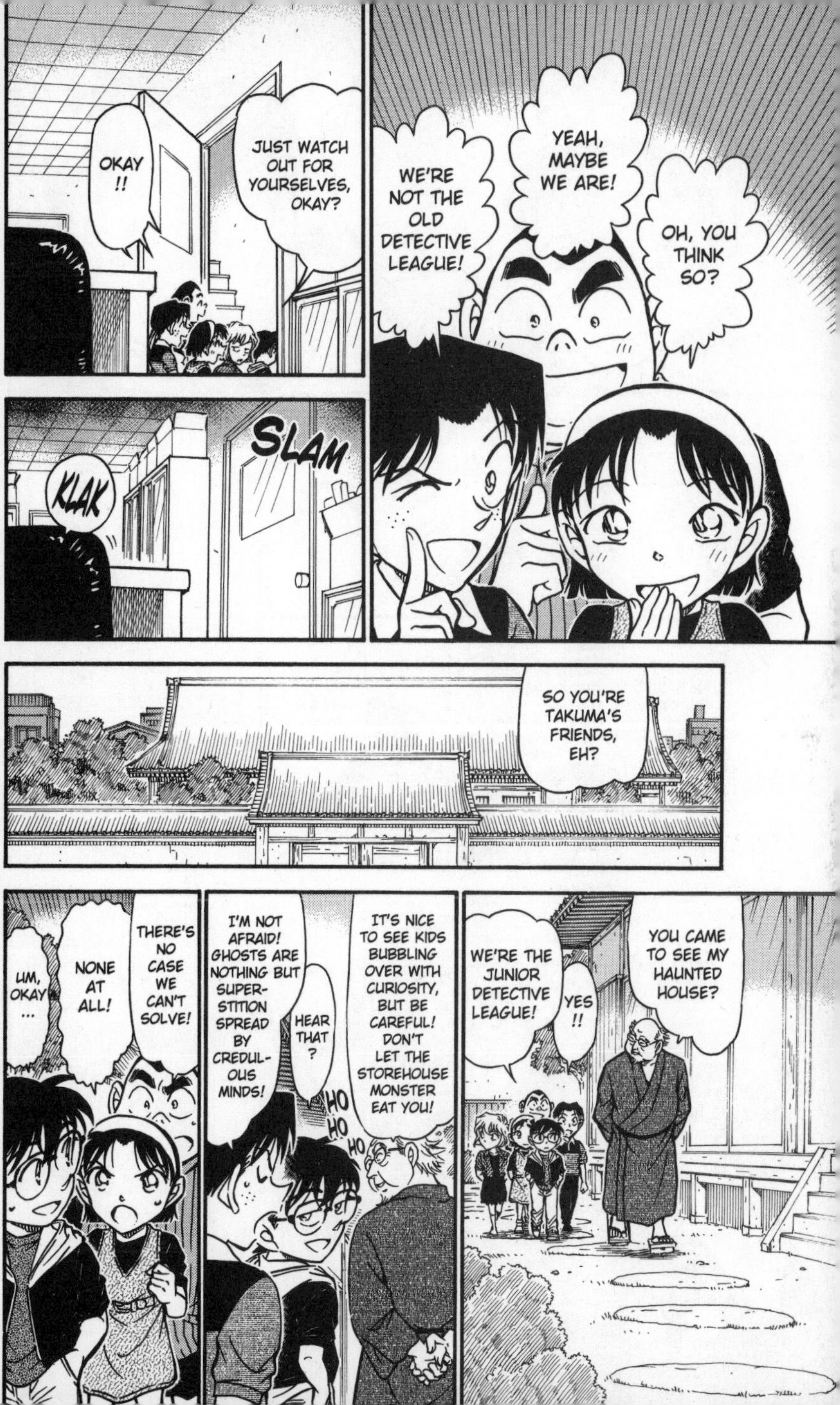
YEAH, MAYBE WE ARE!
OH, YOU THINK SO?
WE'RE NOT THE OLD DETECTIVE LEAGUE!
JUST WATCH OUT FOR YOURSELVES, OKAY?
OKAY !!
SLAM
KLAK
SO YOU'RE TAKUMA'S FRIENDS, EH?
YOU CAME TO SEE MY HAUNTED HOUSE?
YES !!
WE'RE THE JUNIOR DETECTIVE LEAGUE!
IT'S NICE TO SEE KIDS BUBBLING OVER WITH CURIOSITY, BUT BE CAREFUL! DON'T LET THE STOREHOUSE MONSTER EAT YOU!
HO HO HO
HEAR THAT ?
I'M NOT AFRAID! GHOSTS ARE NOTHING BUT SUPER-STITION SPREAD BY CREDUL-OUS MINDS!
THERE'S NO CASE WE CAN'T SOLVE!
NONE AT ALL!
UM, OKAY ...

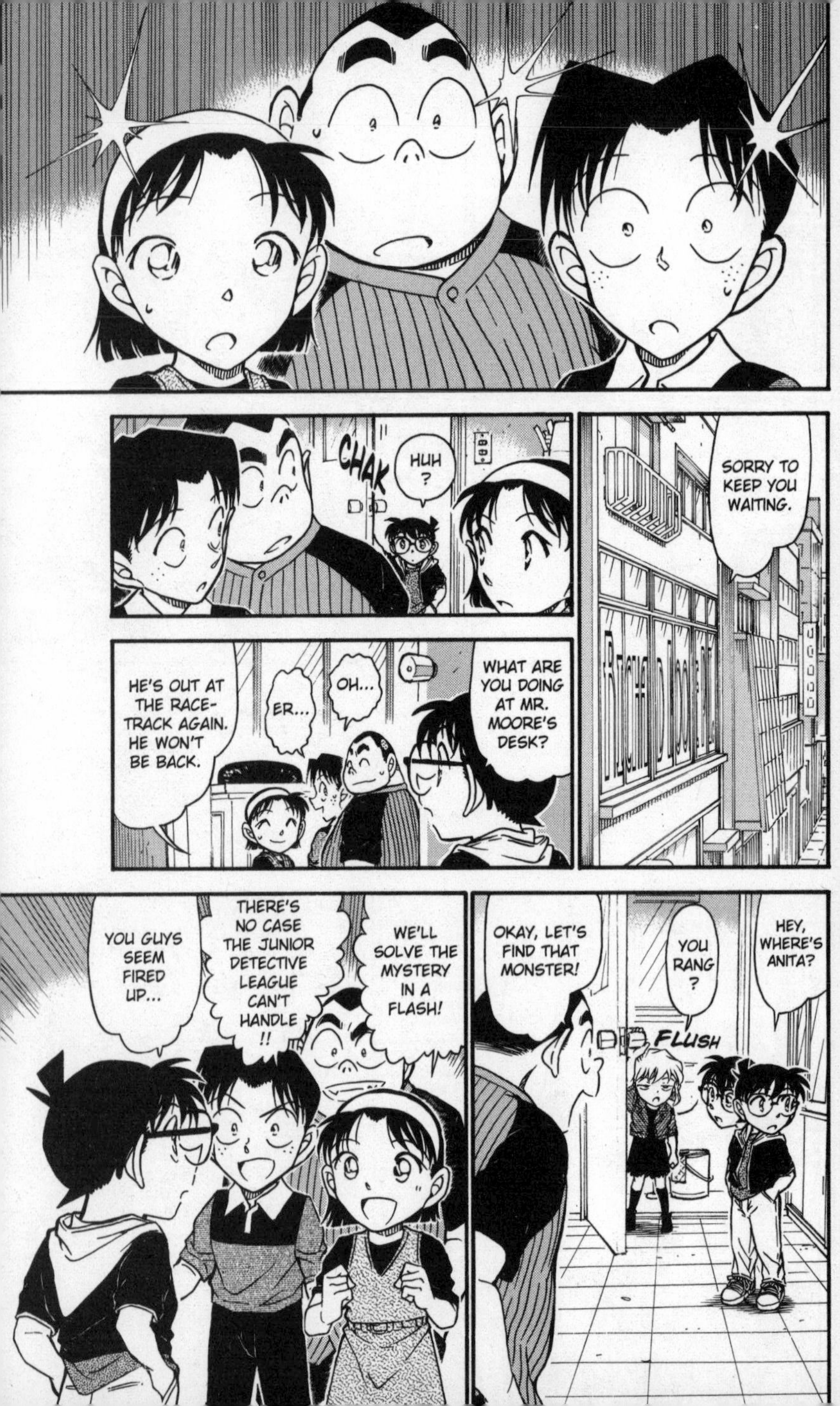
SORRY TO KEEP YOU WAITING.
CHAK
HUH ?
WHAT ARE YOU DOING AT MR. MOORE'S DESK?
OH...
ER...
HE'S OUT AT THE RACE-TRACK AGAIN. HE WON'T BE BACK.
HEY, WHERE'S ANITA?
YOU RANG ?
FLUSH
OKAY, LET'S FIND THAT MONSTER!
WE'LL SOLVE THE MYSTERY IN A FLASH!
THERE'S NO CASE THE JUNIOR DETECTIVE LEAGUE CAN'T HANDLE !!
YOU GUYS SEEM FIRED UP...

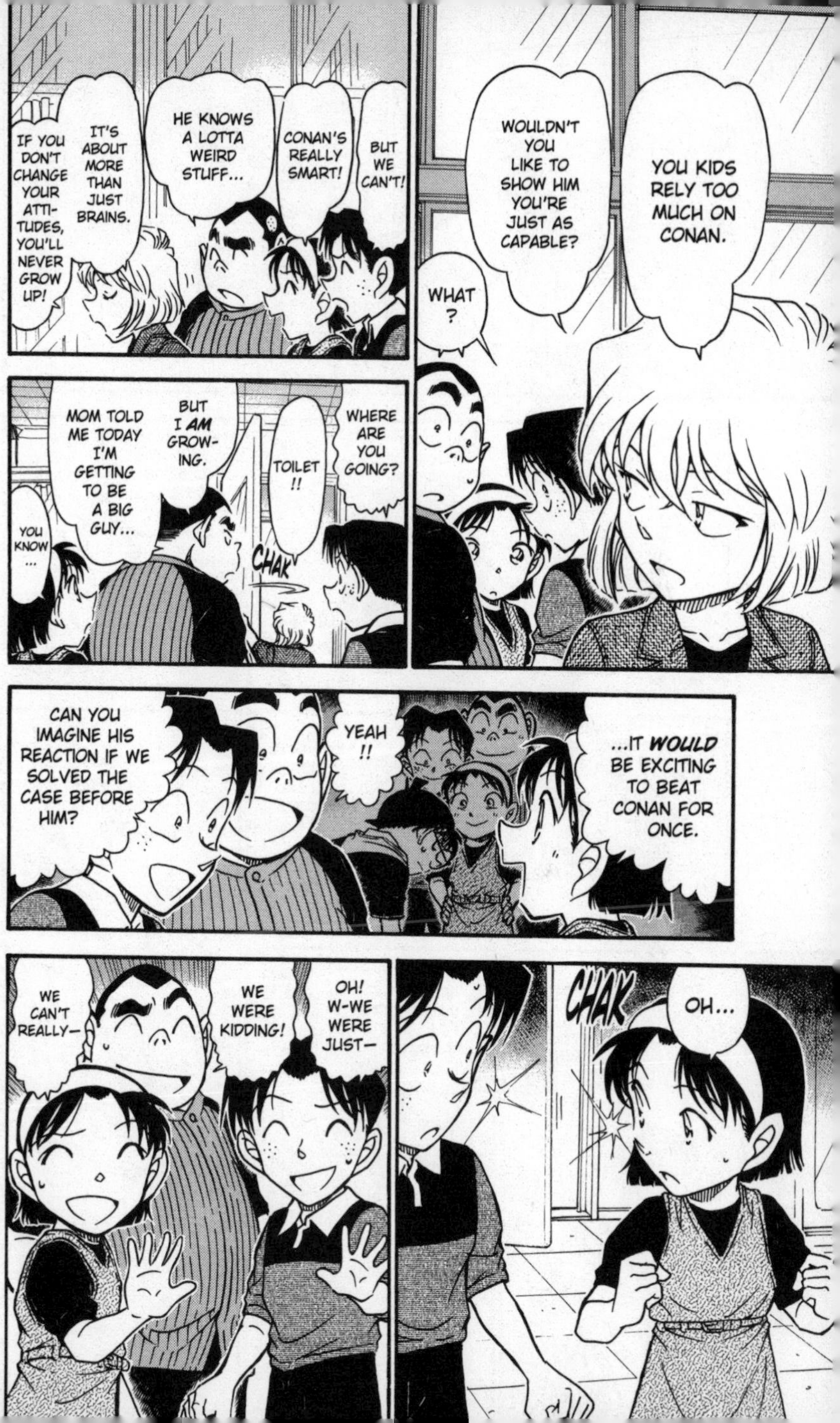
YOU KIDS RELY TOO MUCH ON CONAN.
WOULDN'T YOU LIKE TO SHOW HIM YOU'RE JUST AS CAPABLE?
WHAT?
BUT WE CAN'T!
CONAN'S REALLY SMART!
HE KNOWS A LOTTA WEIRD STUFF...
IT'S ABOUT MORE THAN JUST BRAINS.
IF YOU DON'T CHANGE YOUR ATTITUDES, YOU'LL NEVER GROW UP!
WHERE ARE YOU GOING?
TOILET!!
CHAK
BUT I *AM* GROWING.
MOM TOLD ME TODAY I'M GETTING TO BE A BIG GUY...
YOU KNOW...
...IT *WOULD* BE EXCITING TO BEAT CONAN FOR ONCE.
YEAH!!
CAN YOU IMAGINE HIS REACTION IF WE SOLVED THE CASE BEFORE HIM?
CHAK
OH...
OH! W-WE WERE JUST—
WE WERE KIDDING!
WE CAN'T REALLY—

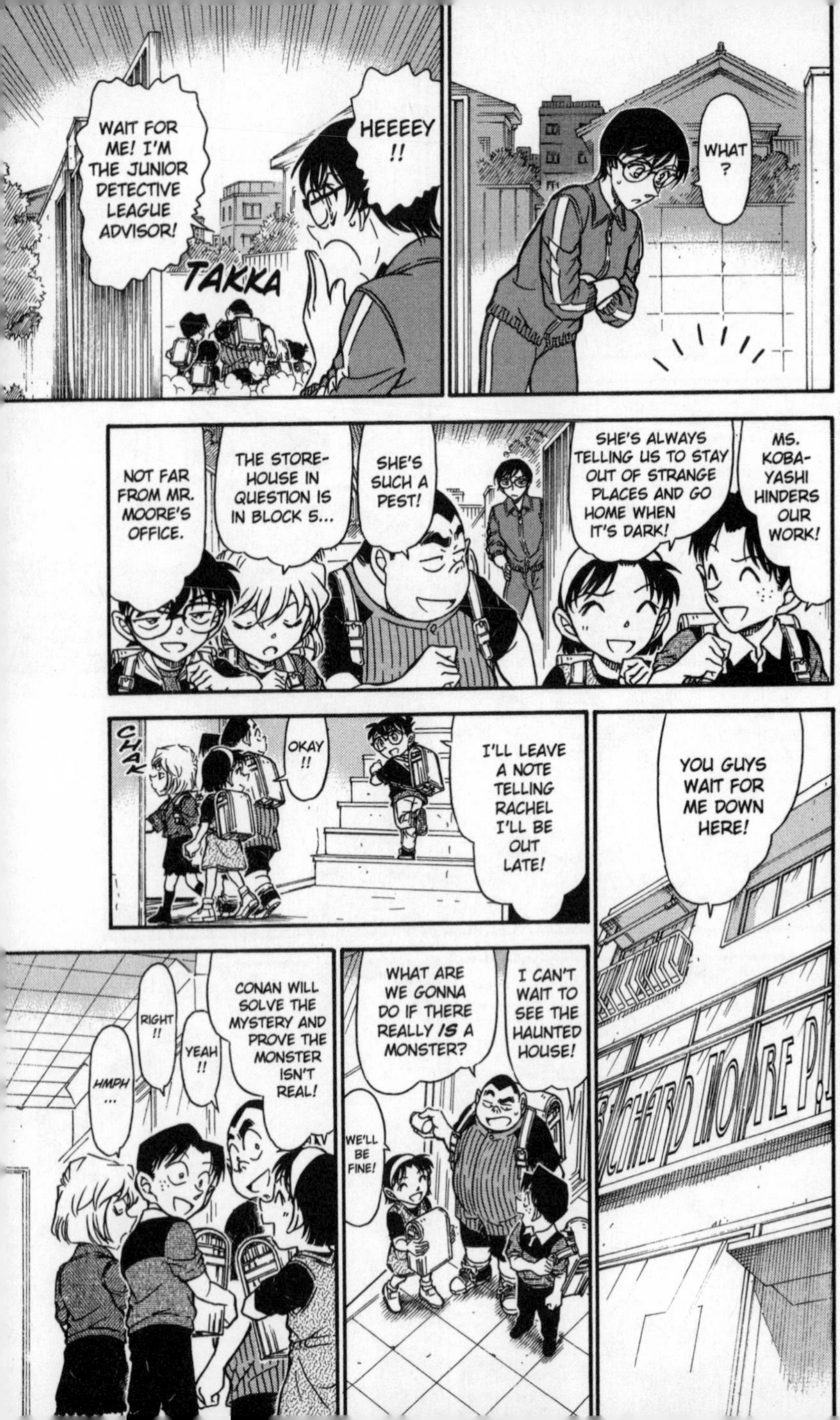
WHAT ?
HEEEEY !!
WAIT FOR ME! I'M THE JUNIOR DETECTIVE LEAGUE ADVISOR!
TAKKA
MS. KOBAYASHI HINDERS OUR WORK!
SHE'S ALWAYS TELLING US TO STAY OUT OF STRANGE PLACES AND GO HOME WHEN IT'S DARK!
SHE'S SUCH A PEST!
THE STOREHOUSE IN QUESTION IS IN BLOCK 5...
NOT FAR FROM MR. MOORE'S OFFICE.
YOU GUYS WAIT FOR ME DOWN HERE!
I'LL LEAVE A NOTE TELLING RACHEL I'LL BE OUT LATE!
OKAY !!
CHAK
I CAN'T WAIT TO SEE THE HAUNTED HOUSE!
WHAT ARE WE GONNA DO IF THERE REALLY IS A MONSTER?
WE'LL BE FINE!
CONAN WILL SOLVE THE MYSTERY AND PROVE THE MONSTER ISN'T REAL!
YEAH !!
RIGHT !!
HMPH ...

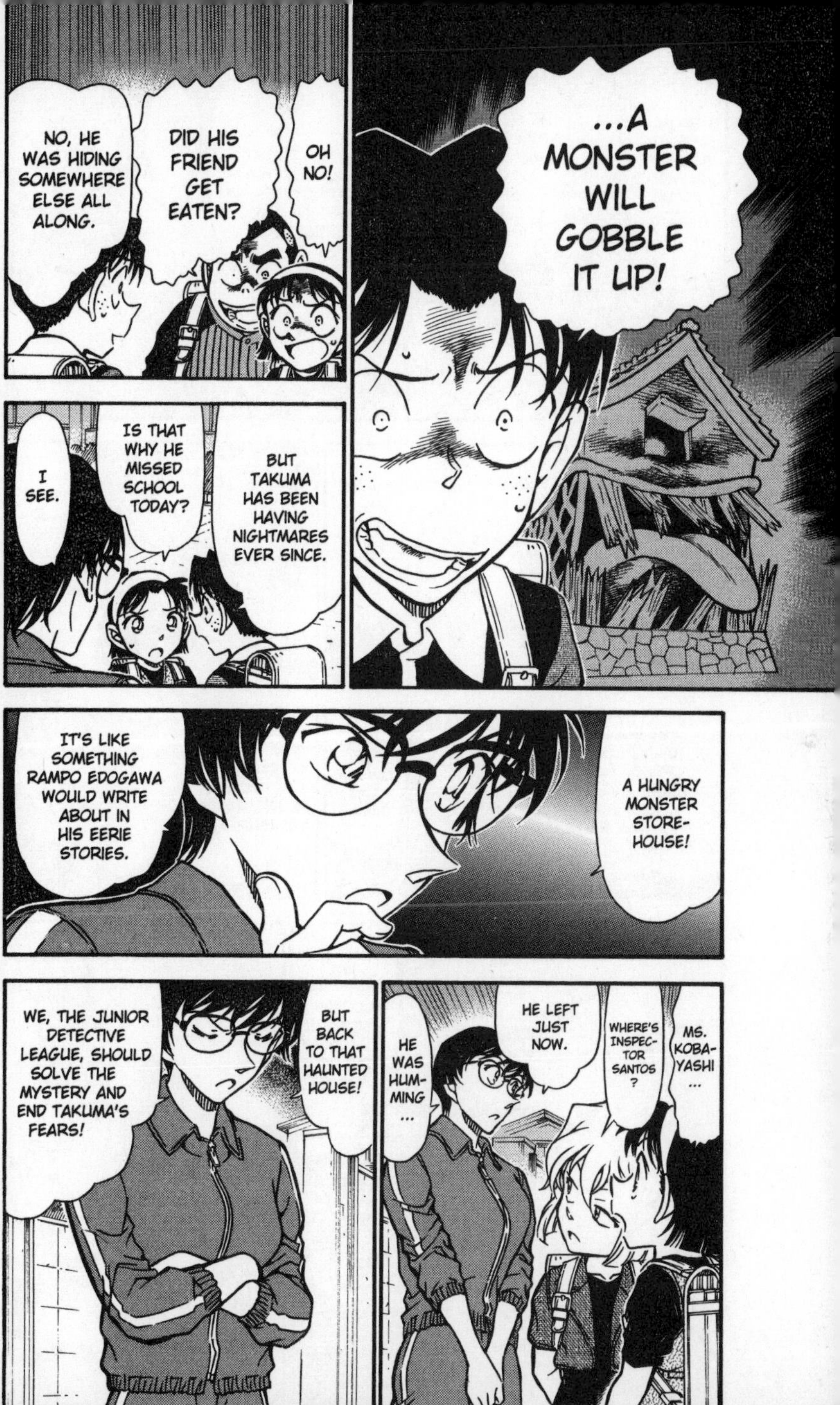
...A MONSTER WILL GOBBLE IT UP!
OH NO!
DID HIS FRIEND GET EATEN?
NO, HE WAS HIDING SOMEWHERE ELSE ALL ALONG.
BUT TAKUMA HAS BEEN HAVING NIGHTMARES EVER SINCE.
IS THAT WHY HE MISSED SCHOOL TODAY?
I SEE.
A HUNGRY MONSTER STORE-HOUSE!
IT'S LIKE SOMETHING RAMPO EDOGAWA WOULD WRITE ABOUT IN HIS EERIE STORIES.
MS. KOBA-YASHI...
WHERE'S INSPEC-TOR SANTOS?
HE LEFT JUST NOW.
HE WAS HUM-MING...
BUT BACK TO THAT HAUNTED HOUSE!
WE, THE JUNIOR DETECTIVE LEAGUE, SHOULD SOLVE THE MYSTERY AND END TAKUMA'S FEARS!

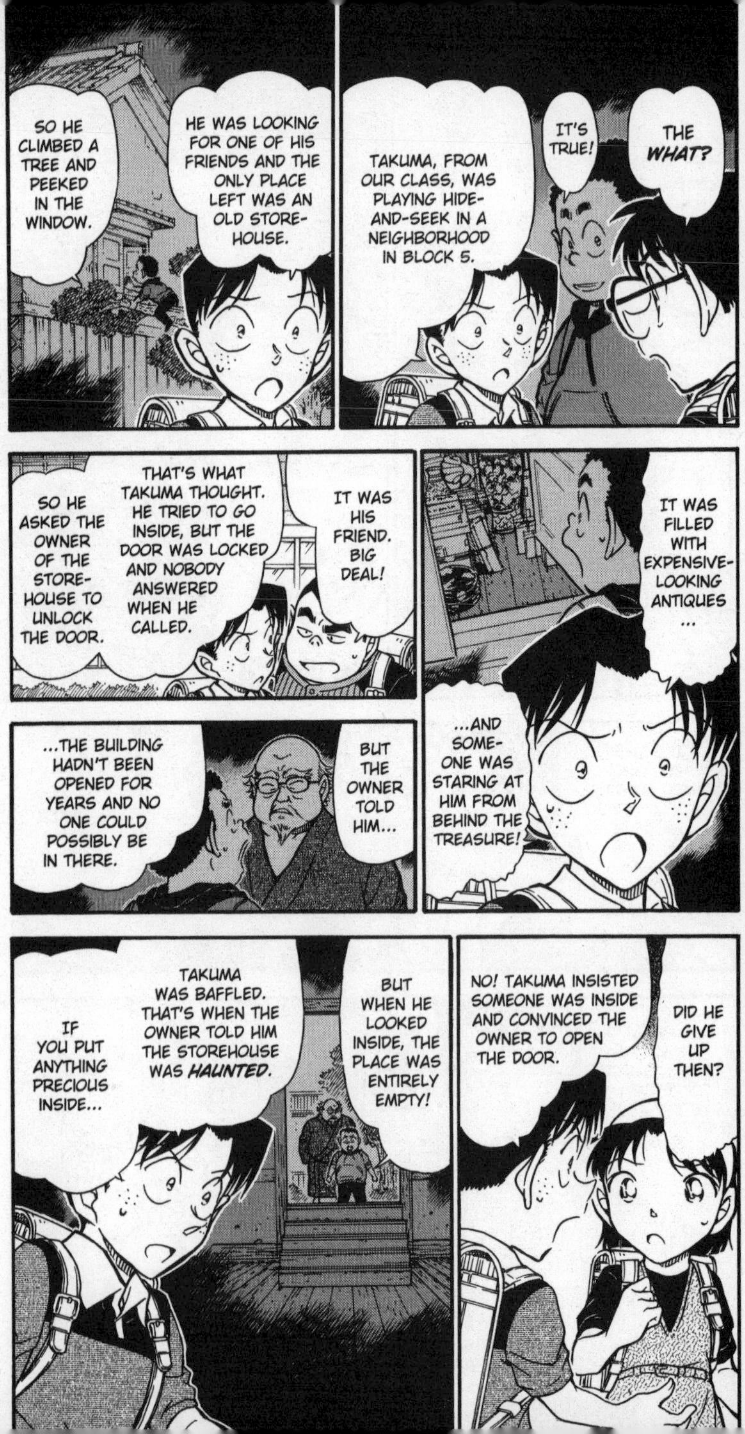
THE *WHAT?*
IT'S TRUE!
TAKUMA, FROM OUR CLASS, WAS PLAYING HIDE-AND-SEEK IN A NEIGHBORHOOD IN BLOCK 5.
HE WAS LOOKING FOR ONE OF HIS FRIENDS AND THE ONLY PLACE LEFT WAS AN OLD STOREHOUSE.
SO HE CLIMBED A TREE AND PEEKED IN THE WINDOW.
IT WAS FILLED WITH EXPENSIVE-LOOKING ANTIQUES...
...AND SOMEONE WAS STARING AT HIM FROM BEHIND THE TREASURE!
IT WAS HIS FRIEND. BIG DEAL!
THAT'S WHAT TAKUMA THOUGHT. HE TRIED TO GO INSIDE, BUT THE DOOR WAS LOCKED AND NOBODY ANSWERED WHEN HE CALLED.
SO HE ASKED THE OWNER OF THE STOREHOUSE TO UNLOCK THE DOOR.
BUT THE OWNER TOLD HIM...
...THE BUILDING HADN'T BEEN OPENED FOR YEARS AND NO ONE COULD POSSIBLY BE IN THERE.
DID HE GIVE UP THEN?
NO! TAKUMA INSISTED SOMEONE WAS INSIDE AND CONVINCED THE OWNER TO OPEN THE DOOR.
BUT WHEN HE LOOKED INSIDE, THE PLACE WAS ENTIRELY EMPTY!
TAKUMA WAS BAFFLED. THAT'S WHEN THE OWNER TOLD HIM THE STOREHOUSE WAS *HAUNTED*.
IF YOU PUT ANYTHING PRECIOUS INSIDE...

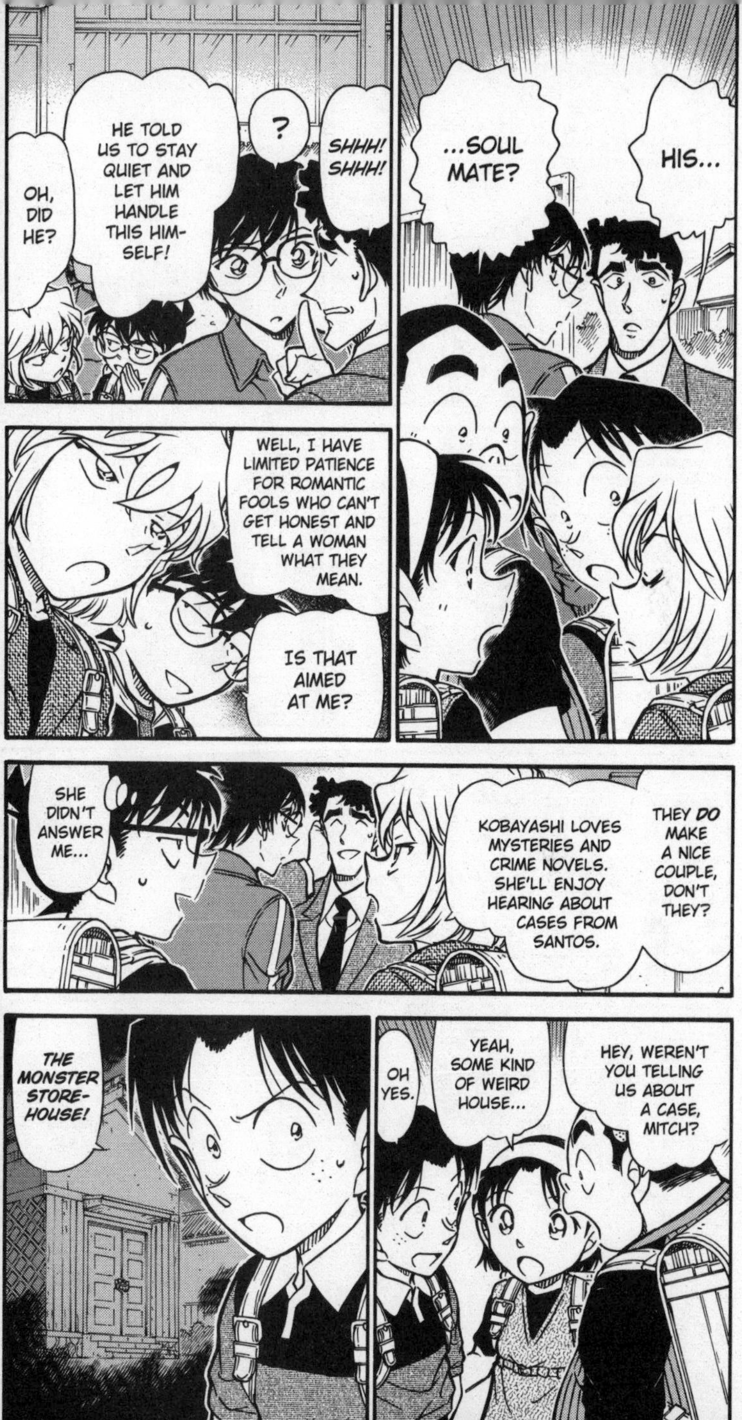
HIS...
...SOUL MATE?
SHHH! SHHH!
?
HE TOLD US TO STAY QUIET AND LET HIM HANDLE THIS HIMSELF!
OH, DID HE?
WELL, I HAVE LIMITED PATIENCE FOR ROMANTIC FOOLS WHO CAN'T GET HONEST AND TELL A WOMAN WHAT THEY MEAN.
IS THAT AIMED AT ME?
THEY *DO* MAKE A NICE COUPLE, DON'T THEY?
KOBAYASHI LOVES MYSTERIES AND CRIME NOVELS. SHE'LL ENJOY HEARING ABOUT CASES FROM SANTOS.
SHE DIDN'T ANSWER ME...
HEY, WEREN'T YOU TELLING US ABOUT A CASE, MITCH?
YEAH, SOME KIND OF WEIRD HOUSE...
OH YES.
THE MONSTER STOREHOUSE!

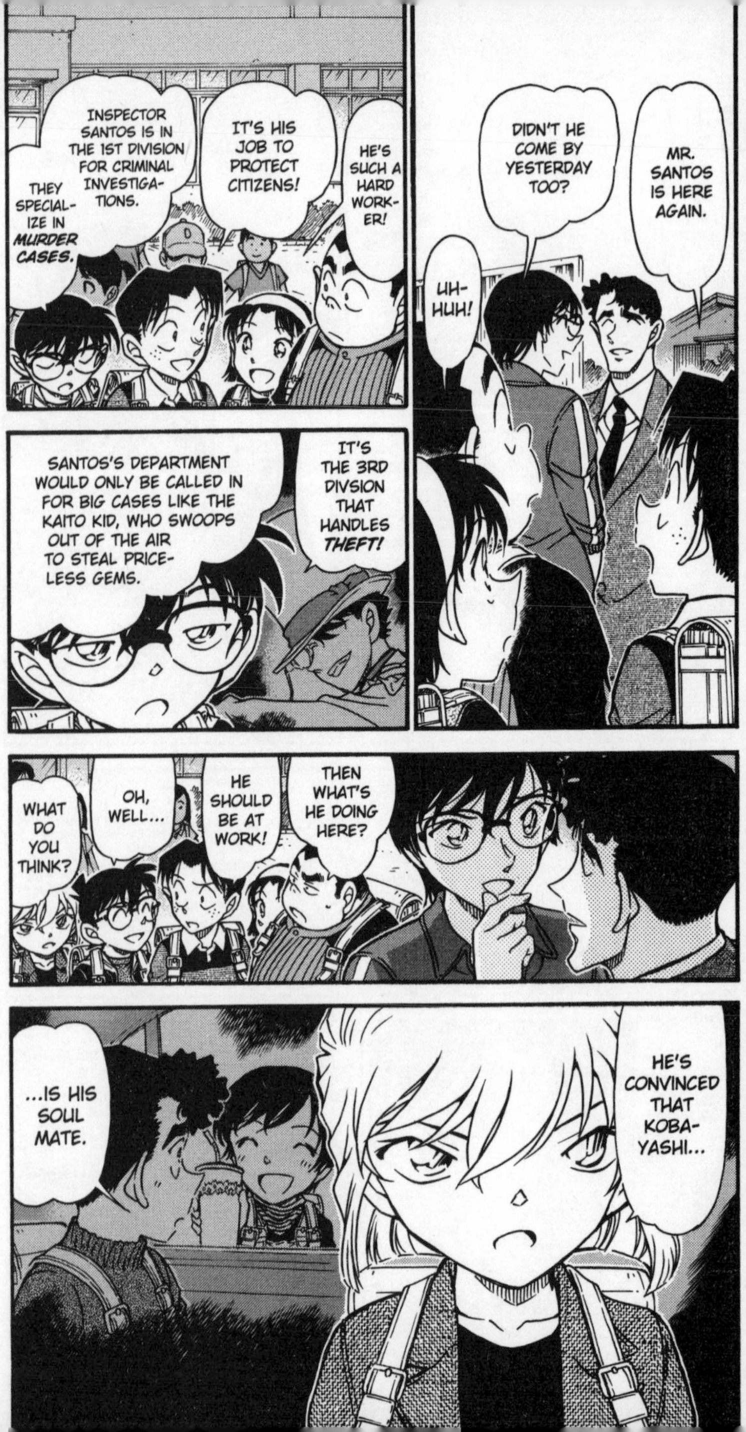
MR. SANTOS IS HERE AGAIN.
DIDN'T HE COME BY YESTERDAY TOO?
UH-HUH!
HE'S SUCH A HARD WORK-ER!
IT'S HIS JOB TO PROTECT CITIZENS!
INSPECTOR SANTOS IS IN THE 1ST DIVISION FOR CRIMINAL INVESTIGA-TIONS.
THEY SPECIAL-IZE IN MURDER CASES.
IT'S THE 3RD DIVSION THAT HANDLES THEFT!
SANTOS'S DEPARTMENT WOULD ONLY BE CALLED IN FOR BIG CASES LIKE THE KAITO KID, WHO SWOOPS OUT OF THE AIR TO STEAL PRICE-LESS GEMS.
THEN WHAT'S HE DOING HERE?
HE SHOULD BE AT WORK!
OH, WELL...
WHAT DO YOU THINK?
HE'S CONVINCED THAT KOBA-YASHI...
...IS HIS SOUL MATE.

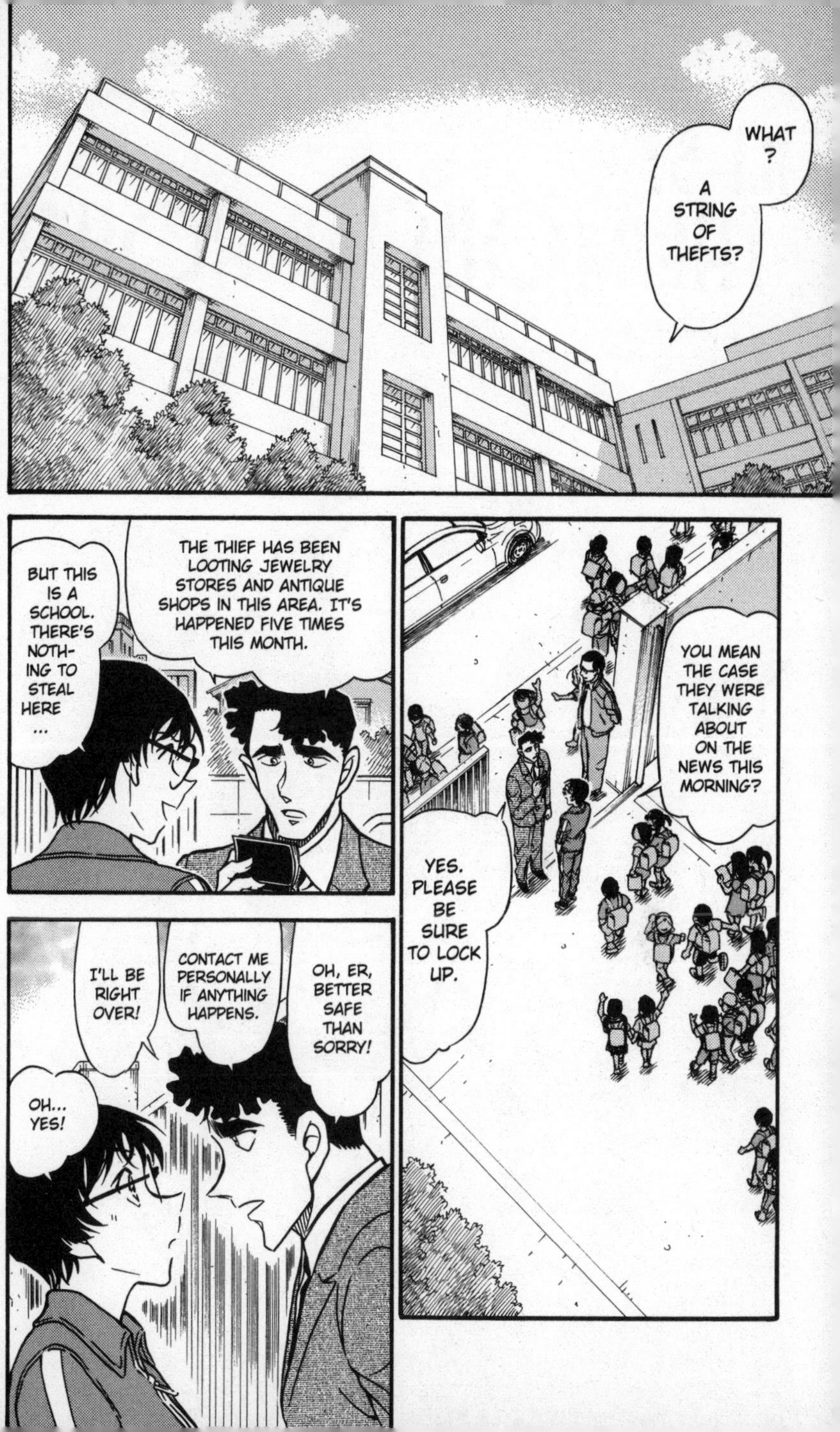
WHAT? A STRING OF THEFTS?
YOU MEAN THE CASE THEY WERE TALKING ABOUT ON THE NEWS THIS MORNING?
YES. PLEASE BE SURE TO LOCK UP.
THE THIEF HAS BEEN LOOTING JEWELRY STORES AND ANTIQUE SHOPS IN THIS AREA. IT'S HAPPENED FIVE TIMES THIS MONTH.
BUT THIS IS A SCHOOL. THERE'S NOTH-ING TO STEAL HERE ...
OH, ER, BETTER SAFE THAN SORRY!
CONTACT ME PERSONALLY IF ANYTHING HAPPENS.
I'LL BE RIGHT OVER!
OH... YES!

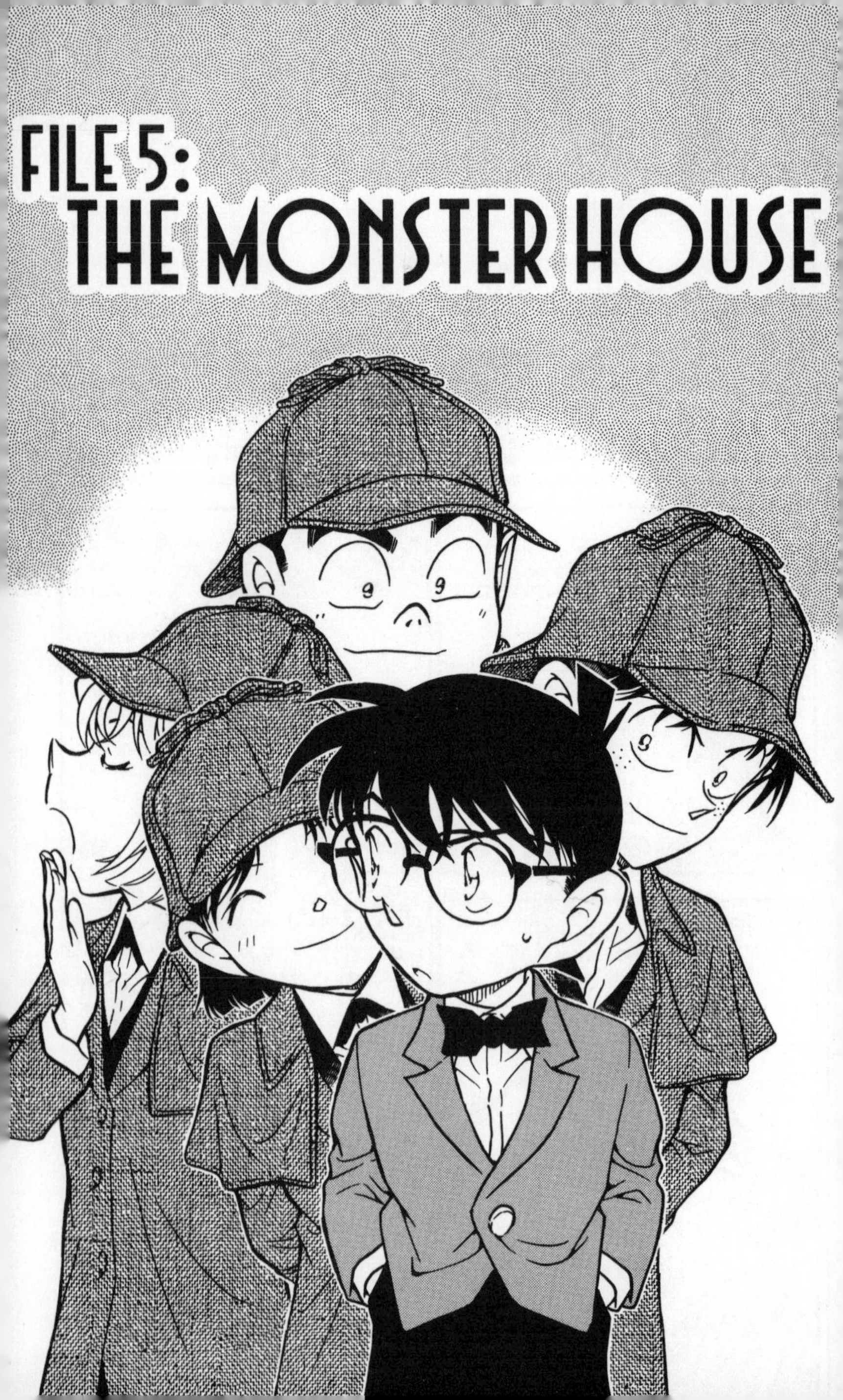
FILE 5:
THE MONSTER HOUSE

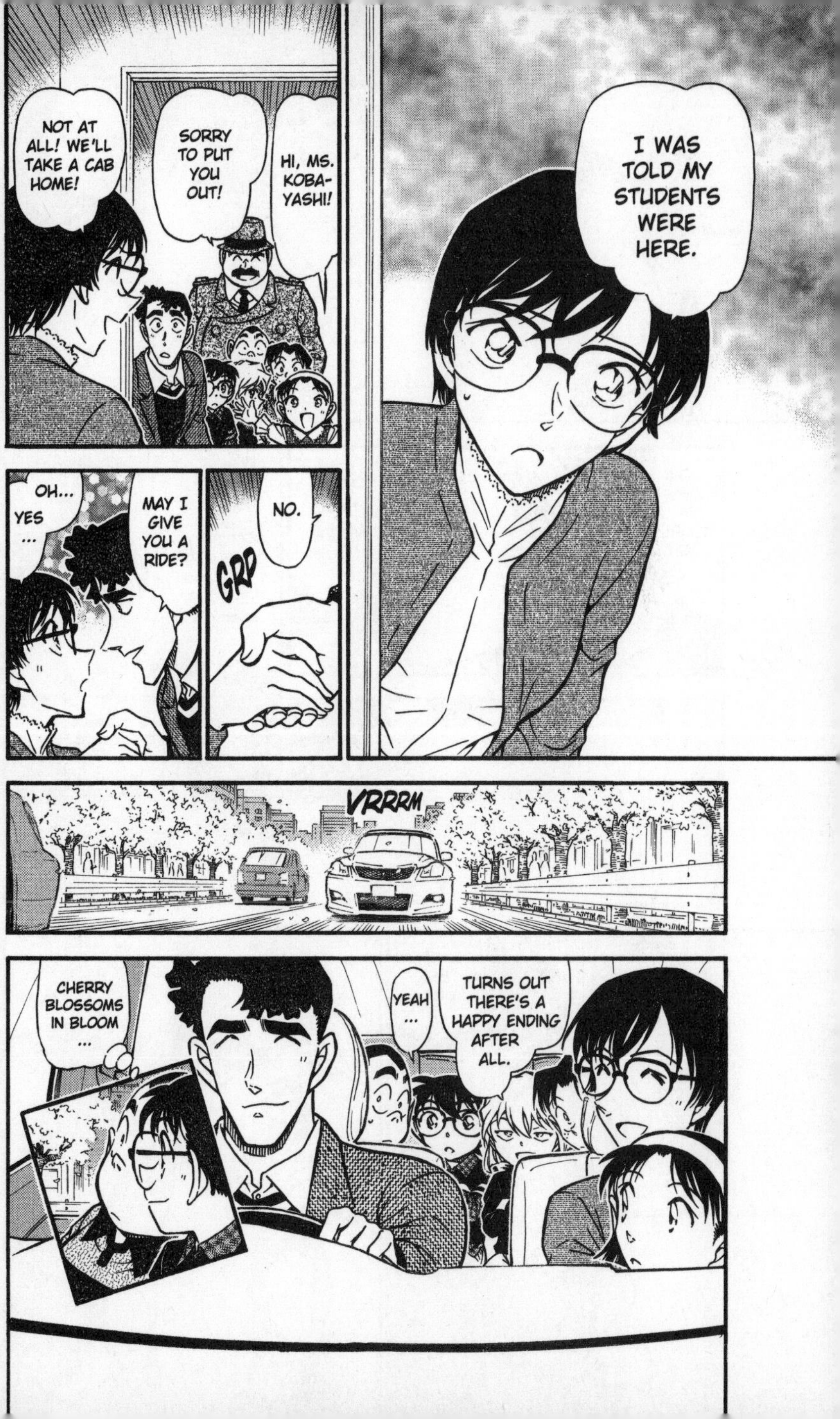
I WAS TOLD MY STUDENTS WERE HERE.
HI, MS. KOBAYASHI!
SORRY TO PUT YOU OUT!
NOT AT ALL! WE'LL TAKE A CAB HOME!
NO.
GRP
MAY I GIVE YOU A RIDE?
OH... YES ...
VRRRM
TURNS OUT THERE'S A HAPPY ENDING AFTER ALL.
YEAH ...
CHERRY BLOSSOMS IN BLOOM ...

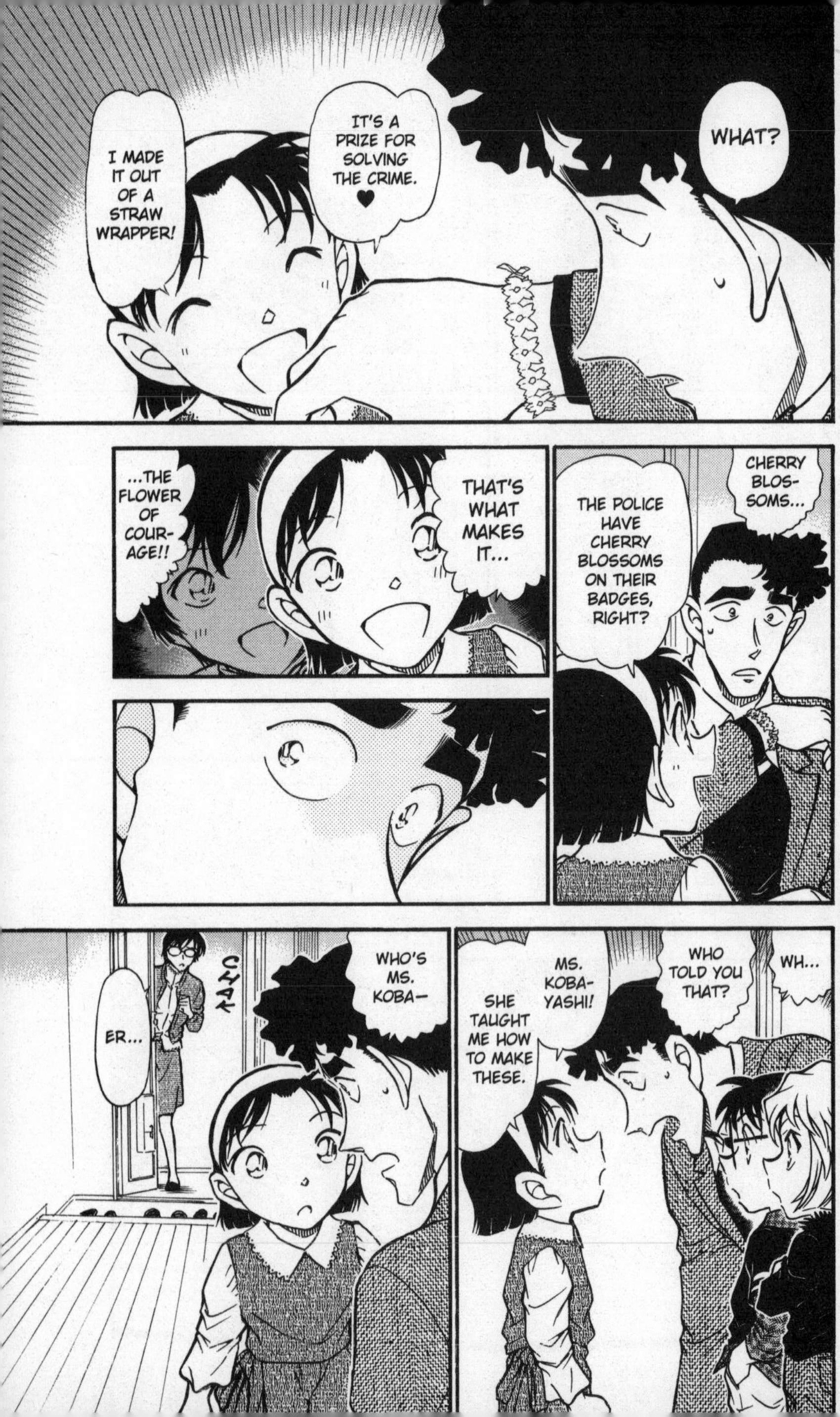
WHAT?
IT'S A PRIZE FOR SOLVING THE CRIME. ♥
I MADE IT OUT OF A STRAW WRAPPER!
CHERRY BLOS-SOMS...
THE POLICE HAVE CHERRY BLOSSOMS ON THEIR BADGES, RIGHT?
THAT'S WHAT MAKES IT...
...THE FLOWER OF COUR-AGE!!
WH...
WHO TOLD YOU THAT?
MS. KOBA-YASHI!
SHE TAUGHT ME HOW TO MAKE THESE.
WHO'S MS. KOBA-
CHAK
ER...

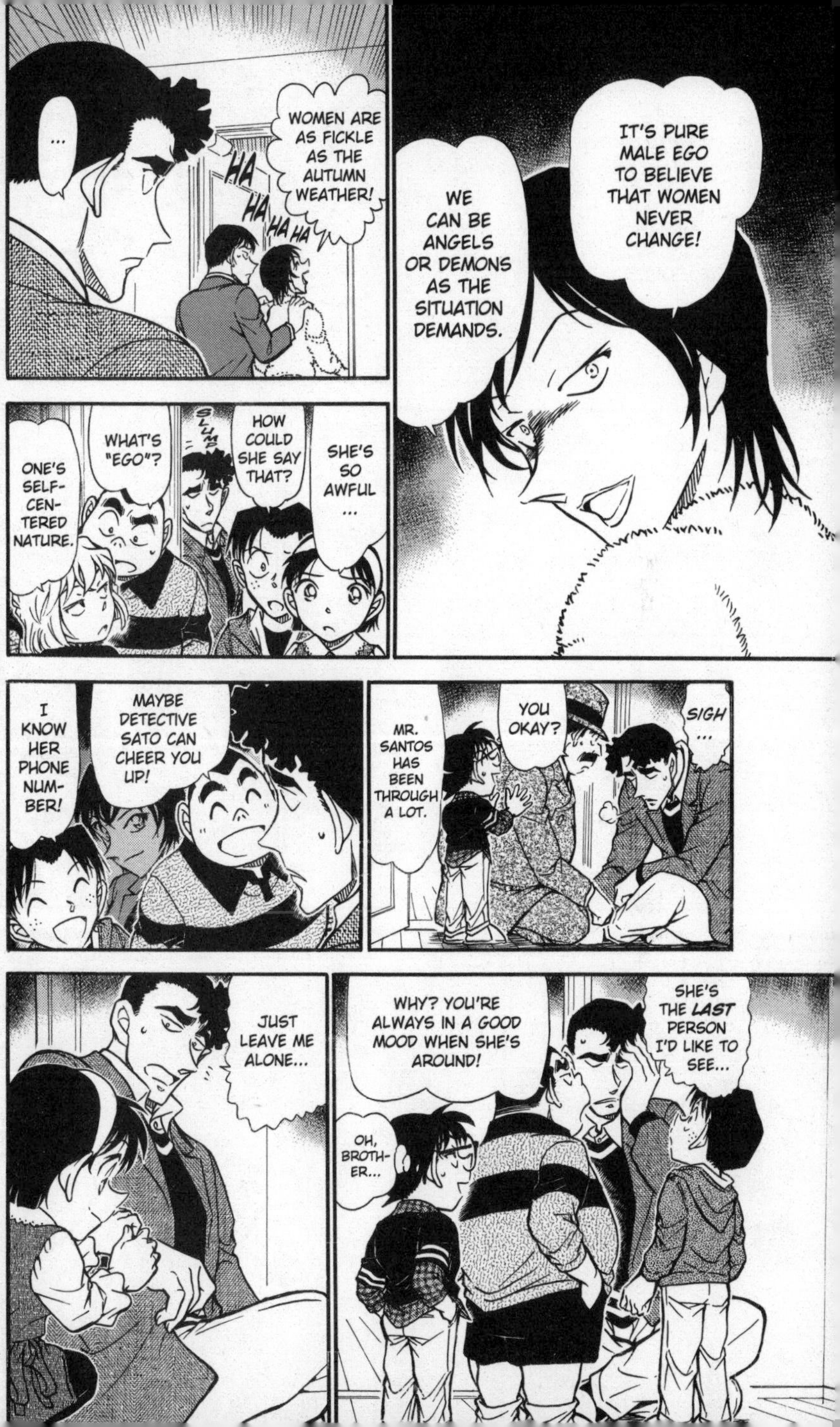
IT'S PURE MALE EGO TO BELIEVE THAT WOMEN NEVER CHANGE!
WE CAN BE ANGELS OR DEMONS AS THE SITUATION DEMANDS.
WOMEN ARE AS FICKLE AS THE AUTUMN WEATHER!
HA HA HA HA
...
SHE'S SO AWFUL...
HOW COULD SHE SAY THAT?
SLUMP
WHAT'S "EGO"?
ONE'S SELF-CENTERED NATURE.
SIGH...
YOU OKAY?
MR. SANTOS HAS BEEN THROUGH A LOT.
MAYBE DETECTIVE SATO CAN CHEER YOU UP!
I KNOW HER PHONE NUMBER!
SHE'S THE *LAST* PERSON I'D LIKE TO SEE...
WHY? YOU'RE ALWAYS IN A GOOD MOOD WHEN SHE'S AROUND!
OH, BROTHER...
JUST LEAVE ME ALONE...

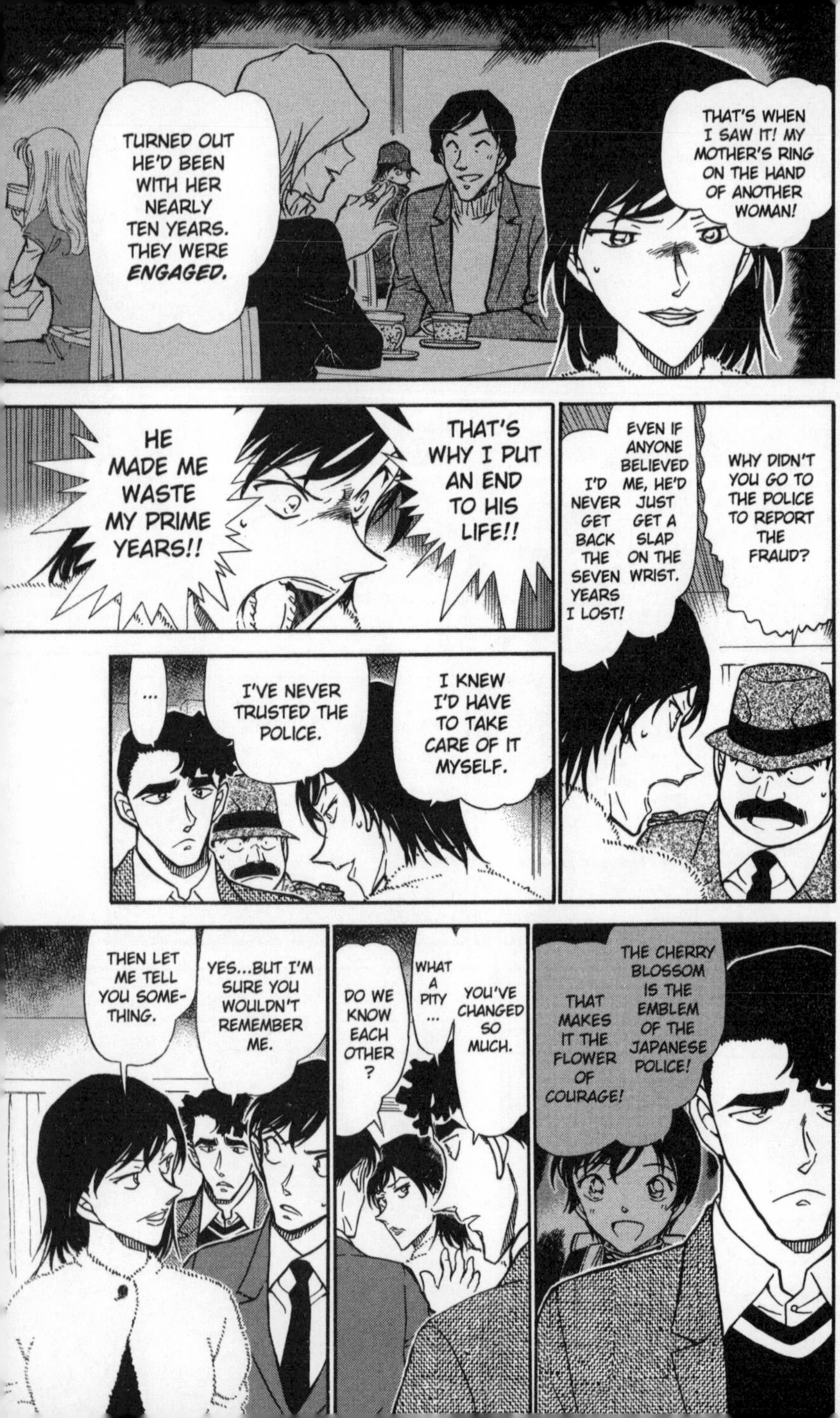
THAT'S WHEN I SAW IT! MY MOTHER'S RING ON THE HAND OF ANOTHER WOMAN!
TURNED OUT HE'D BEEN WITH HER NEARLY TEN YEARS. THEY WERE ENGAGED.
WHY DIDN'T YOU GO TO THE POLICE TO REPORT THE FRAUD?
EVEN IF ANYONE BELIEVED ME, HE'D JUST GET A SLAP ON THE WRIST.
I'D NEVER GET BACK THE SEVEN YEARS I LOST!
THAT'S WHY I PUT AN END TO HIS LIFE!!
HE MADE ME WASTE MY PRIME YEARS!!
I KNEW I'D HAVE TO TAKE CARE OF IT MYSELF.
I'VE NEVER TRUSTED THE POLICE.
...
THE CHERRY BLOSSOM IS THE EMBLEM OF THE JAPANESE POLICE!
THAT MAKES IT THE FLOWER OF COURAGE!
YOU'VE CHANGED SO MUCH.
WHAT A PITY...
DO WE KNOW EACH OTHER?
YES...BUT I'M SURE YOU WOULDN'T REMEMBER ME.
THEN LET ME TELL YOU SOMETHING.

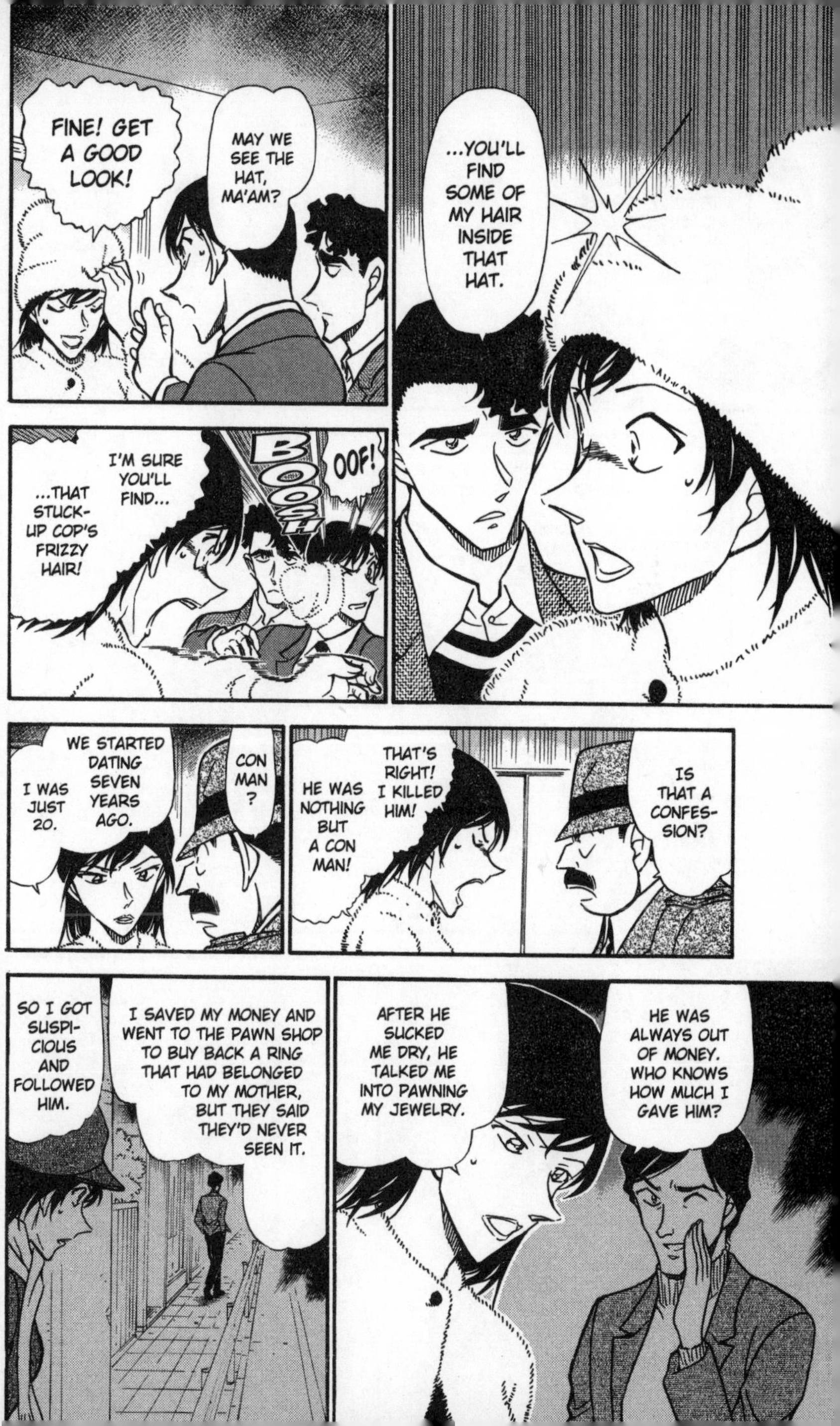
...YOU'LL FIND SOME OF MY HAIR INSIDE THAT HAT.
MAY WE SEE THE HAT, MA'AM?
FINE! GET A GOOD LOOK!
OOF!
BOOSH
I'M SURE YOU'LL FIND...
...THAT STUCK-UP COP'S FRIZZY HAIR!
IS THAT A CONFESSION?
THAT'S RIGHT! I KILLED HIM!
HE WAS NOTHING BUT A CON MAN!
CON MAN?
WE STARTED DATING SEVEN YEARS AGO.
I WAS JUST 20.
HE WAS ALWAYS OUT OF MONEY. WHO KNOWS HOW MUCH I GAVE HIM?
AFTER HE SUCKED ME DRY, HE TALKED ME INTO PAWNING MY JEWELRY.
I SAVED MY MONEY AND WENT TO THE PAWN SHOP TO BUY BACK A RING THAT HAD BELONGED TO MY MOTHER, BUT THEY SAID THEY'D NEVER SEEN IT.
SO I GOT SUSPICIOUS AND FOLLOWED HIM.

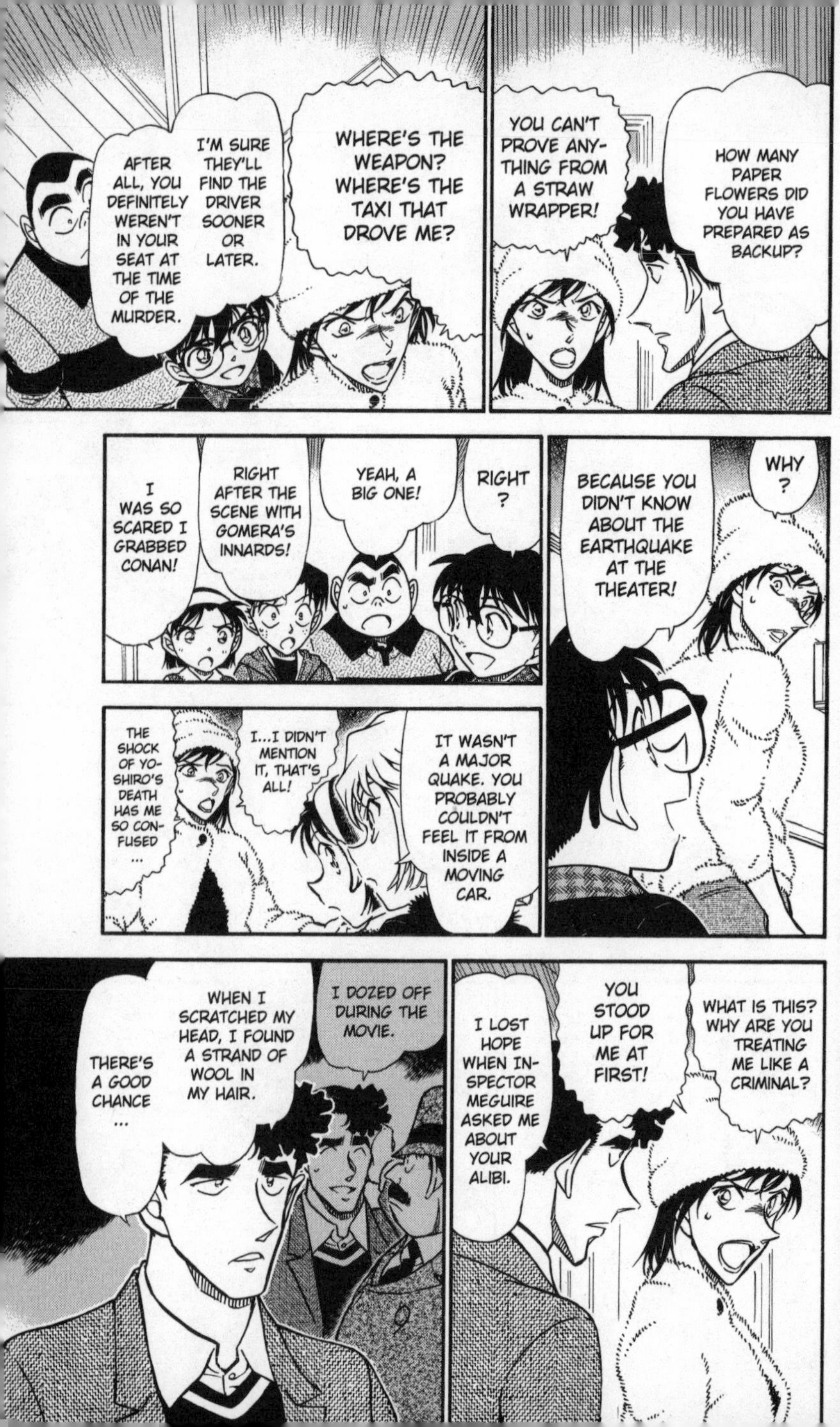
HOW MANY PAPER FLOWERS DID YOU HAVE PREPARED AS BACKUP?
YOU CAN'T PROVE ANYTHING FROM A STRAW WRAPPER!
WHERE'S THE WEAPON? WHERE'S THE TAXI THAT DROVE ME?
I'M SURE THEY'LL FIND THE DRIVER SOONER OR LATER.
AFTER ALL, YOU DEFINITELY WEREN'T IN YOUR SEAT AT THE TIME OF THE MURDER.
WHY?
BECAUSE YOU DIDN'T KNOW ABOUT THE EARTHQUAKE AT THE THEATER!
RIGHT?
YEAH, A BIG ONE!
RIGHT AFTER THE SCENE WITH GOMERA'S INNARDS!
I WAS SO SCARED I GRABBED CONAN!
IT WASN'T A MAJOR QUAKE. YOU PROBABLY COULDN'T FEEL IT FROM INSIDE A MOVING CAR.
I...I DIDN'T MENTION IT, THAT'S ALL!
THE SHOCK OF YOSHIRO'S DEATH HAS ME SO CONFUSED...
WHAT IS THIS? WHY ARE YOU TREATING ME LIKE A CRIMINAL?
YOU STOOD UP FOR ME AT FIRST!
I LOST HOPE WHEN INSPECTOR MEGUIRE ASKED ME ABOUT YOUR ALIBI.
I DOZED OFF DURING THE MOVIE.
WHEN I SCRATCHED MY HEAD, I FOUND A STRAND OF WOOL IN MY HAIR.
THERE'S A GOOD CHANCE...

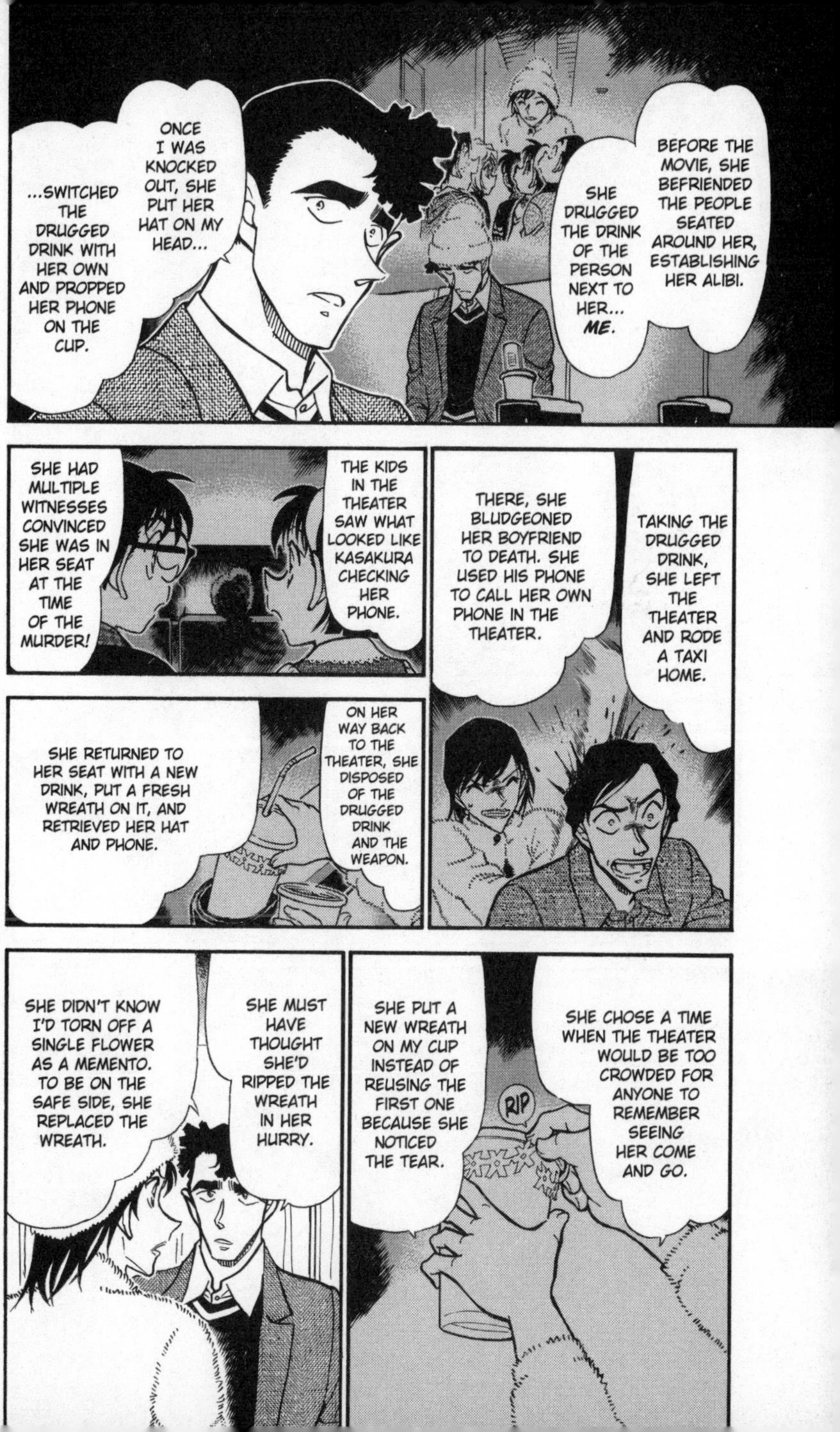
BEFORE THE MOVIE, SHE BEFRIENDED THE PEOPLE SEATED AROUND HER, ESTABLISHING HER ALIBI.
SHE DRUGGED THE DRINK OF THE PERSON NEXT TO HER... ME.
ONCE I WAS KNOCKED OUT, SHE PUT HER HAT ON MY HEAD...
...SWITCHED THE DRUGGED DRINK WITH HER OWN AND PROPPED HER PHONE ON THE CUP.
TAKING THE DRUGGED DRINK, SHE LEFT THE THEATER AND RODE A TAXI HOME.
THERE, SHE BLUDGEONED HER BOYFRIEND TO DEATH. SHE USED HIS PHONE TO CALL HER OWN PHONE IN THE THEATER.
THE KIDS IN THE THEATER SAW WHAT LOOKED LIKE KASAKURA CHECKING HER PHONE.
SHE HAD MULTIPLE WITNESSES CONVINCED SHE WAS IN HER SEAT AT THE TIME OF THE MURDER!
ON HER WAY BACK TO THE THEATER, SHE DISPOSED OF THE DRUGGED DRINK AND THE WEAPON.
SHE RETURNED TO HER SEAT WITH A NEW DRINK, PUT A FRESH WREATH ON IT, AND RETRIEVED HER HAT AND PHONE.
SHE CHOSE A TIME WHEN THE THEATER WOULD BE TOO CROWDED FOR ANYONE TO REMEMBER SEEING HER COME AND GO.
RIP
SHE PUT A NEW WREATH ON MY CUP INSTEAD OF REUSING THE FIRST ONE BECAUSE SHE NOTICED THE TEAR.
SHE MUST HAVE THOUGHT SHE'D RIPPED THE WREATH IN HER HURRY.
SHE DIDN'T KNOW I'D TORN OFF A SINGLE FLOWER AS A MEMENTO. TO BE ON THE SAFE SIDE, SHE REPLACED THE WREATH.

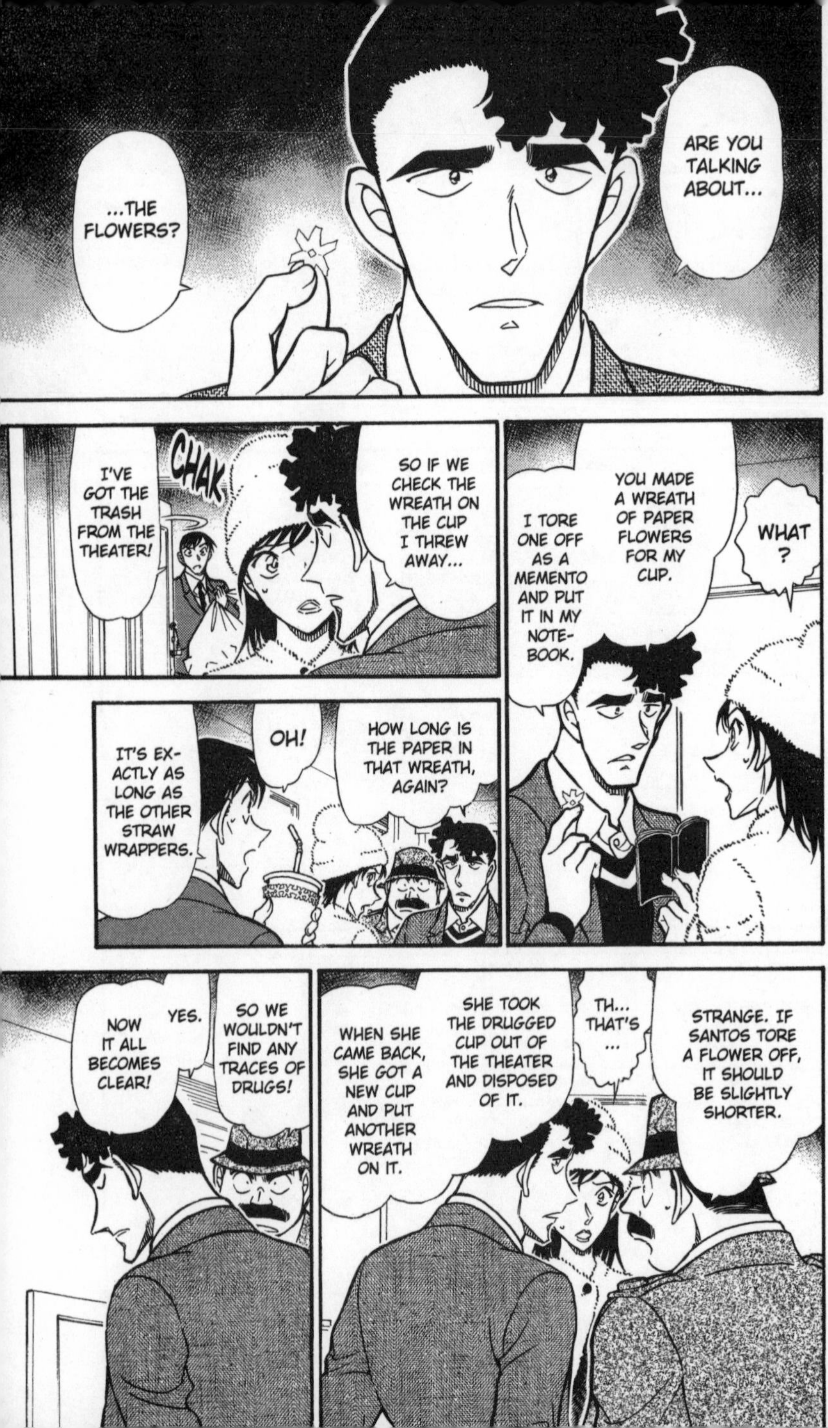
ARE YOU TALKING ABOUT...
...THE FLOWERS?
WHAT?
YOU MADE A WREATH OF PAPER FLOWERS FOR MY CUP.
I TORE ONE OFF AS A MEMENTO AND PUT IT IN MY NOTE-BOOK.
SO IF WE CHECK THE WREATH ON THE CUP I THREW AWAY...
CHAK
I'VE GOT THE TRASH FROM THE THEATER!
HOW LONG IS THE PAPER IN THAT WREATH, AGAIN?
OH!
IT'S EX-ACTLY AS LONG AS THE OTHER STRAW WRAPPERS.
STRANGE. IF SANTOS TORE A FLOWER OFF, IT SHOULD BE SLIGHTLY SHORTER.
TH... THAT'S ...
SHE TOOK THE DRUGGED CUP OUT OF THE THEATER AND DISPOSED OF IT.
WHEN SHE CAME BACK, SHE GOT A NEW CUP AND PUT ANOTHER WREATH ON IT.
SO WE WOULDN'T FIND ANY TRACES OF DRUGS!
YES.
NOW IT ALL BECOMES CLEAR!

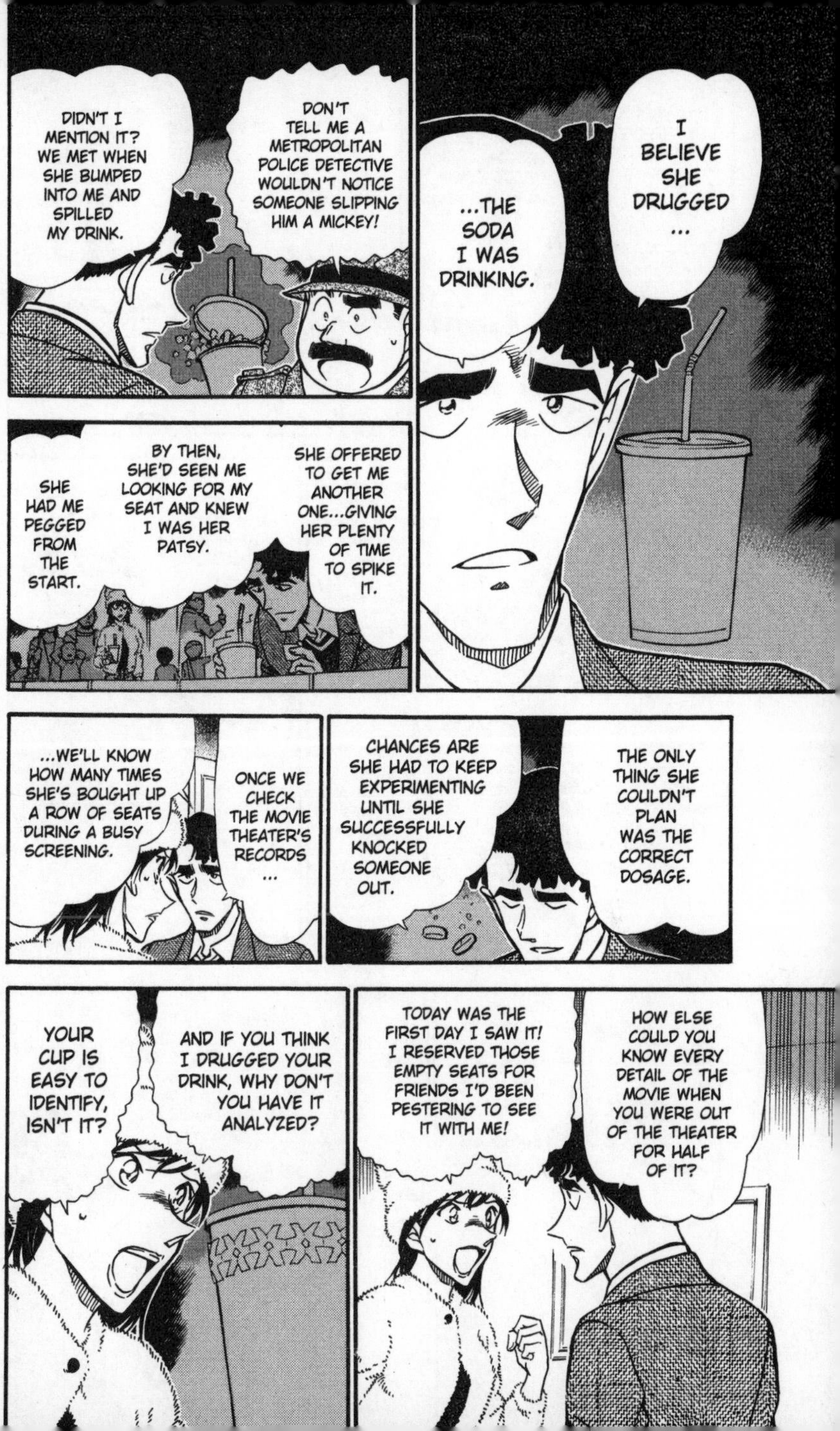
I BELIEVE SHE DRUGGED ...
...THE SODA I WAS DRINKING.
DON'T TELL ME A METROPOLITAN POLICE DETECTIVE WOULDN'T NOTICE SOMEONE SLIPPING HIM A MICKEY!
DIDN'T I MENTION IT? WE MET WHEN SHE BUMPED INTO ME AND SPILLED MY DRINK.
SHE OFFERED TO GET ME ANOTHER ONE...GIVING HER PLENTY OF TIME TO SPIKE IT.
BY THEN, SHE'D SEEN ME LOOKING FOR MY SEAT AND KNEW I WAS HER PATSY.
SHE HAD ME PEGGED FROM THE START.
THE ONLY THING SHE COULDN'T PLAN WAS THE CORRECT DOSAGE.
CHANCES ARE SHE HAD TO KEEP EXPERIMENTING UNTIL SHE SUCCESSFULLY KNOCKED SOMEONE OUT.
ONCE WE CHECK THE MOVIE THEATER'S RECORDS ...
...WE'LL KNOW HOW MANY TIMES SHE'S BOUGHT UP A ROW OF SEATS DURING A BUSY SCREENING.
HOW ELSE COULD YOU KNOW EVERY DETAIL OF THE MOVIE WHEN YOU WERE OUT OF THE THEATER FOR HALF OF IT?
TODAY WAS THE FIRST DAY I SAW IT! I RESERVED THOSE EMPTY SEATS FOR FRIENDS I'D BEEN PESTERING TO SEE IT WITH ME!
AND IF YOU THINK I DRUGGED YOUR DRINK, WHY DON'T YOU HAVE IT ANALYZED?
YOUR CUP IS EASY TO IDENTIFY, ISN'T IT?

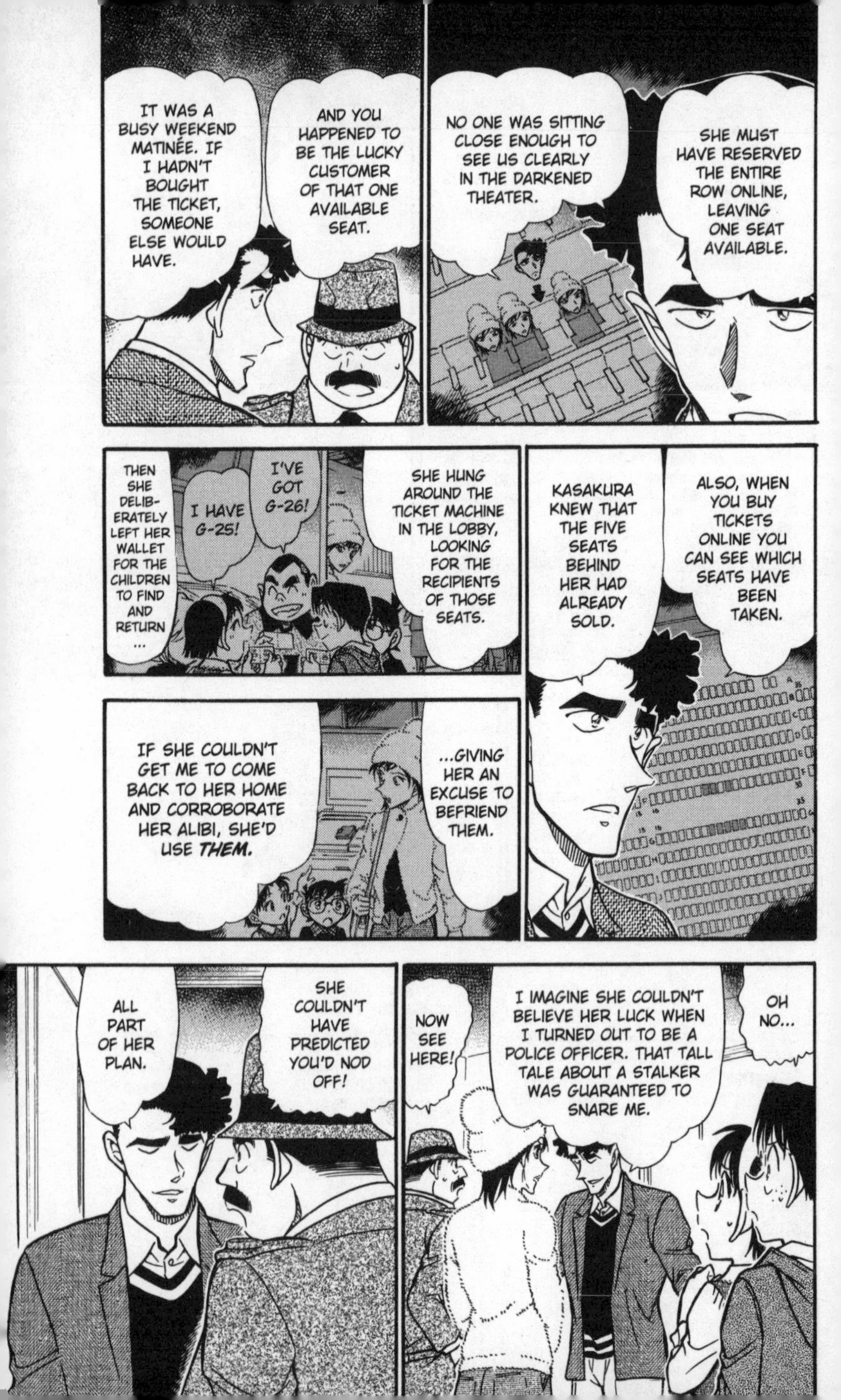
SHE MUST HAVE RESERVED THE ENTIRE ROW ONLINE, LEAVING ONE SEAT AVAILABLE.
NO ONE WAS SITTING CLOSE ENOUGH TO SEE US CLEARLY IN THE DARKENED THEATER.
AND YOU HAPPENED TO BE THE LUCKY CUSTOMER OF THAT ONE AVAILABLE SEAT.
IT WAS A BUSY WEEKEND MATINÉE. IF I HADN'T BOUGHT THE TICKET, SOMEONE ELSE WOULD HAVE.
ALSO, WHEN YOU BUY TICKETS ONLINE YOU CAN SEE WHICH SEATS HAVE BEEN TAKEN.
KASAKURA KNEW THAT THE FIVE SEATS BEHIND HER HAD ALREADY SOLD.
SHE HUNG AROUND THE TICKET MACHINE IN THE LOBBY, LOOKING FOR THE RECIPIENTS OF THOSE SEATS.
I'VE GOT G-26!
I HAVE G-25!
THEN SHE DELIBERATELY LEFT HER WALLET FOR THE CHILDREN TO FIND AND RETURN ...
...GIVING HER AN EXCUSE TO BEFRIEND THEM.
IF SHE COULDN'T GET ME TO COME BACK TO HER HOME AND CORROBORATE HER ALIBI, SHE'D USE ***THEM.***
OH NO...
I IMAGINE SHE COULDN'T BELIEVE HER LUCK WHEN I TURNED OUT TO BE A POLICE OFFICER. THAT TALL TALE ABOUT A STALKER WAS GUARANTEED TO SNARE ME.
NOW SEE HERE!
SHE COULDN'T HAVE PREDICTED YOU'D NOD OFF!
ALL PART OF HER PLAN.

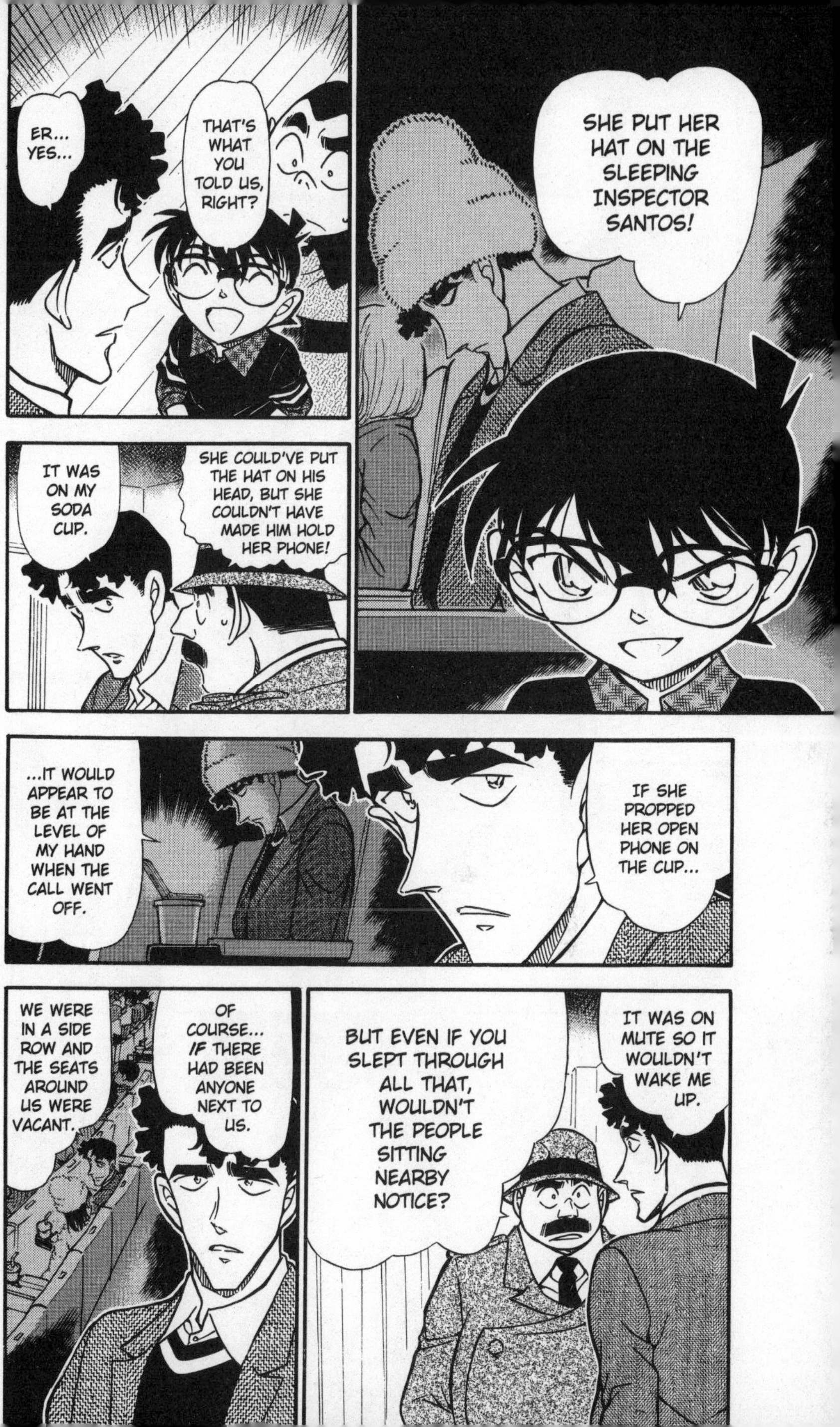
SHE PUT HER HAT ON THE SLEEPING INSPECTOR SANTOS!
THAT'S WHAT YOU TOLD US, RIGHT?
ER... YES...
SHE COULD'VE PUT THE HAT ON HIS HEAD, BUT SHE COULDN'T HAVE MADE HIM HOLD HER PHONE!
IT WAS ON MY SODA CUP.
IF SHE PROPPED HER OPEN PHONE ON THE CUP...
...IT WOULD APPEAR TO BE AT THE LEVEL OF MY HAND WHEN THE CALL WENT OFF.
IT WAS ON MUTE SO IT WOULDN'T WAKE ME UP.
BUT EVEN IF YOU SLEPT THROUGH ALL THAT, WOULDN'T THE PEOPLE SITTING NEARBY NOTICE?
OF COURSE... IF THERE HAD BEEN ANYONE NEXT TO US.
WE WERE IN A SIDE ROW AND THE SEATS AROUND US WERE VACANT.

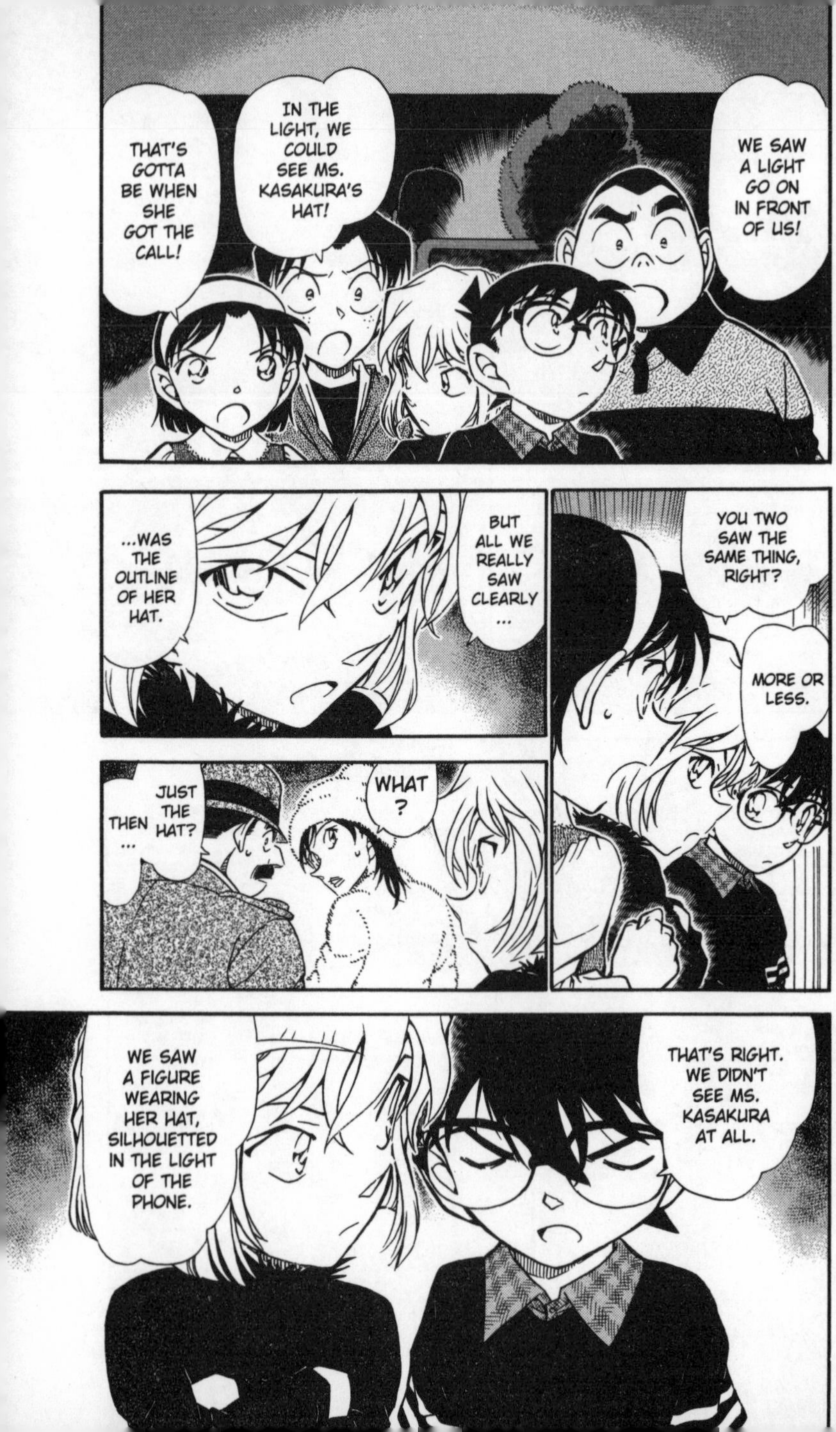
WE SAW A LIGHT GO ON IN FRONT OF US!
IN THE LIGHT, WE COULD SEE MS. KASAKURA'S HAT!
THAT'S GOTTA BE WHEN SHE GOT THE CALL!
YOU TWO SAW THE SAME THING, RIGHT?
MORE OR LESS.
BUT ALL WE REALLY SAW CLEARLY ...
...WAS THE OUTLINE OF HER HAT.
WHAT ?
THEN ... JUST THE HAT?
THAT'S RIGHT. WE DIDN'T SEE MS. KASAKURA AT ALL.
WE SAW A FIGURE WEARING HER HAT, SILHOUETTED IN THE LIGHT OF THE PHONE.

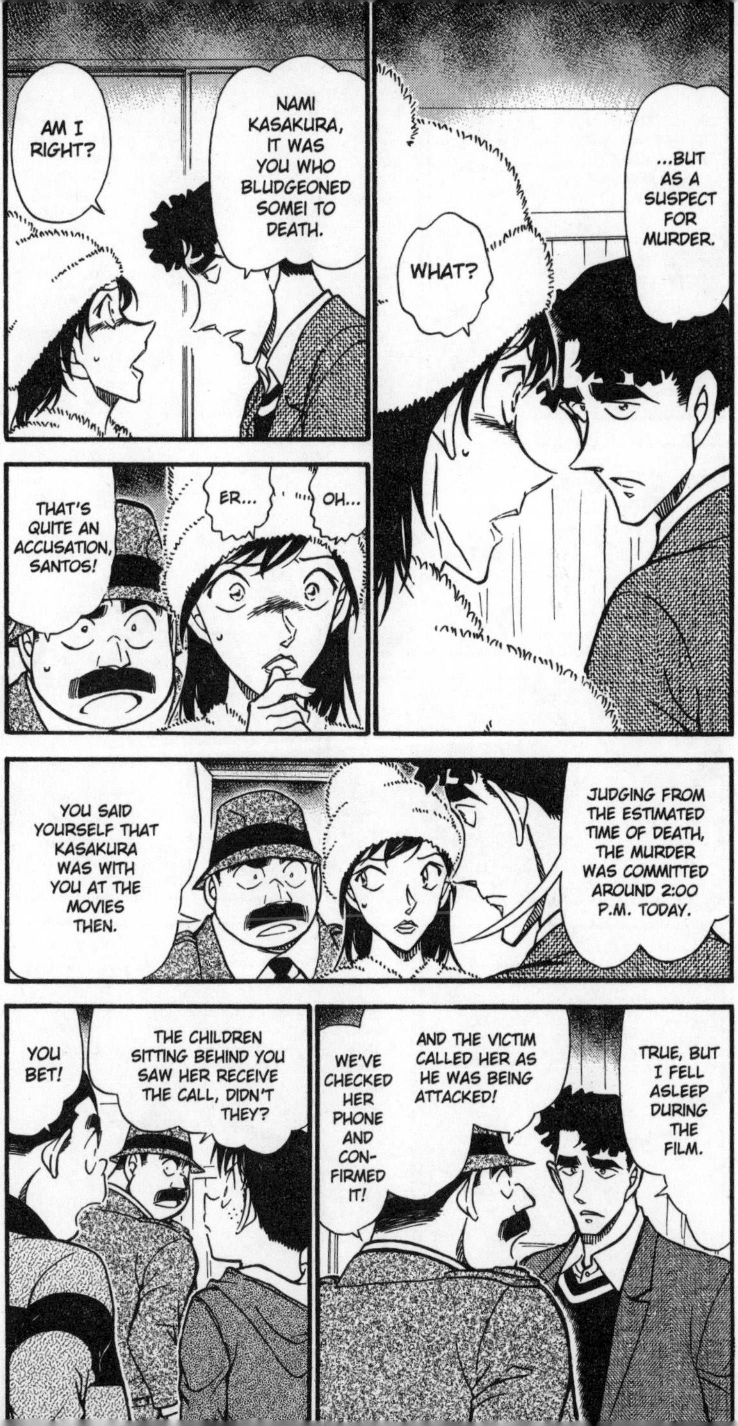
...BUT AS A SUSPECT FOR MURDER.
WHAT?
NAMI KASAKURA, IT WAS YOU WHO BLUDGEONED SOMEI TO DEATH.
AM I RIGHT?
OH...
ER...
THAT'S QUITE AN ACCUSATION, SANTOS!
JUDGING FROM THE ESTIMATED TIME OF DEATH, THE MURDER WAS COMMITTED AROUND 2:00 P.M. TODAY.
YOU SAID YOURSELF THAT KASAKURA WAS WITH YOU AT THE MOVIES THEN.
TRUE, BUT I FELL ASLEEP DURING THE FILM.
AND THE VICTIM CALLED HER AS HE WAS BEING ATTACKED!
WE'VE CHECKED HER PHONE AND CON-FIRMED IT!
THE CHILDREN SITTING BEHIND YOU SAW HER RECEIVE THE CALL, DIDN'T THEY?
YOU BET!

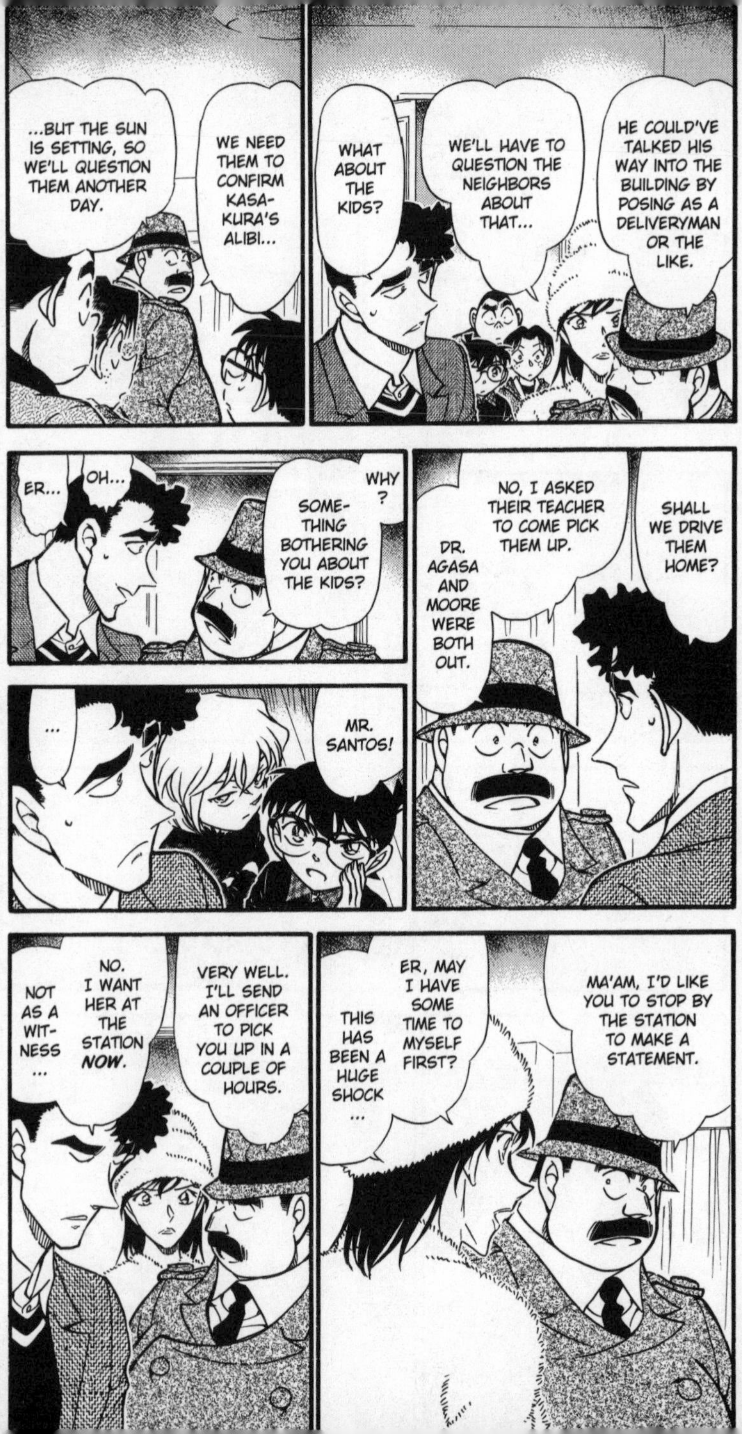
HE COULD'VE TALKED HIS WAY INTO THE BUILDING BY POSING AS A DELIVERYMAN OR THE LIKE.
WE'LL HAVE TO QUESTION THE NEIGHBORS ABOUT THAT...
WHAT ABOUT THE KIDS?
WE NEED THEM TO CONFIRM KASA-KURA'S ALIBI...
...BUT THE SUN IS SETTING, SO WE'LL QUESTION THEM ANOTHER DAY.
SHALL WE DRIVE THEM HOME?
NO, I ASKED THEIR TEACHER TO COME PICK THEM UP.
DR. AGASA AND MOORE WERE BOTH OUT.
WHY?
SOME-THING BOTHERING YOU ABOUT THE KIDS?
OH...
ER...
MR. SANTOS!
...
MA'AM, I'D LIKE YOU TO STOP BY THE STATION TO MAKE A STATEMENT.
ER, MAY I HAVE SOME TIME TO MYSELF FIRST?
THIS HAS BEEN A HUGE SHOCK...
VERY WELL. I'LL SEND AN OFFICER TO PICK YOU UP IN A COUPLE OF HOURS.
NO. I WANT HER AT THE STATION *NOW*.
NOT AS A WIT-NESS...

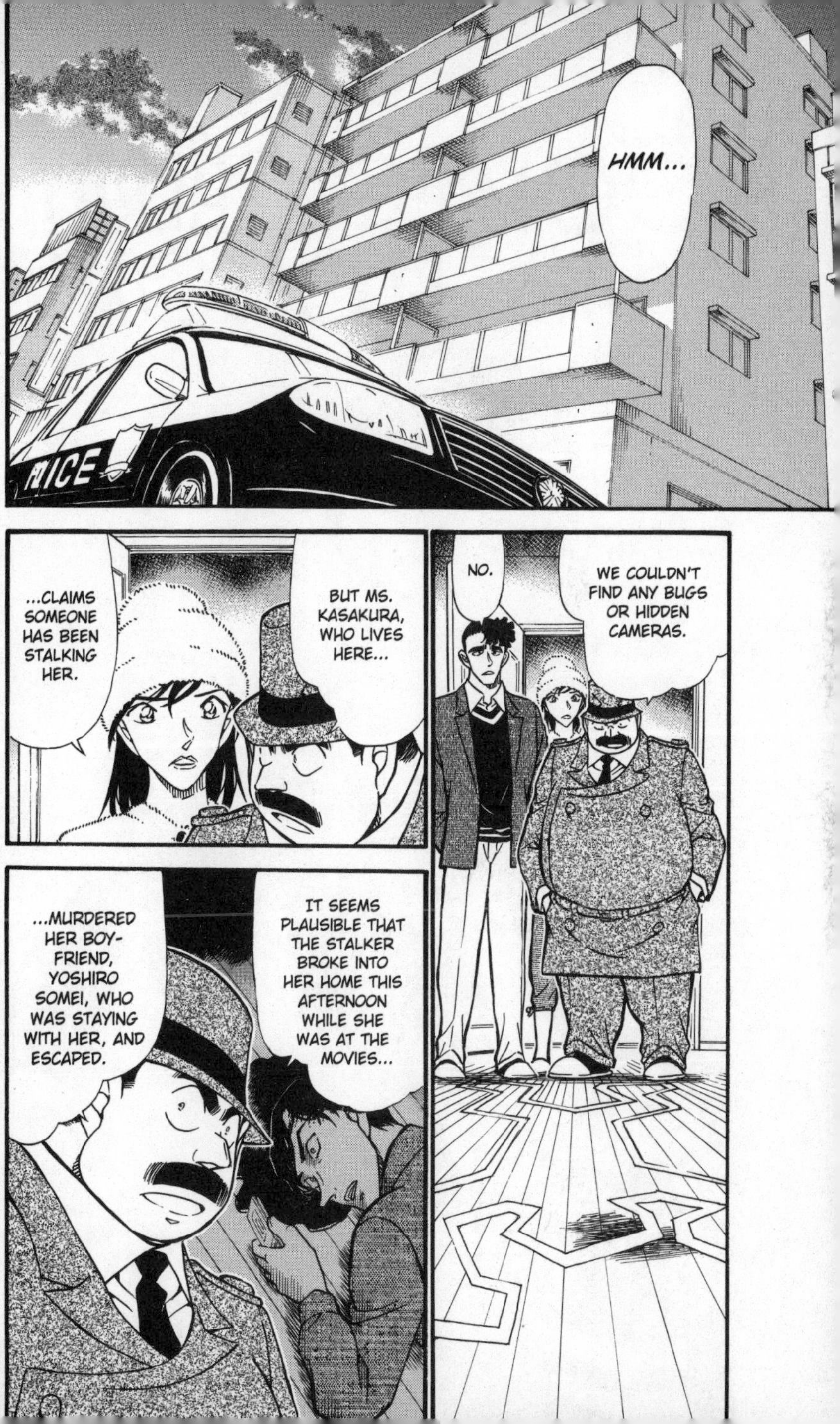
HMM...
WE COULDN'T FIND ANY BUGS OR HIDDEN CAMERAS.
NO.
BUT MS. KASAKURA, WHO LIVES HERE...
...CLAIMS SOMEONE HAS BEEN STALKING HER.
IT SEEMS PLAUSIBLE THAT THE STALKER BROKE INTO HER HOME THIS AFTERNOON WHILE SHE WAS AT THE MOVIES...
...MURDERED HER BOY-FRIEND, YOSHIRO SOMEI, WHO WAS STAYING WITH HER, AND ESCAPED.

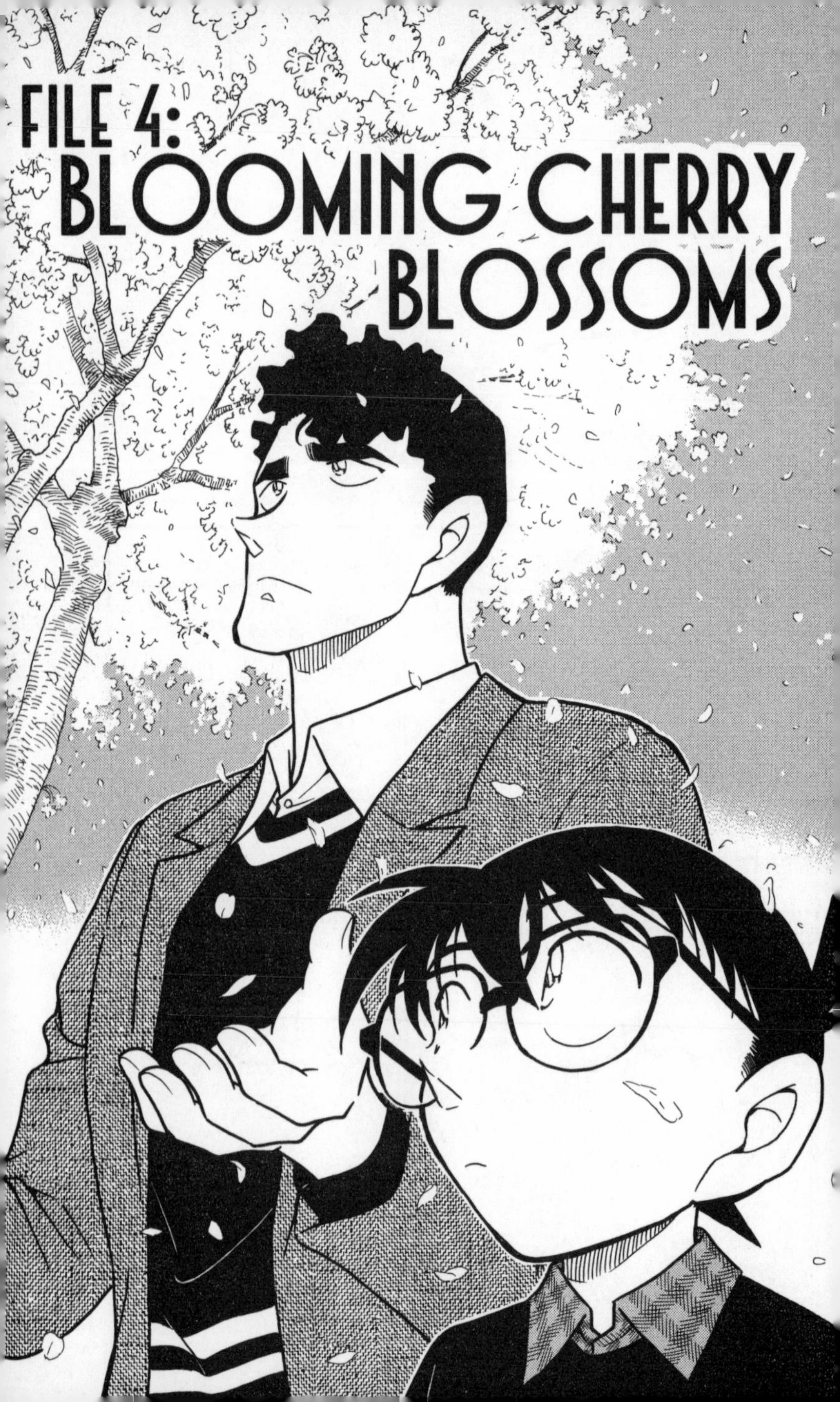
FILE 4:
BLOOMING CHERRY BLOSSOMS

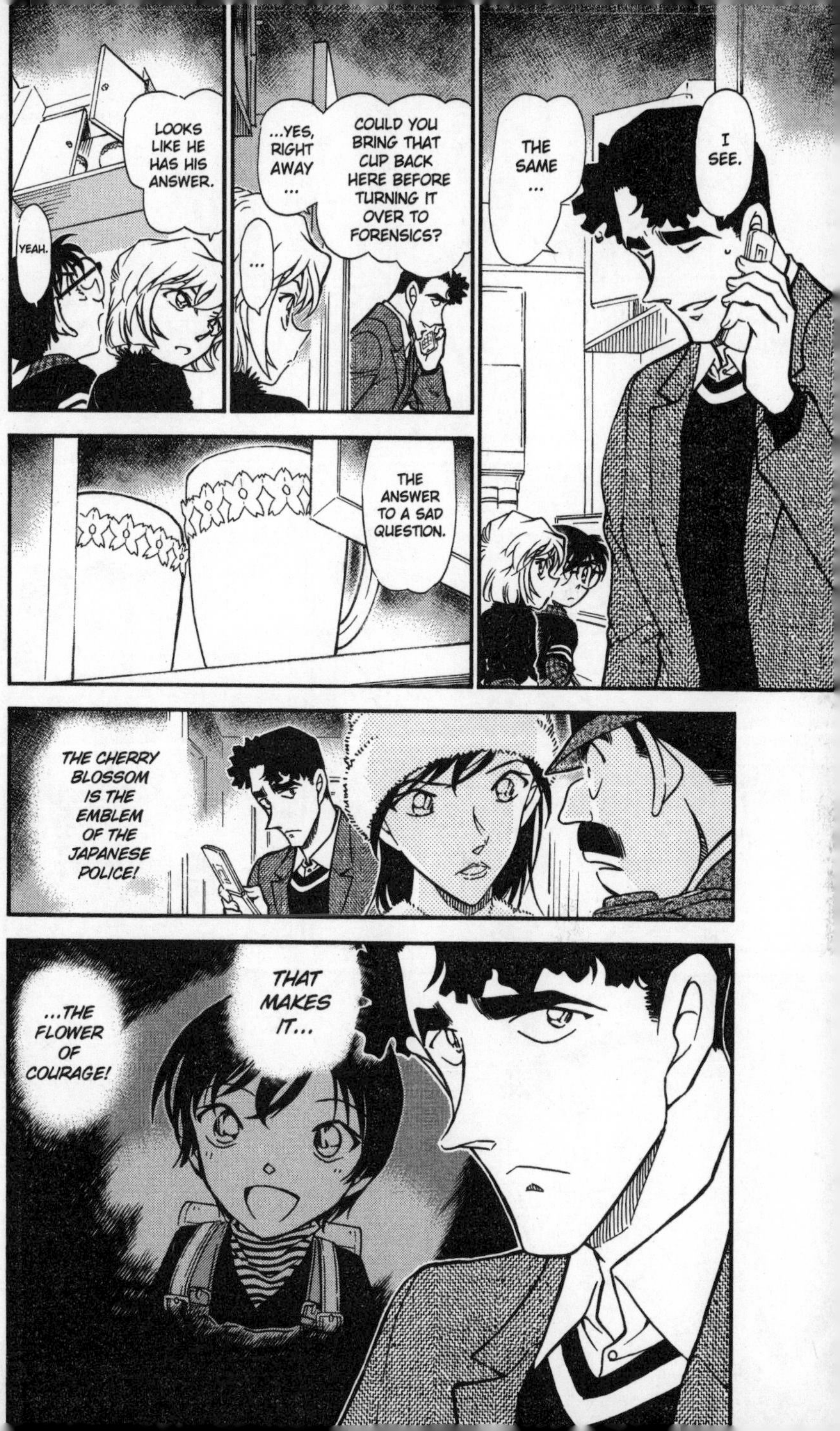
I SEE.
THE SAME ...
COULD YOU BRING THAT CUP BACK HERE BEFORE TURNING IT OVER TO FORENSICS?
...YES, RIGHT AWAY ...
...
LOOKS LIKE HE HAS HIS ANSWER.
YEAH.
THE ANSWER TO A SAD QUESTION.
THE CHERRY BLOSSOM IS THE EMBLEM OF THE JAPANESE POLICE!
THAT MAKES IT...
...THE FLOWER OF COURAGE!

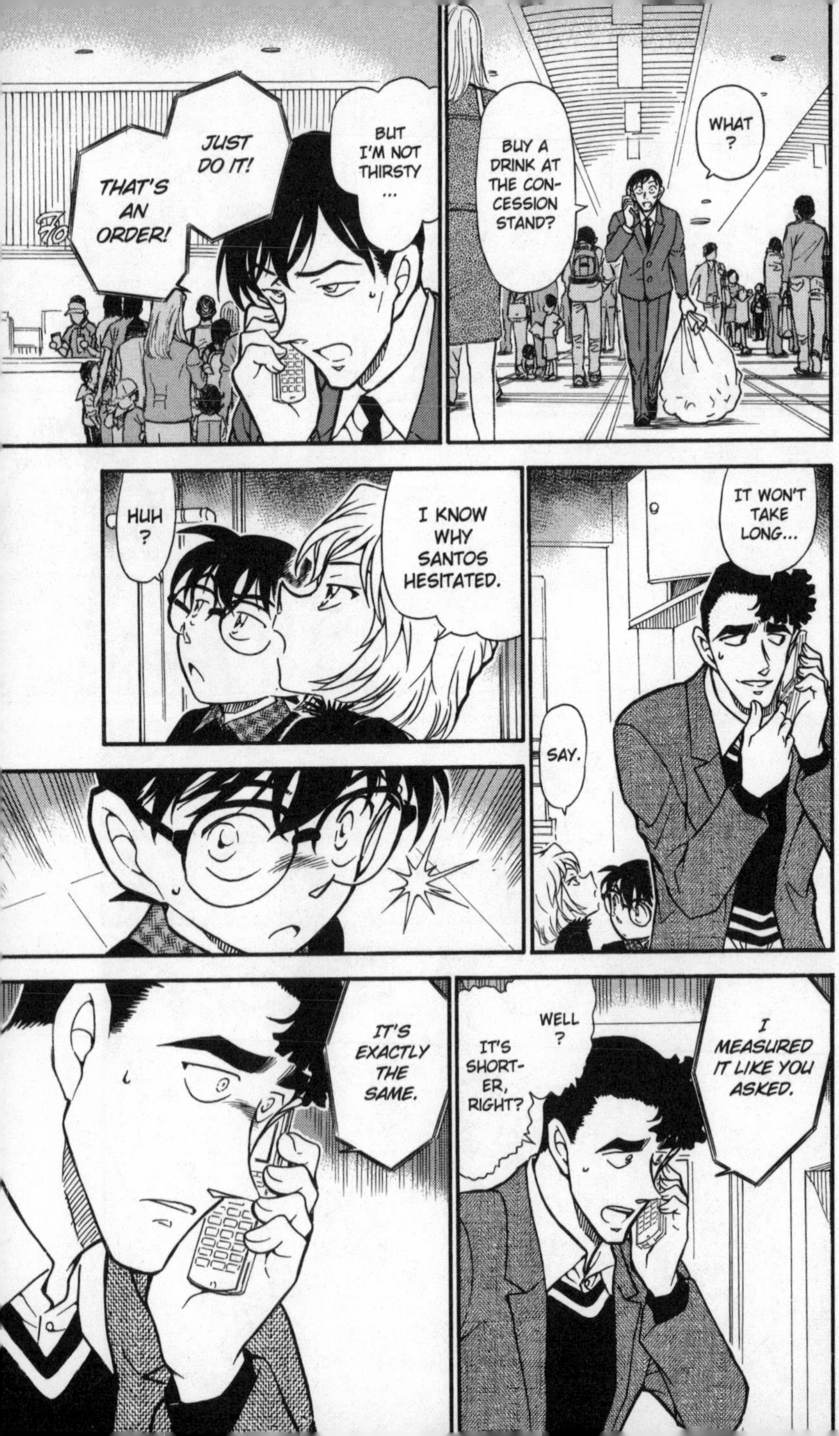
WHAT?
BUY A DRINK AT THE CONCESSION STAND?
BUT I'M NOT THIRSTY...
JUST DO IT!
THAT'S AN ORDER!
IT WON'T TAKE LONG...
SAY.
I KNOW WHY SANTOS HESITATED.
HUH?
I MEASURED IT LIKE YOU ASKED.
WELL?
IT'S SHORTER, RIGHT?
IT'S EXACTLY THE SAME.

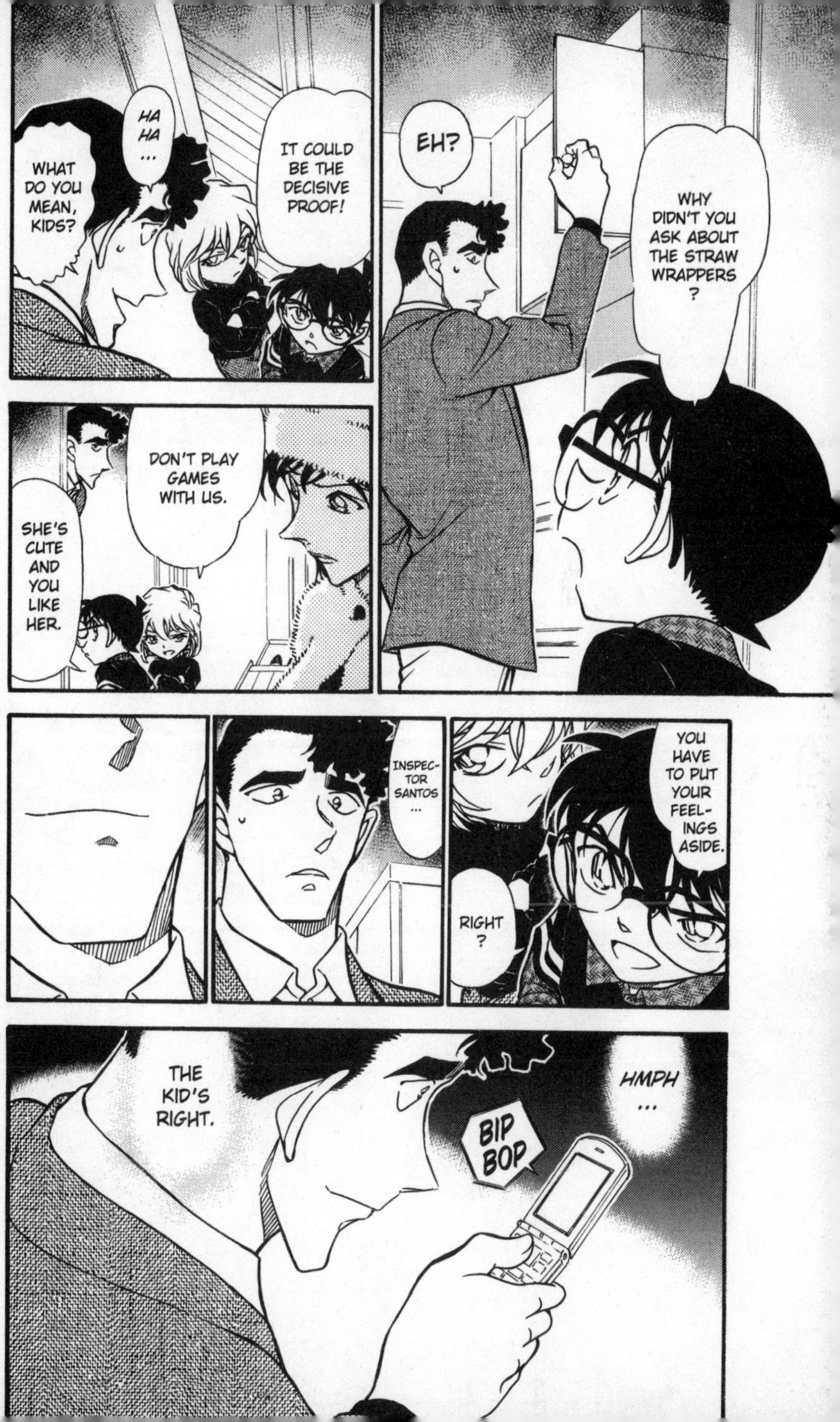
WHY DIDN'T YOU ASK ABOUT THE STRAW WRAPPERS?
EH?
IT COULD BE THE DECISIVE PROOF!
HA HA...
WHAT DO YOU MEAN, KIDS?
DON'T PLAY GAMES WITH US.
SHE'S CUTE AND YOU LIKE HER.
YOU HAVE TO PUT YOUR FEELINGS ASIDE.
RIGHT?
INSPECTOR SANTOS...
HMPH...
BIP BOP
THE KID'S RIGHT.

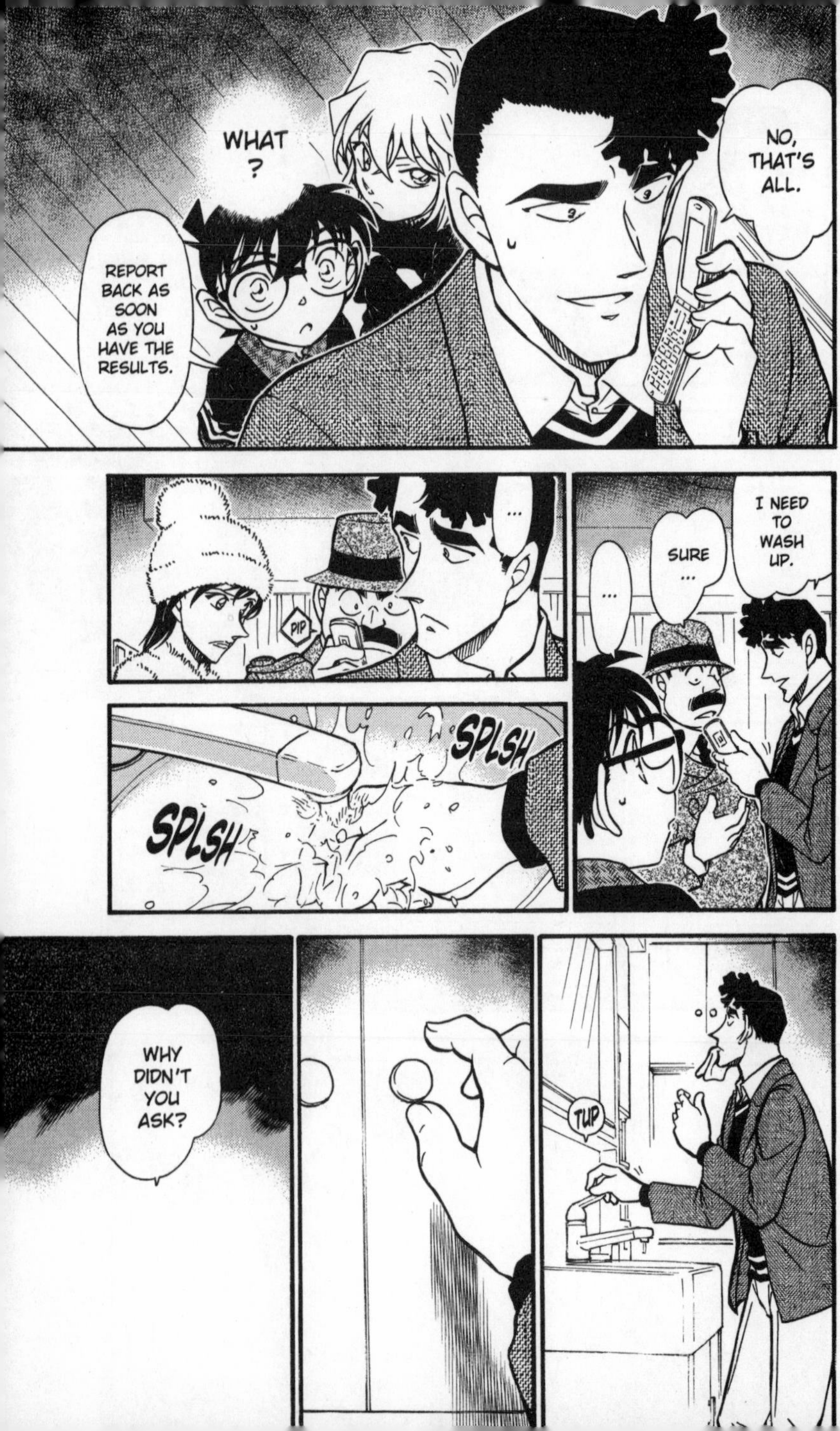
NO, THAT'S ALL.
WHAT ?
REPORT BACK AS SOON AS YOU HAVE THE RESULTS.
I NEED TO WASH UP.
SURE ...
...
...
PIP
SPLSH
SPLSH
TUP
WHY DIDN'T YOU ASK?

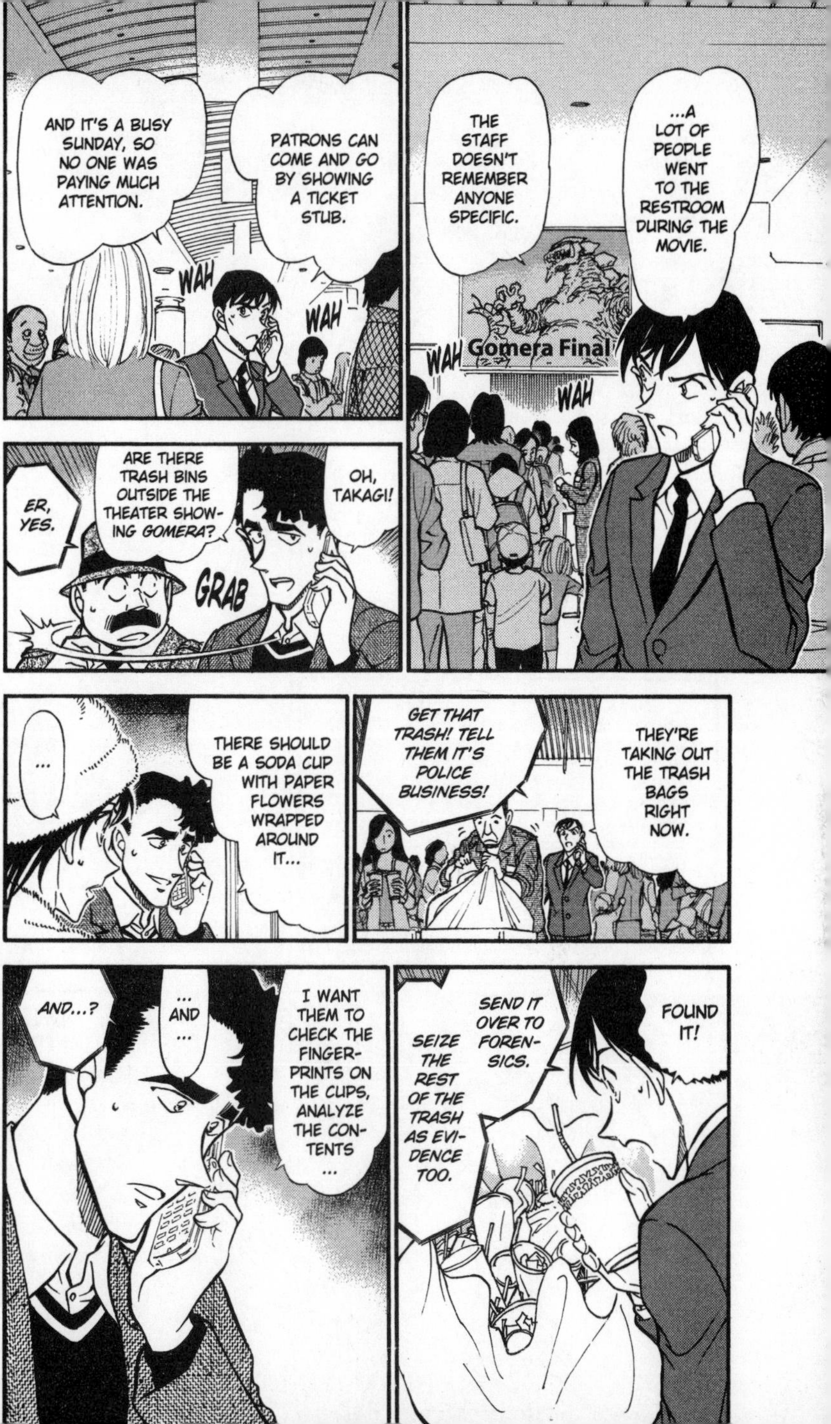
...A LOT OF PEOPLE WENT TO THE RESTROOM DURING THE MOVIE.
THE STAFF DOESN'T REMEMBER ANYONE SPECIFIC.
WAH
Gomera Final
WAH
PATRONS CAN COME AND GO BY SHOWING A TICKET STUB.
AND IT'S A BUSY SUNDAY, SO NO ONE WAS PAYING MUCH ATTENTION.
WAH
WAH
OH, TAKAGI!
ARE THERE TRASH BINS OUTSIDE THE THEATER SHOWING GOMERA?
ER, YES.
GRAB
THEY'RE TAKING OUT THE TRASH BAGS RIGHT NOW.
GET THAT TRASH! TELL THEM IT'S POLICE BUSINESS!
THERE SHOULD BE A SODA CUP WITH PAPER FLOWERS WRAPPED AROUND IT...
...
FOUND IT!
SEND IT OVER TO FORENSICS.
SEIZE THE REST OF THE TRASH AS EVIDENCE TOO.
I WANT THEM TO CHECK THE FINGERPRINTS ON THE CUPS, ANALYZE THE CONTENTS...
...AND...
AND...?

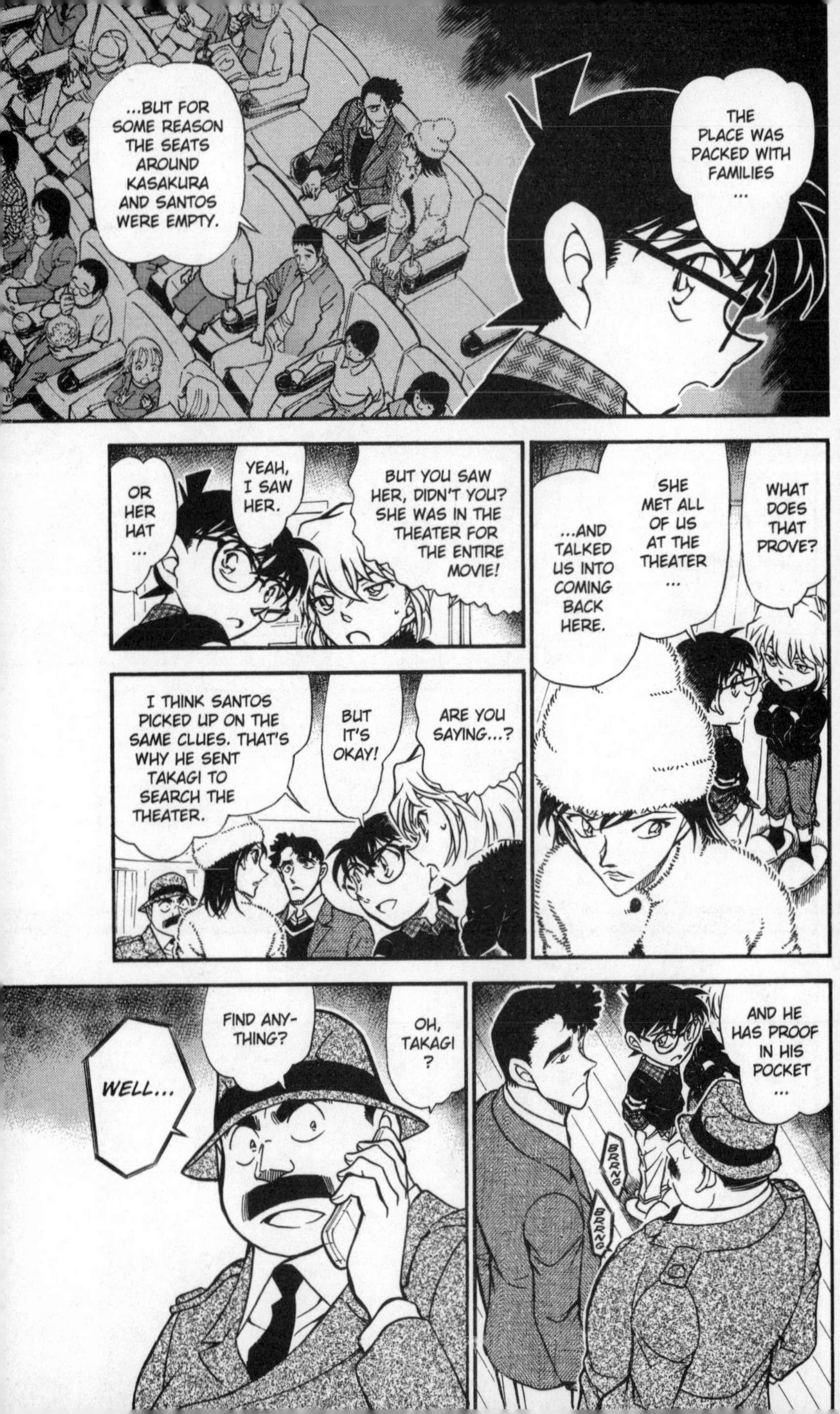
THE PLACE WAS PACKED WITH FAMILIES...
...BUT FOR SOME REASON THE SEATS AROUND KASAKURA AND SANTOS WERE EMPTY.
WHAT DOES THAT PROVE?
SHE MET ALL OF US AT THE THEATER...
...AND TALKED US INTO COMING BACK HERE.
BUT YOU SAW HER, DIDN'T YOU? SHE WAS IN THE THEATER FOR THE ENTIRE MOVIE!
YEAH, I SAW HER.
OR HER HAT...
ARE YOU SAYING...?
BUT IT'S OKAY!
I THINK SANTOS PICKED UP ON THE SAME CLUES. THAT'S WHY HE SENT TAKAGI TO SEARCH THE THEATER.
AND HE HAS PROOF IN HIS POCKET...
BRRNG
BRRNG
OH, TAKAGI?
FIND ANY-THING?
WELL...

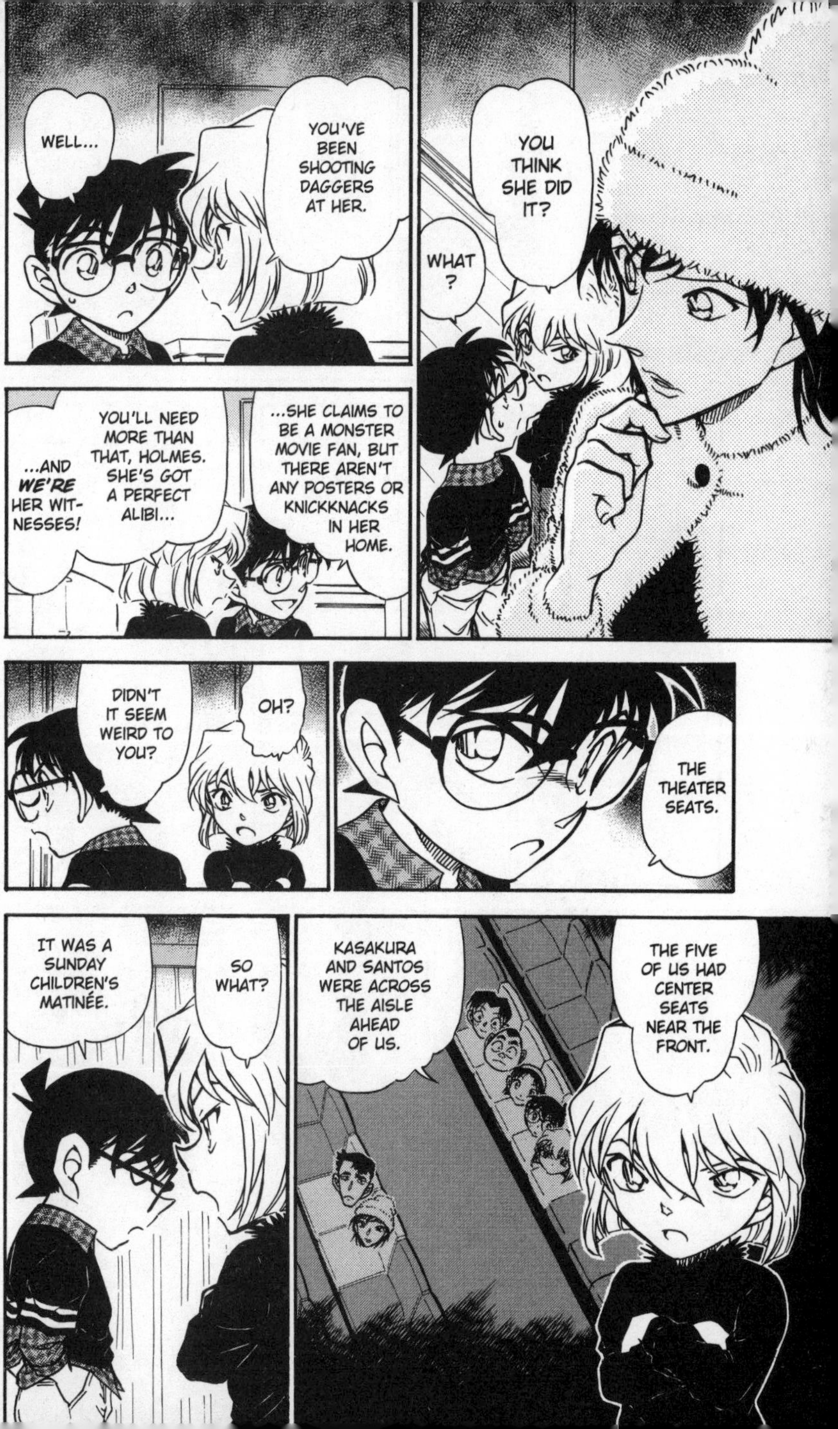
YOU THINK SHE DID IT?
WHAT?
YOU'VE BEEN SHOOTING DAGGERS AT HER.
WELL...
...SHE CLAIMS TO BE A MONSTER MOVIE FAN, BUT THERE AREN'T ANY POSTERS OR KNICKKNACKS IN HER HOME.
YOU'LL NEED MORE THAN THAT, HOLMES. SHE'S GOT A PERFECT ALIBI...
...AND *WE'RE* HER WITNESSES!
THE THEATER SEATS.
OH?
DIDN'T IT SEEM WEIRD TO YOU?
THE FIVE OF US HAD CENTER SEATS NEAR THE FRONT.
KASAKURA AND SANTOS WERE ACROSS THE AISLE AHEAD OF US.
SO WHAT?
IT WAS A SUNDAY CHILDREN'S MATINÉE.

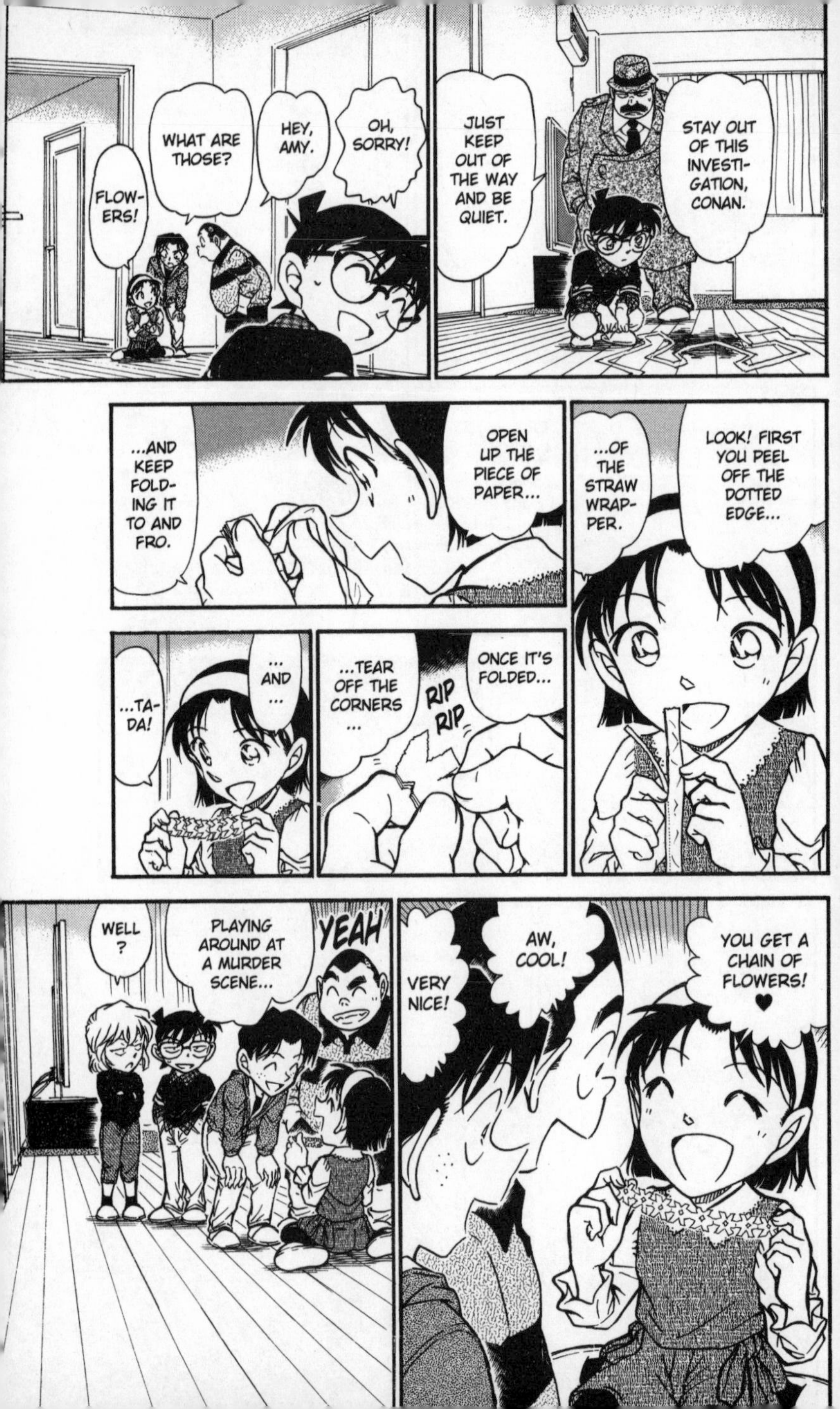
STAY OUT OF THIS INVESTIGATION, CONAN.
JUST KEEP OUT OF THE WAY AND BE QUIET.
OH, SORRY!
HEY, AMY.
WHAT ARE THOSE?
FLOWERS!
LOOK! FIRST YOU PEEL OFF THE DOTTED EDGE...
...OF THE STRAW WRAPPER.
OPEN UP THE PIECE OF PAPER...
...AND KEEP FOLDING IT TO AND FRO.
ONCE IT'S FOLDED...
RIP RIP
...TEAR OFF THE CORNERS ...
... AND ...
...TA-DA!
YOU GET A CHAIN OF FLOWERS! ♥
AW, COOL!
VERY NICE!
YEAH
PLAYING AROUND AT A MURDER SCENE...
WELL ?

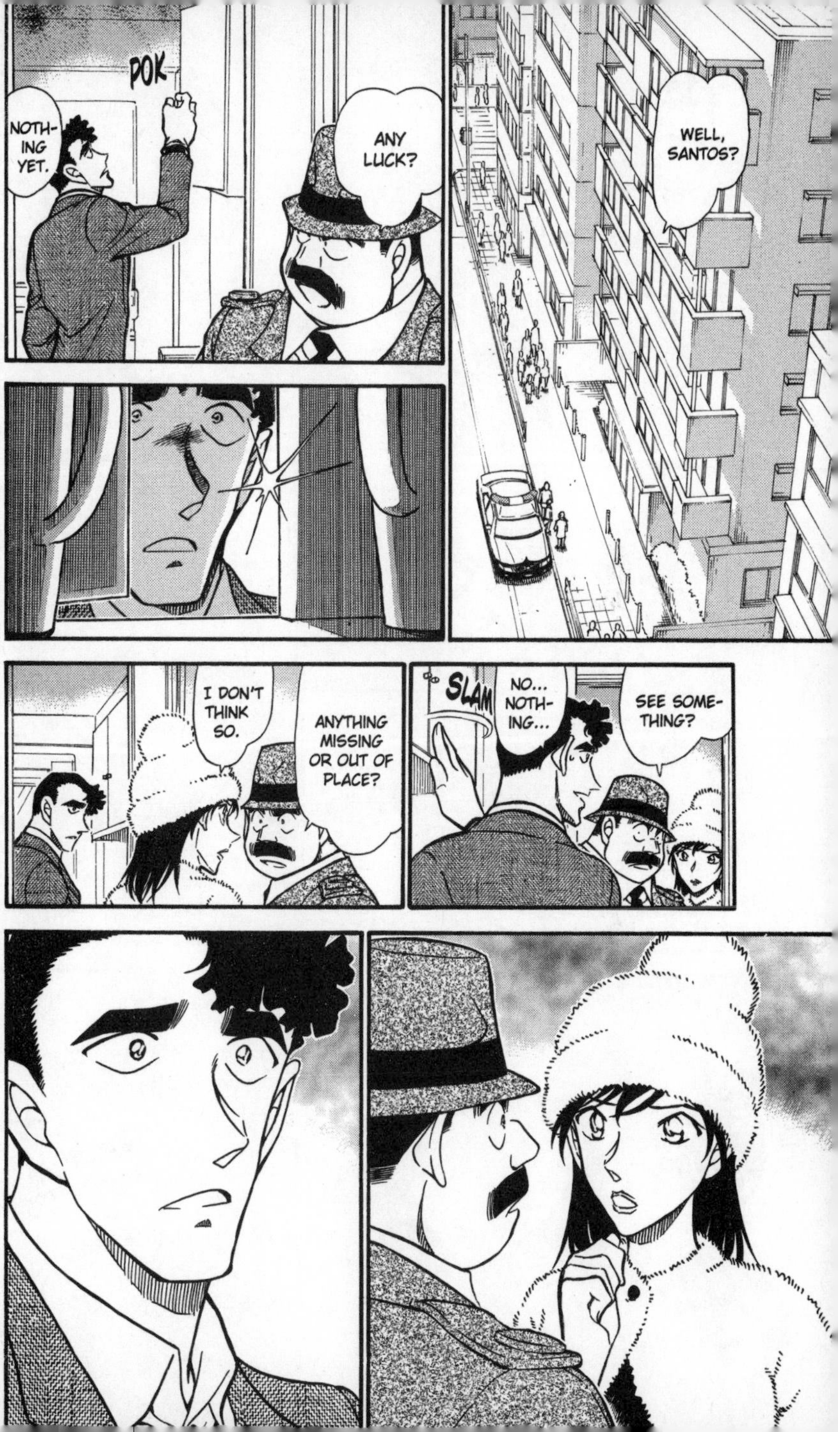
WELL, SANTOS?
ANY LUCK?
POK
NOTH-ING YET.
SEE SOME-THING?
NO... NOTH-ING...
SLAM
ANYTHING MISSING OR OUT OF PLACE?
I DON'T THINK SO.

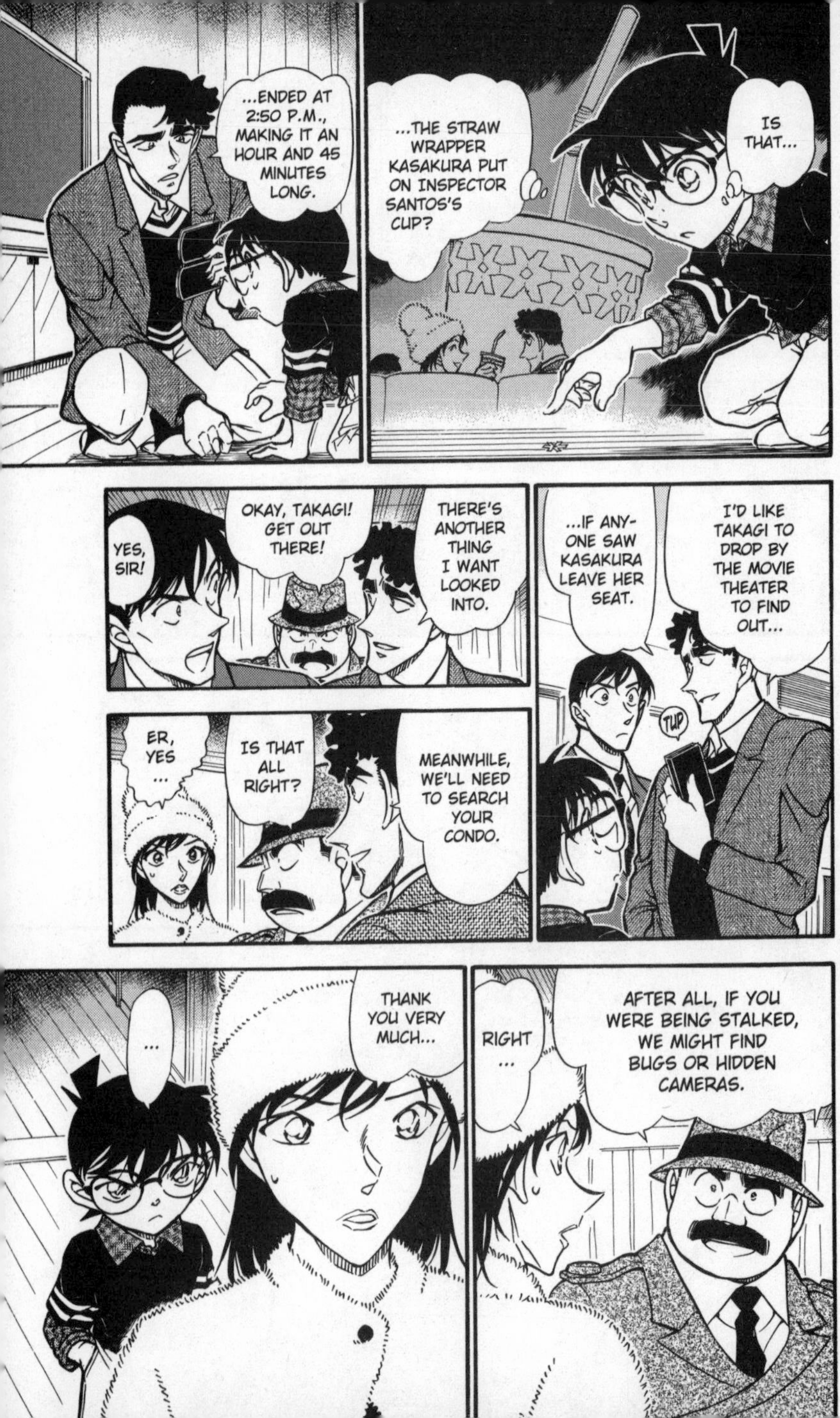
IS THAT...
...THE STRAW WRAPPER KASAKURA PUT ON INSPECTOR SANTOS'S CUP?
...ENDED AT 2:50 P.M., MAKING IT AN HOUR AND 45 MINUTES LONG.
I'D LIKE TAKAGI TO DROP BY THE MOVIE THEATER TO FIND OUT...
...IF ANYONE SAW KASAKURA LEAVE HER SEAT.
TUP
THERE'S ANOTHER THING I WANT LOOKED INTO.
OKAY, TAKAGI! GET OUT THERE!
YES, SIR!
MEANWHILE, WE'LL NEED TO SEARCH YOUR CONDO.
IS THAT ALL RIGHT?
ER, YES ...
AFTER ALL, IF YOU WERE BEING STALKED, WE MIGHT FIND BUGS OR HIDDEN CAMERAS.
RIGHT ...
THANK YOU VERY MUCH...
...

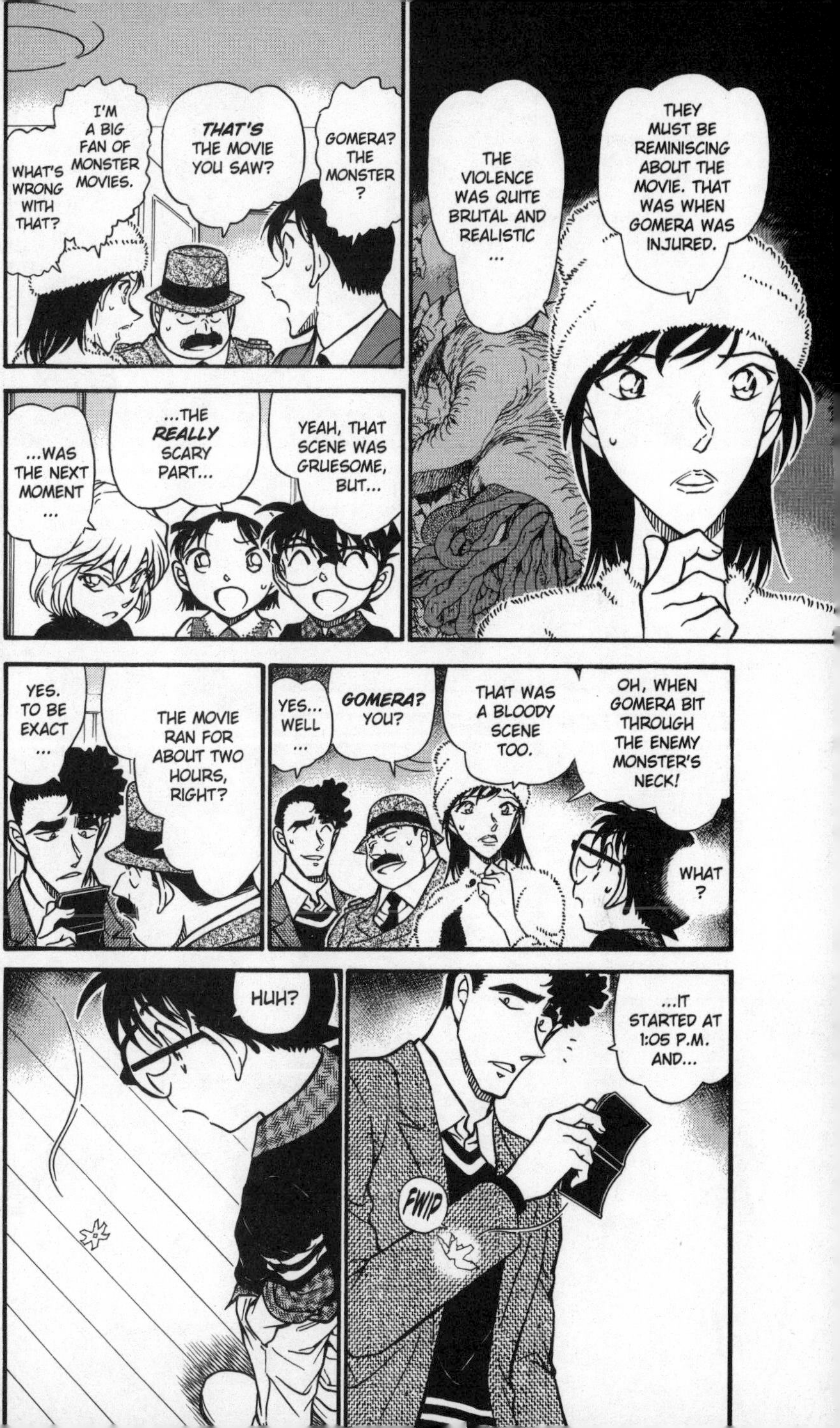
THEY MUST BE REMINISCING ABOUT THE MOVIE. THAT WAS WHEN GOMERA WAS INJURED.
THE VIOLENCE WAS QUITE BRUTAL AND REALISTIC ...
GOMERA? THE MONSTER ?
THAT'S THE MOVIE YOU SAW?
I'M A BIG FAN OF MONSTER MOVIES.
WHAT'S WRONG WITH THAT?
YEAH, THAT SCENE WAS GRUESOME, BUT...
...THE *REALLY* SCARY PART...
...WAS THE NEXT MOMENT ...
OH, WHEN GOMERA BIT THROUGH THE ENEMY MONSTER'S NECK!
THAT WAS A BLOODY SCENE TOO.
GOMERA? YOU?
YES... WELL ...
WHAT ?
THE MOVIE RAN FOR ABOUT TWO HOURS, RIGHT?
YES. TO BE EXACT ...
...IT STARTED AT 1:05 P.M. AND...
FWIP
HUH?

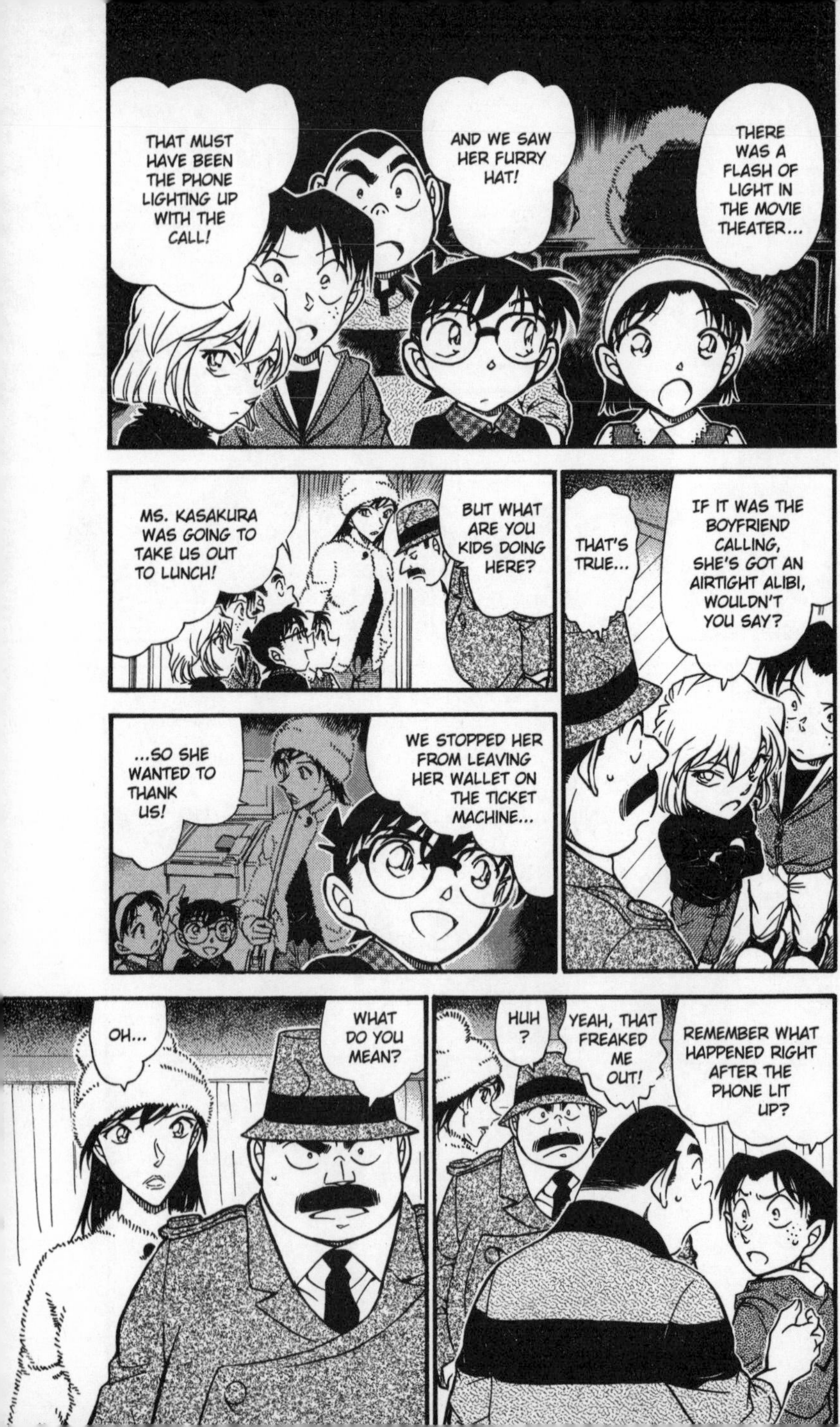
THERE WAS A FLASH OF LIGHT IN THE MOVIE THEATER...
AND WE SAW HER FURRY HAT!
THAT MUST HAVE BEEN THE PHONE LIGHTING UP WITH THE CALL!
IF IT WAS THE BOYFRIEND CALLING, SHE'S GOT AN AIRTIGHT ALIBI, WOULDN'T YOU SAY?
THAT'S TRUE...
BUT WHAT ARE YOU KIDS DOING HERE?
MS. KASAKURA WAS GOING TO TAKE US OUT TO LUNCH!
WE STOPPED HER FROM LEAVING HER WALLET ON THE TICKET MACHINE...
...SO SHE WANTED TO THANK US!
REMEMBER WHAT HAPPENED RIGHT AFTER THE PHONE LIT UP?
YEAH, THAT FREAKED ME OUT!
HUH?
WHAT DO YOU MEAN?
OH...

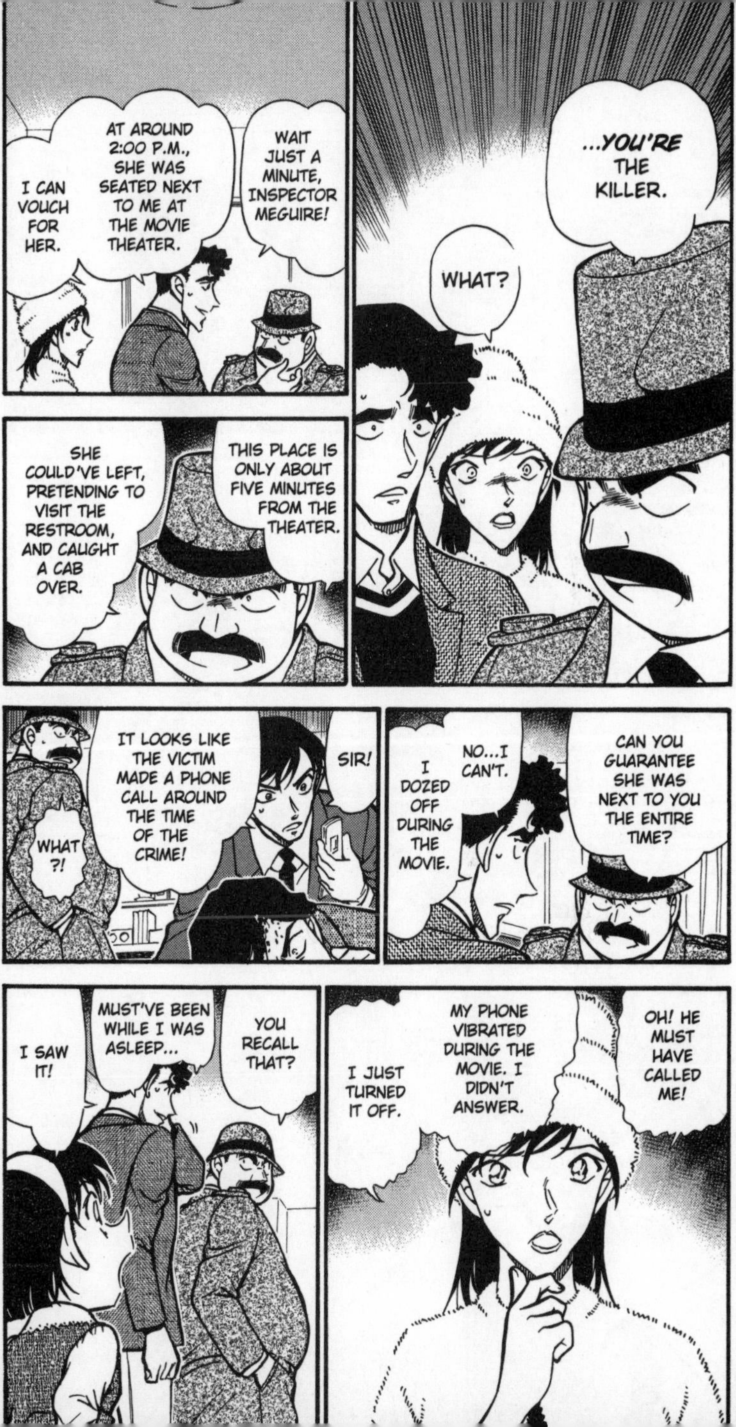

...YOU'RE THE KILLER.
WHAT?
WAIT JUST A MINUTE, INSPECTOR MEGUIRE!
AT AROUND 2:00 P.M., SHE WAS SEATED NEXT TO ME AT THE MOVIE THEATER.
I CAN VOUCH FOR HER.
THIS PLACE IS ONLY ABOUT FIVE MINUTES FROM THE THEATER.
SHE COULD'VE LEFT, PRETENDING TO VISIT THE RESTROOM, AND CAUGHT A CAB OVER.
CAN YOU GUARANTEE SHE WAS NEXT TO YOU THE ENTIRE TIME?
NO...I CAN'T.
I DOZED OFF DURING THE MOVIE.
SIR!
IT LOOKS LIKE THE VICTIM MADE A PHONE CALL AROUND THE TIME OF THE CRIME!
WHAT?!
OH! HE MUST HAVE CALLED ME!
MY PHONE VIBRATED DURING THE MOVIE. I DIDN'T ANSWER.
I JUST TURNED IT OFF.
YOU RECALL THAT?
MUST'VE BEEN WHILE I WAS ASLEEP...
I SAW IT!

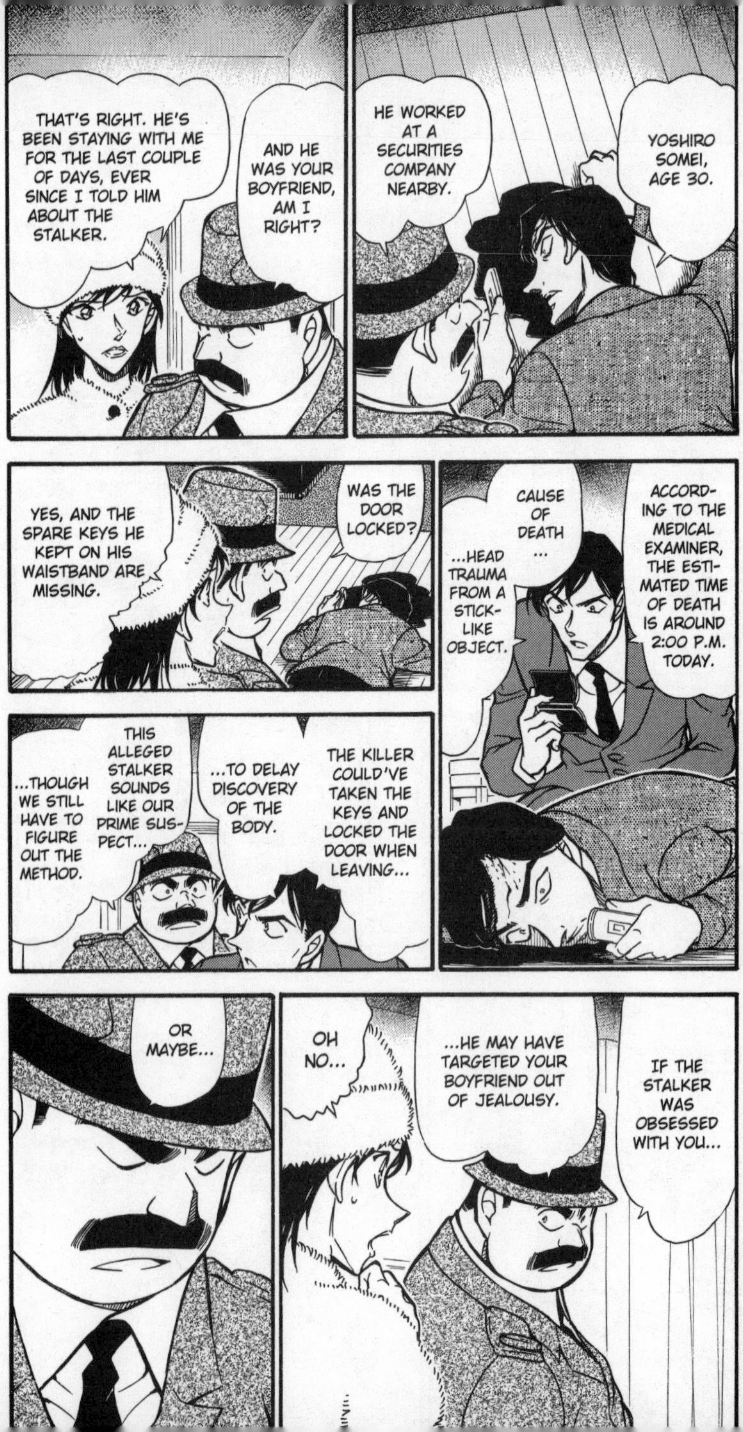
YOSHIRO SOMEI, AGE 30.
HE WORKED AT A SECURITIES COMPANY NEARBY.
AND HE WAS YOUR BOYFRIEND, AM I RIGHT?
THAT'S RIGHT. HE'S BEEN STAYING WITH ME FOR THE LAST COUPLE OF DAYS, EVER SINCE I TOLD HIM ABOUT THE STALKER.
ACCORDING TO THE MEDICAL EXAMINER, THE ESTIMATED TIME OF DEATH IS AROUND 2:00 P.M. TODAY.
CAUSE OF DEATH...
...HEAD TRAUMA FROM A STICK-LIKE OBJECT.
WAS THE DOOR LOCKED?
YES, AND THE SPARE KEYS HE KEPT ON HIS WAISTBAND ARE MISSING.
THE KILLER COULD'VE TAKEN THE KEYS AND LOCKED THE DOOR WHEN LEAVING...
...TO DELAY DISCOVERY OF THE BODY.
THIS ALLEGED STALKER SOUNDS LIKE OUR PRIME SUSPECT...
...THOUGH WE STILL HAVE TO FIGURE OUT THE METHOD.
IF THE STALKER WAS OBSESSED WITH YOU...
...HE MAY HAVE TARGETED YOUR BOYFRIEND OUT OF JEALOUSY.
OH NO...
OR MAYBE...

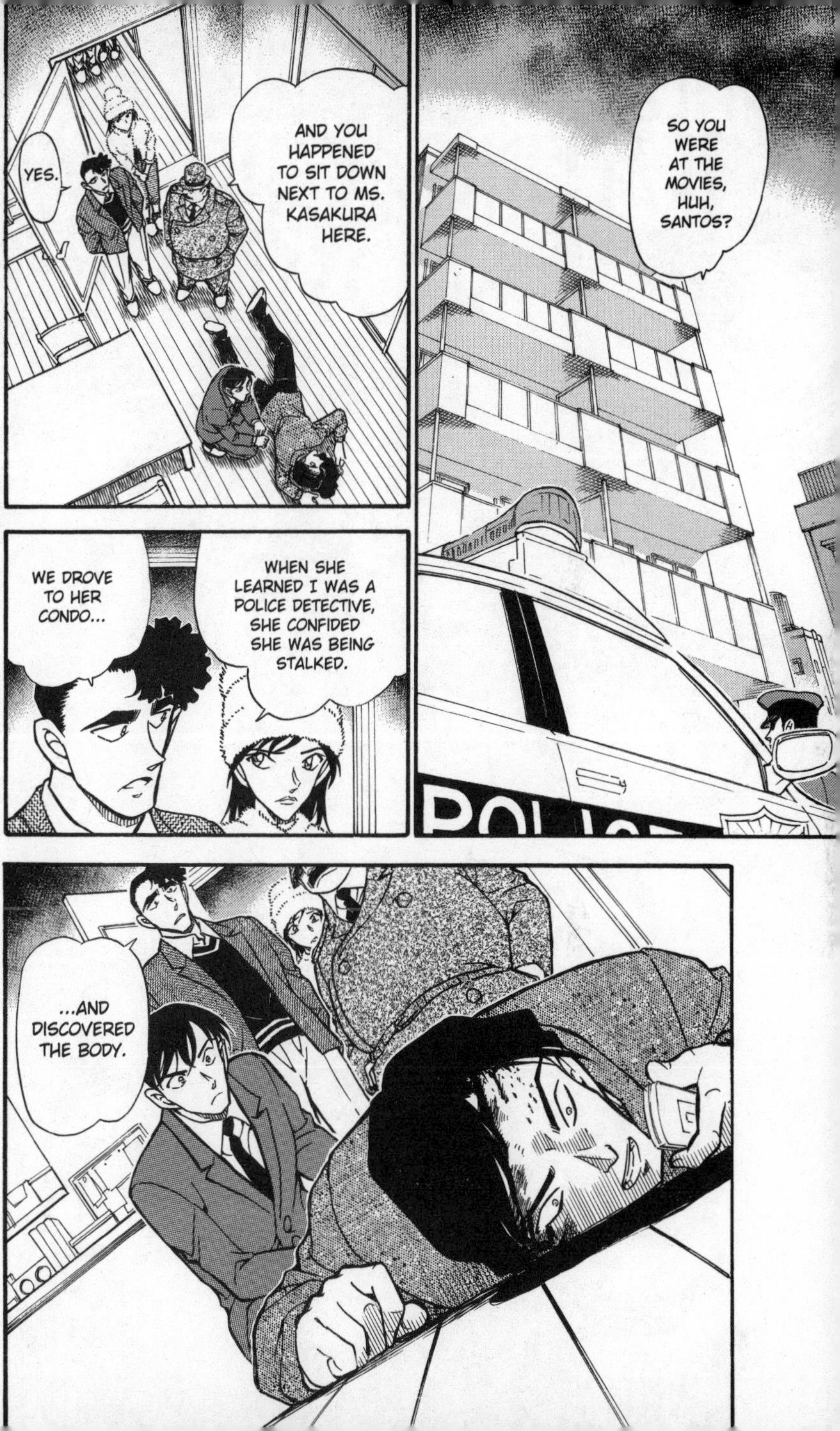
SO YOU WERE AT THE MOVIES, HUH, SANTOS?
AND YOU HAPPENED TO SIT DOWN NEXT TO MS. KASAKURA HERE.
YES.
WHEN SHE LEARNED I WAS A POLICE DETECTIVE, SHE CONFIDED SHE WAS BEING STALKED.
WE DROVE TO HER CONDO...
...AND DISCOVERED THE BODY.

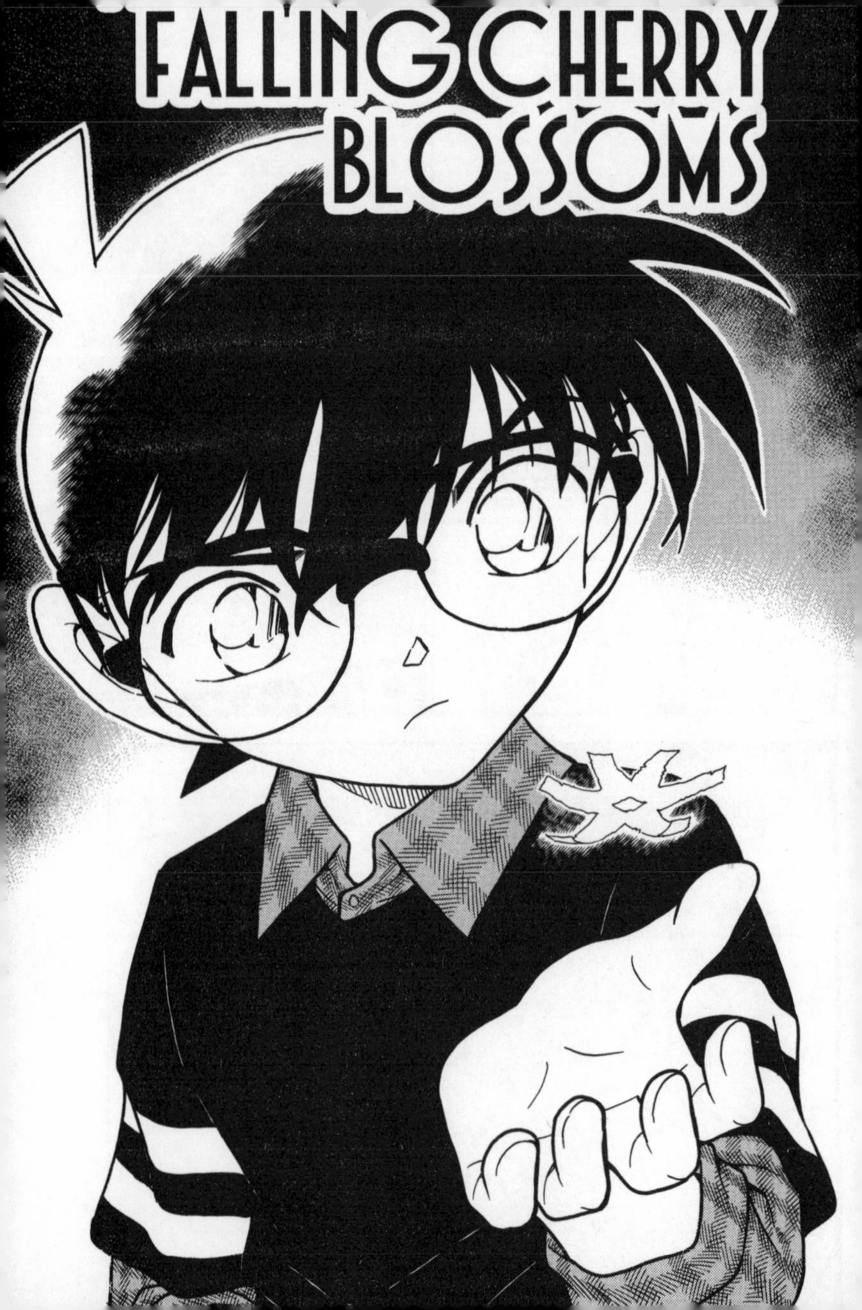
FALLING CHERRY BLOSSOMS

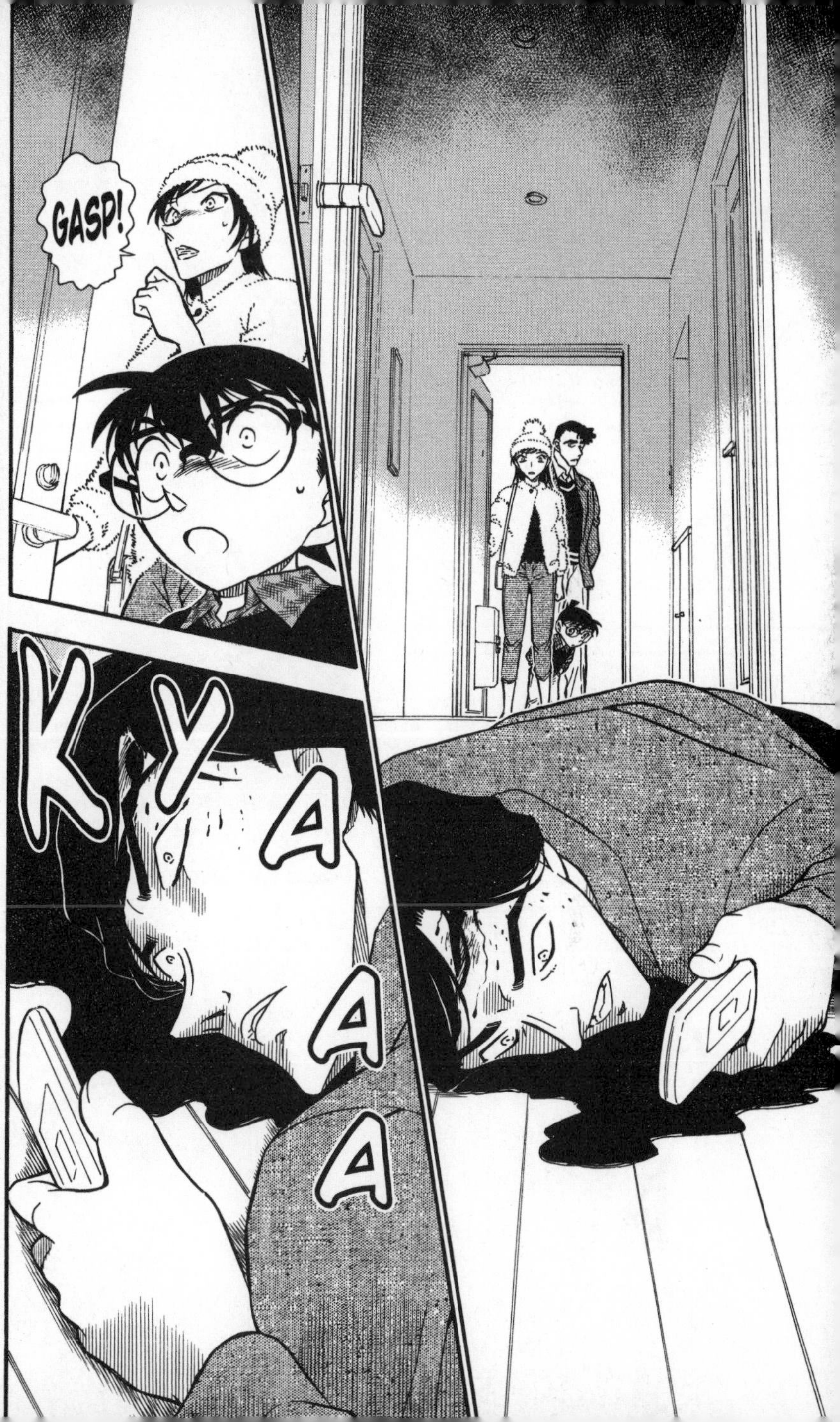
GASP!
KYAAAA

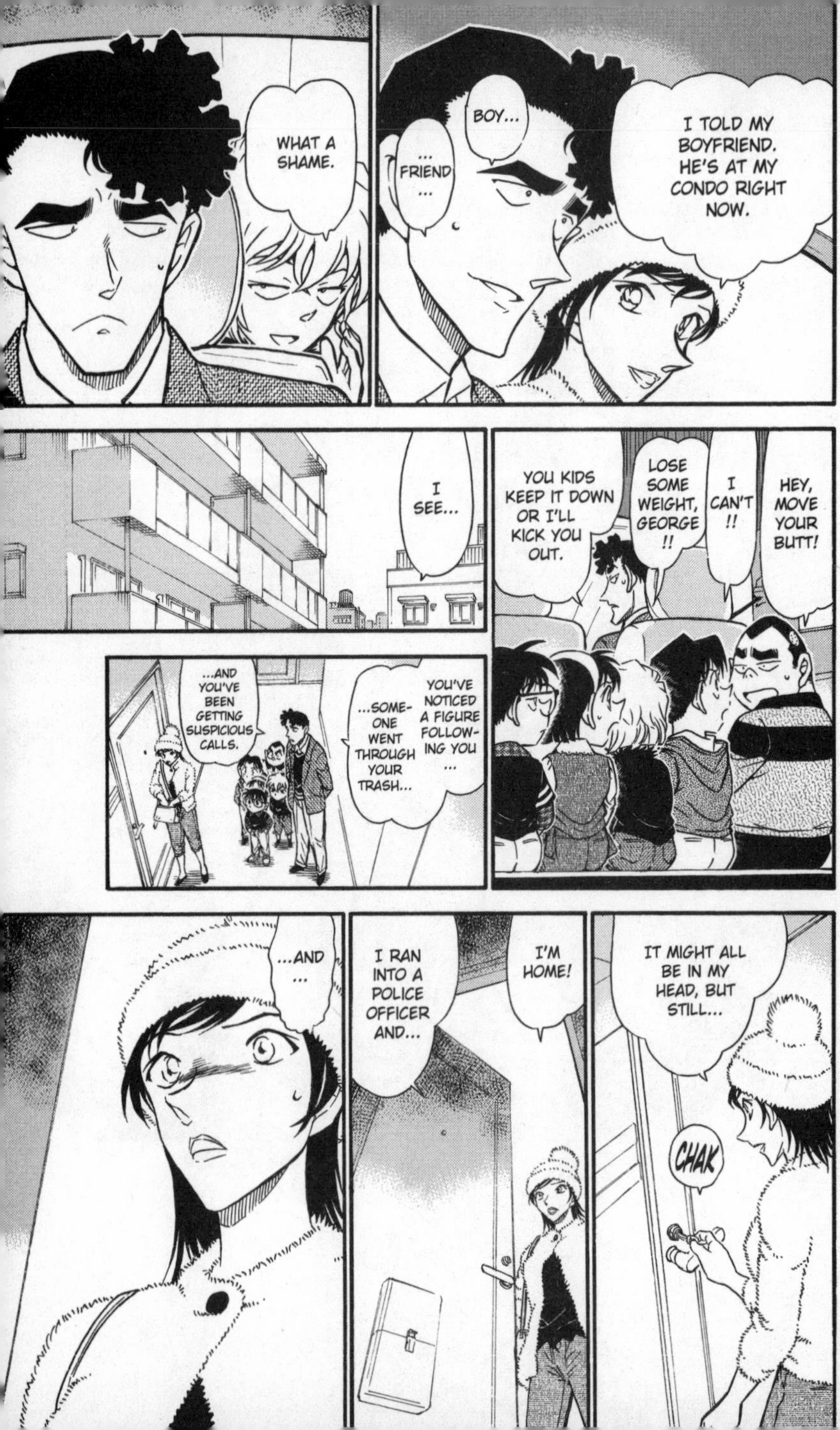
I TOLD MY BOYFRIEND. HE'S AT MY CONDO RIGHT NOW.
BOY...
...FRIEND...
WHAT A SHAME.
HEY, MOVE YOUR BUTT!
I CAN'T!!
LOSE SOME WEIGHT, GEORGE!!
YOU KIDS KEEP IT DOWN OR I'LL KICK YOU OUT.
I SEE...
YOU'VE NOTICED A FIGURE FOLLOWING YOU...
...SOMEONE WENT THROUGH YOUR TRASH...
...AND YOU'VE BEEN GETTING SUSPICIOUS CALLS.
IT MIGHT ALL BE IN MY HEAD, BUT STILL...
CHAK
I'M HOME!
I RAN INTO A POLICE OFFICER AND...
...AND...

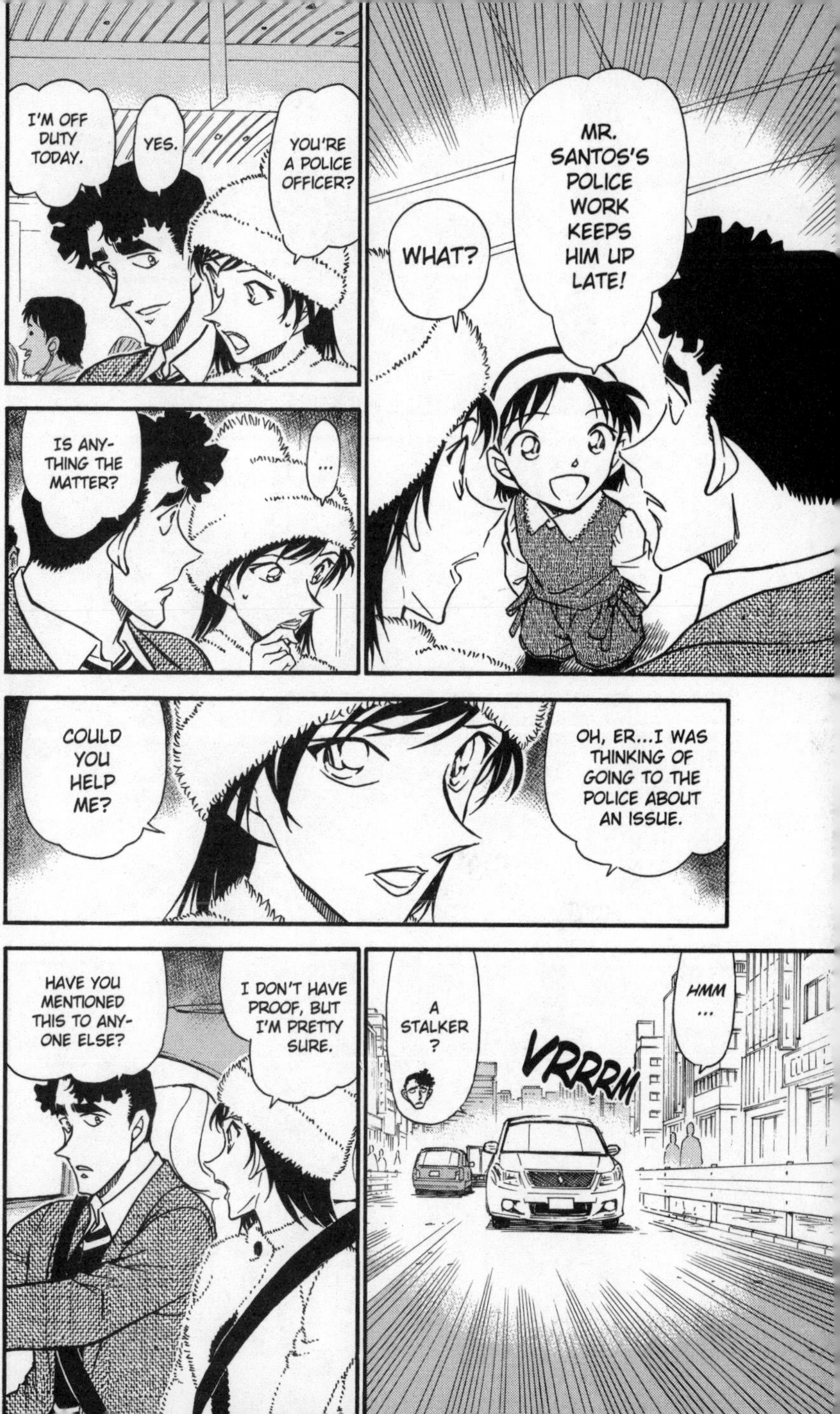
MR. SANTOS'S POLICE WORK KEEPS HIM UP LATE!
WHAT?
YOU'RE A POLICE OFFICER?
YES.
I'M OFF DUTY TODAY.
...
IS ANY-THING THE MATTER?
OH, ER...I WAS THINKING OF GOING TO THE POLICE ABOUT AN ISSUE.
COULD YOU HELP ME?
HMM ...
VRRRM
A STALKER ?
I DON'T HAVE PROOF, BUT I'M PRETTY SURE.
HAVE YOU MENTIONED THIS TO ANY-ONE ELSE?

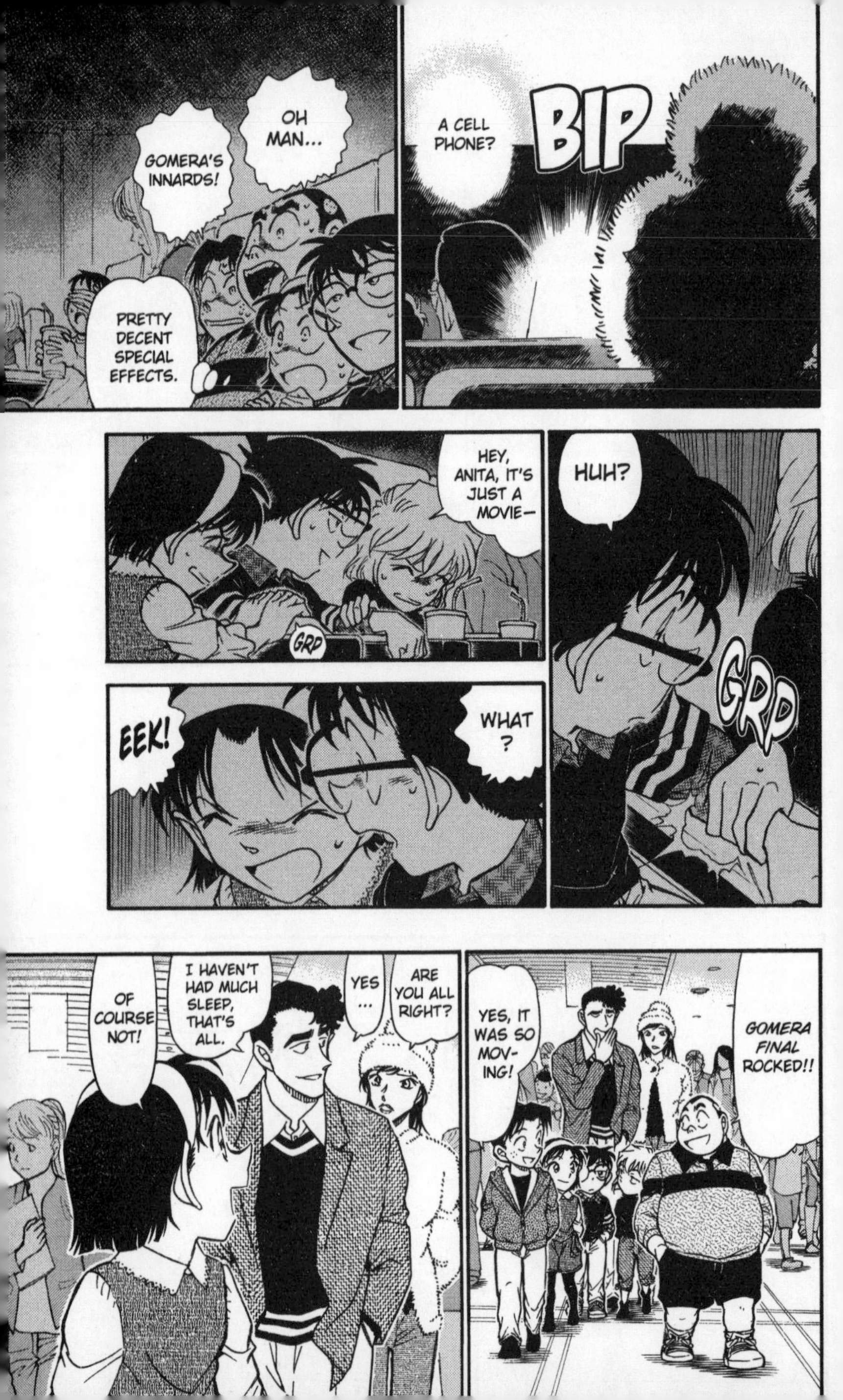
A CELL PHONE?
BIP
OH MAN...
GOMERA'S INNARDS!
PRETTY DECENT SPECIAL EFFECTS.
HUH?
GRP
HEY, ANITA, IT'S JUST A MOVIE—
GRP
WHAT?
EEK!
GOMERA FINAL ROCKED!!
YES, IT WAS SO MOV-ING!
ARE YOU ALL RIGHT?
YES...
I HAVEN'T HAD MUCH SLEEP, THAT'S ALL.
OF COURSE NOT!

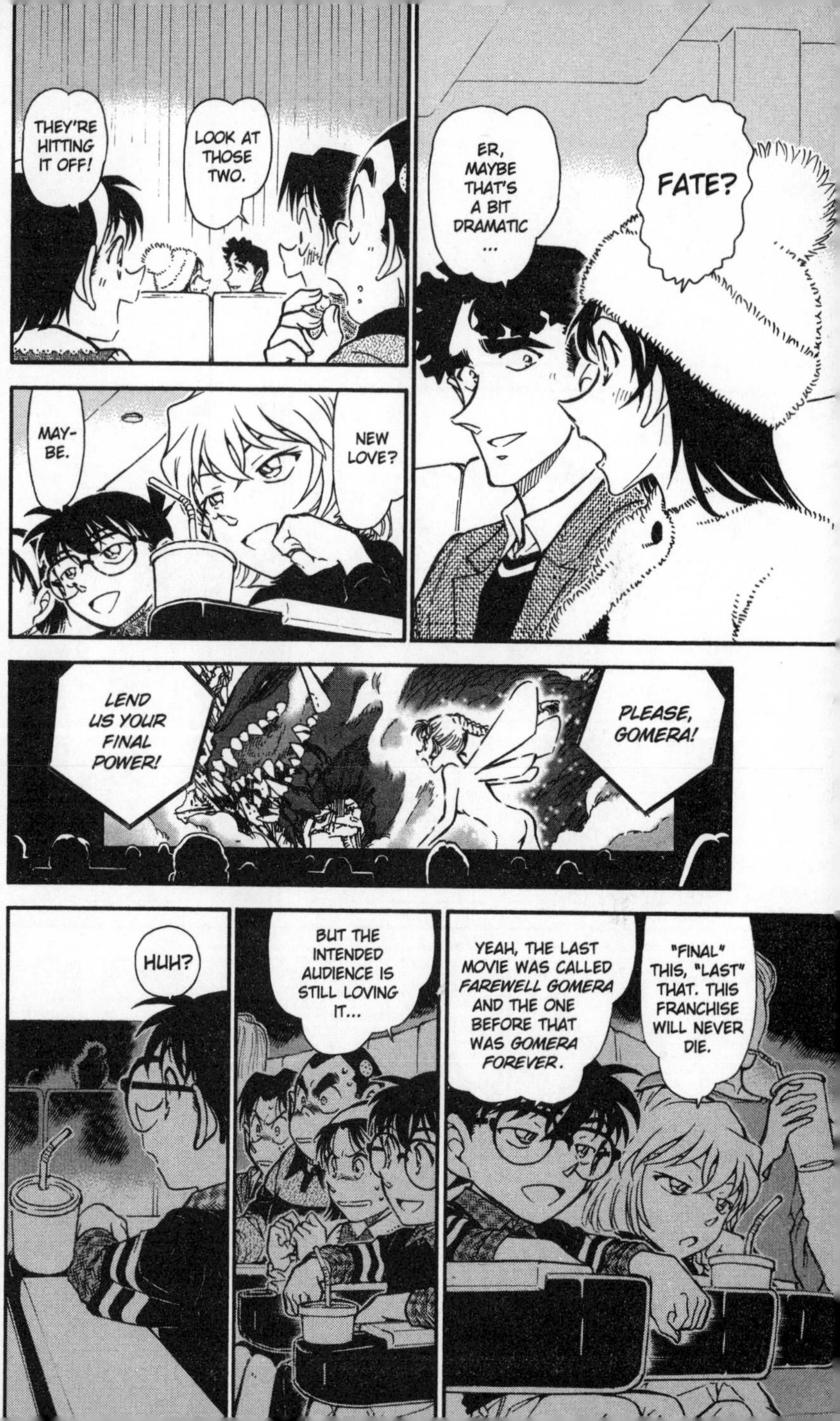
FATE?
ER, MAYBE THAT'S A BIT DRAMATIC ...
LOOK AT THOSE TWO.
THEY'RE HITTING IT OFF!
NEW LOVE?
MAY-BE.
PLEASE, GOMERA!
LEND US YOUR FINAL POWER!
"FINAL" THIS, "LAST" THAT. THIS FRANCHISE WILL NEVER DIE.
YEAH, THE LAST MOVIE WAS CALLED *FAREWELL GOMERA* AND THE ONE BEFORE THAT WAS *GOMERA FOREVER*.
BUT THE INTENDED AUDIENCE IS STILL LOVING IT...
HUH?

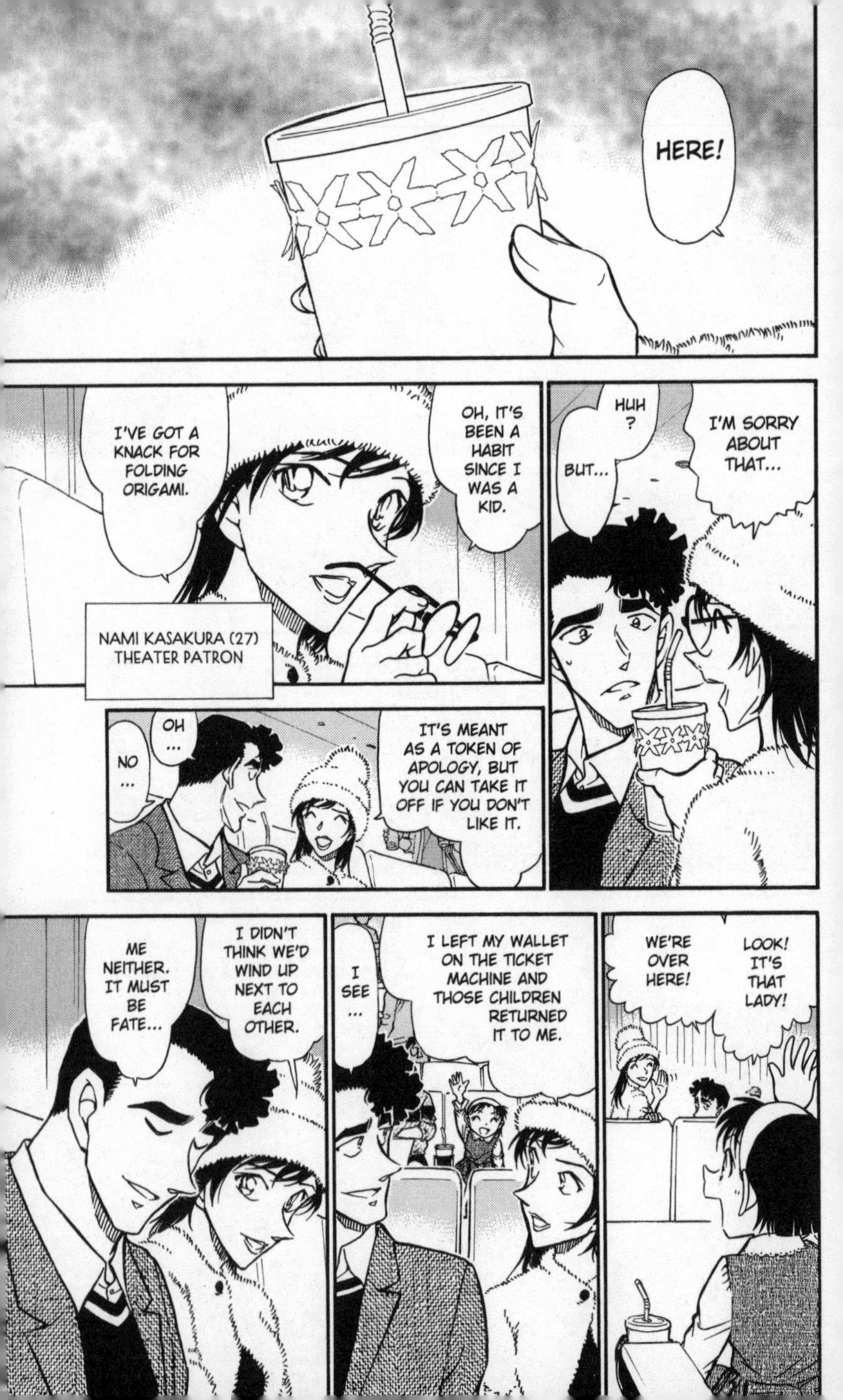
HERE!
I'M SORRY ABOUT THAT...
HUH?
BUT...
OH, IT'S BEEN A HABIT SINCE I WAS A KID.
I'VE GOT A KNACK FOR FOLDING ORIGAMI.
NAMI KASAKURA (27) THEATER PATRON
IT'S MEANT AS A TOKEN OF APOLOGY, BUT YOU CAN TAKE IT OFF IF YOU DON'T LIKE IT.
OH ...
NO ...
LOOK! IT'S THAT LADY!
WE'RE OVER HERE!
I LEFT MY WALLET ON THE TICKET MACHINE AND THOSE CHILDREN RETURNED IT TO ME.
I SEE ...
I DIDN'T THINK WE'D WIND UP NEXT TO EACH OTHER.
ME NEITHER. IT MUST BE FATE...

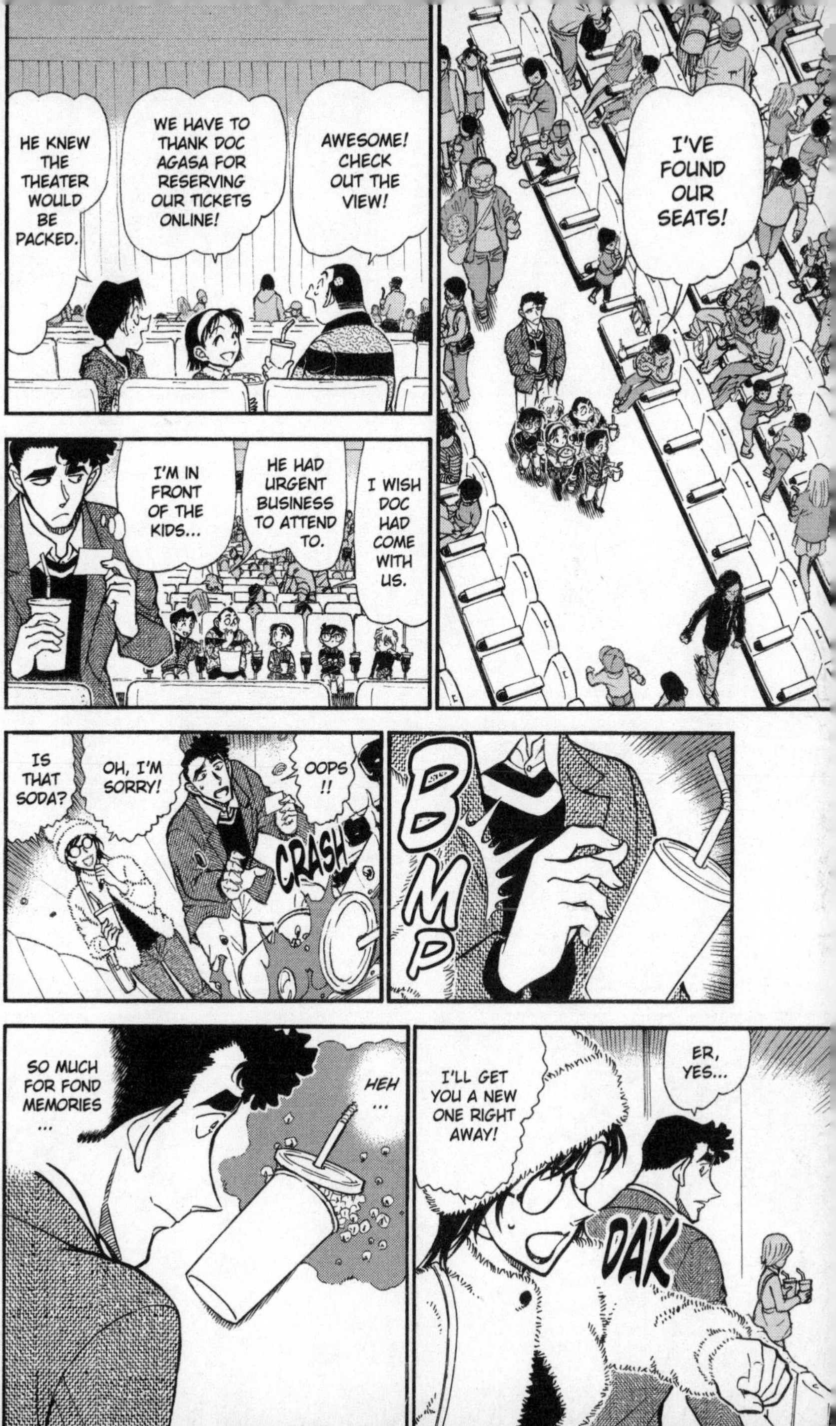
I'VE FOUND OUR SEATS!
AWESOME! CHECK OUT THE VIEW!
WE HAVE TO THANK DOC AGASA FOR RESERVING OUR TICKETS ONLINE!
HE KNEW THE THEATER WOULD BE PACKED.
I WISH DOC HAD COME WITH US.
HE HAD URGENT BUSINESS TO ATTEND TO.
I'M IN FRONT OF THE KIDS...
BMP
OOPS !!
CRASH
OH, I'M SORRY!
IS THAT SODA?
ER, YES...
I'LL GET YOU A NEW ONE RIGHT AWAY!
DAK
HEH ...
SO MUCH FOR FOND MEMORIES ...

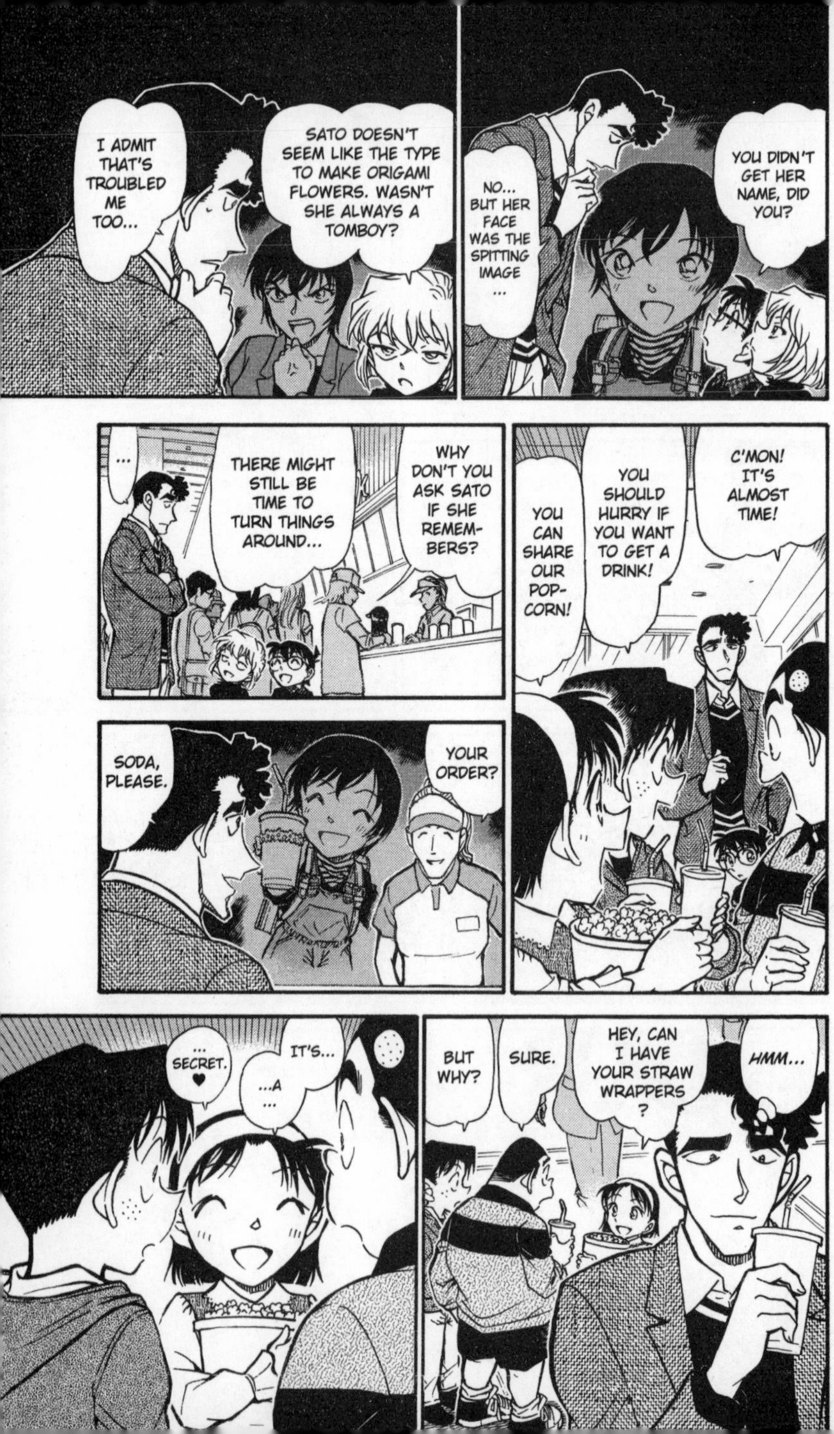
YOU DIDN'T GET HER NAME, DID YOU?
NO... BUT HER FACE WAS THE SPITTING IMAGE ...
SATO DOESN'T SEEM LIKE THE TYPE TO MAKE ORIGAMI FLOWERS. WASN'T SHE ALWAYS A TOMBOY?
I ADMIT THAT'S TROUBLED ME TOO...
C'MON! IT'S ALMOST TIME!
YOU SHOULD HURRY IF YOU WANT TO GET A DRINK!
YOU CAN SHARE OUR POP-CORN!
WHY DON'T YOU ASK SATO IF SHE REMEM-BERS?
THERE MIGHT STILL BE TIME TO TURN THINGS AROUND...
...
YOUR ORDER?
SODA, PLEASE.
HMM...
HEY, CAN I HAVE YOUR STRAW WRAPPERS?
SURE.
BUT WHY?
IT'S...
...A ...
... SECRET. ♥

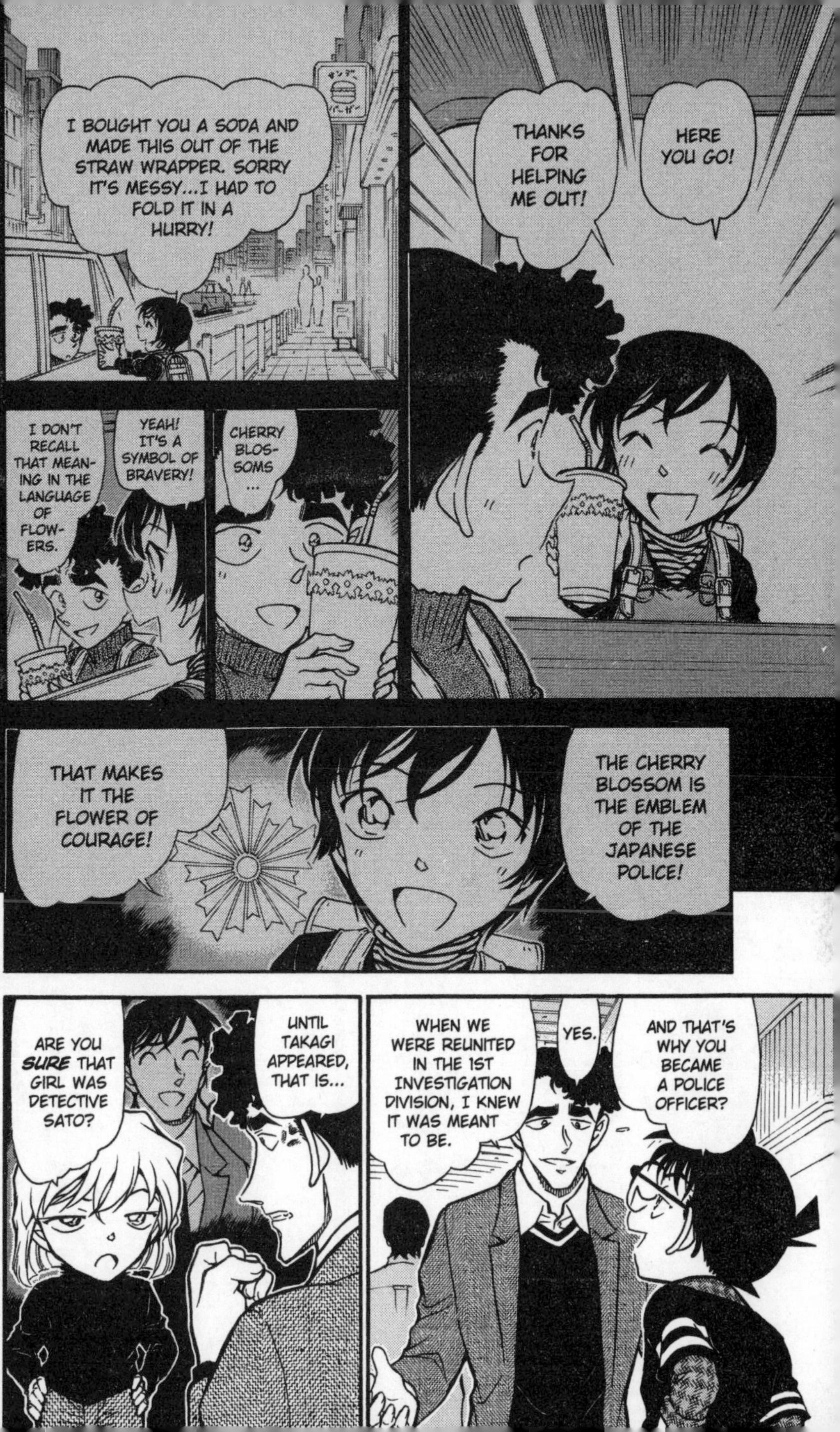
HERE YOU GO!
THANKS FOR HELPING ME OUT!
I BOUGHT YOU A SODA AND MADE THIS OUT OF THE STRAW WRAPPER. SORRY IT'S MESSY...I HAD TO FOLD IT IN A HURRY!
CHERRY BLOSSOMS...
YEAH! IT'S A SYMBOL OF BRAVERY!
I DON'T RECALL THAT MEANING IN THE LANGUAGE OF FLOWERS.
THE CHERRY BLOSSOM IS THE EMBLEM OF THE JAPANESE POLICE!
THAT MAKES IT THE FLOWER OF COURAGE!
AND THAT'S WHY YOU BECAME A POLICE OFFICER?
YES.
WHEN WE WERE REUNITED IN THE 1ST INVESTIGATION DIVISION, I KNEW IT WAS MEANT TO BE.
UNTIL TAKAGI APPEARED, THAT IS...
ARE YOU ***SURE*** THAT GIRL WAS DETECTIVE SATO?

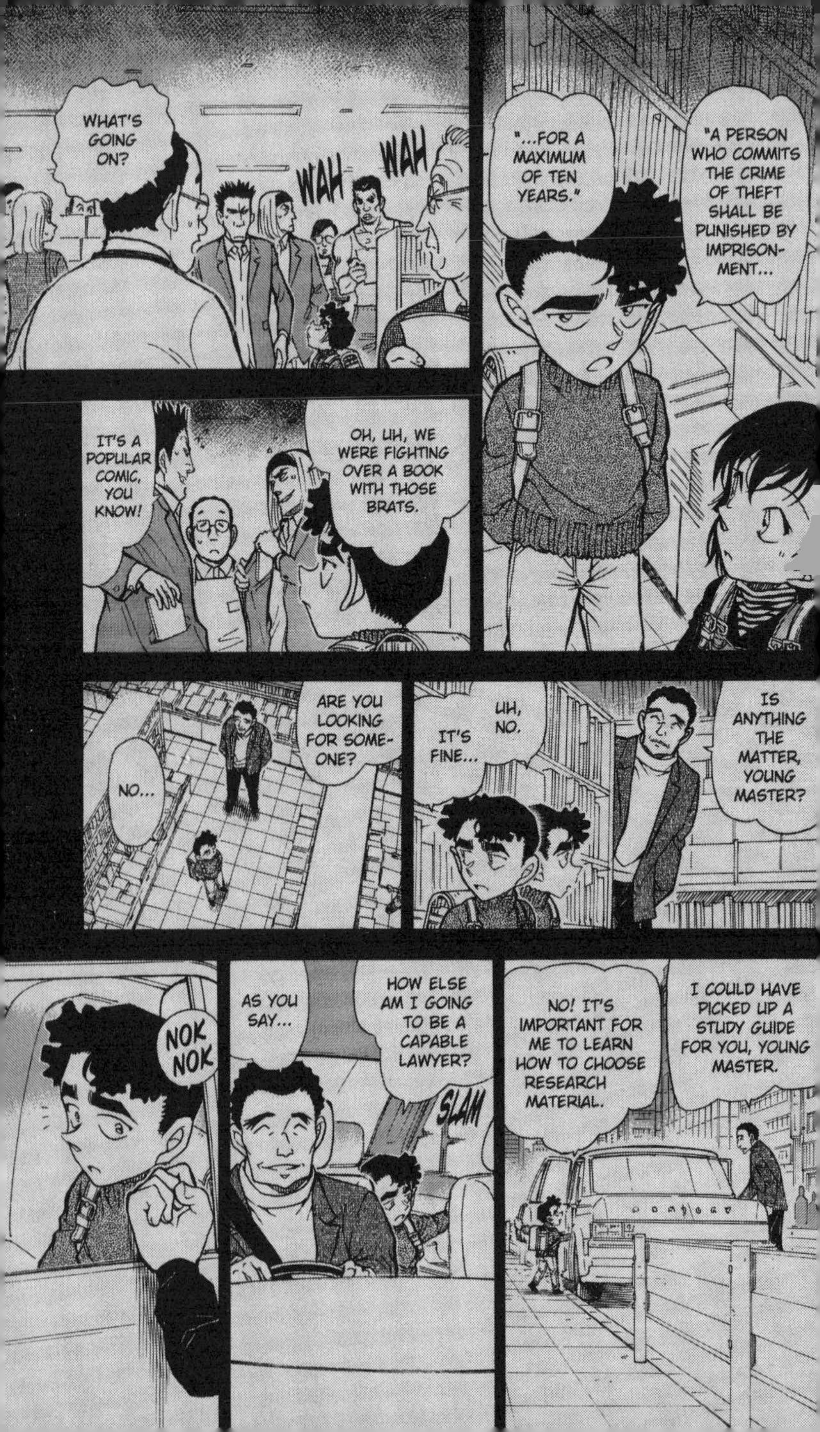
"A PERSON WHO COMMITS THE CRIME OF THEFT SHALL BE PUNISHED BY IMPRISON-MENT...
"...FOR A MAXIMUM OF TEN YEARS."
WAH
WAH
WHAT'S GOING ON?
OH, UH, WE WERE FIGHTING OVER A BOOK WITH THOSE BRATS.
IT'S A POPULAR COMIC, YOU KNOW!
IS ANYTHING THE MATTER, YOUNG MASTER?
UH, NO.
IT'S FINE...
ARE YOU LOOKING FOR SOME-ONE?
NO...
I COULD HAVE PICKED UP A STUDY GUIDE FOR YOU, YOUNG MASTER.
NO! IT'S IMPORTANT FOR ME TO LEARN HOW TO CHOOSE RESEARCH MATERIAL.
HOW ELSE AM I GOING TO BE A CAPABLE LAWYER?
AS YOU SAY...
SLAM
NOK NOK

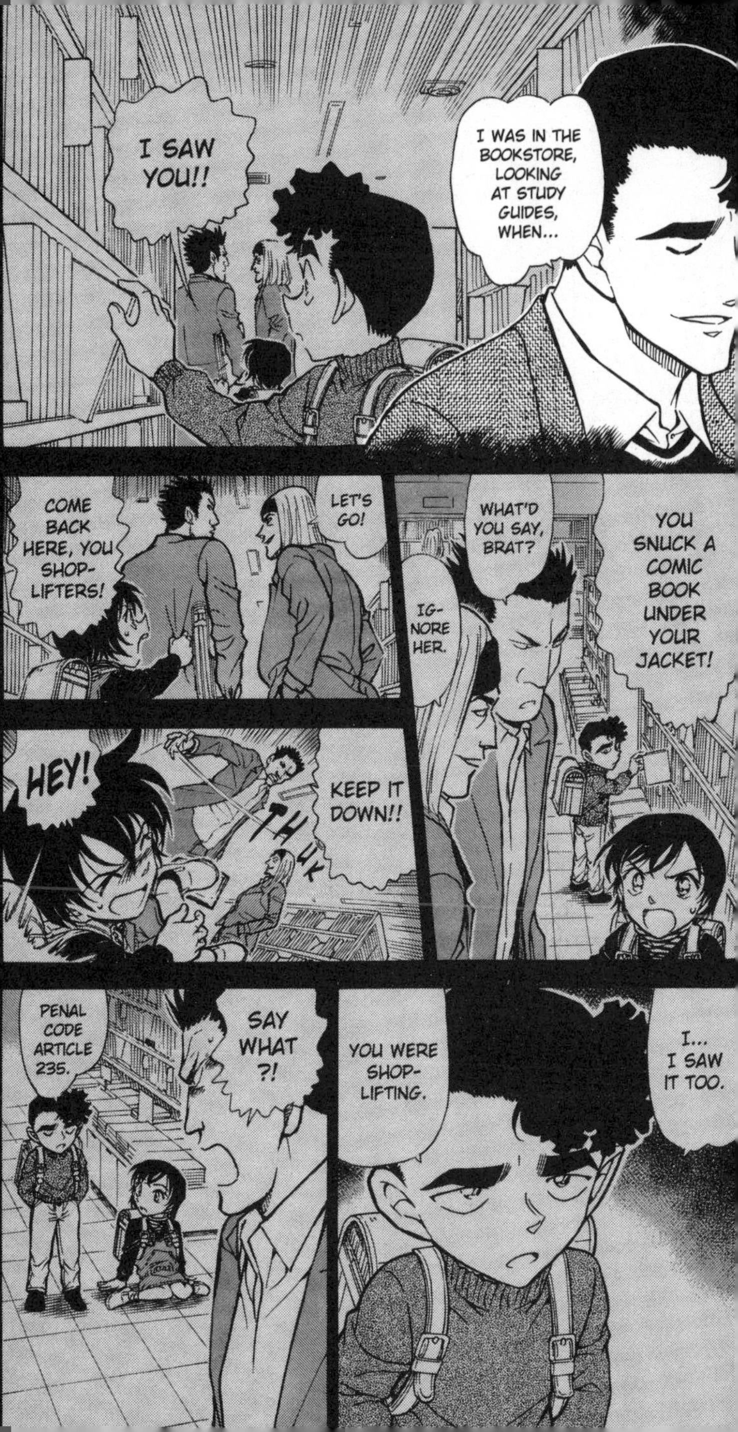
I WAS IN THE BOOKSTORE, LOOKING AT STUDY GUIDES, WHEN...
I SAW YOU!!
YOU SNUCK A COMIC BOOK UNDER YOUR JACKET!
WHAT'D YOU SAY, BRAT?
IG-NORE HER.
LET'S GO!
COME BACK HERE, YOU SHOP-LIFTERS!
KEEP IT DOWN!!
THUK
HEY!
I... I SAW IT TOO.
YOU WERE SHOP-LIFTING.
SAY WHAT?!
PENAL CODE ARTICLE 235.

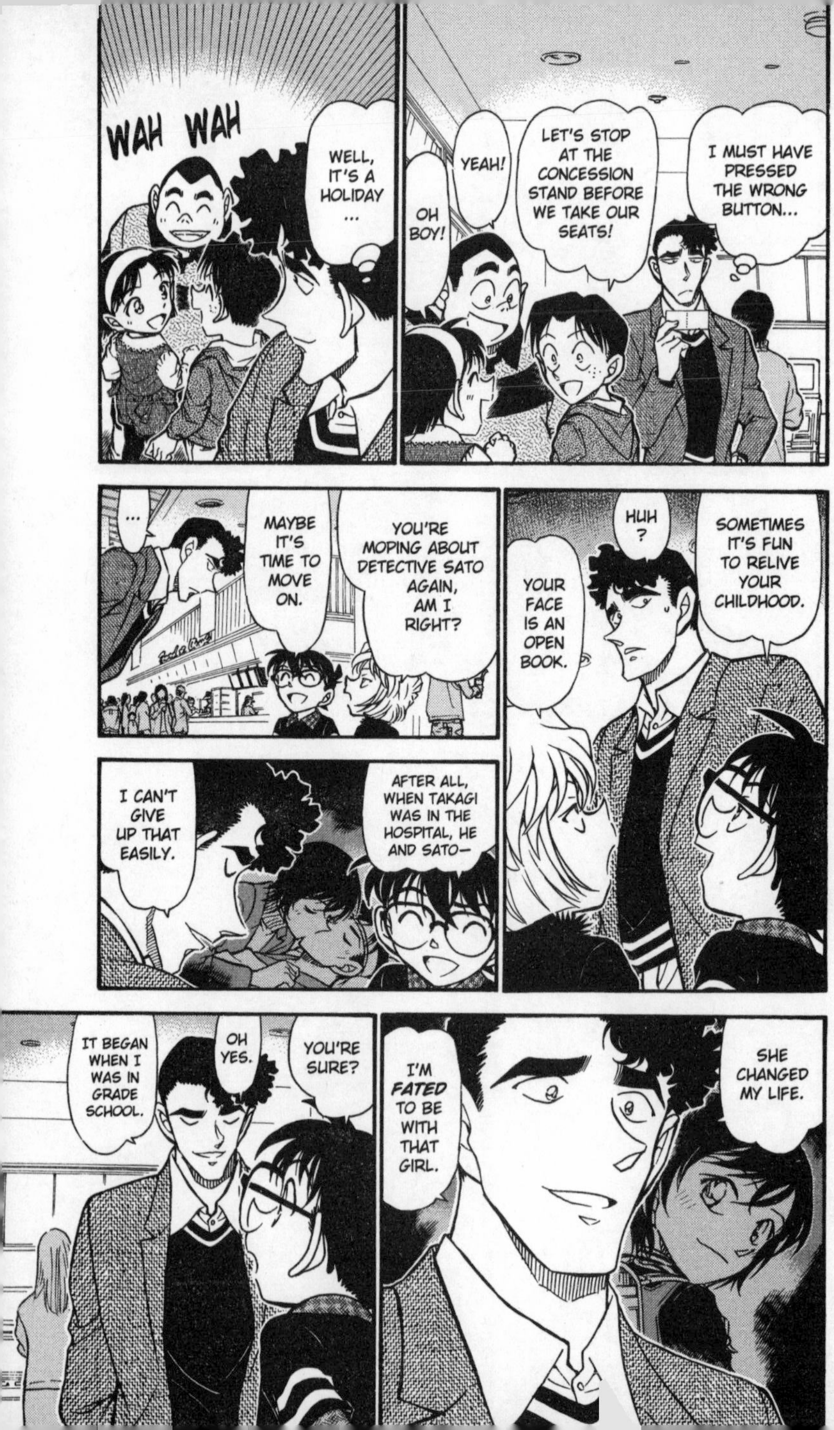
I MUST HAVE PRESSED THE WRONG BUTTON...
LET'S STOP AT THE CONCESSION STAND BEFORE WE TAKE OUR SEATS!
YEAH!
OH BOY!
WELL, IT'S A HOLIDAY ...
WAH WAH
SOMETIMES IT'S FUN TO RELIVE YOUR CHILDHOOD.
HUH ?
YOUR FACE IS AN OPEN BOOK.
YOU'RE MOPING ABOUT DETECTIVE SATO AGAIN, AM I RIGHT?
MAYBE IT'S TIME TO MOVE ON.
...
AFTER ALL, WHEN TAKAGI WAS IN THE HOSPITAL, HE AND SATO—
I CAN'T GIVE UP THAT EASILY.
SHE CHANGED MY LIFE.
I'M *FATED* TO BE WITH THAT GIRL.
YOU'RE SURE?
OH YES.
IT BEGAN WHEN I WAS IN GRADE SCHOOL.

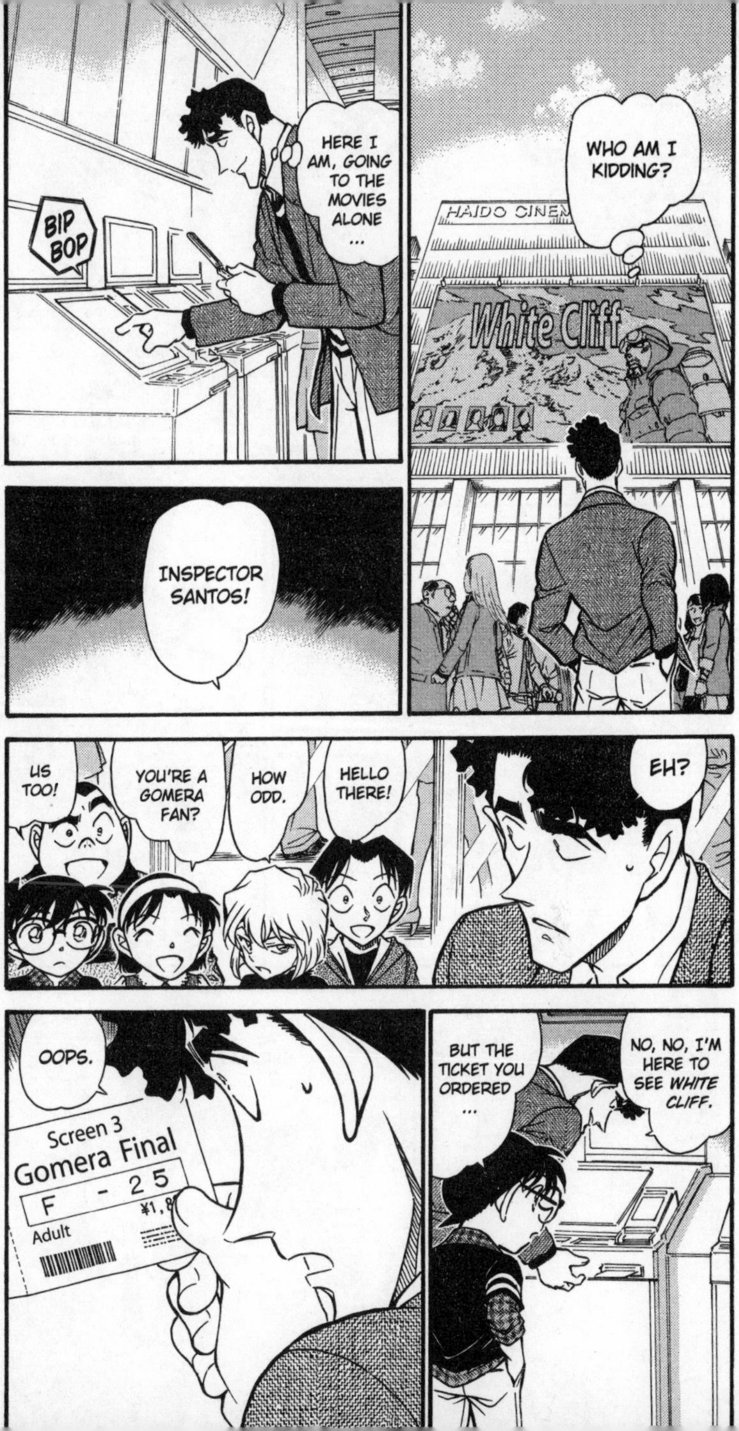
WHO AM I KIDDING?
HAIDO CINEM
White Cliff
HERE I AM, GOING TO THE MOVIES ALONE ...
BIP BOP
INSPECTOR SANTOS!
EH?
HELLO THERE!
HOW ODD.
YOU'RE A GOMERA FAN?
US TOO!
NO, NO, I'M HERE TO SEE *WHITE CLIFF*.
BUT THE TICKET YOU ORDERED ...
OOPS.
Screen 3
Gomera Final
F - 25
¥1,8
Adult

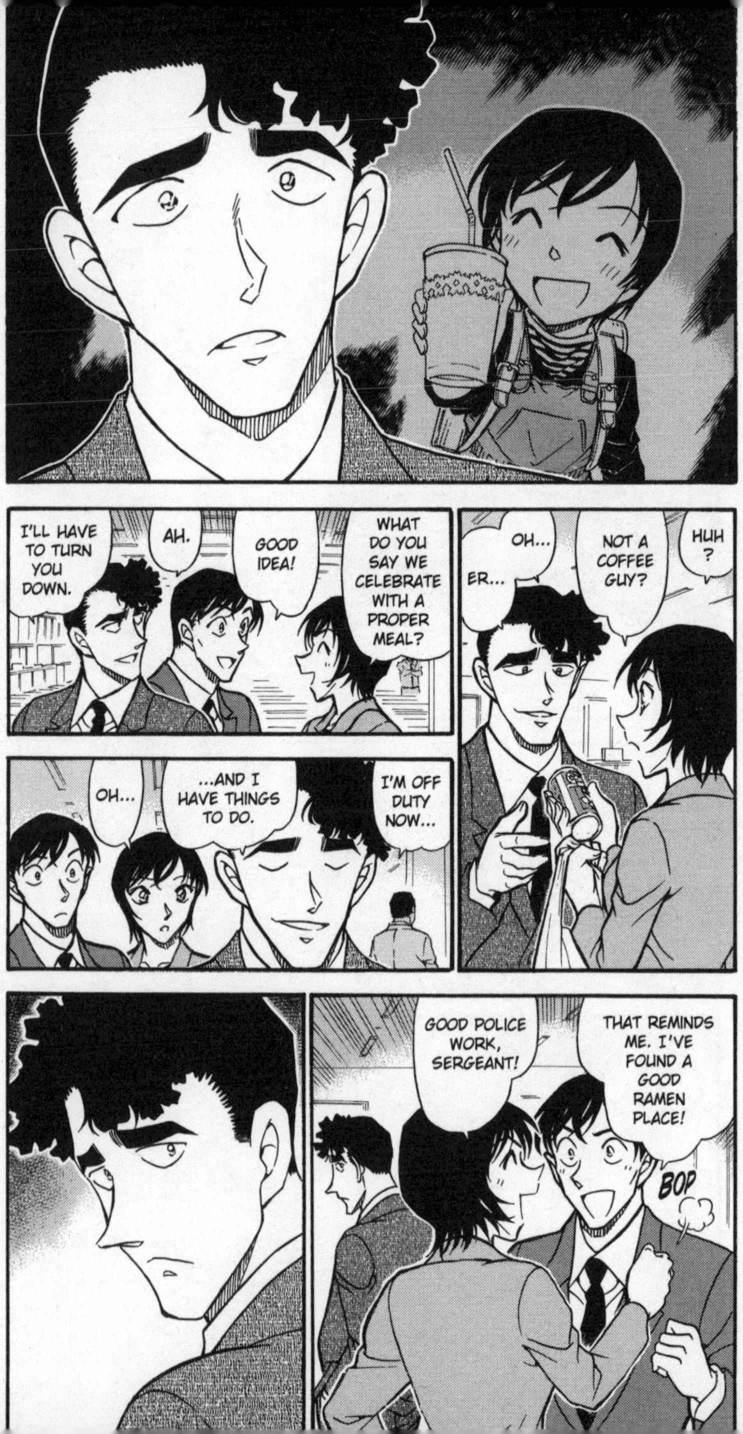
HUH?
NOT A COFFEE GUY?
OH...
ER...
WHAT DO YOU SAY WE CELEBRATE WITH A PROPER MEAL?
GOOD IDEA!
AH.
I'LL HAVE TO TURN YOU DOWN.
I'M OFF DUTY NOW...
...AND I HAVE THINGS TO DO.
OH...
THAT REMINDS ME. I'VE FOUND A GOOD RAMEN PLACE!
GOOD POLICE WORK, SERGEANT!
BOP

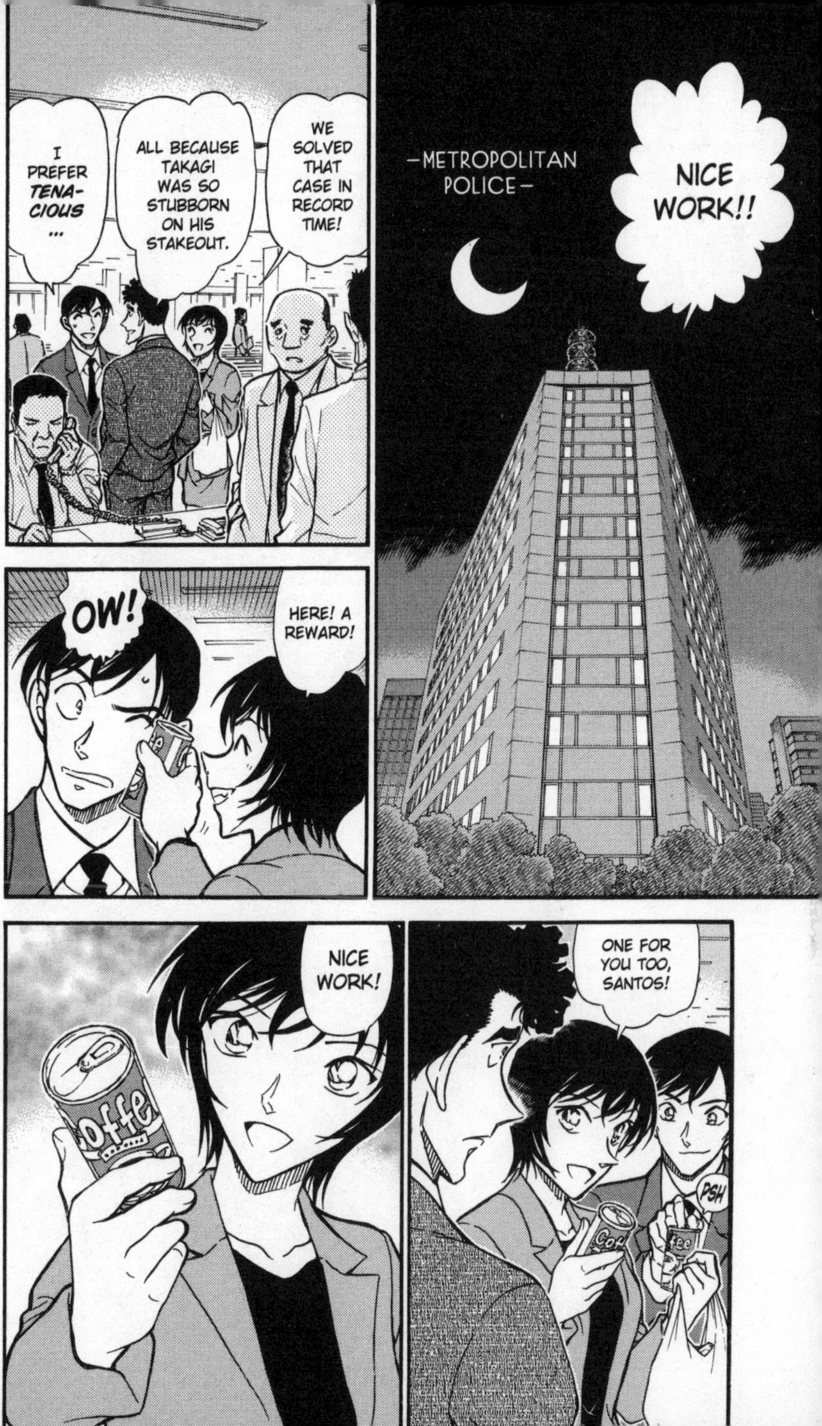

-METROPOLITAN POLICE-
NICE WORK!!
WE SOLVED THAT CASE IN RECORD TIME!
ALL BECAUSE TAKAGI WAS SO STUBBORN ON HIS STAKEOUT.
I PREFER *TENACIOUS*...
HERE! A REWARD!
OW!
ONE FOR YOU TOO, SANTOS!
PSH
NICE WORK!

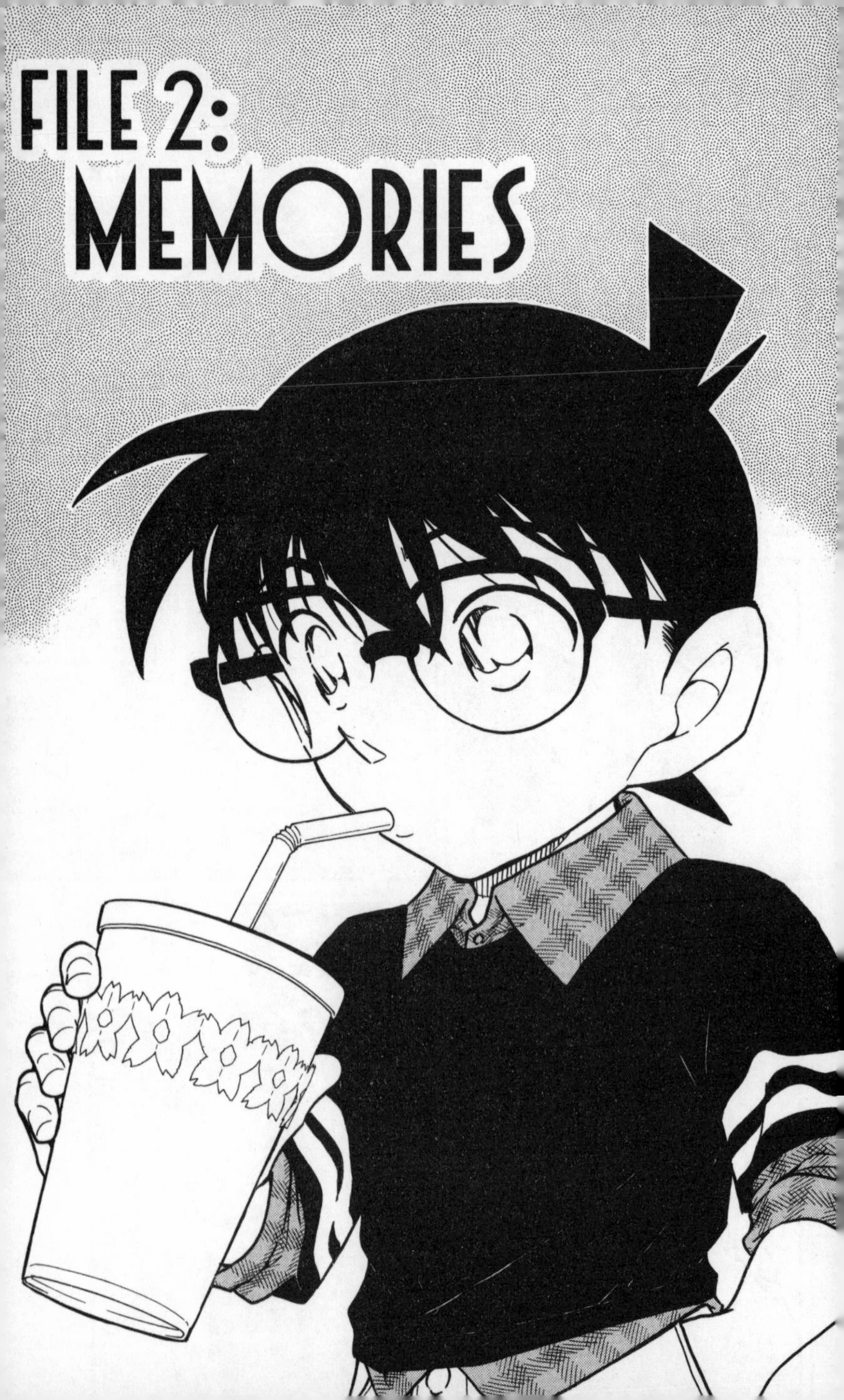
FILE 2:
MEMORIES

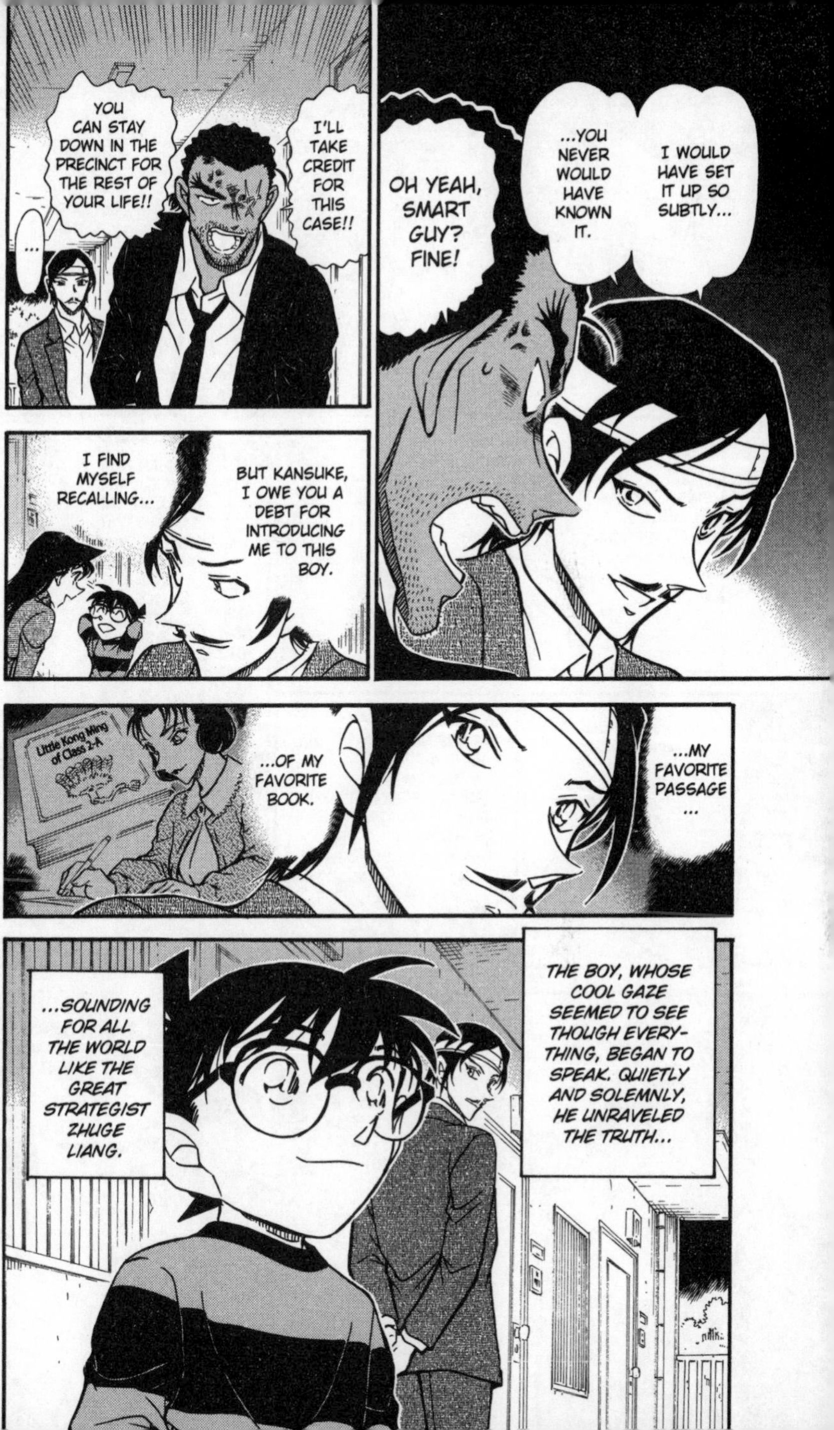
I WOULD HAVE SET IT UP SO SUBTLY...
...YOU NEVER WOULD HAVE KNOWN IT.
OH YEAH, SMART GUY? FINE!
I'LL TAKE CREDIT FOR THIS CASE!!
YOU CAN STAY DOWN IN THE PRECINCT FOR THE REST OF YOUR LIFE!!
...
BUT KANSUKE, I OWE YOU A DEBT FOR INTRODUCING ME TO THIS BOY.
I FIND MYSELF RECALLING...
...MY FAVORITE PASSAGE ...
...OF MY FAVORITE BOOK.
Little Kong Ming of Class 2-A
THE BOY, WHOSE COOL GAZE SEEMED TO SEE THOUGH EVERY-THING, BEGAN TO SPEAK. QUIETLY AND SOLEMNLY, HE UNRAVELED THE TRUTH...
...SOUNDING FOR ALL THE WORLD LIKE THE GREAT STRATEGIST ZHUGE LIANG.

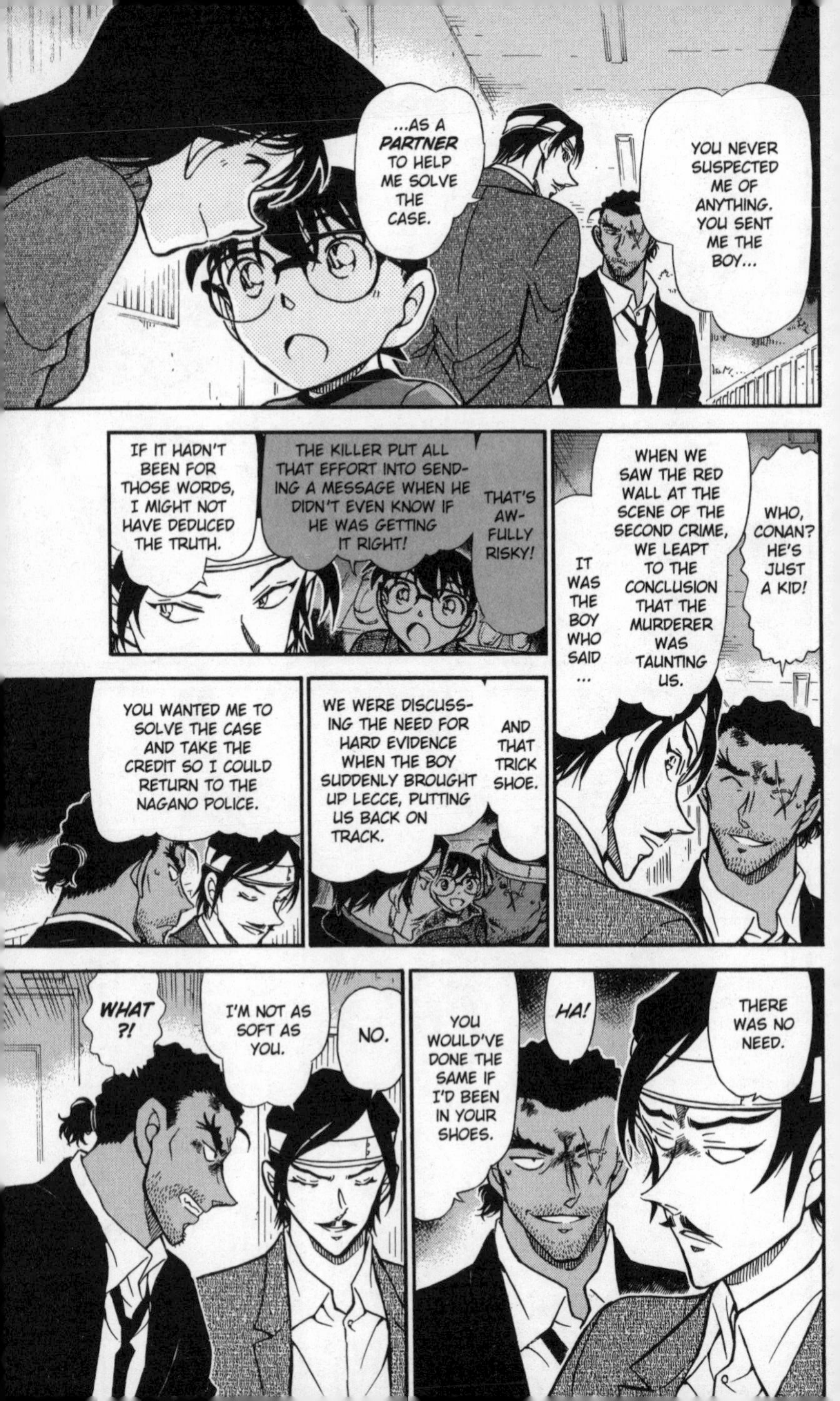
YOU NEVER SUSPECTED ME OF ANYTHING. YOU SENT ME THE BOY...
...AS A *PARTNER* TO HELP ME SOLVE THE CASE.
WHO, CONAN? HE'S JUST A KID!
WHEN WE SAW THE RED WALL AT THE SCENE OF THE SECOND CRIME, WE LEAPT TO THE CONCLUSION THAT THE MURDERER WAS TAUNTING US.
IT WAS THE BOY WHO SAID...
THE KILLER PUT ALL THAT EFFORT INTO SENDING A MESSAGE WHEN HE DIDN'T EVEN KNOW IF HE WAS GETTING IT RIGHT!
THAT'S AWFULLY RISKY!
IF IT HADN'T BEEN FOR THOSE WORDS, I MIGHT NOT HAVE DEDUCED THE TRUTH.
WE WERE DISCUSSING THE NEED FOR HARD EVIDENCE WHEN THE BOY SUDDENLY BROUGHT UP LECCE, PUTTING US BACK ON TRACK.
AND THAT TRICK SHOE.
YOU WANTED ME TO SOLVE THE CASE AND TAKE THE CREDIT SO I COULD RETURN TO THE NAGANO POLICE.
THERE WAS NO NEED.
HA!
YOU WOULD'VE DONE THE SAME IF I'D BEEN IN YOUR SHOES.
NO.
I'M NOT AS SOFT AS YOU.
WHAT?!

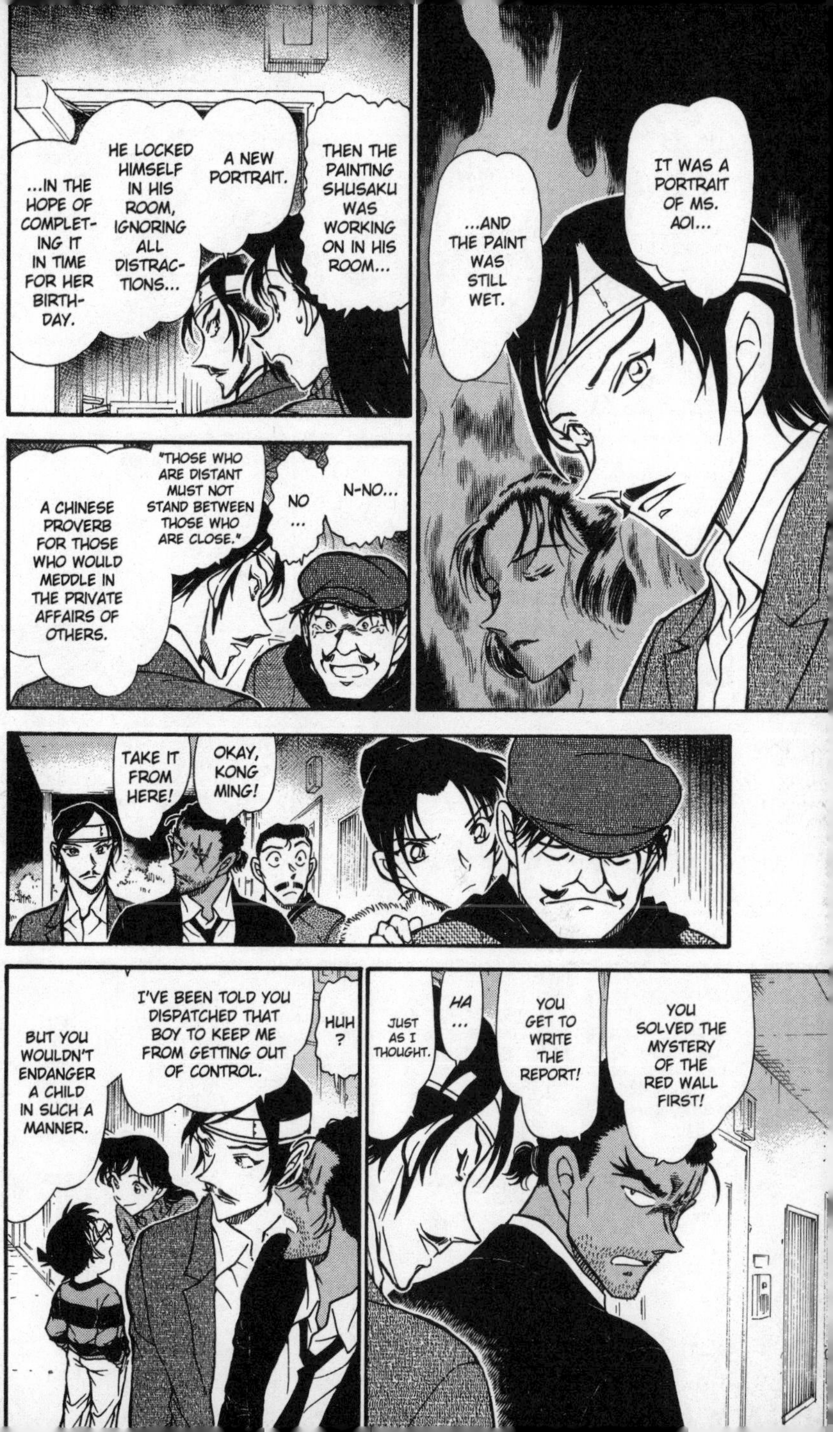
IT WAS A PORTRAIT OF MS. AOI...
...AND THE PAINT WAS STILL WET.
THEN THE PAINTING SHUSAKU WAS WORKING ON IN HIS ROOM...
A NEW PORTRAIT.
HE LOCKED HIMSELF IN HIS ROOM, IGNORING ALL DISTRACTIONS...
...IN THE HOPE OF COMPLETING IT IN TIME FOR HER BIRTHDAY.
N-NO...
NO ...
"THOSE WHO ARE DISTANT MUST NOT STAND BETWEEN THOSE WHO ARE CLOSE."
A CHINESE PROVERB FOR THOSE WHO WOULD MEDDLE IN THE PRIVATE AFFAIRS OF OTHERS.
OKAY, KONG MING!
TAKE IT FROM HERE!
YOU SOLVED THE MYSTERY OF THE RED WALL FIRST!
YOU GET TO WRITE THE REPORT!
HA ...
JUST AS I THOUGHT.
HUH ?
I'VE BEEN TOLD YOU DISPATCHED THAT BOY TO KEEP ME FROM GETTING OUT OF CONTROL.
BUT YOU WOULDN'T ENDANGER A CHILD IN SUCH A MANNER.

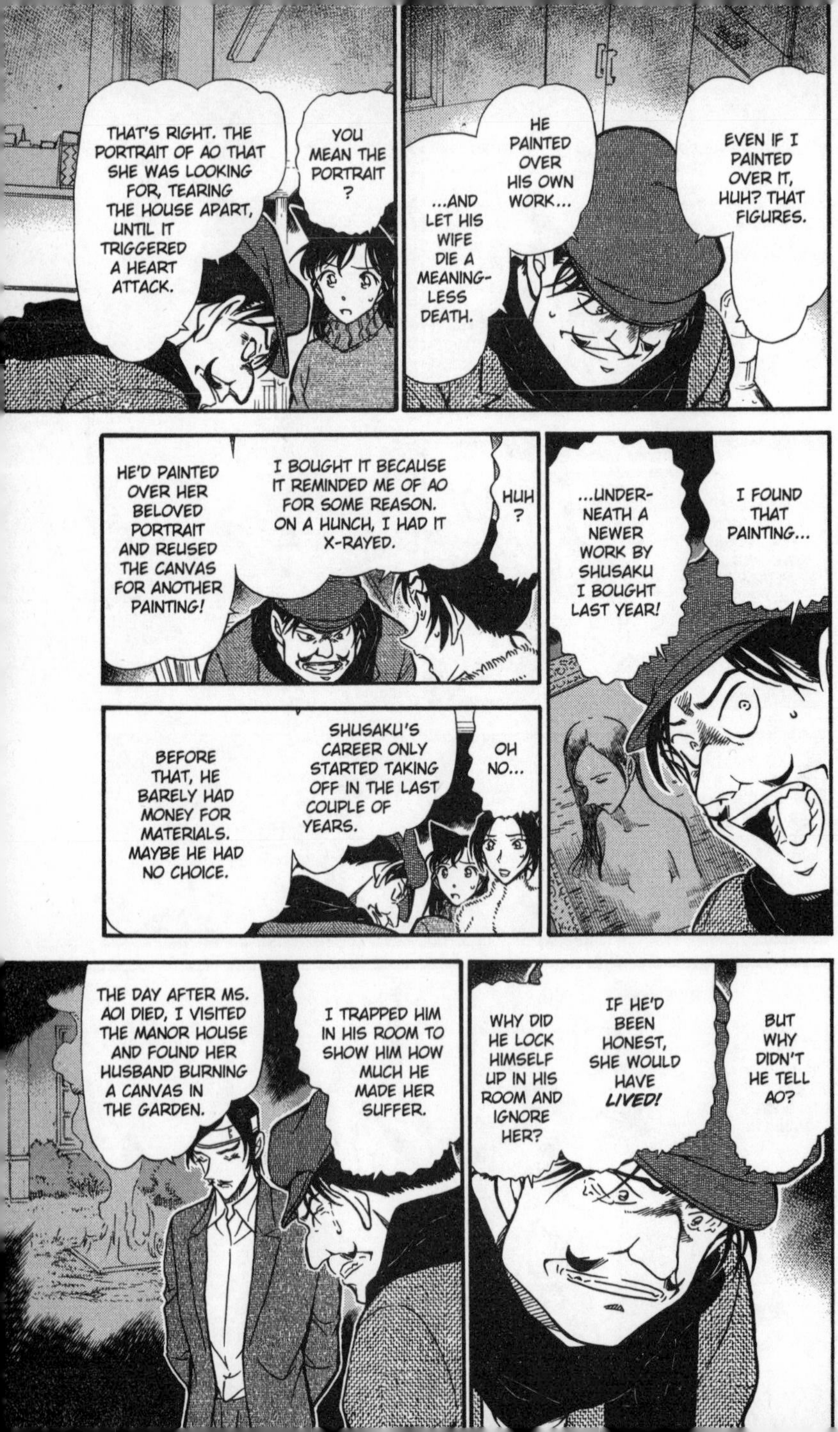
EVEN IF I PAINTED OVER IT, HUH? THAT FIGURES.
HE PAINTED OVER HIS OWN WORK...
...AND LET HIS WIFE DIE A MEANING-LESS DEATH.
YOU MEAN THE PORTRAIT?
THAT'S RIGHT. THE PORTRAIT OF AO THAT SHE WAS LOOKING FOR, TEARING THE HOUSE APART, UNTIL IT TRIGGERED A HEART ATTACK.
I FOUND THAT PAINTING...
...UNDER-NEATH A NEWER WORK BY SHUSAKU I BOUGHT LAST YEAR!
HUH?
I BOUGHT IT BECAUSE IT REMINDED ME OF AO FOR SOME REASON. ON A HUNCH, I HAD IT X-RAYED.
HE'D PAINTED OVER HER BELOVED PORTRAIT AND REUSED THE CANVAS FOR ANOTHER PAINTING!
OH NO...
SHUSAKU'S CAREER ONLY STARTED TAKING OFF IN THE LAST COUPLE OF YEARS.
BEFORE THAT, HE BARELY HAD MONEY FOR MATERIALS. MAYBE HE HAD NO CHOICE.
BUT WHY DIDN'T HE TELL AO?
IF HE'D BEEN HONEST, SHE WOULD HAVE *LIVED!*
WHY DID HE LOCK HIMSELF UP IN HIS ROOM AND IGNORE HER?
I TRAPPED HIM IN HIS ROOM TO SHOW HIM HOW MUCH HE MADE HER SUFFER.
THE DAY AFTER MS. AOI DIED, I VISITED THE MANOR HOUSE AND FOUND HER HUSBAND BURNING A CANVAS IN THE GARDEN.

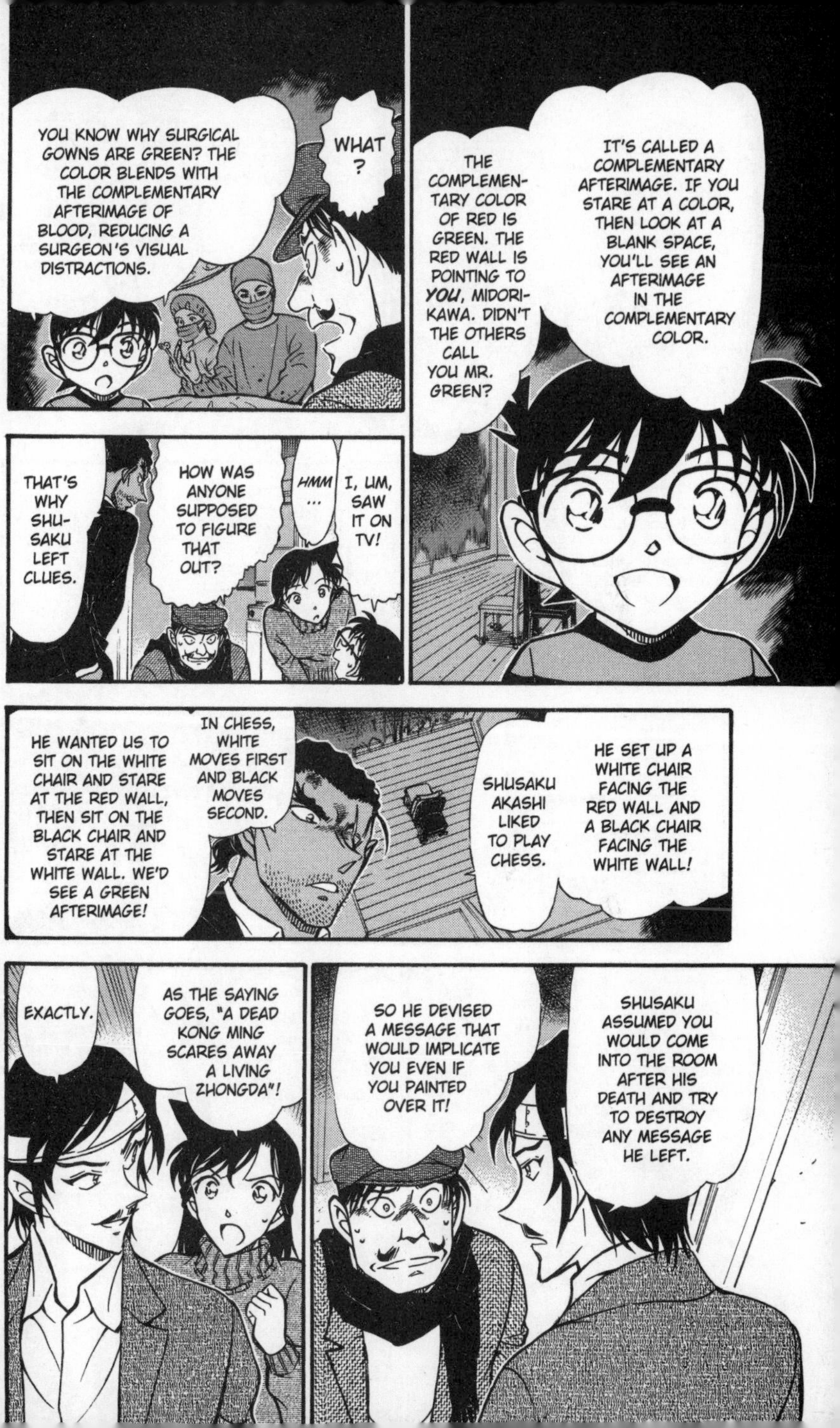
IT'S CALLED A COMPLEMENTARY AFTERIMAGE. IF YOU STARE AT A COLOR, THEN LOOK AT A BLANK SPACE, YOU'LL SEE AN AFTERIMAGE IN THE COMPLEMENTARY COLOR.
THE COMPLEMENTARY COLOR OF RED IS GREEN. THE RED WALL IS POINTING TO *YOU*, MIDORIKAWA. DIDN'T THE OTHERS CALL YOU MR. GREEN?
WHAT ?
YOU KNOW WHY SURGICAL GOWNS ARE GREEN? THE COLOR BLENDS WITH THE COMPLEMENTARY AFTERIMAGE OF BLOOD, REDUCING A SURGEON'S VISUAL DISTRACTIONS.
I, UM, SAW IT ON TV!
HMM ...
HOW WAS ANYONE SUPPOSED TO FIGURE THAT OUT?
THAT'S WHY SHUSAKU LEFT CLUES.
HE SET UP A WHITE CHAIR FACING THE RED WALL AND A BLACK CHAIR FACING THE WHITE WALL!
SHUSAKU AKASHI LIKED TO PLAY CHESS.
IN CHESS, WHITE MOVES FIRST AND BLACK MOVES SECOND.
HE WANTED US TO SIT ON THE WHITE CHAIR AND STARE AT THE RED WALL, THEN SIT ON THE BLACK CHAIR AND STARE AT THE WHITE WALL. WE'D SEE A GREEN AFTERIMAGE!
SHUSAKU ASSUMED YOU WOULD COME INTO THE ROOM AFTER HIS DEATH AND TRY TO DESTROY ANY MESSAGE HE LEFT.
SO HE DEVISED A MESSAGE THAT WOULD IMPLICATE YOU EVEN IF YOU PAINTED OVER IT!
AS THE SAYING GOES, "A DEAD KONG MING SCARES AWAY A LIVING ZHONGDA"!
EXACTLY.

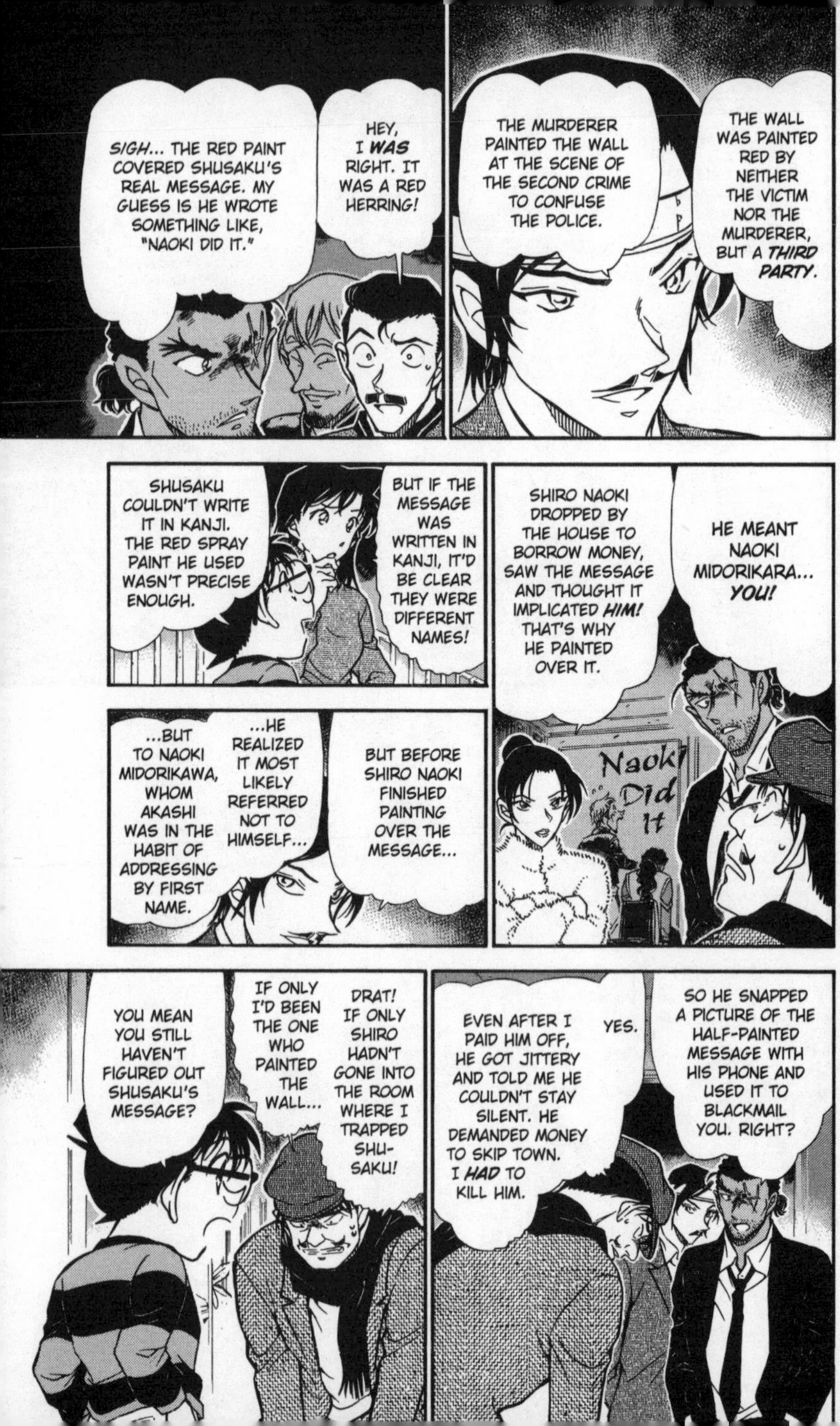
THE WALL WAS PAINTED RED BY NEITHER THE VICTIM NOR THE MURDERER, BUT A *THIRD PARTY*.
THE MURDERER PAINTED THE WALL AT THE SCENE OF THE SECOND CRIME TO CONFUSE THE POLICE.
HEY, I *WAS* RIGHT. IT WAS A RED HERRING!
SIGH... THE RED PAINT COVERED SHUSAKU'S REAL MESSAGE. MY GUESS IS HE WROTE SOMETHING LIKE, "NAOKI DID IT."
HE MEANT NAOKI MIDORIKARA... *YOU!*
SHIRO NAOKI DROPPED BY THE HOUSE TO BORROW MONEY, SAW THE MESSAGE AND THOUGHT IT IMPLICATED *HIM!* THAT'S WHY HE PAINTED OVER IT.
Naoki Did It
BUT IF THE MESSAGE WAS WRITTEN IN KANJI, IT'D BE CLEAR THEY WERE DIFFERENT NAMES!
SHUSAKU COULDN'T WRITE IT IN KANJI. THE RED SPRAY PAINT HE USED WASN'T PRECISE ENOUGH.
BUT BEFORE SHIRO NAOKI FINISHED PAINTING OVER THE MESSAGE...
...HE REALIZED IT MOST LIKELY REFERRED NOT TO HIMSELF...
...BUT TO NAOKI MIDORIKAWA, WHOM AKASHI WAS IN THE HABIT OF ADDRESSING BY FIRST NAME.
SO HE SNAPPED A PICTURE OF THE HALF-PAINTED MESSAGE WITH HIS PHONE AND USED IT TO BLACKMAIL YOU. RIGHT?
YES.
EVEN AFTER I PAID HIM OFF, HE GOT JITTERY AND TOLD ME HE COULDN'T STAY SILENT. HE DEMANDED MONEY TO SKIP TOWN. I *HAD* TO KILL HIM.
DRAT! IF ONLY SHIRO HADN'T GONE INTO THE ROOM WHERE I TRAPPED SHU-SAKU!
IF ONLY I'D BEEN THE ONE WHO PAINTED THE WALL...
YOU MEAN YOU STILL HAVEN'T FIGURED OUT SHUSAKU'S MESSAGE?

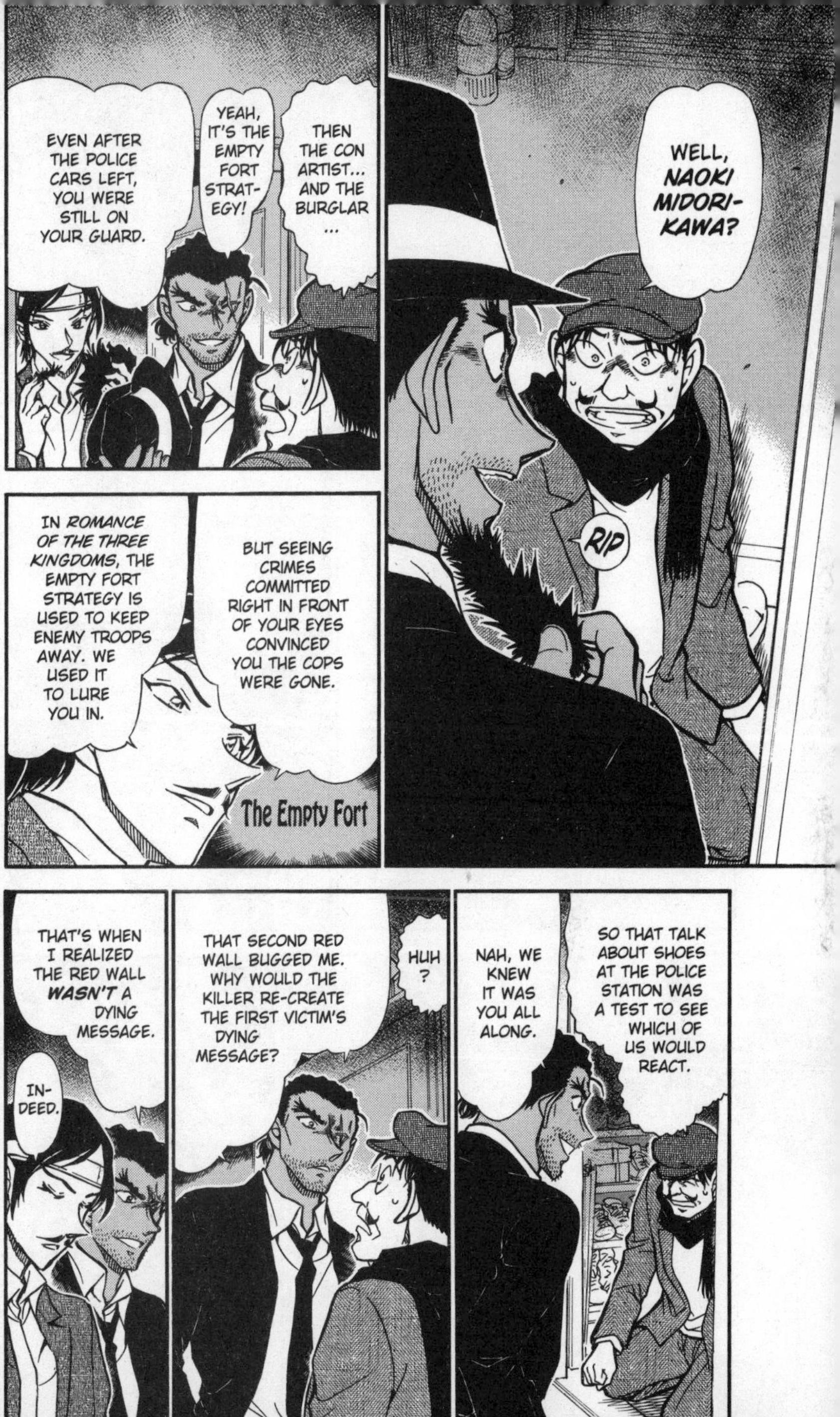
WELL, NAOKI MIDORIKAWA?
RIP
THEN THE CON ARTIST... AND THE BURGLAR ...
YEAH, IT'S THE EMPTY FORT STRATEGY!
EVEN AFTER THE POLICE CARS LEFT, YOU WERE STILL ON YOUR GUARD.
BUT SEEING CRIMES COMMITTED RIGHT IN FRONT OF YOUR EYES CONVINCED YOU THE COPS WERE GONE.
IN *ROMANCE OF THE THREE KINGDOMS*, THE EMPTY FORT STRATEGY IS USED TO KEEP ENEMY TROOPS AWAY. WE USED IT TO LURE YOU IN.
The Empty Fort
SO THAT TALK ABOUT SHOES AT THE POLICE STATION WAS A TEST TO SEE WHICH OF US WOULD REACT.
NAH, WE KNEW IT WAS YOU ALL ALONG.
HUH?
THAT SECOND RED WALL BUGGED ME. WHY WOULD THE KILLER RE-CREATE THE FIRST VICTIM'S DYING MESSAGE?
THAT'S WHEN I REALIZED THE RED WALL ***WASN'T*** A DYING MESSAGE.
INDEED.

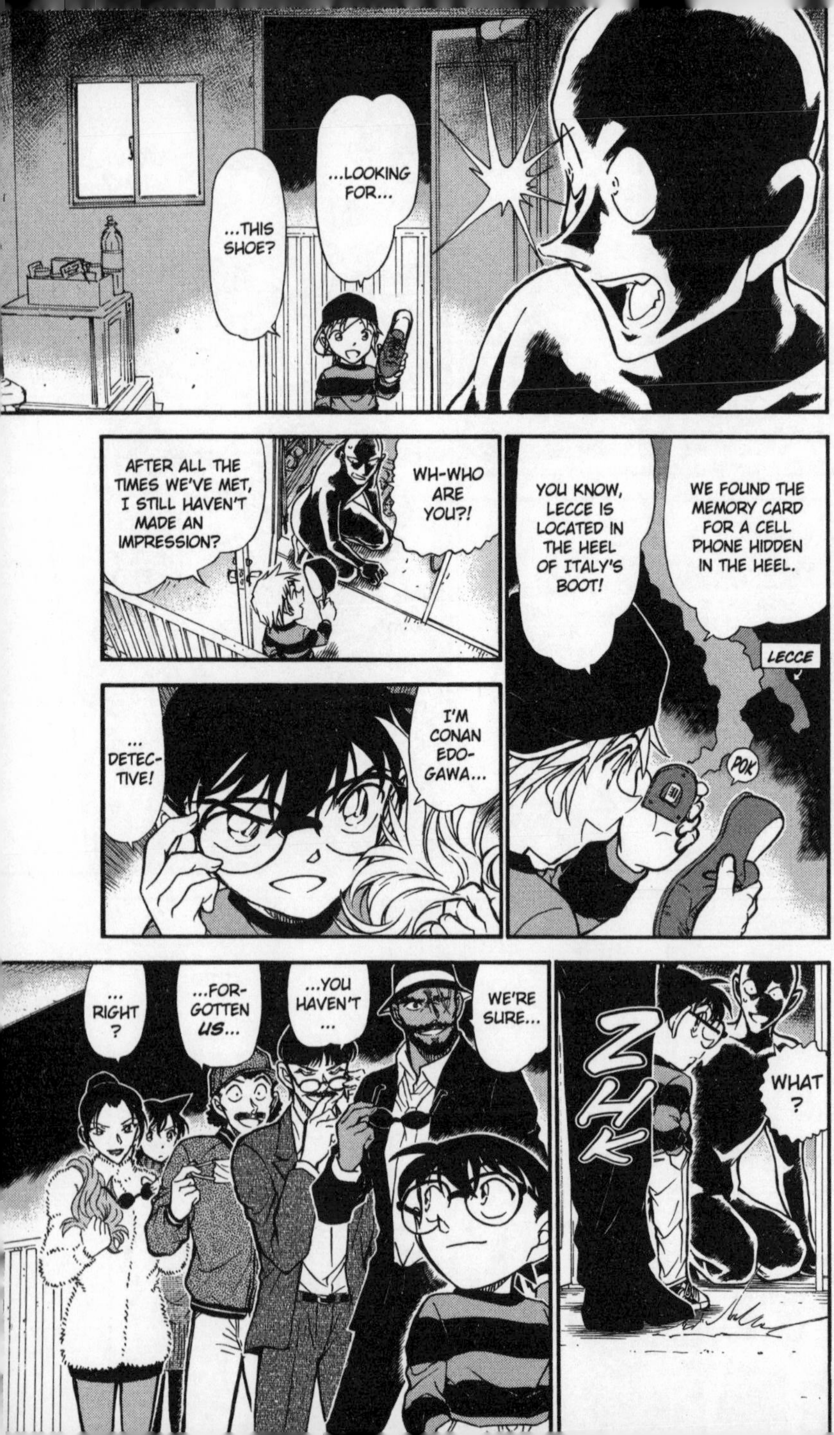
...LOOKING FOR...
...THIS SHOE?
WE FOUND THE MEMORY CARD FOR A CELL PHONE HIDDEN IN THE HEEL.
YOU KNOW, LECCE IS LOCATED IN THE HEEL OF ITALY'S BOOT!
LECCE
POK
WH-WHO ARE YOU?!
AFTER ALL THE TIMES WE'VE MET, I STILL HAVEN'T MADE AN IMPRESSION?
I'M CONAN EDO-GAWA...
...DETECTIVE!
WHAT?
ZHK
WE'RE SURE...
...YOU HAVEN'T...
...FOR-GOTTEN US...
...RIGHT?

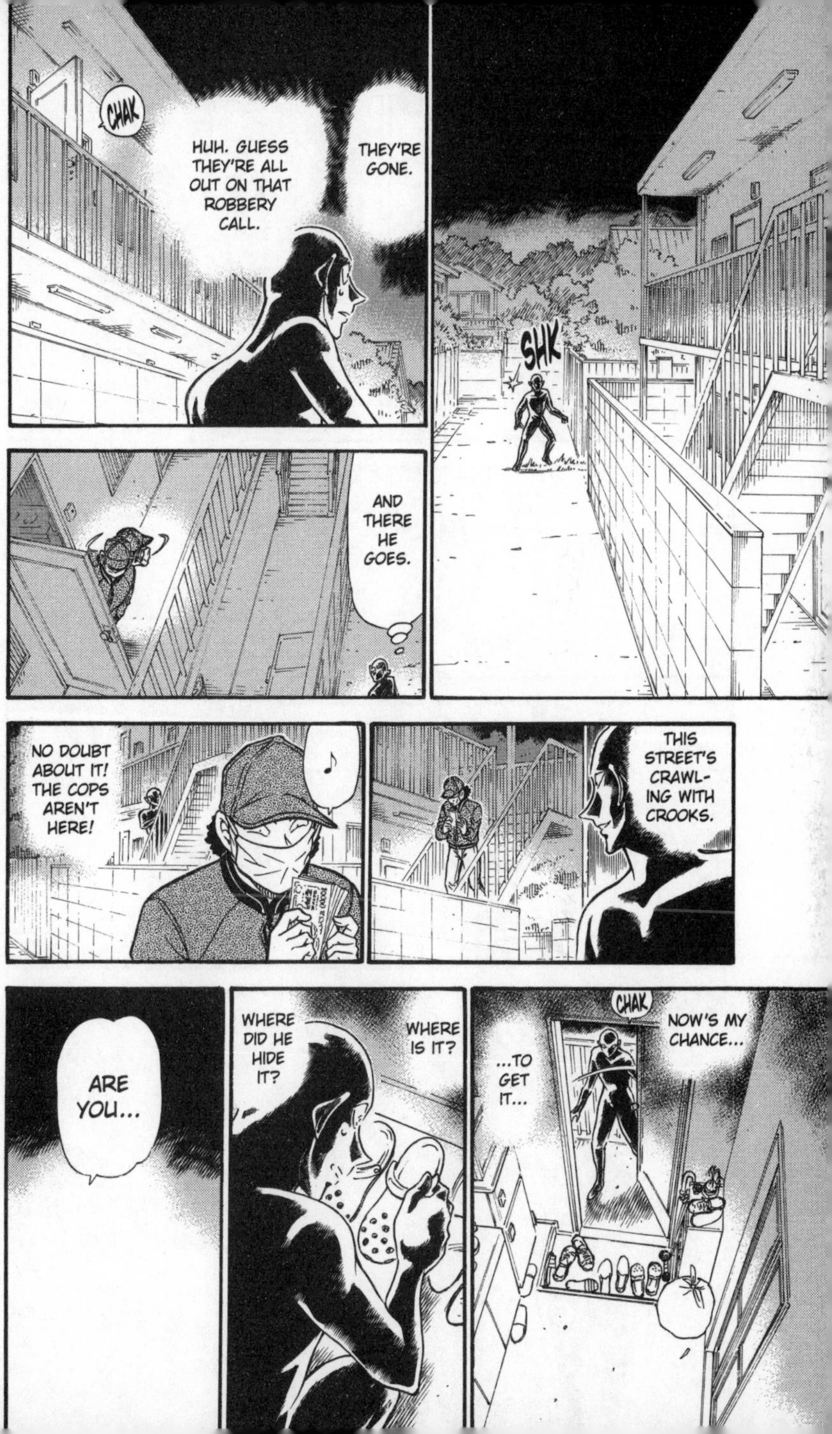

SHK
THEY'RE GONE.
CHAK
HUH. GUESS THEY'RE ALL OUT ON THAT ROBBERY CALL.
AND THERE HE GOES.
THIS STREET'S CRAWL-ING WITH CROOKS.
♪
NO DOUBT ABOUT IT! THE COPS AREN'T HERE!
CHAK
NOW'S MY CHANCE...
...TO GET IT...
WHERE IS IT?
WHERE DID HE HIDE IT?
ARE YOU...

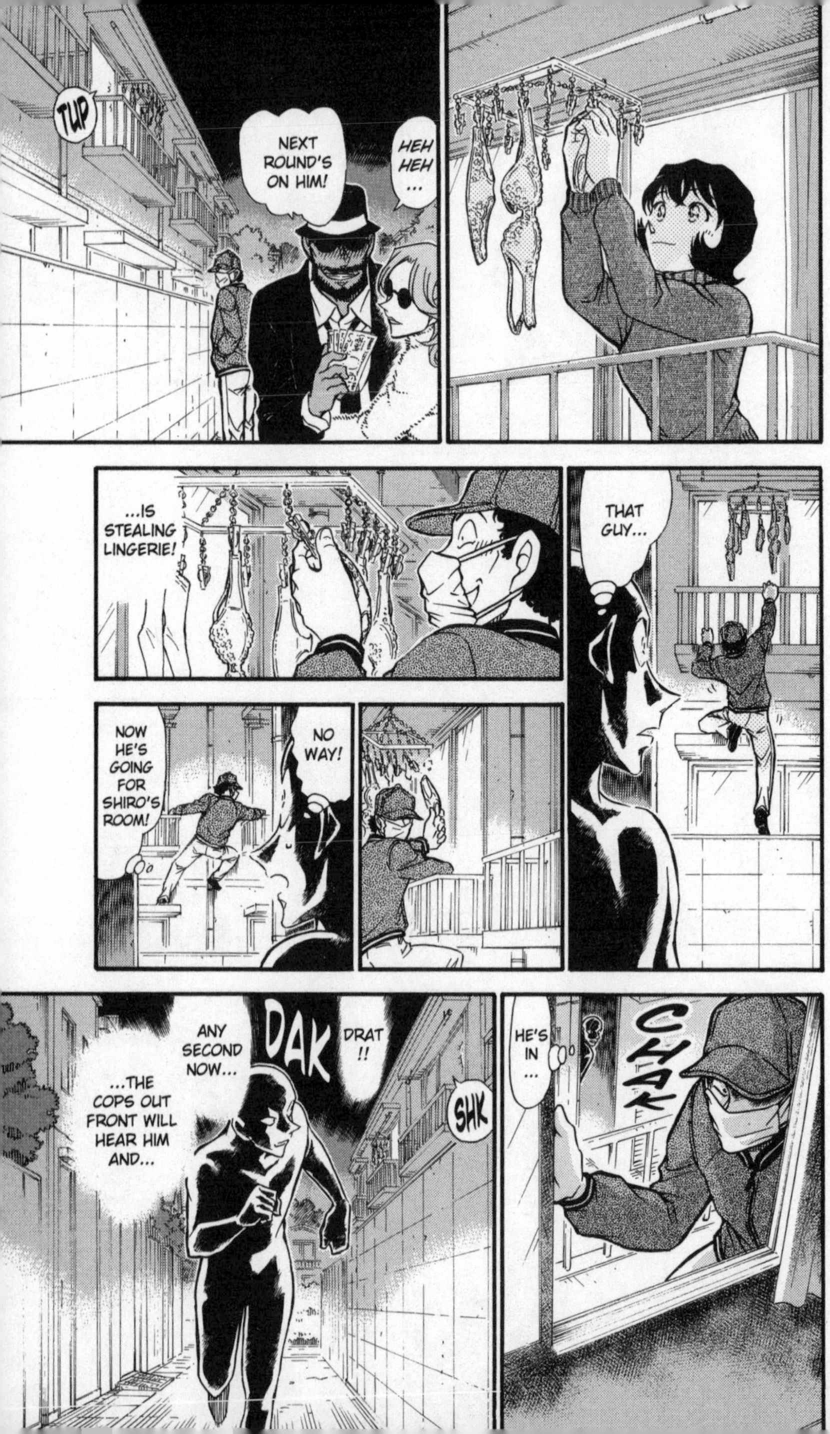
HEH HEH ...
NEXT ROUND'S ON HIM!
TUP
THAT GUY...
...IS STEALING LINGERIE!
NO WAY!
NOW HE'S GOING FOR SHIRO'S ROOM!
CHAK
HE'S IN ...
SHK
DRAT !!
DAK
ANY SECOND NOW...
...THE COPS OUT FRONT WILL HEAR HIM AND...

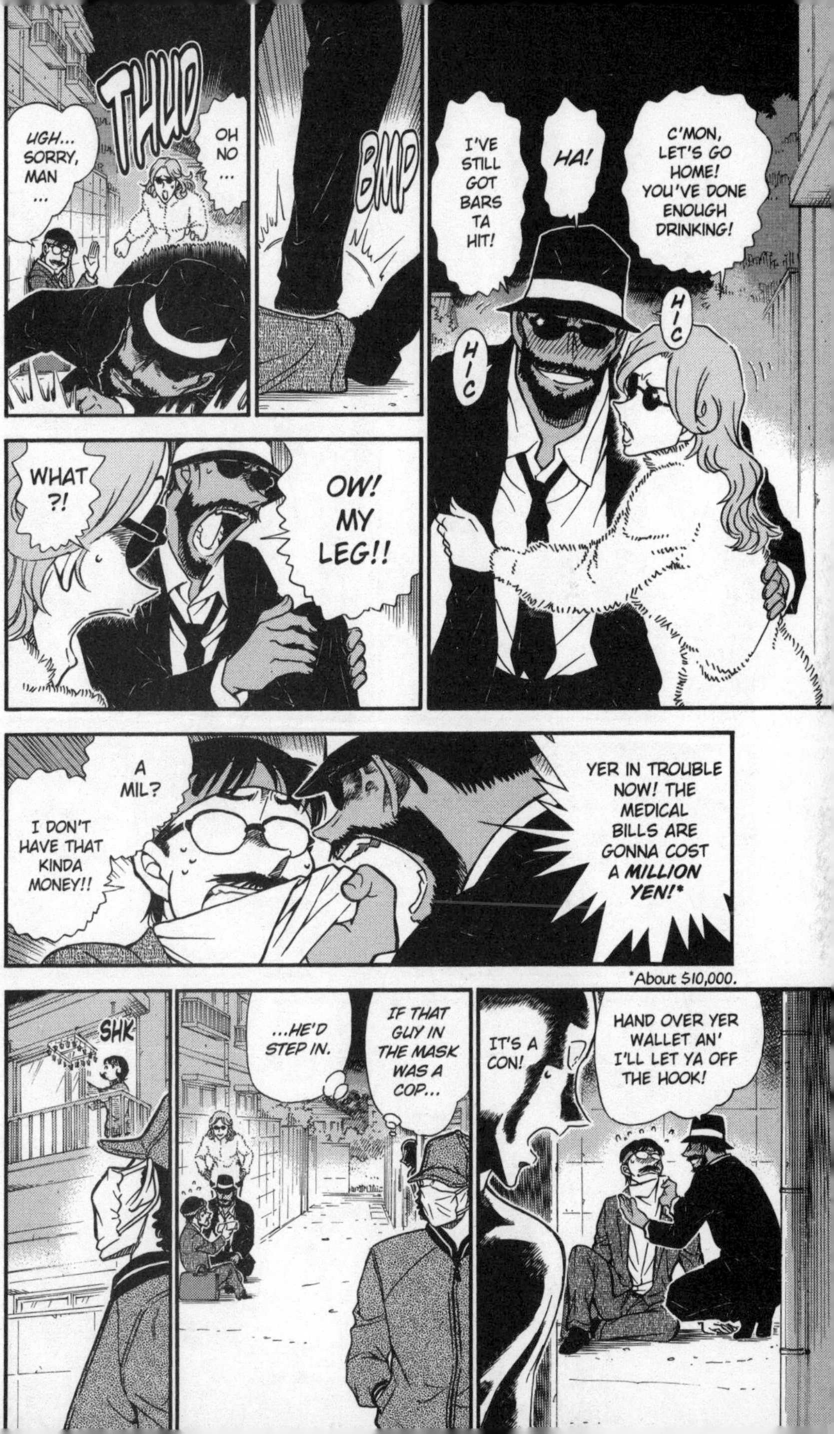
C'MON, LET'S GO HOME! YOU'VE DONE ENOUGH DRINKING!
HA!
I'VE STILL GOT BARS TA HIT!
HIC
HIC
BMP
THUD
OH NO ...
UGH... SORRY, MAN ...
OW! MY LEG!!
WHAT ?!
YER IN TROUBLE NOW! THE MEDICAL BILLS ARE GONNA COST A MILLION YEN!*
A MIL?
I DON'T HAVE THAT KINDA MONEY!!
HAND OVER YER WALLET AN' I'LL LET YA OFF THE HOOK!
IT'S A CON!
IF THAT GUY IN THE MASK WAS A COP...
...HE'D STEP IN.
SHK

*About $10,000.

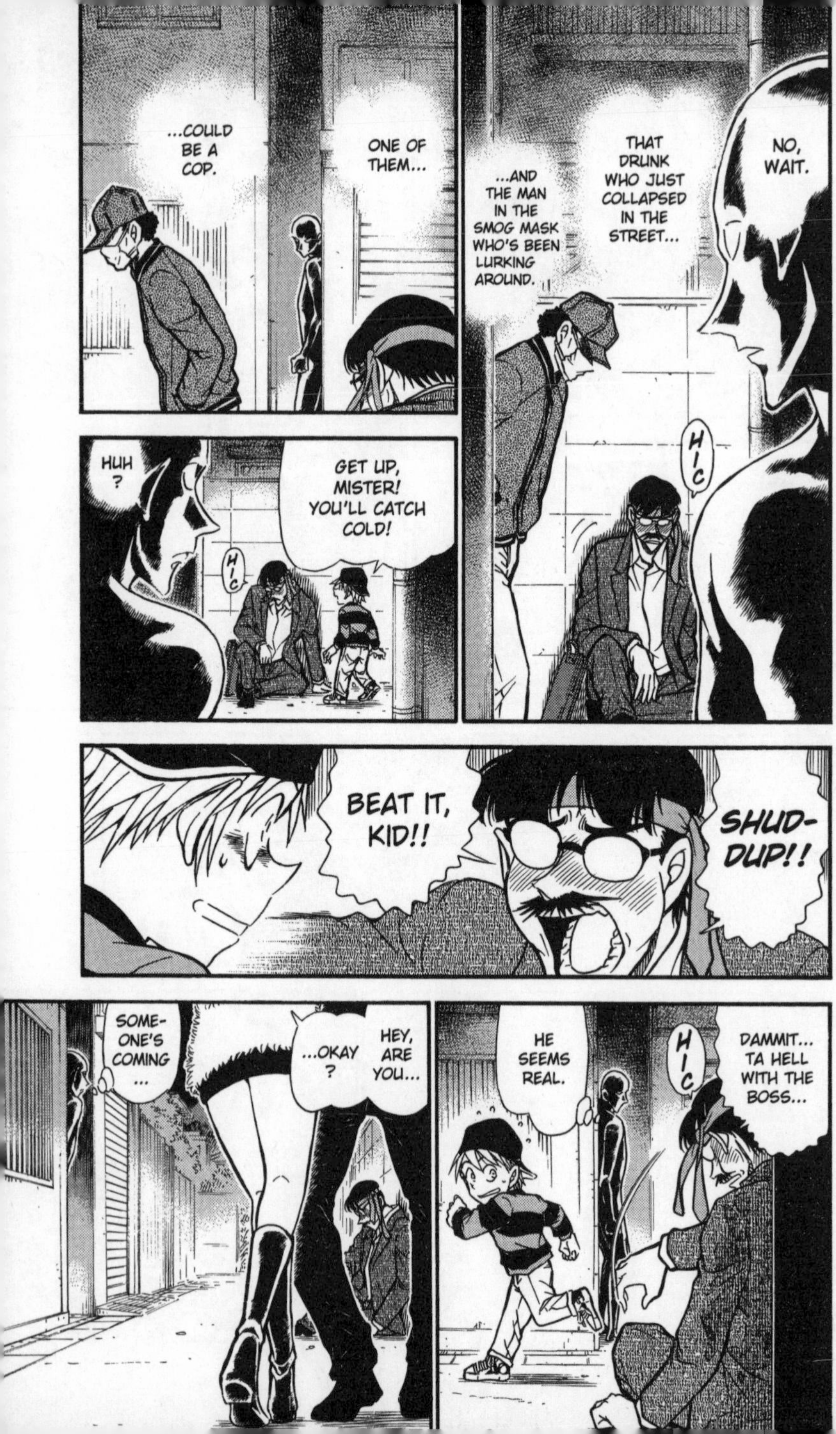
NO, WAIT.
THAT DRUNK WHO JUST COLLAPSED IN THE STREET...
...AND THE MAN IN THE SMOG MASK WHO'S BEEN LURKING AROUND.
HIC
ONE OF THEM...
...COULD BE A COP.
GET UP, MISTER! YOU'LL CATCH COLD!
HIC
HUH?
SHUD-DUP!!
BEAT IT, KID!!
DAMMIT... TA HELL WITH THE BOSS...
HIC
HE SEEMS REAL.
HEY, ARE YOU...
...OKAY?
SOME-ONE'S COMING...

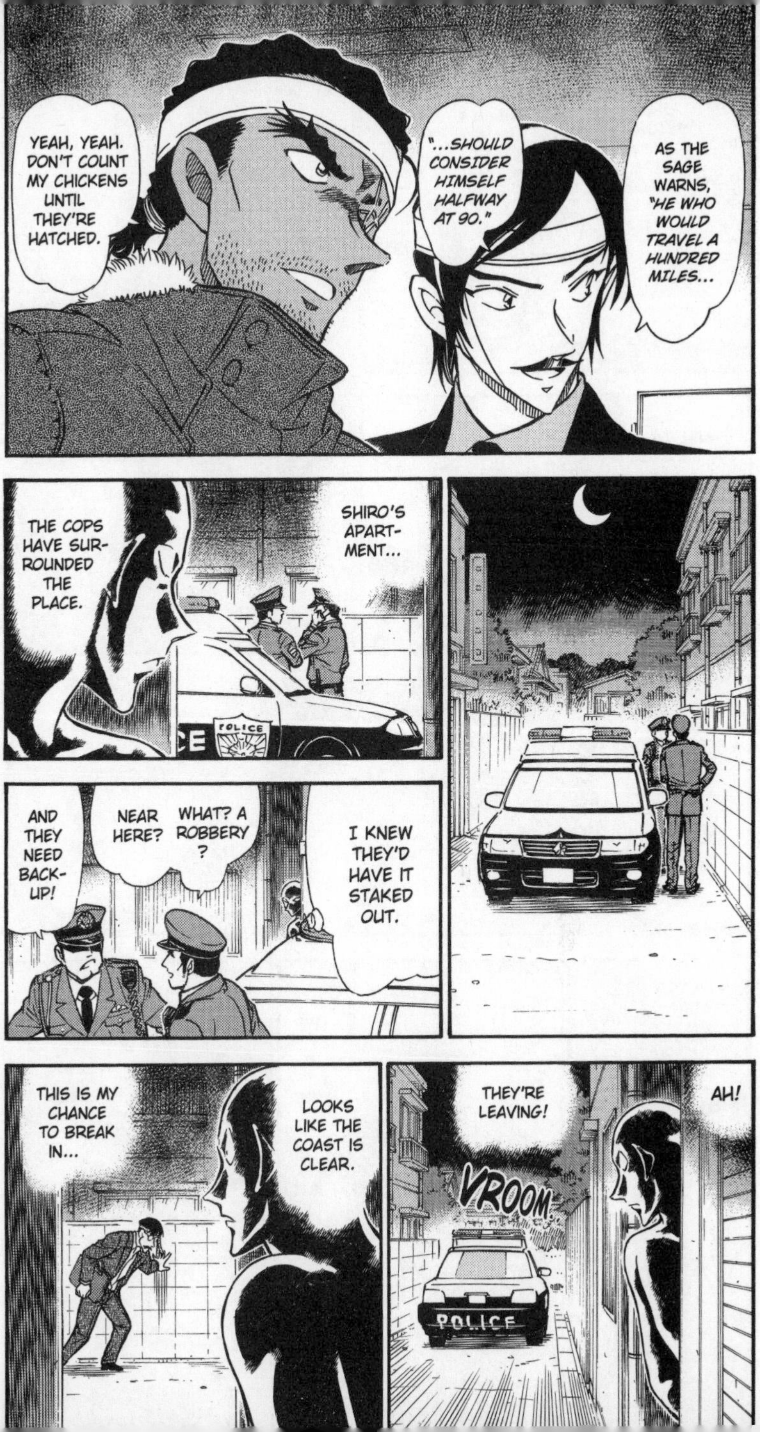
AS THE SAGE WARNS, "HE WHO WOULD TRAVEL A HUNDRED MILES...
"...SHOULD CONSIDER HIMSELF HALFWAY AT 90."
YEAH, YEAH. DON'T COUNT MY CHICKENS UNTIL THEY'RE HATCHED.
SHIRO'S APART-MENT...
THE COPS HAVE SUR-ROUNDED THE PLACE.
POLICE
I KNEW THEY'D HAVE IT STAKED OUT.
WHAT? A ROBBERY?
NEAR HERE?
AND THEY NEED BACK-UP!
AH!
THEY'RE LEAVING!
VROOM
POLICE
LOOKS LIKE THE COAST IS CLEAR.
THIS IS MY CHANCE TO BREAK IN...

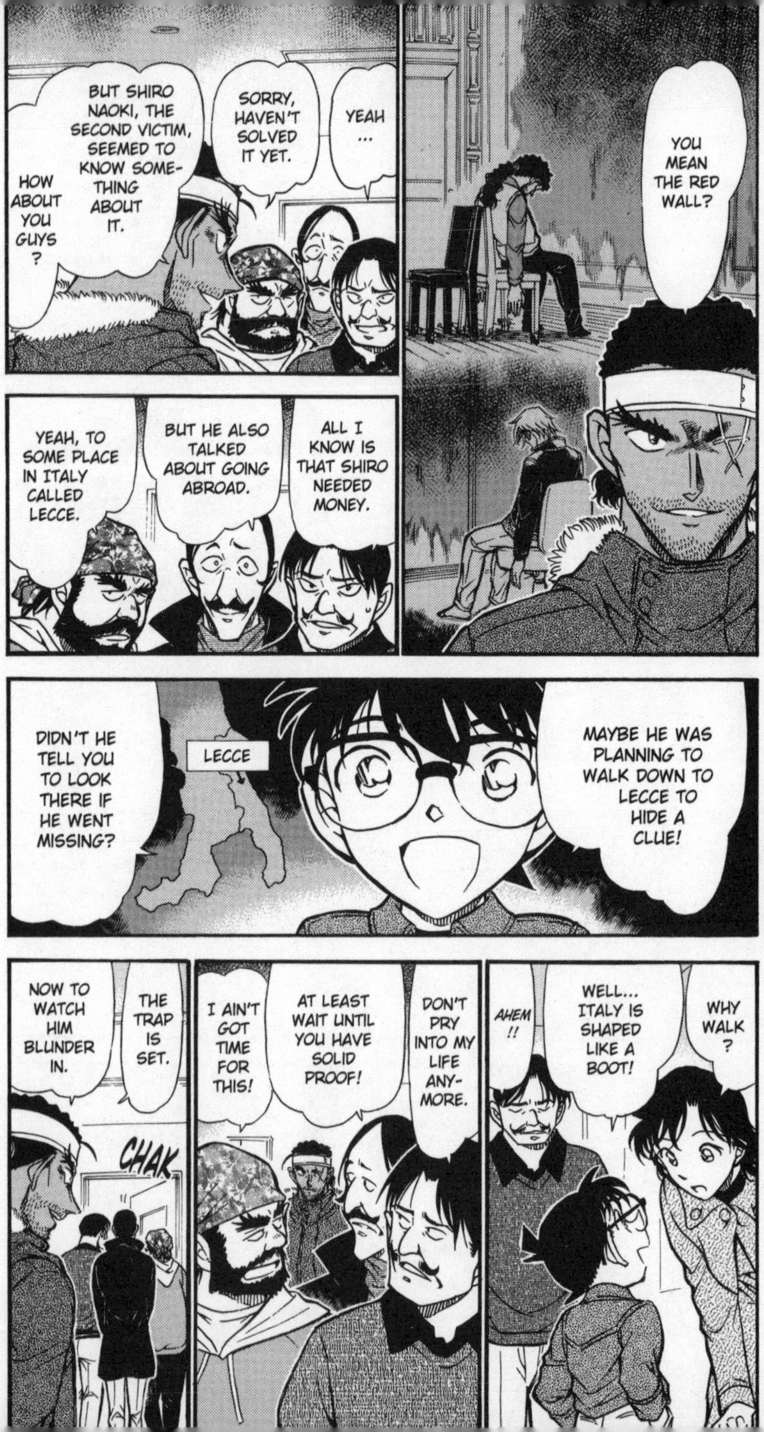
YOU MEAN THE RED WALL?
YEAH ...
SORRY, HAVEN'T SOLVED IT YET.
BUT SHIRO NAOKI, THE SECOND VICTIM, SEEMED TO KNOW SOMETHING ABOUT IT.
HOW ABOUT YOU GUYS?
ALL I KNOW IS THAT SHIRO NEEDED MONEY.
BUT HE ALSO TALKED ABOUT GOING ABROAD.
YEAH, TO SOME PLACE IN ITALY CALLED LECCE.
MAYBE HE WAS PLANNING TO WALK DOWN TO LECCE TO HIDE A CLUE!
LECCE
DIDN'T HE TELL YOU TO LOOK THERE IF HE WENT MISSING?
WHY WALK?
WELL... ITALY IS SHAPED LIKE A BOOT!
AHEM!!
DON'T PRY INTO MY LIFE ANYMORE.
AT LEAST WAIT UNTIL YOU HAVE SOLID PROOF!
I AIN'T GOT TIME FOR THIS!
THE TRAP IS SET.
NOW TO WATCH HIM BLUNDER IN.
CHAK

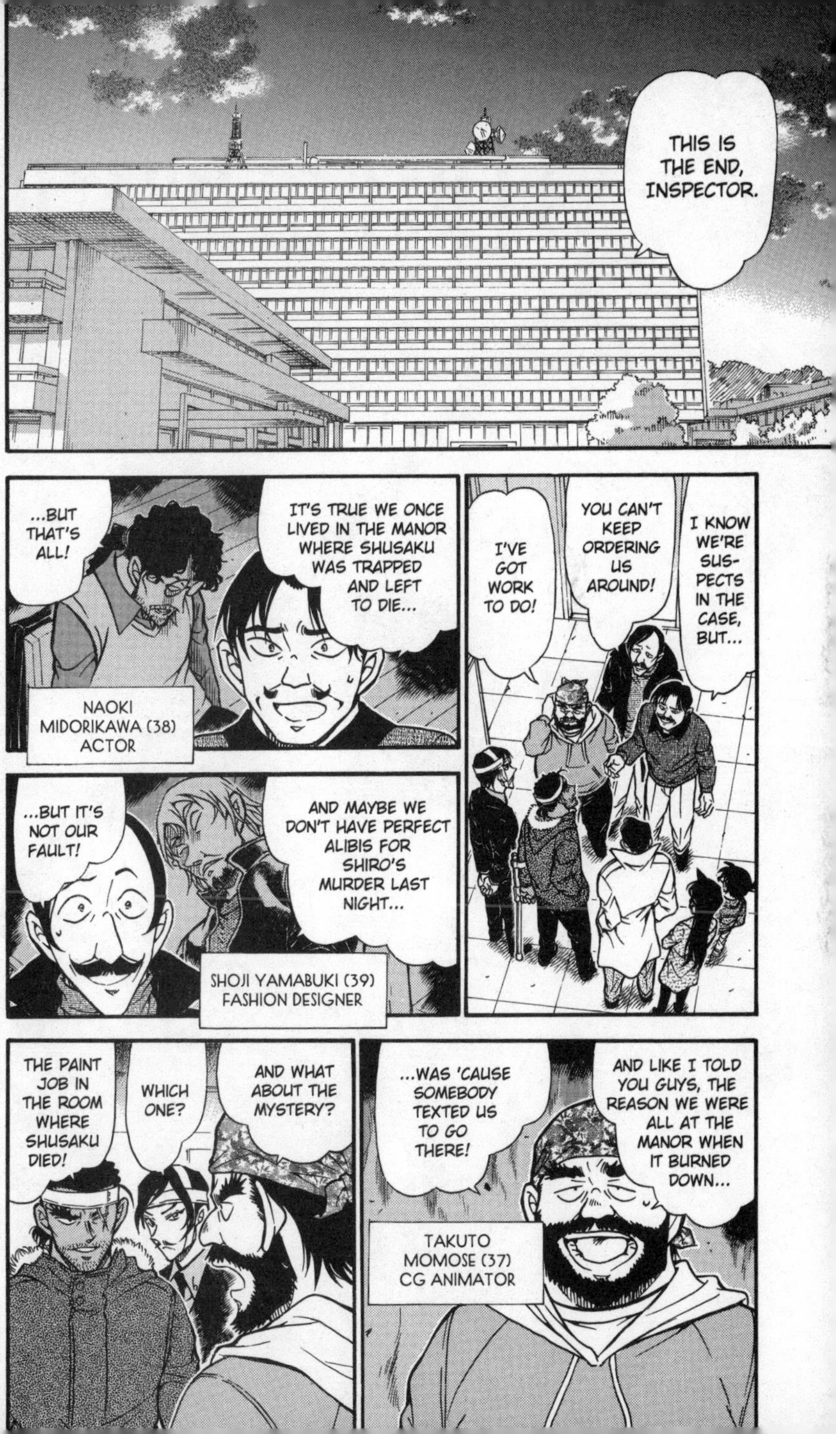

THIS IS THE END, INSPECTOR.
I KNOW WE'RE SUS-PECTS IN THE CASE, BUT...
YOU CAN'T KEEP ORDERING US AROUND!
I'VE GOT WORK TO DO!
IT'S TRUE WE ONCE LIVED IN THE MANOR WHERE SHUSAKU WAS TRAPPED AND LEFT TO DIE...
...BUT THAT'S ALL!
NAOKI MIDORIKAWA (38) ACTOR
AND MAYBE WE DON'T HAVE PERFECT ALIBIS FOR SHIRO'S MURDER LAST NIGHT...
...BUT IT'S NOT OUR FAULT!
SHOJI YAMABUKI (39) FASHION DESIGNER
AND LIKE I TOLD YOU GUYS, THE REASON WE WERE ALL AT THE MANOR WHEN IT BURNED DOWN...
...WAS 'CAUSE SOMEBODY TEXTED US TO GO THERE!
TAKUTO MOMOSE (37) CG ANIMATOR
AND WHAT ABOUT THE MYSTERY?
WHICH ONE?
THE PAINT JOB IN THE ROOM WHERE SHUSAKU DIED!

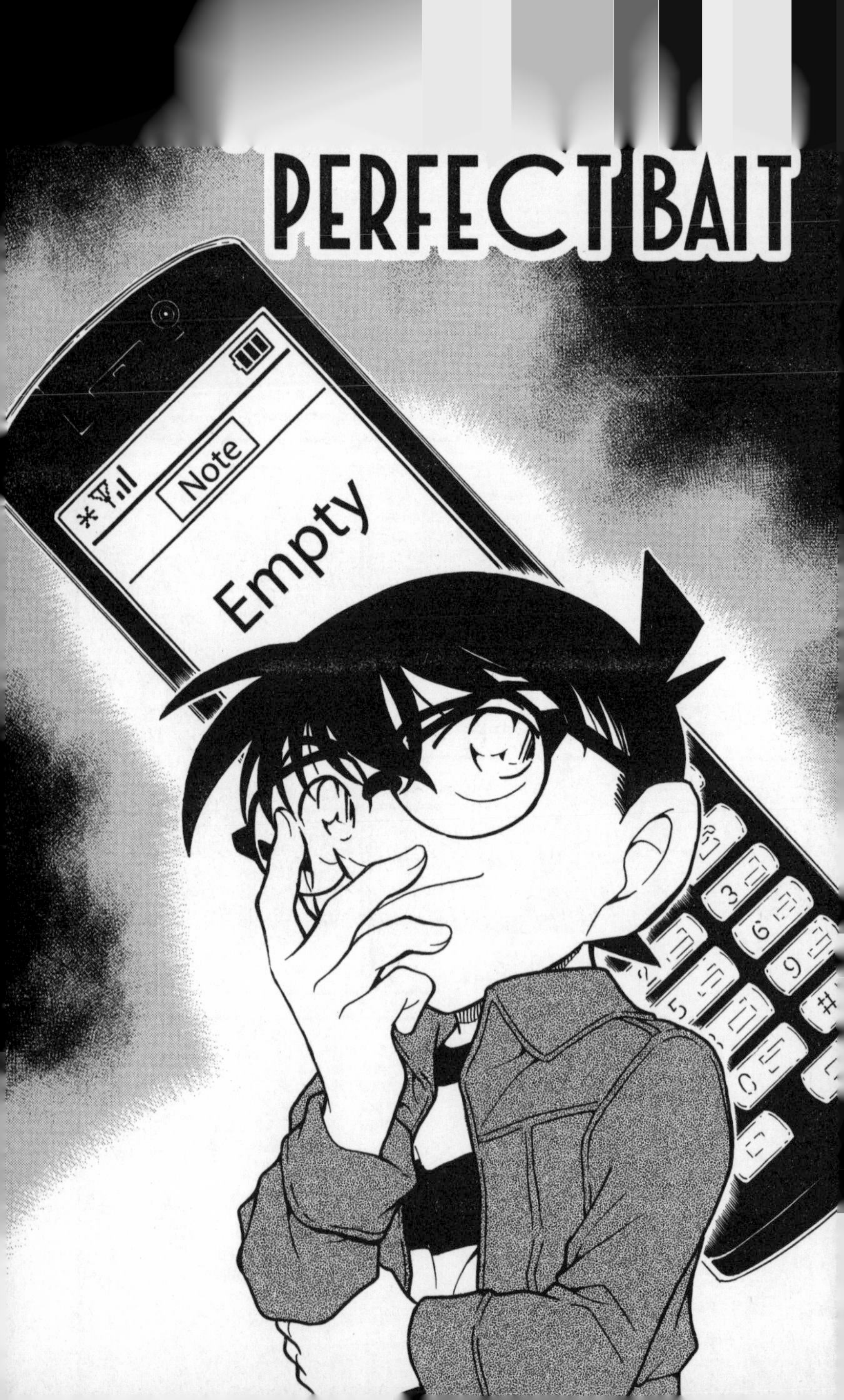
PERFECT BAIT
Note
Empty

CASE CLOSED

Volume 66
Shonen Sunday Edition

Story and Art by GOSHO AOYAMA

MEITANTEI CONAN Vol. 66
by Gosho AOYAMA
© 1994 Gosho AOYAMA
All rights reserved.
Original Japanese edition published by SHOGAKUKAN.
English translation rights in the United States of America, Canada,
the United Kingdom and Ireland arranged with SHOGAKUKAN.

Translation
Tetsuichiro Miyaki

Touch-up & Lettering
Freeman Wong

Cover & Graphic Design
Andrea Rice

Editor
Shaenon K. Garrity

Printed in the U.S.A.

Published by VIZ Media, LLC
P.O. Box 77010
San Francisco, CA 94107

10 9 8 7 6 5 4 3 2 1
First printing, April 2018

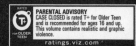

Table of Contents

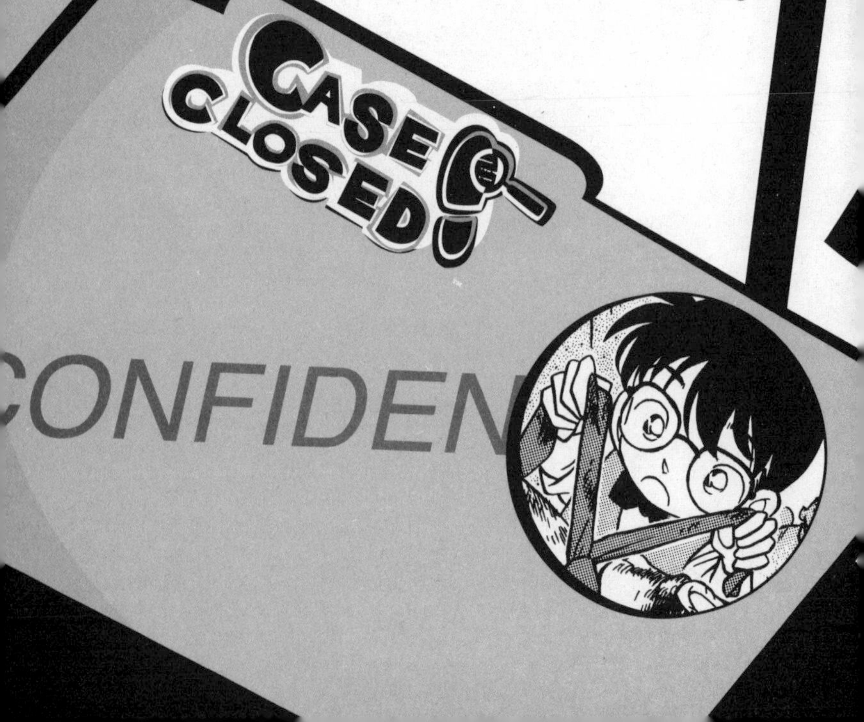

CASE CLOSED
CONFIDEN

Case Briefing:

Subject:
Occupation:
Special Skills:
Equipment:

Jimmy Kudo, a.k.a. Conan Edogawa
High School Student/Detective
Analytical thinking and deductive reasoning, Soccer
Bow Tie Voice Transmitter, Super Sneakers,
Homing Glasses, Stretchy Suspenders

The subject is hot on the trail of a pair of suspicious men in black when he is attacked from behind and administered a strange substance which physically transforms him into a first grader. When the subject confides in the eccentric inventor Dr. Agasa, they decide to keep the subject's true identity a secret for the safety of everyone around him. Assuming the new identity of first-grader Conan Edogawa, the subject continues to assist the police force on their most baffling cases. The only problem is that most crime-solving professionals won't take a little kid's advice!

CASE CLOSED™

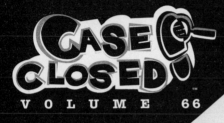

VOLUME 66

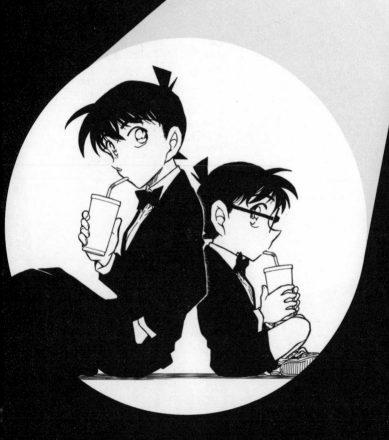

Gosho Aoyama